SOCIAL NETWORKS AND TRUST

THEORY AND DECISION LIBRARY

General Editors: W. Leinfellner (*Vienna*) and G. Eberlein (*Munich*)

Series A: Philosophy and Methodology of the Social Sciences

Series B: Mathematical and Statistical Methods

Series C: Game Theory, Mathematical Programming and Operations Research

Series D: System Theory, Knowledge Engineering an Problem Solving

SERIES C: GAME THEORY, MATHEMATICAL PROGRAMMING
AND OPERATIONS RESEARCH

VOLUME 30

Scope: Particular attention is paid in this series to game theory and operations research, their formal aspects and their applications to economic, political and social sciences as well as to socio-biology. It will encourage high standards in the application of game-theoretical methods to individual and social decision making.

The titles published in this series are listed at the end of this volume.

SOCIAL NETWORKS AND TRUST

by

VINCENT BUSKENS
*Department of Sociology,
Utrecht University, Utrecht, The Netherlands*

KLUWER ACADEMIC PUBLISHERS
BOSTON / DORDRECHT / LONDON

A C.I.P. Catalogue record for this book is available from the Library of Congress.

ISBN 1-4020-7010-1

Published by Kluwer Academic Publishers,
P.O. Box 17, 3300 AA Dordrecht, The Netherlands.

Sold and distributed in North, Central and South America
by Kluwer Academic Publishers,
101 Philip Drive, Norwell, MA 02061, U.S.A.

In all other countries, sold and distributed
by Kluwer Academic Publishers,
P.O. Box 322, 3300 AH Dordrecht, The Netherlands.

Printed on acid-free paper

Printed in the Netherlands

To my parents, for always
stimulating me without
pushing me beyond my limits

Contents

List of Figures xi
List of Tables xiii
Preface xv

1. INTRODUCTION: EMBEDDED TRUST 1
   - 1.1 Examples 1
   - 1.2 Trust 5
     - 1.2.1 Defining Trust 5
     - 1.2.2 Trust in Isolated Encounters 9
     - 1.2.3 Trust in Repeated Transactions 10
     - 1.2.4 Trust in Social Networks 15
     - 1.2.5 Arrangements to Reduce the Trust Problem 23
   - 1.3 Research Questions 26
   - 1.4 Overview 29

2. SOCIAL NETWORK ANALYSIS AND GAME THEORY 31
   - 2.1 Social Network Analysis 32
   - 2.2 Game Theory 42

3. A GAME-THEORETIC MODEL FOR CONTROL EFFECTS IN SOCIAL NETWORKS 53
   - 3.1 Introduction 53
   - 3.2 Construction of the Model 55
   - 3.3 Solution of the Model 62
   - 3.4 Properties of the Solution 66
   - 3.5 Approximation Using Linearization 71
   - 3.6 Approximation Using Simulation 74
     - 3.6.1 Methods 74
     - 3.6.2 Analyses for Simulated Data 78
   - 3.7 Substantive Implications 86
   - 3.8 Discussion 89

4. A STOCHASTIC MODEL FOR INFORMATION DIFFUSION IN SOCIAL NETWORKS 93
4.1 Introduction 93
4.2 The Model 96
4.2.1 Assumptions and Main Theorem 96
4.2.2 Diffusion Times and Centrality Measures 101
4.3 Analytic Results for Diffusion Times 104
4.4 The Simulation 109
4.4.1 Methods 109
4.4.2 Analyses for Simulated Data 112
4.5 Substantive Implications Related to Trust 119
4.6 Discussion 121

5. CONTRACTING IN INFORMATION TECHNOLOGY TRANSACTIONS: A SURVEY 125
5.1 Introduction 125
5.2 Data and Hypotheses 130
5.2.1 Description of the Data 130
5.2.2 Operationalizations 132
5.2.3 Summary Statistics of the Variables 142
5.2.4 Hypotheses 143
5.3 Analyses 146
5.3.1 Methods 146
5.3.2 Tests of the Hypotheses 147
5.3.3 Interpretation of the Network Effects 152
5.4 Conclusions and Discussion 158

6. BUYING A USED CAR: AN EXPERIMENT 163
6.1 Introduction 163
6.2 The Vignette Experiment 166
6.2.1 The Setting 166
6.2.2 Independent Variables 167
6.2.3 Method of Paired Comparison 170
6.2.4 Vignette Selection 173
6.2.5 Subject Characteristics 177
6.3 Data Collection 178
6.4 Analyses 179
6.4.1 Methods 179
6.4.2 Tests of the Hypotheses 181
6.4.3 Presentation Effects 185
6.4.4 Subject Effects 186
6.5 Conclusions and Discussion 187

7. SUMMARY AND NEW PERSPECTIVES 191
7.1 Results 191
7.2 Discussion 198
7.3 Suggestions for Further Research 204

Appendices 212
A– Mathematical Details 213
B– Network Construction Methods for Valued Networks 225
C– Information on the MAT95 Questionnaire 229
D– The Vignette Experiment 235

References 245

About the Author 261

Author Index 263

Topic Index 267

List of Figures

1.1	Extensive form of a Trust Game	7
1.2	Which trustors can trust the trustee most?	27
1.3	Overview	30
2.1	Example of a network of trustors	33
2.2	Extensive form of a Trust Game with incomplete information	43
3.1	Extensive form of a Heterogeneous Trust Game	56
3.2	A sequence of transactions	57
3.3	Example of a network of trustors	59
4.1	A four-person network as an example	98
4.2	Markov chain belonging to the four-person network	99
4.3	Transmitter centrality for homogeneous networks	108
4.4	The effect of outdegree on transmitter centrality	114
4.5	The effect of density on transmitter centrality	114
4.6	The effect of network size on transmitter centrality	115
5.1	Selectivity in the sample of transactions	157
6.1	Example of a pair of vignettes	172
6.2	Example of a pair of vignettes comparing past and future	175

List of Tables

2.1 Conjectures on the effects of network parameters on information diffusion rates 41
3.1 Summary statistics and correlations of the network parameters for the constructed networks 75
3.2 Tobit-like regression of the trust thresholds 79
3.3 Tobit-like regression of the normalized thresholds 84
4.1 Linear regression of (transformed) transmitter centrality 113
4.2 Linear regression of (transformed) transmitter centrality including detailed network parameters 117
5.1 Frequencies and Mokken scale analysis relating to the 24 issues of the contract 134
5.2 Principal components analysis for components and complexity 140
5.3 Principal components analysis for dependence 141
5.4 Principal components analysis for monitoring problems 141
5.5 Summary statistics of the key variables 143
5.6 Hypotheses on effects on safeguards 145
5.7 Linear regression of safeguards 148
5.8 Linear regression of degree 153
6.1 Description of the variables in the vignette experiment 168
6.2 Hypotheses on effects on the attractiveness of a vignette 171
6.3 The 6 possible divisions of 10 pairs of variables in 2 disjunct cycles of 5 pairs 176
6.4 Probit analyses of the choice of vignettes 181
6.5 Comparison of choices for pairs of vignettes that differ in exactly two variables 182
6.6 Probit analyses of the choice of vignettes including interaction effects 184

Preface

From my mountain walks I know that the most difficult paths leading to the highest peaks are remembered the longest, at times because of the splendid views, then again because of the extreme exhaustion. But the feeling at the end is almost always gratifying. Binmore (1994) warns us at the beginning of his book that "[t]hose who tread every step of the way are often weary at the end." Although I do not want to suggest that this book is worth reading from "cover to cover" for every single reader, I want to encourage the reader at least not to skip all the harder parts, because looking only from the valleys gives a limited and one-sided view of the mountains. My advice for the reader under time-pressure (as we almost all are) is to start with the general overview of the scenery as described in Chapter 1. Then, skip to the final chapter in which I present "snapshots" from the more important discoveries along the road and from some perspectives of mountains that could not be climbed. Based on these pictures, the reader can determine on which treks into the mountains he wants to follow me.

This book deals primarily with trust problems involving two actors. In a trust problem, there is one actor (the trustor) who can choose to place trust and another actor (the trustee) who might honor or abuse trust. In specific applications of trust problems, they are called buyers and suppliers, respectively. It turns out that people easily mix up who is whom. To facilitate the distinction for the reader, I address the trustors with female pronouns and the trustees with male pronouns.[1]

While some of the chapters are derived from previously published articles (Buskens 1998; Buskens and Yamaguchi 1999; Buskens, Raub, and Weesie 2000; Buskens and Weesie 2000a, 2000b), I trust that the integrating Chapters 1,

[1] I am not the first one who uses female pronouns for the "good guys" and male pronouns for the (possibly) "bad guys" (see Klein 1997b).

2, and 7 and the cross-references between the chapters provide added value. They ensure that this monograph tells one consistent story. Chapters 1 through 4 discuss the theory, Chapters 5 and 6 provide empirical evidence, and Chapter 7 concludes.

About seven years ago, I entered the environment of the social sciences almost as a stranger. I owe many people my gratitude for helping me to get around. Jeroen Weesie and Werner Raub saved me from losing my way in the vast social science landscape. Moreover, they showed me the way to places I would never have reached otherwise. They pursued me everywhere with their continuing and inescapable comments. Chris Snijders had always time to listen to my questions. If he did not have an answer himself, he was almost always able to rephrase my questions in such a way that I could find the answers myself. I am also grateful to all the other colleagues working in the Pionier research program "The Management of Matches" who provided a very inspiring and critical research environment. Particularly, Ronald Batenburg made a major effort in collecting the data analyzed in Chapter 5. In addition, I thank Henk Flap and Andreas Flache for pointing out some flaws in my original thesis that are corrected in this new edition. Finally, I thank all my other colleagues at the sociology department at Utrecht University for their comments and for providing a pleasant working environment.

During a research visit at the University of Chicago, I obtained valuable support from Ronald Burt and Kazuo Yamaguchi. I thank them for commenting on my papers, especially my vignette experiment, and providing me with research facilities. Marilyn Minderhoud-Jones carefully read my manuscript and corrected my sloppy English. Lambèr Royakkers was, as an outsider, a useful proof-reader and gave some good comments on the manuscript. Furthermore, I thank the Interuniversity Center for Social Science Theory and Methodology (ICS) for providing a supportive research environment and the Netherlands Organization for Scientific Research (NWO) for financial support through the Pionier program "The Management of Matches."

Last but not least, I thank Wilma for her unconditional support during all the years I have been working on this book, especially since I know that my writing is not her favorite reading material.

VINCENT BUSKENS

Chapter 1

INTRODUCTION: EMBEDDED TRUST

> *A fruitful analysis of human action requires us to avoid the atomization of under- and oversocialized conceptions. Actors do not behave or decide as atoms outside a social context, nor do they adhere slavishly to a script written for them by the particular intersection of social categories that they happen to occupy. Their attempts at purposive actions are instead embedded in concrete ongoing systems of social relations.*
>
> —Granovetter (1985: 487)

In this book a complex scientific puzzle is presented. A scientific puzzle differs from an ordinary jig-saw puzzle in that it has no clear borders and is characterized by more than two dimensions. In the book, selected parts of the "social networks and trust" puzzle are put together. At the end, other parts worthy of further study are discussed. In this chapter, some illustrative examples are discussed in Section 1.1. Section 1.2 offers a more formal overview of the most important dimensions of the puzzle. Section 1.3 introduces the research questions, while Section 1.4 provides an overview of the topics treated elsewhere in this book.

1.1 EXAMPLES

Transactions in interdependent relations often include an element of risk, because outcomes depend not only on the actions of a single actor, but on the actions of a number of actors. Trust relations are a particular type of interdependent relations. In trust relations, *one* actor takes a risk. Whether the outcome of a transaction in a trust relation is favorable to this actor depends on the performance of the other actors (see Coleman 1990: 91). The following examples show that the behavior of actors in a trust relation can be influenced by the "social context" of that trust relation. I will refer to these examples again later in the book.

Example 1: Buying a Software Package

Consider a firm that wants to buy a tailor-made software package. The risk this firm takes in buying the software package originates in time and information asymmetries. The buyer may have to pay for the product *before* it is completed and it is not certain whether the product will be delivered on time. Moreover, the supplier often has *better information* than the buyer about the quality and value of the product. The buyer needing the software package has to trust the supplier to deliver the product on time and to the specifications agreed upon.

Problems that may occur during such a transaction can have different backgrounds. The problems may arise from events outside the control of the actors concerned. For example, flu strikes the employees of the supplier and, as a result, he is unable to deliver the software package on time.[1] Here, the problem does not arise because of untrustworthy behavior on the part of the supplier. Other problems may arise because of deliberate opportunistic behavior by the supplier as, for instance, when he has an incentive to withhold information from the buyer or to deliver the product after the agreed delivery time.

The supplier is probably better able to judge which software package is best suited to the buyer's situation. The supplier is thus in a position where he can try to make an additional profit by selling software that is more elaborate than the software actually required. Another example of opportunistic behavior is when the supplier delivers a software package too late, because by doing so he can earn an additional profit by serving another customer first.

A buyer of a software package is assumed to realize the risks described above. If she knows beforehand that the supplier will deliver the product late or is likely to withhold essential information about the product, she would certainly choose another supplier. Still, the buyer can have convincing reasons for trusting that the supplier will not behave opportunistically. If the buyer has had positive experiences in previous transactions with the supplier, the buyer may rely on the supplier's trustworthiness even though she knows that the supplier has incentives to abuse trust. However, even in a first transaction with a supplier, the buyer may realize that the supplier not only has short-term incentives to act opportunistically, but also long-term incentives to act in a trustworthy way and deliver a well-suited software package at the appointed time. The reason for this is that good performance on the part of the supplier increases the probability that the buyer will return to him again and request that he supplies her with new products. Therefore, if the buyer is convinced that the supplier's long-term incentives of future transactions exceed his short-term

[1] To facilitate the distinction between the actor who has to trust (trustor or buyer) and the actor who is trusted (trustee or supplier), I will refer to the trustor with female pronouns and to the trustee with male pronouns as I explained in the preface.

incentives of opportunistic behavior in this transaction, the buyer can trust the supplier to handle the transaction properly.

Because buyers of information technology (IT) products buy new products and updates frequently, the assumption of repeated transactions is reasonable in this case. However, repeated transactions are less common in many other types of transactions. This raises the question of why buyers trust a supplier if they do not expect to do business with that supplier frequently again. I now turn to such an example.

Example 2: Buying a Used Car

Consider a student with a tight budget who wants to buy a used car. It is the student's first car and she is not a car expert. Given this lack of expertise, she runs the risk of buying a "lemon" (Akerlof 1970). Because the student can hardly see the difference between a good car and a bad one, a dealer has an incentive to sell her a bad car for the price of a good one. As a first-time buyer, the student has not built up any previous experience with the dealer in earlier transactions. Further, in contrast with the IT market, it is improbable that the student will buy many used cars from the same dealer. Perhaps the student knows other students who have bought used cars from this dealer. These students can provide information about the quality of cars sold by the dealer. If a student receives positive information about the dealer, she might trust the dealer on that basis. But, as in the case of the individual buying the software package, the student's trust need not be based on information from past transactions alone. She also knows that the dealer takes into account that she may tell her friends about the quality of the car he has sold her. These friends are potential car buyers. The more friends the student has, the more important it is for the dealer to sell her a good car. If he builds up a good reputation, his business will flourish, if his reputation sours, his business will suffer.[2] In reasoning this way it is essential that the dealer expects the student to be acquainted with other potential used-car buyers.

In the first example where the purchase of software was at issue, a bilateral social relationship was argued to facilitate trust. Of course, buyers of IT products may know other potential buyers and the supplier should take this into account. But in both examples, it is unlikely that the buyer and the supplier are closely related in any social context other than their business relationship. The Jewish diamond merchants in New York provide a classic example of a very dense society in which trust is omnipresent (Wechsberg 1966: 81–86).

[2] I apply the term "reputation" in the commonly used sense of "a characteristic or attribute ascribed to one person (firm, industry, etc.) by another" (Wilson 1985: 27). This usually represents a prediction about future behavior and "[i]ts predictive power depends on the supposition that past behavior is indicative of future behavior" (Wilson 1985: 28).

Example 3: The Diamond Merchants

The Jewish diamond merchants in New York form a closely-knit community. They go to the same synagogues and live in the same neighborhood. The merchants often hand diamonds to each other for inspection prior to a transaction. The diamonds are taken home without any safeguards or formal arrangements. Although there are considerable incentives to "lose" a diamond or to change a high-quality diamond for one of lower quality, the merchants trust each other because the sanctions for cheating are severe. If a merchant is found untrustworthy, this will quickly become known throughout the dense community. "Ostracism" will not only drive cheaters out of business, but will also result in them being expelled from their social context. Thus, in such densely connected societies, the consequences of untrustworthy behavior are beyond the boundaries of business relations, and extend into personal relationships as well.

Example 4: The Stock Exchange

An additional example in which informal third-party sanctions facilitate trust is Weber's (1921: 191–193) description of the stock exchange market. Weber describes transactions arranged through hand signals. If stock prices suddenly change, dealers might regret their transactions. Moreover, it will be hard to prove that a transaction was agreed upon. Weber argues that among dealers there is what he calls "Einverständnis": transactions are not to be canceled and dealers are not to have transactions with those who are known for canceling transactions. Because dealers at the stock exchange know each other quite well and meet regularly, untrustworthy dealers are easily detected. Dealers who get a reputation for being unreliable in honoring agreements will find it difficult to secure partners for new transactions. This will severely damage their business.

THE PUZZLE

The examples discussed above show that trust can emerge and can be stabilized in interdependent relations through the social context of the relationships. These examples can be kept in mind and help to facilitate the understanding of the more abstract theoretical puzzles addressed in Chapters 3 and 4. In these chapters, trust relations and the effects of social context are investigated using mathematical models. Specific attention will be paid to the two kinds of effects discussed in the examples. First, the social context of trustors (or buyers) provides them with *information* through which they can *learn* whether a trustee (or supplier) is expected to be trustworthy. Second, the social context offers trustors the possibility of *controlling* an untrustworthy trustee through her own sanctions or third-party sanctions. I will distinguish two aspects of the social context. First, *temporal embeddedness* is the extent to which two actors have transactions over time, i.e., have had transactions in the past and expect new transactions in the future. Example 1 illustrates that temporal embeddedness influences a trustor's opportunities for learning and control. Second, *network embeddedness* is the extent to which actors are linked to third parties 1in a social network (Raub 1997; Raub and Weesie 1993a, 2000a). Although these examples show that trust may emerge in dense networks, not much is known about the precise effects of social networks on trust. *This book mainly studies how learning and control differ from one social network of trustors to another as well as between trustors within a social network.*

Before more detailed research questions can be formulated, I will try to give a more precise account of how trust is conceptualized in this book, and how the theory to be developed can be placed within the context of existing research.

1.2 TRUST

1.2.1 DEFINING TRUST

Before embarking on a discussion of the relationship between social networks and trust, I examine the essential characteristics of trust relations. The sociological literature on trust has been extensively reviewed by Misztal (1996). She describes the role of trust in classical sociological literature and focuses on the importance of trust in obtaining social order. Misztal (1996: Chapter 3) identifies trust as having three functions. First, she discusses the *integrative function of trust*. Parsons' work (for example, Parsons 1937) reflects this function. He considers system-level trust in normative systems as the main source of social order. This means that social order is a result of norms prescribing trustful and trustworthy behavior. Parsons rejects more individualistic explanations of trust according to which rational self-interest might be considered to be a basis for trust. Luhmann's (1988) research provides insights into the second function of trust: the *reduction of complexity*. Luhmann argues that actors increasingly need trust because of the growing complexity of modern society and because the consequences of decisions are becoming more uncertain. Both Luhmann and Parsons consider trust as being beneficial for the social system as a whole, whether this involves the integrative function of trust or the reduction of complexity. However, they fail to explain why trust emerges *in individual cases*, and what reasons individuals have for trusting each other.

Research in line of the third function of trust, "trust as a *lubricant for co-operation*" (Arrow 1974: 23), emphasizes the individual-level explanation of trust. This book also treats trust in this way. Most of the research on this third function of trust has been carried out within a rational choice approach.[3] It is assumed that trust is only possible if, for the trustor, the expected outcome of

[3] I do not want to discuss justifications for the rational choice approach. For a theoretical point of view, see Coleman (1990). For reviews on empirical support, I refer the reader to Friedman and Hechter (1988) and Hechter and Kanazawa (1997).

placing trust is preferred over the expected outcome of not placing trust. By taking such an individual-level approach, variations in trust within the same group of actors can be explained.

Even within the literature on trust from a rational choice perspective, there is no uniformity about the definition of trust. Coleman (1990: 97–99) distinguishes four elements that define a trust situation between a trustor and a trustee.

1. Placing trust by the trustor allows the trustee *to honor or abuse trust.* This action would not have been possible without placing trust by the trustor.

2. The trustor *regrets* placing trust *if trust is abused*, but *benefits from honored trust.*

3. The trustor *voluntarily* places resources in the hands of the trustee *without formal safeguards.*

4. There is a *time lag* between placement of trust and the action of the trustee.

The Trust Game as shown in Figure 1.1 is a game-theoretic representation of a transaction that closely resembles Coleman's definition of a trust situation (see also Dasgupta 1988; Kreps 1990a). The Trust Game starts with a move made by the trustor, who chooses between placing trust and not placing trust. If the trustor does not place trust, the game is over and the trustor obtains a payoff P_1, while the trustee receives P_2. If the trustor places trust, the trustee chooses between honoring trust and abusing trust. If the trustee honors trust, the trustor and trustee receive, respectively, $R_1 > P_1$ and $R_2 > P_2$. If the trustee abuses trust, the trustor receives $S_1 < P_1$ and the trustee $T_2 > R_2$. Throughout this study, I assume that these payoffs represent *utilities* for the actors that correspond to the outcomes of the game.[4,5]

Assume that the Trust Game with all payoffs is known to both actors in the game. The trustee will abuse trust if trust is placed, because the payoff for abusing trust is larger than the payoff for honoring trust ($T_2 > R_2$). The trustor realizes that the trustee will abuse trust if trust is placed. Thus, because the trustor is better off not placing trust than when she does place trust and trust is abused ($S_1 < P_1$), a rational trustor will not place trust. The expected

[4]In experiments where the payoffs are directly related to monetary outcomes, one has to take into account that utility not necessarily coincides with money. For example, because of feelings of fairness, subjects might also be concerned about the money received by their partners. This implies that subjects in such experiments transform the payoffs into their subjective utilities (see Kelley and Thibaut 1978; Weesie 1994; Snijders 1996: 48).

[5]Empirically, the size of the payoffs depends on transaction characteristics such as the monetary value of the transaction. Subsection 1.2.5 refers to relevant transaction characteristics in a discussion about transaction cost theory (Williamson 1985).

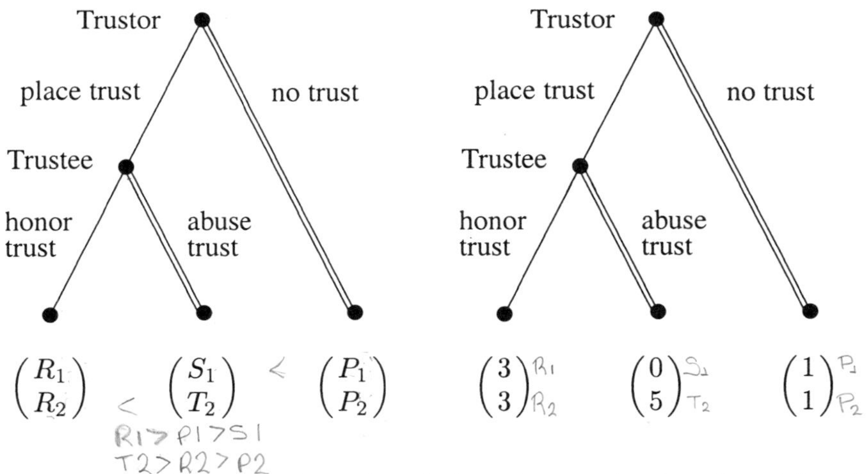

Figure 1.1. Extensive form of a Trust Game Γ. $R_1 > P_1$, $R_2 > P_2$, $P_1 > S_1$, and $T_2 > R_2$. The right-hand Trust Game is a numerical example. The double lines indicate the equilibrium path of play (see Chapter 2).

moves are indicated by double lines in Figure 1.1. Note that "abuse trust" is not observed if trust is not placed. The outcome constitutes a *social dilemma* because both actors are worse off in the situation that trust is not placed, which is the expected outcome, than in the case where trust is placed and honored ($R_1 > P_1$ and $R_2 > P_2$).[6]

Definition of a trust situation. A *trust situation* is a transaction between two actors that resembles a Trust Game.

Comparing the Trust Game with Coleman's definition shows that the trustee indeed has a choice to abuse or honor trust if the trustor places trust. Furthermore, the trustor will regret placing trust if trust is abused and benefits if trust is honored. The payoff difference $P_1 - S_1$, can be considered as the "resources" the trustor places in hands of the trustee if she places trust. Clearly, the order of decisions can be interpreted as a time-lag between the placement of trust and the action of the trustee in the Trust Game. The difference between the Trust Game

[6]The Trust Game can be seen as a one-sided version of the well-known Prisoner's Dilemma (see, for example, Luce and Raiffa 1957). In the Prisoner's Dilemma, both actors choose simultaneously between "cooperate" or "defect." If both actors cooperate they both obtain R. If both actors defect they both obtain $P < R$. If one actor cooperates and the other defects, the cooperative actor obtains $S < P$, while the defective actor obtains $T > R$. This implies that both actors are better off individually if they defect, whatever the other actor does. Consequently, it is expected that both actors defect and obtain P, while R is possible but does not satisfy the incentive constraint. The disadvantage of studying the Prisoner's Dilemma is that being trustful and trustworthy coincide, while these two aspects can be disentangled in the Trust Game.

and Coleman's definition of a trust situation is that Coleman does not specify the *incentives for the trustee*. In Coleman's definition, the choice between honoring and abusing trust is regarded as an exogenous chance mechanism. However, I consider it an explicit choice made by an actor.[7]

Studying trust in terms of the Trust Game reveals two relevant concepts. First, the *trustfulness* of the trustor, i.e., the extent to which the trustor places trust in the trustee. Second, the *trustworthiness* of the trustee, i.e., the extent to which the trustee honors trust if trust is placed. The analysis of the Trust Game suggests that the trustfulness of the trustor largely depends on her expectation of the trustworthiness of the trustee. If the trustor expects the trustee to abuse trust, she will not place trust. Although I will focus on explaining the trustfulness of the trustor in this book, it should be noted that the (expected) trustworthiness of the trustee will be the main predictor of trustfulness. In the remainder of this book, the term "trust" refers to the trustfulness of the trustor.

Definition of trust. *Trust* is the trustfulness of a trustor: the extent to which the trustor is willing to take the risk of trust being abused by the trustee.

A lack of trust is costly for both the trustor and the trustee. One reason for this is that the trustor may not want to enter a transaction with the trustee if trust is lacking. In this case, the loss of the trustee involves foregoing the benefits of a transaction with the trustor. The trustor incurs extra costs in finding alternatives to the transaction she wants to conduct with the trustee. In Subsection 1.2.4, this interpretation of "no trust" will be discussed in the context of the extent to which it is possible for social networks to provide alternatives for the trustor. Another reason is that if the trustor has to do business with the trustee, some kind of arrangement such as a formal contract is necessary in order to overcome the lack of trust.[8] The effect of such an arrangement might be fourfold. It decreases the incentive ($T_2 - R_2$) for the trustee to abuse trust; it compensates the trustor for the loss ($R_1 - S_1$) that would be due to abused trust by the trustee; it increases the trustor's opportunities for sanctioning the trustee ($R_2 - P_2$); or it adjusts the trustor's beliefs about the trustworthiness of the trustee. Some of these arrangements will be discussed in Subsection 1.2.5. If such an arrangement is used, the trustor can trust the trustee and buy, for example, the used car or software package.

[7]Although Coleman *models* the probability that trust is abused by the trustee exogenously, he pays considerable attention to the arguments of the trustee to choose between honoring and abusing trust (1990: 108–115).

[8]See, for example, Macaulay (1963) or Lyons (1994) on the (limited) use of contracts.

1.2.2 TRUST IN ISOLATED ENCOUNTERS

So far, the Trust Game has been analyzed for "isolated encounters." These are single encounters without any information or incentive connection to other encounters in which the two actors are involved. There is also no connection to the encounters between these two actors and other actors.

Snijders (1996) has mainly studied trust in isolated encounters in experimental contexts. In spite of the reasoning given above, he finds that aggregated over a variety of Trust Games with different monetary payoffs, trust is placed in 37% of all the Trust Games in his experiments and honored in 36% (see Snijders 1996: Table 4.1). To explain trustfulness and trustworthiness in these experiments, Snijders used the payoffs as well as the personal characteristics of the subjects in the experiments.

In analyzing the experiments, one important conclusion was that payoffs are more important than the personal characteristics of the subjects when it comes to explaining trustfulness and trustworthiness. The trustworthiness of the trustee was explained primarily by the *temptation* ($\frac{T_2-R_2}{T_2-S_1}$) that might encourage the trustee to abuse trust.[9] More specifically, trustworthiness decreases with temptation. The explanation is straightforward. $T_2 - R_2$ is the incentive for the trustee to abuse trust. The larger the incentive, the smaller the probability that the trustee honors trust. $T_2 - S_1$ equals the difference between the outcomes for the trustee and trustor if trust is abused. In the experiment, payoffs are directly related to monetary outcomes and not to the utilities actors derive from a certain outcome of the game. Therefore, the increase of trustworthiness with $T_2 - S_1$ can be explained by the fact that the trustee feels more "guilty" due to abuse of trust if $T_2 - S_1$ is larger, and this has a negative effect on the utility the trustee derives from abusing trust (see Snijders 1996: Section 2.4). Because I assume that the outcomes represent utilities for the actors in this study, rather than temptation, I focus on the incentive to abuse trust ($T_2 - R_2$).

As far as the behavior of the trustor is concerned, Snijders finds that trustfulness, just as trustworthiness, depends mainly on the payoffs of the game, in particular on the "monetary" *risk* ($\frac{P_1-S_1}{R_1-S_1}$) of the trustor and on temptation for the trustee.[10] The monetary risk is the ratio of what the trustor can lose if trust is abused compared to not placing trust ($P_1 - S_1$) and what she can gain by placing trust and taking the risk of trust being abused ($R_1 - S_1$). The main finding is that trustfulness decreases with the monetary risk of the trustor as well as with the temptation of the trustee. Thus, a trustor is more reluctant if

[9]Snijders (1996: 8) only considers symmetric Trust Games and omits indices for the payoffs. I add the indices to show whose payoffs are used in the definition of temptation.

[10]Note that I generally refer to risk as a combination of the probability that the trustee abuses trust *and* the money at stake in a Trust Game. Snijders defines risk purely via the money that is at stake for the trustor in a Trust Game ($\frac{P_1-S_1}{R_1-S_1}$).

more money is at stake. Moreover, the trustor seems to be concerned with the payoffs for the trustee, and—with good reason—her expectation that the trustee will honor trust is smaller if the temptation is larger. Although the effect of the monetary risk was substantial in Snijders' analyses, I conclude that the trustor also takes into account the incentive for the trustee to abuse trust.

The examples in Section 1.1 show that most trust situations cannot meaningfully be conceived as isolated encounters but rather as transactions embedded in a social context (see Granovetter 1985). Actors often have multiple transactions with each other and third parties might learn about what happens in transactions between two actors. In the following two subsections, I discuss the effects of temporal embeddedness and network embeddedness.

1.2.3 TRUST IN REPEATED TRANSACTIONS

Often, trust situations among actors do not simply occur once, but are recurrent over time, because actors live together, work together, or meet regularly. Although the temporal embeddedness of transactions influences the behavior of both the trustor and the trustee, I focus on the behavior of the trustor. What is important is that the behavior of the trustor depends on *her anticipation* of the behavior of the trustee.

In repeated transactions, two types of effects on the behavior of the trustor can be distinguished: *learning* and *control*. These are the two types of effects that play a central role in the book. Learning indicates the extent to which a trustor can modify her *expectations* about characteristics of a trustee from observing his behavior in past transactions. Control indicates the extent to which the trustor can influence the trustee's *behavior* via sanctions anticipated by the trustee. In this subsection, these two types of effects are discussed for repeated transactions between two actors. In Subsection 1.2.4, learning and control effects are discussed for transactions embedded in a social network. Subsections 1.2.3 and 1.2.4 end with a review of empirical evidence for learning and control in repeated transactions and transactions in a social network. I refer the reader to Buskens and Raub (2002) for a more extensive review on these topics.

Learning through Temporal Embeddedness

Learning indicates the extent to which a trustor obtains information about the incentives and abilities of a trustee from past transactions with this trustee. A buyer who is involved in an initial transaction with a supplier of IT products does not fully know the extent to which a supplier may be trying to make large profits in a short time and run away with the money. Nevertheless, a trustor will have some beliefs (expectations) about the incentives and abilities of the supplier, perhaps based on her experiences with other suppliers. After a transaction, the trustor will adjust her initial beliefs about the abilities of the trustee and about the trustee's efforts and incentives to keep the trustor as a long-term customer. Consequently, the extent to which she trusts the trustee may change with these experiences. After positive experiences in transactions with the trustee, the trustor's trust in the trustee will generally increase. This effect is frequently discussed in the sociological literature (Granovetter 1985: 400; Coleman 1990: 102–104). In general, a trustee would be wise to take into account how the trustor's observation of his behavior influences the expectations, and hence the behavior of the trustor in subsequent transactions, because the trustee's reputation is affected by his past behavior. In Section 2.2, I will briefly discuss how learning effects can be analyzed using game-theoretic models and present some of the results. However, modeling learning in strategic interactions is beyond the scope of this book.

CONTROL THROUGH TEMPORAL EMBEDDEDNESS

While sociologists generally focus on the explanation of trust as a result of past experiences and, consequently, on learning, economists tend to focus on control (see Burt and Knez 1995b: Chapter 1). Control is based on the anticipation of the trustee about transactions in the future with the same trustor (or, as will be seen in Subsection 1.2.4, with other trustors). The trustee realizes that a trustor might refrain from placing trust again if he abuses trust now. A trustor can also take specific measures to sanction the trustee after trust has been abused. The trustor realizes that she can control the behavior of the trustee with these implicit or explicit threats. Therefore, the trustor will place trust if the long-term costs of her sanctions are larger for the trustee than his short-term gains from abusing trust. Other authors refer to the mechanism underlying control as *reciprocity* (Gouldner 1960; Blau [1964] 1996) or *conditional cooperation* (Taylor 1987). An actor behaves cooperatively as long as a partner also cooperates, and behaves non-cooperatively as soon as the partner provides reasons for doing so.[11]

In terms of repeated Trust Games, the trustor can punish the trustee after abusing trust by withholding trust for one or more transactions. If the trustor does not place trust, the trustee receives P_2, which is his worst outcome. This punishment is more severe for the trustee if he considers future transactions more important (see Kreps 1990a). If the trustor is uncertain about the time preferences of the trustee, it can be difficult for the trustor to rely on sanctions in future transactions. Therefore, the effects of learning and control are to some extent interrelated. For the moment, I conclude with the expectation that the

[11]Tit-for-Tat (Axelrod 1984) is one of the "strategies" based on the principle of conditional cooperation. It was able to sustain stable cooperation in Axelrod's computer experiment on repeated Prisoner's Dilemmas. The idea of modeling cooperation via reciprocity in repeated games has been introduced in sociology by Voss (1982, 1985: Chapters 3 and 4).

trust of the trustor increases with a "positive shadow of the past" and with the "shadow of the future" (Axelrod 1984).

Empirical Evidence on Effects of Temporal Embeddedness

There is much empirical evidence on effects of temporal embeddedness via learning and control in repeated encounters. Trust is indicated by different phenomena in relations between organizations. The extent to which partners invest in making formal arrangements to overcome a lack of trust is one such indicator. This indicator will also be used in Chapter 5. The continuity of relations is a second indicator for trust. *Empirical research on relations between organizations* emphasizes the effects of past transactions on trust. Expectations about future transactions have only been included in a few recent studies.

In a field study of four enterprises, Larson (1992) illustrates that relations between firms start with small transactions. Transactions become larger over time as trust emerges if the transactions progress smoothly. After the "trial period," cooperative efforts can become more extensive, while the transactions are controlled through social relations only: " 'they trust us to pay and we trust them to give us a reasonable price' " (Larson 1992: 95). In an ethnographic study, Uzzi (1996, 1997) shows that failure rates of dress apparel firms are lower the stronger the relationship between partners. Uzzi explains this as a result of the comparative advantage of trust in strong relationships.

Gulati (1995a, 1995b) finds that the probability that firms form alliances with partners is larger if they have been involved in alliances before. Gulati interprets this finding as an indication that previous, probably positive, experiences enlarges trust among partners. Moreover, the probability that partners in alliances use equity as a formal governance mechanism decreases with the number of previous alliances between the partners. Similarly, Baker, Faulkner, and Fisher (1998) find that interorganizational ties between advertising agencies and their clients have a smaller probability of being dissolved if they have already existed for a longer period. Gulati and Gargiulo (1999) is one of the recent studies in which more specific network properties such as centrality are used to explain, in this case, alliance formation.

Three studies are particularly noteworthy for addressing the effects of temporal embeddedness on the investment in formal arrangements. In a study on 72 subcontracting relationships, Lyons (1994) finds that the probability for arranging the relationship with a formal contract decreases with the number of years subcontractors have been trading with their most important customers. Blumberg (1997: Section 4.2) uses a complex measure for the investment in formal arrangements (comprising both the time and money invested in formal arrangements and negotiations) and the length of the contract. He finds that both measures decrease and, thus, that trust increases with the extent to which the partners had transactions in the past. Blumberg does not find an effect of the transactions the partners expect in the future. Batenburg, Raub, and Snijders (2002) study relations between buyers and suppliers of IT products. Their dependent variable is a combination of time and money spent in searching for a partner, negotiating with the partner, and the length of the contract. They find that these investments decrease if the partners had transactions in the past. Furthermore, they find that the investments decrease even more if the partners already had past transactions *and* expect more transactions in future. They do not find an effect of expected future transactions if the partners had no previous transactions. Their explanation is that it is worthwhile to invest more in formal arrangements in a first transaction if more future transactions are expected, because these investments can be used again in subsequent transactions.[12] Still, less formal arrangements need to be made if more future transactions are expected because of the sanction opportunities from subsequent transactions. Combining these two arguments, it is unclear what the total effect of future transactions will be in initial transactions between two partners.

In *experimental research*, cooperative relations are extensively studied using repeated Prisoner's Dilemmas. An overview and major references can be found in Colman (1982: Chapter 7). Relevant findings in this context are that subjects regularly end up in cooperative play, but also might run into mutually defective choices, which reflects that subjects, to some extent, test whether the other subject is trustworthy. This can lead to mutually cooperative choices. Defective choices of untrustworthy partners probably result in mutually defective choices with partners who are trustworthy. Yamagishi and his co-workers (e.g., Yamagishi and Kakiuchi 2000) also focus on behavior in Prisoner's Dilemmas, although they try to distinguish behavior of actors who agree on statements such as "most people are trustworthy" with behavior of actors who do not agree on such statements. This study differs from Yamagishi's work, since Yamagishi mainly tries to explain differences in cooperative behavior between actors who differ in "intrinsic trust," while I try to explain differences in trusting behavior for actors in various trust situations.

More directly related to the issues discussed here are the experiments by Camerer and Weigelt (1988) and Neral and Ochs (1992). In these experiments, games are played that consist of eight or six times repeated Trust Games with incomplete information in which the trustors are not sure whether the trustee has an incentive to abuse trust. Thus, there is a positive probability that a trustor meets a trustee for whom $T_2 < R_2$, which implies that such a trustee will never abuse trust. All other elements of the Trust Game are the same.[13] These experiments show that trustees care more about their reputation in the initial periods of play than at the end of the eight or six periods to be played.

[12] Note that I ignored such relation-specific investments in the discussion about learning and control.

[13] Some details about the formal properties of this game can be found in Section 2.2 and Figure 2.2.

Moreover, trustors test whether the trustee is trustworthy, especially in the earlier periods. The more positive experiences the trustor has, the more she is convinced that she is playing with a trustee who does not have any incentive to abuse trust. However, the observed probability of placing trust by the trustor does not increase as the end of the game comes nearer. The trustor realizes that also the trustee has an incentive to make her believe that he does not have an incentive to abuse trust, but he will abuse trust in the last game. This corresponds with findings by Gautschi (2002), who did experiments on two and three times repeated Trust Games. His results show that trust increases with positive past experiences and decreases with negative past experiences. Moreover, recent experiences are more important than experiences that happened longer ago. In addition, trust increases in Gautschi's experiments with the number of periods to be played, i.e., with a longer future. Of course, contrary to these experiments, actors in real-life situations hardly ever know in advance which transaction with the partner will be the last one.

Kollock (1994) studies trust experimentally in situations in which buyers are uncertain about the quality of a seller's products. Two groups of four subjects ("buyers" and "sellers") can trade with each other for twenty rounds. In each round, buyers and sellers are given five minutes to make offers about prices, while the sellers advertise the quality of their good. The sellers can choose from three levels of quality at which they want to produce. The advertisement about quality does not need to be trustworthy. After each round the buyers are informed about the quality of the product they bought. Profit margins are largest for low-quality products sold for high prices. But selling high-quality products for high prices is preferred by all parties over selling low-quality products for low prices. Also in these experiments, most sellers seek to obtain a reputation for selling high-quality products and for obtaining high prices for their products. Sellers who start to sell low-quality products for high prices eventually end up with mutually sub-optimal outcomes, namely, selling low-quality products for low prices.[14]

Summarizing, empirical studies about relations between firms show considerable evidence for learning effects and some evidence for control effects in bilateral relations. Experimental research also provides evidence for the combination of learning and control effects.

[14]A difference between Kollock's experiments and the repeated Trust Games experiments of Camerer and Weigelt (1988) is that in Kollock's experiment the game with twenty rounds was played *only once*, while Camerer and Weigelt let the subjects play the eight times repeated Trust Games *75–100 times* with changing partners. Camerer and Weigelt show that subjects need some time to experience what the better strategies are. In the initial games in their experiments, a considerable number of subjects end up in sub-optimal outcomes, but this number decreases with experience in playing the repeated games.

1.2.4 TRUST IN SOCIAL NETWORKS

Network embeddedness was introduced at the end of Subsection 1.2.2 as the extent to which actors have relations with third parties. Relations might be business relations or friendship relations. Of course, not all third-party relations of two actors engaged in a transaction have a similar influence on the trust situation between these two actors. I will only consider relations of the trustor that are also, in some way, important for the trustee. Consider again the example of the student buying a used car. Here, only students who have information about the dealer of used cars or students who have plans to buy a used car and are known to the dealer will be considered.[15] In the example of the diamond merchants, one can consider all members of this society of merchants as being essential third parties because untrustworthy trustees are expected to be sanctioned by the whole group.

Other types of network ties not discussed earlier can also affect a trust situation. If a buyer of IT products has business relations with a large number of suppliers of IT products, the buyer has alternative suppliers. Such a buyer is less dependent on a supplier than a buyer with fewer alternative suppliers. A supplier should perform better if he has to maintain a good relation with a buyer who has many alternative suppliers (Hirschman 1970). Consider buying a software package, for example. It could be that a buyer purchases software that is tailor-made and that adjustments can only be made by the same supplier. In such a situation, considerable expense will be incurred if the buyer wants to change to another supplier, who has to start developing software from scratch. Thus, the supplier who originally developed the software need not be afraid that the buyer will change to another supplier.

The two types of network ties distinguished above correspond to the distinction made by Hirschman (1970): exit and voice. An *exit network* provides alternatives such that the trustor can choose other trustees. A *voice network* provides opportunities for the trustor to complain about the behavior of the trustee. In addition, the actors in the voice network may be able to provide information about behavior of the trustee in the past.

It is important to note that I focus on the network contacts of trustors, and not on those of the trustees.[16] This focus is based on the argument that the trustee is the only actor who has an incentive to abuse trust in a Trust Game. Hence, the effects of information concerning the behavior of the trustee and the effects of sanction threats against untrustworthy behavior on the part of the

[15] Other friends of a student can play a role because they give support if the student is deceived by the dealer. However, because these friends do not provide relevant information about the dealer and will not sanction the dealer, they are not included in the discussion about network effects.

[16] I disregard networks of trustees who may communicate information about trustors, for example, about timely payment of trustors.

trustee are more interesting than the effects of information about or sanctions against the trustor. The trustor will trust if she has sufficient reason to believe that the trustee will honor trust and if she does not have a reason to punish the trustee for abusing trust in the past. I avoid the fact, for example, that a trustor might want a reputation for sanctioning every abuse of trust rigorously. I will elaborate on the reasons and consequences of this assumption in Chapter 3.

Parallel to the discussion of temporal embeddedness, I distinguish learning and control effects of network embeddedness, and focus on the voice network of the trustor. The exit network is discussed in relation to the control the trustor exerts on the trustee.

Learning through Network Embeddedness

Trustors can obtain information about the past behavior of a trustee from other trustors or third parties. Using this information, trustors can "update" their beliefs about abilities or incentives of a trustee.

It cannot be expected that the information trustors obtain from third parties will be as easily interpreted as the trustor's own experience with a trustee. Even in a trustor's own transaction with a trustee, it can be difficult to distinguish whether bad performance by the trustee is caused by unforeseeable circumstances or due to opportunistic behavior. Information from third parties will often be less accurate than information from one's own experiences with a trustee (Granovetter 1985; Lorenz 1988), because an outsider may be less informed about the circumstances that lead to abused trust than those actors directly involved. It is particularly complicated to interpret third-party information if third parties provide ambiguous information. Some trustors, for example, may be very satisfied with a trustee, while others experience considerable problems with the same trustee. In this situation trustors may find it hard to draw conclusions from different and inconsistent pieces of third-party information.

Burt and Knez (1995a, 1995b; Burt 2001) find that, in dense networks, actors obtain consistent information about others; as a result, actors in dense networks tend to have more extreme opinions about the trustworthiness of others than actors in less dense networks. Extreme opinions can veer in the direction of trust as well as distrust. Burt and Knez argue that consistency of information is caused by the fact that actors in dense networks prefer to confirm each others opinion instead of arguing about disagreements. Especially in situations in which trustors do not need to disclose all their information about a trustee's behavior, they will disclose the information that is consistent with the other trustor's beliefs about the trustee's behavior. Therefore, actors in dense networks may rely heavily on consistency of information from third parties, while the consistency is driven more by the self-confirming tendency within a dense network than by the actual and consistent experiences third parties may have with the trustee.

The finding that not only trust but also distrust is amplified by more information in dense networks demonstrates that learning effects do not only depend on the amount of information received but also on the *content* of that information. Earlier studies—and the diamond merchants study is a good example—have emphasized that dense networks promote trust. However, the effect on distrust is often disregarded.[17] Explaining trust through learning, for example, allows for a simultaneous explanation of trust within groups and distrust between groups in segregated societies. If actors within groups are positive about group members and negative about others, actors who only obtain within-group information will soon be convinced that they can only trust actors from their own group.[18] Thus, learning can explain trust as well as distrust, although explanatory power depends on the knowledge of the content of information transmitted through the network.

Control through Network Embeddedness

Control is based on the anticipation of a trustee that trustors will sanction untrustworthy behavior and that these sanctions will affect long-term profits. In addition to the control effect of temporal embeddedness, social networks provide options for control through third parties. These can affect the long-term profits of the trustee in addition to and often even more extensively than through future sanctions imposed by the trustor herself.

Rational trustors are aware of the fact that a trustee anticipates on future sanctions. Therefore, trustors may trust the trustee more if they have more sanction opportunities through third parties. These sanctions can vary according to social context and can either be positive or negative. A student buying a good used car can "advertise" this experience among her peer students to the benefit of the dealer. Other students trust a dealer because they obtained information on positive experiences from other students. Students can decide to trust a dealer only if they are assured by the information that he did not sell bad cars. This is a case of *generalized conditional cooperation*: actors will act cooperatively only if their partners act cooperatively with them and also with others in the course of transactions.

Sanctions in social networks can go even further than the termination of business relationships with a trustee who has abused trust. The example of diamond merchants shows that untrustworthy merchants can fall victim to social

[17] Another example for the swift fluctuations in trust causing different and extreme opinions can be found in Coleman's (1990: 189–191) example of extensive communication among faculty about students.

[18] If actors within a network are aware of the selectivity of the information they obtain in a dense network, they should take the selectivity into account in "updating" their beliefs. I will not consider this complication here.

ostracism and lose all social and religious contacts. This sanction is so severe that, in this type of society, trust becomes almost self-evident and sanctions are hardly ever necessary. It is important to note the counterintuitive aspect of this argument, namely, that the more severe the trustors' sanctions may be, the better it is *not only* for the trustors, *but also* for the trustee himself. If the sanctions are more severe the trustors can trust the trustee more, because the trustee has less incentives to abuse trust. Consequently, the cooperative outcome preferred by both actors is reached more often than the uncooperative "no trust" outcome.

Sanctioning through withholding trust is costly not only for the trustee who is sanctioned, but also for the trustors who execute a sanction. If "no trust" means that the trustor does not enter into a (new) transaction with the trustee, the trustor will have to find an alternative. First, she might manufacture the product herself or do without it. The costs related to this option depend on the ability of the trustor to make the product. Second, the trustor may select another partner. The costs of this option depend on the "exit network" of the trustor. The more alternative trustees for a transaction, the lower her costs for finding an alternative trustee. If a trustor has already done business with the trustee for some transactions, it is possible that she made specific investments in this relationship (Williamson 1985: 52–56). Here, exit has additional costs, namely, the loss of these relation-specific investments. These different kinds of costs make the development of a theory about exit networks complicated. A number of authors have studied exit opportunities (for example, Schüßler 1989; Vanberg and Congleton 1992; Lahno 1995; Weesie 1996; Blumberg 1997). These studies show that exit threats can discipline actors to act cooperatively. Weesie (1996) analyzes a model in which voice and exit are combined. Even without modeling networks in detail, such models are highly complex. Because I want to model networks in detail, I concentrate on the effects of voice in social networks. Exit will only be incorporated in the sense that sanctioning an untrustworthy trustee becomes less costly if there are more exit possibilities for the trustor. In terms of the Trust Game, the costs of not placing trust for the trustor $(R_1 - P_1)$ are smaller if she has more alternatives for similar transactions with other trustees.

Some Problems with Control Effects

A number of authors have argued that control through social networks is unlikely to be effective (see, for example, Lorenz 1988; Williamson 1996: 153–155; and the survey in Blumberg 1997: 208–210). Most arguments addressing the lack of effectiveness of third-party sanctions emphasize that third parties will be reluctant to incur the costs of imposing sanctions, which makes the sanction threats less credible. The willingness of third parties to sanction the trustee will largely depend on whether the execution of the sanctions is individually rational. As long as a trustor is uncertain as to whether a trustee is indeed untrustworthy, in particular in a transaction with herself, it can be individually rational to trust the trustee in spite of "rumors" about his untrustworthiness. I summarize these arguments for a network of trustors having transactions with one trustee.

- The effectiveness of control through social networks largely depends on the possibilities of accurate communication among trustors. If other trustors cannot verify whether a problem between a trustor and the trustee is caused by "force majeure" or by opportunistic behavior of the trustee, they will be careful to execute extensive sanctions, losing the profits they may earn if the trustee is trustworthy.

- If trustor A already has positive experiences with the trustee or is convinced that she can arrange her transactions with the trustee better than other trustors, trustor A will not be persuaded by a trustor B who claims that she is deceived by the trustee. Trustor A will be convinced that she can obtain profits from the trustworthy behavior of the trustee. Consequently, trustor A will frustrate sanctions against the trustee.

- If the trustee asks for forgiveness after he has abused trust, trustors who are not deceived themselves are much more inclined to forgive the trustee than the deceived trustor. This weakens third-party sanctions.

- Goods produced by the trustee are not always homogeneous. For example, a producer of software may produce different programs. The bad performance of one specific program does not imply that the producer will perform badly in all the programs he develops. If trustors consider the bad performance to be product-specific, it is not likely that they will sanction the trustee if they purchase another good.

- If the trustee is a large firm, the actors who represent the trustee are not always the same. Similar to the argument above concerning the heterogeneity of products, trustors who are trading with different agents of the trustee might consider the untrustworthy behavior of the trustee to be caused by the agent and may not expect such behavior from their agent.

- Control effects work particularly well if trustors can convincingly inform other trustors not only about the deceits against themselves, but also about deceits committed against other trustors. Such indirect "rumors" might lose their persuasive force easily.

- If the trustors are competitors, it is questionable whether they are willing to provide reliable information to each other. If one trustor loses investments due to the untrustworthy behavior of the trustee, she may want other trustors to lose as well in order to avoid finding herself in a disadvantaged position. Thus, even if a trustor receives information from another trustor, she might question the value and accuracy of the information.

- Finally, accusing the trustee of untrustworthy behavior includes risks for the accusing trustor. She might acquire a reputation for arranging her transactions badly or for being a trouble-maker. This could seriously damage her business and, therefore, she will be reluctant to make far-reaching accusations against the trustee.

Despite these arguments, control effects will play an important role in this book. I realize that the arguments presented above have to be taken seriously. I argue that they place an element of uncertainty into the extent to which control will be effective not only for the trustors but also for the trustee. The trustee also does not know how effective the sanctions of trustors will be. Therefore, the trustee still has to take into account that some careful trustors might not trust him if they hear rumors about untrustworthy behavior. Moreover, it is difficult for the trustee to determine how trustors value the information they obtain from each other. There may be groups of friends among the trustors who inform each other accurately. Consequently, the trustee should take into account that his reputation might be damaged considerably if he abuses trust placed by a trustor who is influential in the network of trustors.

To conclude, it is hypothesized that trustors who are better embedded in social networks will *learn faster* from other trustors and are in a *better* position to *control* the trustee because they *receive more information* and *transmit information faster* through the network.

Empirical Evidence on Effects of Network Embeddedness

In the sociological literature, cohesive social structures and trust are often seen as being almost equivalent. Gellner (1988: 143), for example, states this explicitly and repeatedly. In these studies, trust is treated as being either present or absent in a society. Actors know each other and have similar norms that lead to trustworthy behavior. Diamond merchants (Wechsberg 1966) and the stock exchange market (Weber 1921) form cohesive societies where trust reaches high levels. Ellickson (1991) describes an example of "high trust" among farmers in Shasta County, California. Disputes between the farmers arise when trespassing cattle damage neighboring fields or there are collisions between cattle and vehicles. However, as long as the disputes are not too great, neighbors are able to settle them informally, thereby saving the cost of law-suits. Formal law is used to settle conflicts only in exceptional cases. Anthropological studies also provide examples where reciprocal behavior without formal arrangements is the rule rather than the exception in close communities (see Sahlins 1972: Chapter 5). For example, Ensminger (2001) illustrates the importance of close family ties among the Omar in East Africa who have to hire herders for cattle herding. Cattle is much more easily entrusted to close relatives than to hired herders with whom one has no family ties.[19]

Although these studies provide evidence that trust can be extensive in cohesive networks, they hardly explain why trust emerged and continues to exist. Learning could be part of the explanation, because newcomers will not receive negative information about actors in the network. Moreover, imitation will lead to trustful behavior after some positive experiences. However, if trust is exclusively based on learning, the situation does not seem to be very stable. One untrustworthy actor could easily invade a society where trust is omnipresent and exploit the trustful actors. Therefore, control is important in maintaining a stable level of trust. Actors who are untrustworthy must be expelled or punished severely enough for other actors to see that untrustworthy behavior is only worthwhile in the very short term.[20]

The evidence also suggests that control alone is not sufficient for the emergence and maintenance of trust. As I mentioned in the explanation of learning through network embeddedness, Burt and Knez (1995a, 1995b) show that not only trust emerges in dense social networks, but trust and distrust may occur simultaneously in the same group of actors. Moreover, strong trust as well as strong distrust are especially prevalent in dense parts of the network. Control effects, in principle, only explain the emergence of trust. The reason is that in a dense network control is effective and trustees do not have an incentive to abuse trust. However, the fact that distrust might increase with the density of the network is a strong indication that trustors adjust their beliefs about the trustworthiness of a trustor on the basis of information they obtain from network contacts.

In recent years, several collections of papers have reported the results of studies into the relations between organizations with respect to *network governance* (Nohria and Eccles 1992; Swedberg 1993; Smelser and Swedberg 1994; Kramer and Tyler 1996). The term "network governance" is used for a group of firms that engage in exchange relationships. The explicit implementation of the term network governance varies considerably between the studies (see Jones, Hesterly, and Borgatti 1997). Most of the research is merely descriptive, enumerating the kinds of networks that emerge, and which firms are more likely to be in the center of a network (see Barley, Freeman, and Hybels 1992). Kogut, Shab, and Walker (1992) show that biotechnology firms tend to search

[19]Ensminger (2001) makes some of the mechanisms that can solve this trust problem explicit by discussing various incentives structures that provide control opportunities with herders who are relatives and with herders who are non-relatives.

[20]In game-theoretic terms, a combination of strategies in which abuse of trust is not sanctioned cannot be a Nash equilibrium (see Section 2.2). A similar situation can be found in Axelrod's (1984) computer experiments, in which naive cooperators in Prisoner's Dilemmas are exploited by strategies that initiate defection.

for partners within a cluster of firms with whom they can work cooperatively. However, the causes and consequences of the choices made by these firms are mostly ignored. Gerlach (1992) goes one step further, showing that Japanese firms are more tightly connected in organizational networks than American firms. Therefore, Japanese firms can rely more on interfirm networks of supply and distribution than American firms. As a result, Japanese firms are smaller than American firms because the latter more frequently incorporate production processes within the firms. Finally, Gulati (1995b) finds that social networks help firms to obtain information about facilities and the abilities of potential partners. The result is that alliances occur more often among partners who have more common ties with third parties. Unfortunately, theory about the effects of specific network properties other than the number of ties is lacking in research about the relations between organizations. Therefore, the studies have an illustrative function for the more general theory I want to develop in the subsequent chapters.

Burt's theory of structural holes (1992, 1993) is a theory that tries to use more specific structural properties of a network as explanatory mechanisms for promotion opportunities. Burt argues that a person has a limited number of ties because of time and money constraints. Therefore, one should "organize" the limited number of ties one can mobilize in an optimal way. According to Burt, optimality is reached if redundancy is minimal. A "structural hole" is the absence of a tie between two actors who are connected to a focal actor. If an actor's contacts communicate frequently among themselves, they will provide similar information to the focal actor. Therefore, actors rich in structural holes are expected to obtain more divers and less redundant information than actors with the same number of densely connected contacts. Burt demonstrates empirically that actors rich in structural holes get promoted faster than actors who have few structural holes in their network. In this way, the social network is a "social resource" or "social capital" (Flap and De Graaf 1986; Flap 1988; Coleman 1990: Chapter 12) and helps an actor to achieve his or her goals. In this book, I aim at similar predictions for the amount of trust a trustor can have in a trustee depending on the position of the trustor in her network and, hence, the extent to which the network position of an actor helps her to reach efficient, mutually cooperative outcomes in trust relations.

I realize that the evidence for learning and control through social networks shown above is far from extensive. Although there is enough evidence that trust can emerge in dense social networks, it is still far from clear what drives the emergence of trust. Is it learning or is control through the threat of sanctions more important? Probably, the empirical evidence is limited because theoretical explanations guiding the search for empirical evidence are scarce. I will return to this issue later in the concluding chapter.

1.2.5 ARRANGEMENTS TO REDUCE THE TRUST PROBLEM

Although formal arrangements are not the focus of this book, this section intends to show that the presence of costly bilateral arrangements can be used to indicate a lack of trust between actors in a transaction. Moreover, institutions that arose voluntarily to facilitate communication of information are described. These institutions provide evidence that actors value information about possible partners in a transaction and realize that effective control can prevent opportunistic behavior.

I have already referred to what can happen when a trustor cannot trust a trustee. A student who really needs a used car or a firm that needs a software package has to find a supplier with whom she can make an appropriate deal. In the foregoing subsections, I discussed the way in which temporal and network embeddedness can decrease the trust problem between two partners. In the discussion of exit networks, I have argued that a trustor who does not trust trustee A may search for another trustee, with whom she has, for example, more third-party contacts. However, searching for and selecting an alternative partner costs time and money. An alternative option for the trustor is to lessen the trust problem with trustee A using formal arrangements that reduce the trustee's incentives for behaving opportunistically or reduce the amount of damage that may be caused if trust is abused. Such formal arrangements can include contracts or other bilateral agreements. Moreover, third parties can play a mediating role in trust relations. In this subsection, I discuss some of the arrangements for solving trust problems.

Transaction cost theory (Williamson 1975, 1985) discusses the different ways in which actors formally manage transactions. Williamson assumes that actors will follow incentives for opportunistic behavior, thereby abusing trust (1985: 47–49). Hence, it makes sense for actors to invest in the management of transactions by choosing an appropriate "governance structure" to prevent this kind of opportunistic behavior. The costs of this management are called *transaction costs*. These costs depend on the size of the opportunism potential of a transaction. Opportunism potential depends on three key characteristics of the transaction (Williamson 1985: Chapter 2).[21] The first of Williamson's characteristics is *asset specificity*. Asset specificity refers to the degree to which investments in a transaction are of value only in transactions with the same actor. An example is the investment made by a buyer of tailor-made software in a particular software package. This investment is lost—at least to some degree—if the buyer switches to a package sold by another supplier. If such an investment

[21] How these three characteristics relate to payoffs in a Trust Game will be discussed in Chapter 5, where I seek empirical support for my theory.

is large, the management of a transaction becomes more important. The second characteristic, *uncertainty*, refers to a lack of information on relevant parameters of the transaction. This may involve trustworthiness or the abilities of the partner, an actor's difficulties in assessing the quality of a product, and even developments in the market or developments of new technologies concerning the product she wants to buy. If trustors have a hard time assessing whether a trustee has sold a high-quality product, it is relatively simple for the trustee to abuse trust. Thus, the larger the uncertainty of the actors in a transaction, the more they are inclined to invest in the formal management of the transaction. The third factor is *frequency*. Williamson argues that frequency is important because detailed management is only profitable if it can be used in a series of transactions. I want to add an additional argument about the importance of repeated transactions, namely, the possibilities available to a trustor to sanction the abuse of trust by the trustee in subsequent transactions.

Bilateral Arrangements

Initially, Williamson (1975) only distinguished between "markets" and "hierarchies" as governance structures. If the opportunism potential of actors in a transaction is low, the costs of management for the transaction will be small. Such a transaction can be arranged within the market without extensive formal arrangements. However, if the opportunism potential is high, for instance, because the uncertainty of the partners is high or extensive specific investments have to be made for a transaction, market governance may become inefficient because careful transaction management is required. In such situations, partners may choose for *vertical integration*, i.e., a hierarchical governance structure in which one partner completely determines the course of a transaction. However, such a strict dichotomization of transactions ignores the importance of "hybrid forms" of transaction management (see Williamson 1985: 83–84; Kreps 1990a: 99; Stinchcombe 1990: 233). Williamson (1985: Chapter 3) himself later distinguished bilateral and trilateral contractual arrangements. Within these two types of arrangements one can study the degree of elaboration involved in the contracts. Transaction cost theory then becomes consistent with the argument that more trust and fewer incentives for opportunistic behavior reduce the necessity for elaborated formal contracts (see Chiles and McMackin 1996: 91–92).

Bilateral arrangements are a commonly used option to counter the problem of trust in certain transactions. In the examples provided by buying a used car or a software package, a contract is an option commonly used to diminish trust problems. In the contract, the supplier will make commitments such as the provision of warranties and after-sales services to compensate the buyer if the supplier performs poorly (see Raub and Keren 1993). If there is a considerable development phase in designing a product, the partners may establish bonds to prevent that one partner breaks the relation and, thus, makes investments made by the other partner worthless. Commitments can also be used as signals. For example, if buyers are uncertain about the time preferences of a supplier, the supplier can signal that his business goals are long-term by investing in high-quality equipment.[22]

Institutions for Social Learning and Control

Instead of choosing to arrange transactions with extensive bilateral agreements, actors may seek ways to institutionalize *social* control mechanisms. Schwartz (1954) and Merry (1984) discuss small-scale societies in which the communication of information is institutionalized in such a way that reputational mechanisms work effectively and that include sanctioning actors who do not participate in the communication process. Klein (1997a, 2000) draws on studies that show the emergence of institutions involving reputational mechanisms that prevent actors from acting opportunistically. Most of these institutions make the communication of information either more effective or less costly by using middlemen (Klein 1997b) or law merchants (Milgrom, North, and Weingast 1990) or by forming coalitions (Greif 1989), for example. Middlemen and law merchants keep records of the behavior of possible partners and this information can be purchased from them and used in subsequent encounters. By forming such "centers of information," information can be easily transmitted between traders, and frequent contacts among the traders themselves become less necessary. In this way, the traders can easily get an accurate picture about who does and does not trade trustfully. Consequently, the punishment imposed against untrustworthy traders can be both more severe and more extensive. Moreover, traders who refrain from sanctioning untrustworthy others are detected in these systems and can be sanctioned as well. Thus, control via reputational mechanisms is more effective within such institutions, because uncertainty about which traders are actually untrustworthy is reduced and traders who do not want to take part in sanctions are sanctioned themselves. Coalitions consist of members providing each other with agency services. Members profit from these services, but they are excluded from membership if they are caught cheating. The control mechanism works within these coalitions because information about untrustworthy behavior is transmitted rapidly among the members of the coalition. Members are not allowed to trade with excluded members. If they do, they will be excluded themselves. The long-term profits for members from the agency services is generally greater than the short-term profits from cheating today (Greif 1989).

[22]Actors may use other signals such as wearing an expensive suit. It is questionable whether such signals are reliable as mimicry is so simple. For some game-theoretic considerations on this issue see, for example, Spence (1973), Kreps (1990b: 645–650), Raub and Weesie (2000b), Bacharach and Gambetta (2001), or Snijders and Buskens (2001).

While institutions such as middlemen and law merchants combine learning and control, the next example concerns an institution that focuses primarily on learning. Although communication of information might be relatively cheap, it can be problematic to find *essential* information. Nohria (1992) provides a nice example of an institution that illustrates the importance of searching for a reliable business partner. The "128 Venture Group" organizes meetings in the region of Route 128, a high-technology area around Boston known for its success in creating and building up high-technology ventures (Nohria 1992: 241; Piore and Sabel 1984). These meetings are meant for investors who want to start enterprises, but who only have one or two of the necessary resources such as capital, technology, and knowledge. During the meeting, they can look out for possible partners who might have complementary resources. Actors do not only search for specific skills but explicitly search for people with whom they are better embedded: "Since trust is largely process based and relies on reputation credibility built on occupational history, certification of mutually known contacts, and the prospect of future exchange—participants from outside the region have a hard time in this market" (Nohria 1992: 257).

1.3 RESEARCH QUESTIONS

The problem dealt with in this book is analyzing the effects of network embeddedness on solving trust problems. One essential point in analyzing network effects is understanding the *communication of information* between trustors. The most extreme assumptions, "no communication is possible" or "everybody knows what everybody is doing," are unrealistic and not very satisfactory, because neither assumption distinguishes between the individual trustors in a network. Some theoretical implications of network embeddedness for control effects have been studied with different types of models (Coleman 1990: Chapters 5 and 8; Raub and Weesie 1990; Weesie, Buskens, and Raub 1998). These models can explain the emergence of trust in dense networks such as in the example of the diamond merchants. However, networks are mostly modeled on the basis of one parameter that indicates the number of ties or the density of the network of trustors, which makes it impossible to distinguish between individual trustors in a network.[23]

In this book, I study the way in which the effects of social networks on trust depend on the way the network is structured, i.e., on who exactly has ties to whom. I distinguish network parameters at two levels in order to explain trust with these network effects. First, I consider *global* network parameters such as the number of ties in the network. Global network parameters are properties

[23]Although Raub and Weesie (1990) model networks in more detail, the assumptions for transmission of information are such that the equilibria, ceteris paribus, depend only on one global network characteristic, namely, the minimal number of relations a trustor has in the network.

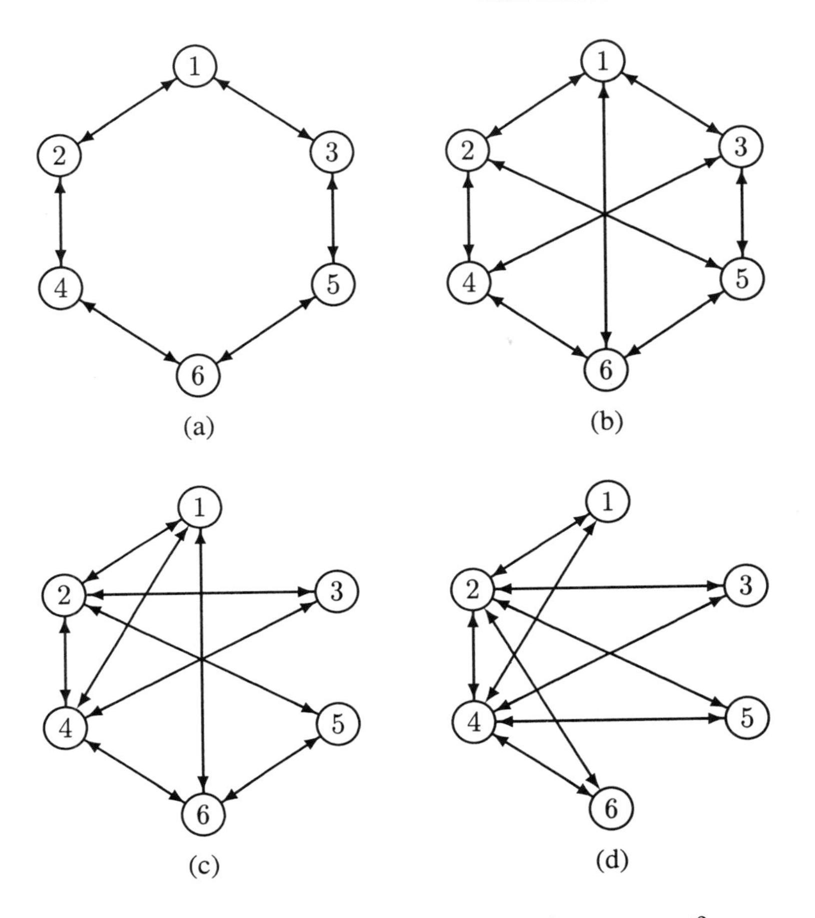

Figure 1.2. Which trustors can trust the trustee most?

of the network as a whole. They can explain why trustors in one network can place more trust in a trustee than trustors in another network. Second, I consider network parameters at the *individual* level such as the number of ties a trustor has. Individual network parameters are properties of a trustor within a network. They can explain why one trustor in a network can place more trust in a trustee than another trustor in the same network. In the light of my earlier discussion, it can be expected that trustors in networks with more ties trust a trustee more than trustors in networks with fewer ties, and that trustors with more ties themselves trust a trustee more than trustors with fewer ties. In this sense, I expect that learning effects and control effects differ not only *between* networks but also *within* networks.

Figure 1.2 shows four networks to illustrate some of the network parameters that will be used in subsequent chapters. Each network consists of six trustors. All trustors are potential partners of the same trustee who is not a member of the network himself. Arrows indicate which trustors transmit information to which other trustors.[24] Now, consider which of these networks is more appropriate to fostering trust and, within networks, which of the trustors is more likely to trust. In network (a) and network (b), all trustors have a similar position ("automorphic equivalence"). This means that the trustors in these networks will receive and transmit information to the same extent as the other trustors in the same network. Therefore, no differences in trust are expected for the trustors within one of these networks. The difference between network (a) and (b) is that network (b) has more ties. Therefore, trustors in network (b) transmit and receive more information than trustors in network (a). Thus, network effects will be stronger in network (b) than in network (a), and the expectation is that trustors in network (b) can place more trust in the trustee than trustors in network (a). Network (c) and (d) have the same number of ties as network (b) and, hence, the same density, but the network structure is different. In network (c), there are individual differences. Trustors 2 and 4 communicate information with four other trustors, trustors 1 and 6 with three others, and trustors 3 and 5 only communicate information with two others. Again, reasoning is straightforward. For trustors who transmit information to more others, control effects will be larger, while learning effects will be larger for trustors who receive information from more others. As long as information is positive, this implies that trustors who communicate with more other trustors can place more trust in the trustee than other trustors within the same network. There are other structural aspects that could have an influence on the diffusion of information and the reasoning here is less straightforward. For example, is there an effect of the number of trustors a focal trustor can reach in two steps, i.e., through one other trustor? Does this effect exist even in addition to the effects of the number of ties in a network and the number of ties a trustor has? What is the consequence on trust if a network is completely centralized around one or a few trustors, as in network (d)? In other words, can trustors in network (b) "on average" place more trust in the trustee than trustors in network (d)?

In this study, the first and most prevalent extension of earlier research is that the explanation of trust will be made more "structural," in the sense that I explain the level of trust a trustor can have in a trustee as a function of *individual* and *global* network parameters. Second, I will distinguish the control ("economic") explanation and the learning ("sociological") explanation of these network effects. Although I do not present an integrated model in which control and learning effects are combined, I do develop hypotheses for both kinds of

[24]The ties in all networks are symmetric (trustors who send information to another trustor also receive information from that trustor), but that will not be a prerequisite in later chapters. Furthermore, in the examples I use discrete networks, but in the models I will use ties that can vary in strength indicating how frequently a trustor transmits information to another trustor.

network effects and the empirical chapters demonstrate that the distinction of learning and control is highly relevant to understand network effects.

RESEARCH QUESTIONS

1. What are the effects of *learning* through social networks on trust of trustors in a trustee, and how are these effects related to individual and global parameters of the social network of trustors?
2. What are the effects of *control* through social networks on trust of trustors in a trustee, and how are these effects related to individual and global parameters of the social network of trustors?
3. How important are *individual compared to global network parameters* for the description of various network effects on trust?

1.4 OVERVIEW

The structure of the book is summarized in Figure 1.3. Before starting to develop new models, I will introduce the two most important conceptual and theoretical tools: social network analysis and game theory (see Chapter 2). In Chapters 3 and 4 I describe two models. Readers who are interested simply in the hypotheses derived from the models can refer to the conclusions of these chapters. Mathematical details that are not essential for an understanding of the substance of the models can be found at the end of the book in Appendix A. Chapter 3 describes a game-theoretic model of a trustee who plays repeated Trust Games with a network of trustors. Hypotheses concerning control effects are derived for some network parameters. Chapter 4 presents a model for stochastic information diffusion through heterogeneous networks. In this chapter, hypotheses are derived about control effects as well as learning effects. These hypotheses are based on the amount of information transmitted or received by a trustor in a network of trustors.

The empirical part of the book begins in Chapter 5, where the models are tested using a data set on transactions between buyers and suppliers of information technology products. Some but not all of the effects of networks are corroborated although the data are not suitable for distinguishing control and learning effects. The chapter addresses some of the theoretical problems related to the models and the empirical problems arising from the data collections. Chapter 6 presents a vignette experiment used to test the models in a situation that is more controlled than that of the survey. Temporal embeddedness and network embeddedness are the main aspects manipulated in the experiment on buying used cars. Moreover, I make a direct attempt to disentangle control effects and learning effects. The experiment offers the first evidence for the simultaneous occurrence of these two kinds of network effects.

Finally, some parts of the puzzle appear to be solved. The results of the models and empirical tests are summarized in the last chapter where their limitations are also discussed. I have made some suggestions about how to address limitations in the future in order to "solve more parts of the puzzle."

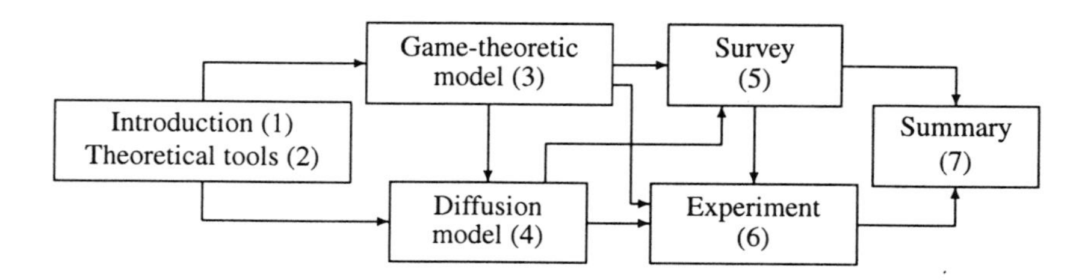

Figure 1.3. Overview (number of chapter in parentheses).

Chapter 2

SOCIAL NETWORK ANALYSIS AND GAME THEORY: BASIC CONCEPTS AND ASSUMPTIONS

I use social network analysis and game theory in the models developed in this book. It is useful to discuss the basic concepts associated with these two "tools" before I begin. Readers familiar with social network analysis should check the formal definitions of a social network and the related network parameters in Section 2.1, because these definitions are somewhat different than those used in most network studies. Section 2.2 has nothing new for readers familiar with game theory, although some readers might be interested in the specific results for Trust Games presented in this section.

Social networks analysis is rich in conceptualization. Wasserman and Faust (1994) offer an extensive overview of concepts and operationalizations. However, social network analysis lacks testable implications (see Granovetter 1979). There are few theoretical predictions about what positions in a network can be expected to have what effect on a dependent variable. And, if phenomena can be explained by the structural aspects of a network, the arguments underlying the explanation are often rather informal and open to many theoretical counterarguments. For example, in the theory of structural holes (Burt 1992), the concept of a structural hole is defined in mathematical detail. Furthermore, the association between an actor who is "rich in structural holes" and the actor's performance is empirically convincing. However, the theoretical arguments underlying the association remain informal. As a consequence, it is hard to argue that network properties rather than personal characteristics that correlate with structural holes drive the performance (see Burt, Jannotta, and Mahoney 1998). In Section 2.1, I introduce the network parameters used in this book. These parameters summarize core structural properties of social networks. After introducing the network parameters, I present informal arguments about the effects they have on information communication processes. As discussed in Chapter 1, the effects of social networks on trust depend, at least in my theory, primarily on how fast trustors in a network can transmit information to other trustors and how quickly they receive information. Expectations on network effects based on my informal arguments will be referred to as "conjectures." In Chapters 3 and 4, I develop theoretical models from which I formally derive the effects of network parameters on trust. Conjectures that do turn out to be indeed logical consequences of the models will then be referred to as "hypotheses."

Game theory is a behavioral theory that is rich in implications. The theory assumes that actors are utility maximizers, and that actors decide upon their behavior taking into account that other actors are utility maximizers as well. Therefore, using actors' utilities for different outcomes in a game, it is possible to make predictions about actors' behavior. Chapter 3 contributes to an integration of social network analysis and game theory by providing a game-theoretic model of trust in a network of actors. The core concepts and basic assumptions of game theory needed to develop this model are introduced in Section 2.2 and models on trust are used as examples. Obviously, the emergence and maintenance of trust among rational actors will not only depend on network parameters but also on payoffs associated with transactions and on the temporal embeddedness of transactions between a trustor and trustee, for example. Section 2.2 provides on overview of related hypotheses that follow from game-theoretic analyses.

2.1 SOCIAL NETWORK ANALYSIS

I wish to explain the effects of social networks on the extent to which trustors can trust a trustee. Because I try to explain trust through learning and control effects, it is essential to know how fast trustors receive and transmit information in the network. Another element I want to include is the "importance" of a given trustor for the trustee. For instance, when a trustor who is involved in half of the trustee's transactions no longer trusts the trustee, this will be more problematic for the trustee than when a trustor who is involved in a much smaller proportion of transactions no longer trusts him. Consequently, the sanctions of a more important trustor can be more severe for the trustee than the sanctions of a less important trustor.[1]

To include these elements, social networks are conceived as *valued directed graphs with weighted nodes*. Figure 2.1 gives an example of such a network. Valued directed graphs are commonly used to represent (finite) networks (see, for example, Harary, Norman, and Cartwright 1965; Wasserman and Faust 1994). A *graph* is a set of nodes and ties between these nodes. If the set of nodes consists of n elements, the ties can be represented by an $n \times n$ matrix

[1]The generalization that trustors may be of varying importance is included in the definitions of network parameters and in the model in Chapter 3. The implications of Chapters 3 and 4 are based on networks in which all trustors are equally important.

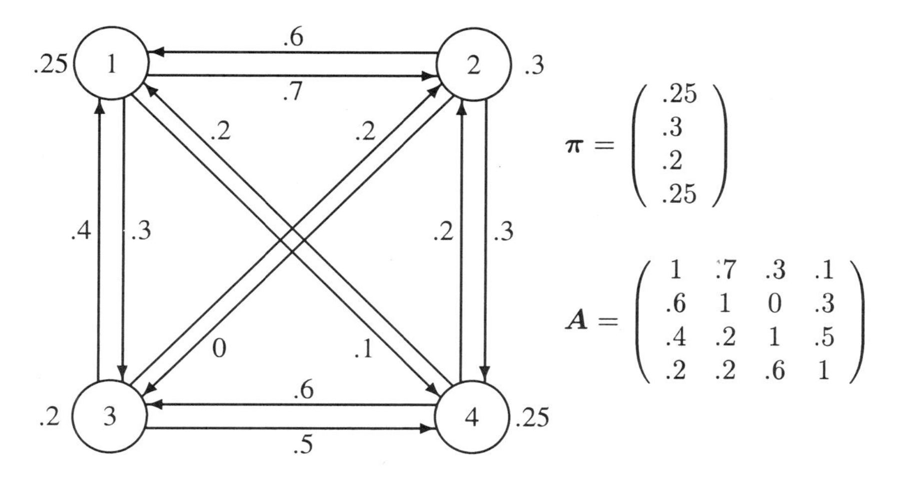

Figure 2.1. Example of a network of trustors.

$\boldsymbol{A}$. In a *discrete* graph, the matrix $\boldsymbol{A}$ indicates only whether certain ties exist, i.e., the elements α_{ij} of $\boldsymbol{A}$ are 0 or 1. In a *directed* graph, the ties are directed from one node to another. This implies that the matrix $\boldsymbol{A}$ is not necessarily symmetric. In a *valued* graph, values are added to the ties to indicate, for example, the importance of a tie. If $\alpha_{ij} > 0$, a tie exists from actor i to actor j. I add *weights* to the nodes (actors) of the network, indicating the importance of a node (actor). I use the term "discrete network" for a network described by a discrete graph. Similarly, I use the terms "valued networks" and "valued networks with weighted nodes."

The formal notation of a valued network with weighted nodes representing n actors is a pair $(\boldsymbol{\pi}, \boldsymbol{A})$, where $\boldsymbol{\pi}$ is an n-vector of weights indicating the importance of each actor with $\sum_{i=1}^{n} \pi_i = 1$, $\pi_i > 0$ for all i, and $\boldsymbol{A}$ is an $n \times n$-matrix where α_{ij}, $0 \leq \alpha_{ij} \leq 1$, is the importance of the tie from actor i to actor j.[2] By definition, $\alpha_{ii} = 1$ for $i = 1, \ldots, n$.[3]

A network is called *homogeneous* if $\alpha_{ij} = \alpha$ for all $i \neq j$. In this study, I am interested in heterogeneous networks and in the effects of heterogeneity on trust. In heterogeneous networks, some ties are stronger than others. Ties can be strong within subgroups of a network and weak between subgroups of a network. Networks might resemble a chain, a circle, or a star. All these

[2]I use boldface for vectors (lowercase) and matrices (uppercase).

[3]The same representation is directly applicable to stochastic blockmodels (see, for example, Wasserman and Faust 1994), where $\boldsymbol{\pi}$ indicates the percentage of actors in a block, while the matrix $\boldsymbol{A}$ represents the percentage of ties present between the blocks. Here, the diagonal elements should represent the percentage of ties within blocks and, hence, need not be constrained to 1.

properties might hinder or facilitate information diffusion. Network parameters such as the centrality of an actor in a network (see Freeman 1979) measure certain aspects of heterogeneity. Network parameters are usually defined for discrete networks in the literature, although sometimes informal indications are given about generalizations of network parameters for valued networks. In this book, network parameters are formally defined for valued networks with weighted nodes.

Although the list of network parameters below might seem a rather ad hoc selection, they cover the main structural properties that are frequently discussed in social network literature. In Chapter 1, I explained that I want to study network properties at the individual and global level. Therefore, I have differentiated between individual and global network parameters. Individual network parameters measure the properties of an actor within a network and can explain "within-network" effects. Global network parameters measure the properties of a network as a whole and can explain "between-network" effects. On the individual level, I focus on three properties:

- the extent to which an individual actor is connected to other actors in the network (outdegree and indegree),
- the extent to which the neighbors of an actor are connected to other actors (degree quality), and
- the extent to which neighbors of the focal actors are mutually connected (local density).

On the global level, four properties are distinguished:

- the density of the network,
- the extent to which the network is centralized around one or a few actors (outdegree variance, indegree variance, outdegree-indegree covariance),
- the transitivity of the network, i.e., a measure for the existence of dense subgroups with limited connectivity among these subgroups, and
- the number of actors in the network (network size).

I also describe intuitive expectations about the effects of the network parameters on information *transmission* and *reception rates*, i.e., how fast information is transmitted and received by actors in the network. I start with the individual network parameters.

OUTDEGREE

Outdegree is a parameter for the extent to which an actor in a network communicates information to other actors. For discrete networks, outdegree is defined as the number of ties an actor has divided by the maximal number of ties that are possible for an actor (Freeman 1979). For example, if there are five actors in a network and a focal actor has ties to three of the four other actors, the focal actor's outdegree is $\frac{3}{4}$. For valued networks, outdegree is defined as the sum of the values of the ties starting from the focal actor, divided by the highest possible value. Generalizing outdegree for valued networks with weighted nodes, the values of the ties are weighted by the importance of the actors at the other end of these ties. In this way, an actor who is connected to more important other actors has a higher outdegree than an actor who is connected to the same extent, but with less important others. Because actors cannot have ties to themselves, standardization is used such that the outdegree is 1 if an actor is "perfectly" connected to all other actors.[4] Formally, the outdegree for actor i is defined as

$$D_{out}(i) = \frac{1}{1 - \pi_i} \sum_{j \neq i} \pi_j \alpha_{ij}. \tag{2.1}$$

Because an actor with a higher outdegree transmits information more often to other actors, I conjecture that an actor with a higher outdegree will transmit information faster to other actors than an actor with a lower outdegree. On the other hand, outdegree does not have an influence on the extent to which an actor receives information. Therefore, I do not expect an effect of outdegree on the time needed for an actor to receive information.

INDEGREE

Indegree is a parameter for the extent to which an actor receives information from other actors. The indegree is the number of incoming ties to the focal actor relative to its maximal value. Indegree is also called *degree prestige* (Freeman 1979). Incorporating weighted nodes, indegree can be defined here analogously to outdegree as

$$D_{in}(i) = \frac{1}{1 - \pi_i} \sum_{j \neq i} \pi_j \alpha_{ji}. \tag{2.2}$$

Indegree and outdegree are identical for *symmetric* networks, i.e., if $\alpha_{ij} = \alpha_{ji}$ for all i and j.

If the indegree of an actor is higher, she will receive information more frequently from other actors and, therefore, I expect she will receive information sooner. The indegree of an actor does not influence the transmission of infor-

[4] The weights are chosen in such a way for all network parameters that these parameters are directly generalizable for stochastic blockmodels. The necessary adjustments for stochastic blockmodels involve the inclusion of ties *within* blocks (see Buskens 1998).

mation to other actors. Therefore, no effect is expected from indegree on how fast an actor transmits information.

DEGREE QUALITY

Outdegree and indegree are strictly local parameters of network position. These parameters could be made "less local" by studying the (weighted) proportion of actors an actor can reach in two, three, or more steps. *Outdegree quality* and *indegree quality* measure the extent to which actors can reach others or can be reached by others in two steps. Thus, these parameters indicate the extent to which an actor is linked to actors who have high degrees themselves. For example, if an actor communicates with only one actor who, however, communicates with all actors in the network, the first actor might still be able to transmit information relatively fast. An actor who receives information from only one other actor will receive information slower if this other actor receives information from only one actor. This is in contrast with the situation where this other actor is informed by a large number of third actors. The parameters outdegree quality $Q_{out}(i)$ and indegree quality $Q_{in}(i)$ are formally defined as the weighted covariance between the value of a tie to (from) an actor and the outdegree (indegree) of that actor.[5] Ties are weighted such that ties to (from) intermediate actors who are more important obtain a larger weight. Formally,

$$Q_{out}(i) = \frac{1}{1-\pi_i} \sum_{j \neq i} \pi_j \Big(a_{ij} - D_{out}(i) \Big) \left(D_{out}(j) - \frac{1}{1-\pi_i} \sum_{k \neq i} \pi_k D_{out}(k) \right)$$

and

$$Q_{in}(i) = \frac{1}{1-\pi_i} \sum_{j \neq i} \pi_j \Big(a_{ji} - D_{in}(i) \Big) \left(D_{in}(j) - \frac{1}{1-\pi_i} \sum_{k \neq i} \pi_k D_{in}(k) \right). \quad (2.3)$$

Thus, an actor has high outdegree quality if outgoing ties are toward actors with high outdegrees. Rogers (1995: 289) finds that actors search information from opinion leaders or those with high status who are expected to have higher outdegrees or indegrees. A positive effect of indegree quality on the diffusion of information might indicate that these actors use a "rational" strategy when choosing their ties.

As outdegree quality and indegree quality are extensions of outdegree and indegree, respectively, the conjectures for these parameters are the same as for

[5]In an earlier paper (Buskens 1998), these parameters are called *individual outdegree centralization* and *individual indegree centralization*, but this terminology is confusing because centralization usually refers to global network parameters.

outdegree and indegree. I conjecture that higher outdegree quality facilitates a rapid transmission of information through the network and that outdegree quality does not have an effect on how quickly an actor receives information. Moreover, I expect that the time information needs to reach an actor will decrease with indegree quality, and indegree quality will not have an effect on how fast an actor transmits information in a network.

LOCAL DENSITY

The following individual network parameters are *local outdegree density* and *local indegree density*. Local density measures the extent to which an actor's contacts have contacts among themselves. It is expected that information is transmitted more slowly through the network if an actor informs two actors who have also frequent contacts among themselves than if the actor informs two actors who never have contacts with each other, because the probability is relatively high that these actors obtain the same information from multiple sources (Granovetter 1973).[6] Again, outdegree and indegree versions of this parameter are distinguished. The local outdegree density $LD_{out}(i)$ of actor i measures the extent to which actor i transmits information to connected neighbors. Local indegree density $LD_{in}(i)$ of actor i measures the extent to which actor i obtains information from connected neighbors. A tie is weighted with the product of the importance of the receiver and the transmitter, because the contribution of such a tie to the local density depends on the importance of the receiver as well as the importance of the transmitter.[7] Formally, the parameters are defined as

$$LD_{out}(i) = \frac{\sum_{j \neq i} \sum_{k \neq i, k \neq j} \pi_j \pi_k \alpha_{ij} \alpha_{ik} \alpha_{jk}}{\sum_{j \neq i} \sum_{k \neq i, k \neq j} \pi_j \pi_k \alpha_{ij} \alpha_{ik}}, \tag{2.4}$$

and

$$LD_{in}(i) = \frac{\sum_{j \neq i} \sum_{k \neq i, k \neq j} \pi_j \pi_k \alpha_{ji} \alpha_{ki} \alpha_{jk}}{\sum_{j \neq i} \sum_{k \neq i, k \neq j} \pi_j \pi_k \alpha_{ji} \alpha_{ki}}. \tag{2.5}$$

The local density parameters described above are only defined if actor i has at least two ties to other actors. Local density is defined as 0 if an actor has at most one tie.

Because a higher local outdegree density makes redundant information transmission more likely, I expect that a high local density will inhibit fast trans-

[6] This argument is similar to the redundancy argument in Burt's theory on structural holes. See Burt (1992: Chapter 1) for precise definitions and examples. Local degree density resembles the opposite of what Burt defines as the "effective size" of a network for an actor (1992: 52), but it is not a straightforward generalization.

[7] Other forms such as the sum of the importance of the two actors connected by a tie are possible. One argument in favor of the product is that for stochastic blockmodels the proportion of actual ties from one block to another equals the product of the proportions of the actors in these blocks times the density of ties between the two blocks.

mission of information in a social network when density has been controlled. Therefore, an actor with a higher local outdegree density will transmit information more slowly through a network than an actor with a lower local outdegree density. No effect of local outdegree density is expected on the time information needs to reach a focal actor. For local indegree density the argument is somewhat different. If an actor receives information from other actors who frequently receive information from each other, information that has reached the neighborhood of the focal actor is also quickly received by many neighbors and, therefore, can be expected to be known fairly soon by the focal actor. Consequently, I conjecture that an actor with a higher local indegree density will receive information sooner than an actor with a lower local indegree density. I expect the local indegree density will not have an effect on the speed with which an actor transmits information through the network.

DENSITY

Density is the first global network parameter to be discussed. In discrete networks, the density of a network is defined as the number of ties divided by the number of possible ties. In valued networks, the density (Δ) is the sum of all values of the ties in the network divided by the sum of all maximal values of the ties. Ties are weighted with the product of the importance of the two actors adjacent to the tie. Formally,

$$\Delta = \frac{\sum_{i=1}^{n} \sum_{j \neq i} \pi_i \pi_j \alpha_{ij}}{\sum_{i=1}^{n} \sum_{j \neq i} \pi_i \pi_j}. \tag{2.6}$$

This corresponds with the average of all outdegrees or indegrees only if $\pi_i = \frac{1}{n}$ for all i. Then,

$$\Delta = \frac{1}{n} \sum_{i=1}^{n} D_{out}(i) = \frac{1}{n} \sum_{i=1}^{n} D_{in}(i). \tag{2.7}$$

I expect that information will be communicated faster through networks with a higher density than through networks with a lower density. Therefore, I conjecture that, on average, actors will transmit and receive information faster in a dense network than in a sparse network.

CENTRALIZATION

Global centralization parameters are always related to individual centrality parameters. Since I used outdegree and indegree as centrality parameters earlier, I discuss centralization parameters based on outdegree and indegree. *Centralization* of a network measures the differences in outdegrees or indegrees of the actors in a network. A suitable parameter for measuring this difference is the variance of actor degrees: degree variance (Snijders 1981). I define *outdegree variance* and *indegree variance* as the average variance in the outdegrees and indegrees of the actors in the network, with each term weighted by the importance of the actor. Note that the average outdegrees and indegrees could have been replaced by density if all actors are equally important. Formally, the outdegree variance is defined as

$$V_{out} = \sum_{i=1}^{n} \pi_i \left(D_{out}(i) - \sum_{j=1}^{n} \pi_j D_{out}(j) \right)^2, \tag{2.8}$$

and, similarly, the indegree variance is defined as

$$V_{in} = \sum_{i=1}^{n} \pi_i \left(D_{in}(i) - \sum_{j=1}^{n} \pi_j D_{in}(j) \right)^2. \tag{2.9}$$

It can be expected that centralization accelerates information diffusion if the central actors are also the important actors in the diffusion process. In an earlier paper (Buskens and Weesie 2000a) on the model proposed in Chapter 3, I derived the result that trustors trust a trustee to a relatively large extent in a network where trustors who receive a large amount of information (have a high indegree) are the same trustors as those who transmit a large amount of information (have a high outdegree). I try to cover this aspect with a third network centralization measure: *outdegree-indegree covariance*. This network parameter is defined as

$$V_{out,in} = \sum_{i=1}^{n} \pi_i \left(D_{out}(i) - \sum_{j=1}^{n} \pi_j D_{out}(j) \right) \left(D_{in}(i) - \sum_{j=1}^{n} \pi_j D_{in}(j) \right). \tag{2.10}$$

Other centralization parameters are proposed in the literature. Freeman (1979), for example, compares degrees in a network with the maximal degree in the network to obtain a centralization parameter. Freeman's parameter correlates highly with the centralization parameters defined above. I use degree variance instead of Freeman's parameter, because Freeman's parameter is too strongly related to the actor with the maximal degree. Yamaguchi (1994a, 1994b; Buskens and Yamaguchi 1999) proposes the "coefficient of variation" in degrees as a centralization parameter. This parameter is defined as the square-root of the variance in degrees divided by the average degree or density of the network and could be used for outdegrees as well as indegrees. Because the coefficient of variation correlates more with density, outdegree, and indegree than outdegree variance and indegree variance, it is not used in the following chapters. The higher the correlations among network parameters, the more problematic it becomes to disentangle the effects of the different parameters.

There are no clear conjectures for centralization parameters. If actors with a high indegree also have a high outdegree, central actors will receive *and* transmit information at a high rate. In such a network, I expect information will be transmitted and received faster by all trustors. Thus, actors in a networks with higher outdegree-indegree covariance will transmit and receive information on average more quickly than actors in a network with a lower outdegree-indegree covariance. Controlling for outdegree-indegree covariance, I expect that outdegree variance and indegree variance will inhibit the transmission of information, as it seems to be inefficient if actors who obtain information frequently, do not communicate this information to others or if actors who are able to transmit information to many others receive very little information. Thus, I conjecture that the information transmission rate and the information reception rate decrease with outdegree variance and indegree variance.

TRANSITIVITY

To define transitivity, I recall some definitions. A *triad* consists of three actors (i, j, k) in a network. A discrete network is called *transitive* if the existence of a tie from actor i to actor j and from actor j to actor k implies that there is a tie from actor i to actor k. A discrete network is called *intransitive* if it is not transitive; thus, intransitivity implies that there is a triad (i, j, k) such that ties from actor i to actor j and from actor j to actor k exist, while a tie from actor i to actor k is absent. I define the extent to which a triad (i, j, k) is transitive as $\alpha_{ij}\alpha_{ik}\alpha_{jk}$ for a valued network. To obtain network *transitivity*, the transitivity of each triad is summed over all triads and weighted by the product of importance of the three actors involved, divided by the maximal possible value on the basis of all pairs of ties of the actors:

$$Tr = \frac{\sum_{i=1}^{n} \sum_{j \neq i} \sum_{k \neq i, k \neq j} \pi_i \pi_j \pi_k \alpha_{ij} \alpha_{ik} \alpha_{jk}}{\sum_{i=1}^{n} \sum_{j \neq i} \sum_{k \neq i, k \neq j} \pi_i \pi_j \pi_k \alpha_{ij} \alpha_{ik}}. \tag{2.11}$$

Transitivity as described above is defined only if at least one actor has two or more ties. Transitivity is defined as 0 if all actor have at most one tie.

Transitivity is related to density. For example, if all α_{ij} are equal to 1, transitivity as well as density are equal to 1. If density is low, transitivity measures the extent to which ties are concentrated in subgroups of actors within the network. I expect that high transitivity slows down information diffusion through the network, because information can be caught within subgroups of actors. Information will need a relatively long time to reach other actors in the network. This argument corresponds with Granovetter's (1973: 1374) statement that trusting a leader is more problematic for the followers if the network of followers is fragmented. Therefore, I conjecture that transitivity has a negative effect on the time needed for information to reach actors in the network as well as on the time actors need to spread information in the network.

Table 2.1. Conjectures on the effects of network parameters on information diffusion rates.

	Transmission rate	Reception rate
INDIVIDUAL NETWORK PARAMETERS		
Outdegree	+	0
Indegree	0	+
Outdegree quality	+	0
Indegree quality	0	+
Local outdegree density	−	0
Local indegree density	0	+
GLOBAL NETWORK PARAMETERS		
Density	+	+
Outdegree variance	−	−
Indegree variance	−	−
Outdegree-indegree covariance	+	+
Transitivity	−	−
Network size	?	?

NETWORK SIZE

The last network parameter, which does not need extensive explanation, is *network size* n. This is simply the number of actors in the network. Because I generally assume that $\pi_i = \frac{1}{n}$ for all i, the number of actors in the network can certainly have effects on information diffusion. In larger networks, more time may be needed to inform the same proportion of actors than in smaller networks. The effects of network size are important as far as generalizations of results to large networks are concerned. If network size has a considerable additive effect on information diffusion, generalizing results from small networks to large networks will not be straightforward. In the simulations, I only consider networks with between two and ten actors. Therefore, if the effects of network parameters depend on the size of the network, it is more difficult to predict what the effects of these networks will be for networks with more than ten actors.

THE CONJECTURES SUMMARIZED

In conclusion, Table 2.1 gives an overview of the conjectures relating to the effects of network parameters on the rate of information transmission and reception amongst actors in a network. The relationship with conjectures relating to trust is straightforward. Trustors who transmit information more quickly are expected to place more trust in the trustee because they have more extensive control opportunities. Trustors who receive information more quickly place more trust in the trustee if the information is positive and place less trust if the information is negative.

2.2 GAME THEORY

[R]epeated games may be a good approximation of some long-term relationships ...—particularly those where "trust" and "social pressure" are important, such as when informal agreements are used to enforce mutually beneficial trades without legally enforced contracts.

—Fudenberg and Tirole (1991: 145)

Game theory allows predictions to be made about behavior of actors in interdependent choice situations. In Subsection 1.2.1, I argued that the trustor would not place trust in the Trust Game. This, in fact, is the game-theoretic solution of a one-shot Trust Game that is played without any connection being made to past or future transactions. In general, I define the *solution* of a game as the outcome that results from a combination of strategies played by rational actors.[8] In this section, I will explain how such a solution can be found.

Some concepts are needed for this explanation.[9] The Trust Game in Figure 1.1 is a representation of the game in extensive form. The *extensive form* is a configuration of nodes and branches, without any loops and originating from a single node. This is often referred to as the *game tree*. At each node there is a description as to which actor has to *move*. In my case, actors are the trustor or the trustee. A *move* made by an actor is a choice he or she makes at a given node. In the Trust Game, the trustor can choose between the moves "placing trust" and "not placing trust." An *end node* is a node with no outgoing move. At every end node, the payoffs for the actors are specified. I added labels at the branches of the game tree to indicate the interpretation of the moves.

Before or during a game, events might occur that are not under the control of the actors in the game, but which nevertheless influence the course of the game. These events can be included in the extensive form of the game by using "chance" moves. A chance move is said to be played by *Nature*. For example, the value of T_2 in the Trust Game may be unknown before the game begins, but might be chosen from a given distribution at the start of the game. This would be indicated by an additional node at the top of the game tree (see Figure 2.2). If Nature chooses between two or three values, each of these choices will be indicated by a different branch giving the probabilities of each choice at each branch, respectively. This case is illustrated in Figure 2.2, where Nature chooses $T_{2,1}$ with probability 0.6 and $T_{2,2}$ with probability 0.4. In Chapter 3, a game is analyzed in which payoffs are chosen from a continuous distribution. This will be indicated by specifying the distribution from which Nature "chooses."

[8]See Harsanyi's solution concept that consists of solution payoffs and a set of joint strategies that realize these payoffs (1977: 135–137).

[9]For a general introduction to game theory see Rasmusen (1994), for example.

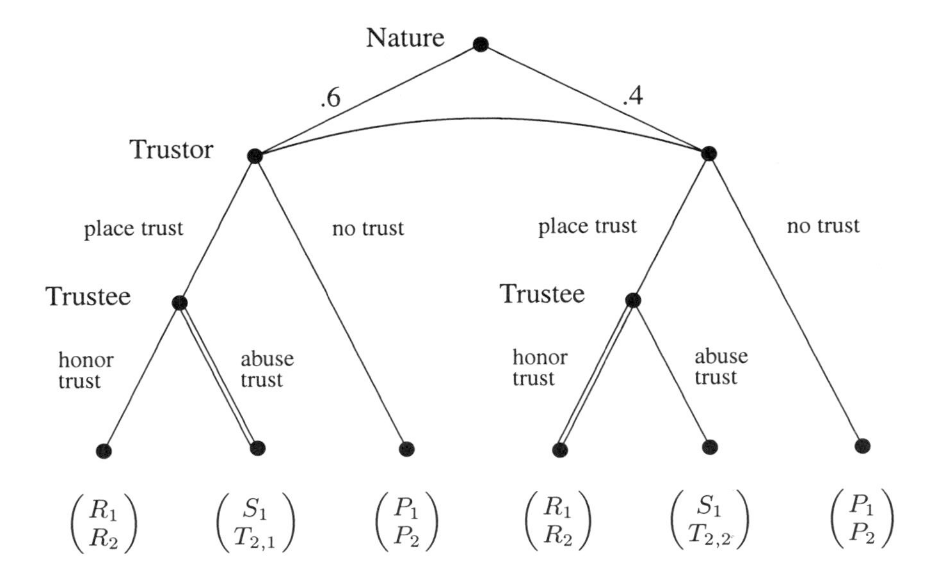

Figure 2.2. Extensive form of a Trust Game with incomplete information Γ^I, where $R_i > P_i, (i = 1, 2)$, $P_1 > S_1$, $T_{2,1} > R_2$, and $T_{2,2} < R_2$.

Moves in a game may or may not be observed by actors in a game before the actors concerned have to move themselves. Information sets in the extensive form of a game indicate whether an actor is able to observe a certain move. The actor's *information set* is a set of nodes among which the actor is not able to distinguish this by direct observation (see Rasmusen 1994: 40). In Figure 2.2, the line between the two nodes in which the trustor has to move indicates that they belong to the same information set for the trustor. This line means that the trustor could not observe the initial move by Nature, and she does not know which of the two nodes the game reached at the moment she has to move. An information set that consists of one single node is called a *singleton.* In analyzing games, there is an implicit assumption that the actors know the game tree. It is also assumed that the actors know that other actors know the game tree. The term *common knowledge* is used for information of which everybody is aware, and everybody knows that everybody knows and so on.

A *strategy* of an actor is a rule that prescribes the moves of an actor for each of his or her information set in the game. For example, a strategy for the trustee can specify that he will abuse trust if trust is placed by the trustor.

A *Nash equilibrium* is a combination of actor strategies such that no actor can obtain a higher payoff by changing to another strategy under the assumption that the other actors do not change their strategies (Nash 1951). In the Trust Game, the strategy for the trustor "never place trust" and the strategy for the trustee "always abuse trust if trust is placed" form a Nash equilibrium. The reason is that given that the trustee will abuse trust, the trustor prefers not to place trust because $S_1 < P_1$. And, given that the trustor never places trust, the trustee will obtain P_2 whatever his strategy might be. Thus, he cannot improve his payoff by changing to another strategy. A Nash equilibrium is the minimal requirement for a combination of strategies to be a candidate for the solution in a game. A combination of strategies that does not form a Nash equilibrium cannot be part of the solution, because if one player can obtain a higher payoff by changing to another strategy, he or she is expected to do so.

In many games, however, there are multiple Nash equilibria that lead to different outcomes of the game. In such cases, I need arguments as to why rational actors prefer some equilibria to others. Ideally, I would like to have one outcome that could be selected as the solution. Assume that $\frac{R_1+S_1}{2} < P_1$ in the Trust Game. Then, the strategies "never place trust" of the trustor and "choose with equal probability between abuse and honor trust if trust is placed" of the trustee also form a Nash equilibrium. This is a Nash equilibrium because the trustor is still better off not placing trust and the trustee cannot improve his payoff by changing to another strategy. The reason why this equilibrium is not considered realistic is that if trust were in fact placed, the trustee's best option would be to abuse trust. Below, it will be argued that the strategies "not placing trust" by the trustor and "always abusing trust if trust is placed" form the most "reasonable" Nash equilibrium for the Trust Game, and therefore the outcome "trust is not placed by the trustor" can be considered as the solution. Before I formalize some equilibrium selection arguments, I will introduce some additional concepts concerning information in a game.

Information in Games

Rasmusen (1994: Section 2.3) presents a suitable classification for information in a game. A game with *perfect information* is a game in which all nodes are singletons. Where this is not the case, a game is one with *imperfect information*. Thus, in a game with perfect information, actors observe all moves by Nature and by other actors that occur before they have to move. Moreover, actors never move simultaneously in a game with perfect information. The Trust Game is an example of a game with perfect information. A game of *certainty* is a game in which Nature never moves after an actor has moved. A game of uncertainty can still be a game with perfect information if the moves by Nature are observed immediately by all the actors. An example of such a game is analyzed in Chapter 3.

Two special types of games with imperfect information are games with asymmetric and games with incomplete information. In a game with *incomplete information*, Nature moves first and this move cannot be observed by at least one of the actors. In a game with *symmetric information*, an actor's information set at any node where an actor chooses an action or at an end node contains at least the same elements as the information sets of every other actor. An example of a game with asymmetric information is a game in which Nature moves first and this move is not observed by all actors. The Trust Game with incomplete information Γ^I in Figure 2.2 is an example of a game with incomplete and asymmetric information. If the trustee would also be unable to observe the move by Nature, the game would be one with symmetric information.

EQUILIBRIUM SELECTION

The *equilibrium path* is the path through the game tree that is followed in equilibrium. However, also the responses at the nodes that are never reached in equilibrium have to be specified in the (equilibrium) strategies. Above, I have mentioned two possible strategies followed by the trustee that prescribe what the trustee does after the trustor places trust although that move of the trustee is not part of equilibrium play. The *perfectness* of an equilibrium is related to whether a strategy of an actor is still optimal on paths away from the equilibrium path (Selten 1965).

In order to provide a formal definition of a *subgame-perfect equilibrium*, I first define a *subgame*. A *subgame* is a game that starts at a node that is a singleton for every actor and includes all the branches and nodes that follow this singleton. In the Trust Game, the game starting at the node where the trustee moves is a subgame; the whole Trust Game is a subgame of itself. A combination of strategies form a *subgame-perfect equilibrium* if it is a Nash equilibrium for the entire game and the induced strategies form a Nash equilibrium for all subgames. The double lines in Figure 1.1 indicate equilibrium play in the two relevant subgames. In general, one can find a subgame-perfect equilibrium in a finite game with perfect information by *backward induction*: start at the end of the tree, and find the equilibrium paths from the last moves in the tree; given these moves at the end of the tree, find the equilibrium paths from the last but one moves, and continue this procedure up to the top of the tree. Note that this procedures does not work in Figure 2.2 because the trustor's move does not start a subgame. The information set in which the trustor has to move consists of two nodes.

Because the only Nash equilibrium for the subgame that starts at the trustee's node prescribes abusing trust by the trustee, the only subgame-perfect equilibrium is the equilibrium in which the trustor never places trust and the trustee always abuses trust if trust is placed. I will use the subgame-perfect equilibrium concept to analyze the game in Chapter 3. In games with imperfect information, the concept of a subgame-perfect equilibrium is not always useful because there are no subgames with the exception of the whole game tree. Adjusted concepts for perfect equilibria are *perfect Bayesian equilibria* and *sequential equilibria* (see, for example, Rasmusen 1994: Chapter 6). I will not use these concepts in this book.

Another important equilibrium selection criterion is *payoff dominance*. In dynamic games that are more complex than the Trust Game, such as the repeated Trust Game, there will usually be a large number of subgame-perfect equilibria. In such situations, the set of equilibria can often be restricted by only considering payoff dominant equilibria. A payoff dominant equilibrium (Harsanyi and Selten 1988: 80–81) is an equilibrium for which no other equilibrium exist that is a Pareto improvement, i.e., an equilibrium for which at least one actor is better off and the others are not worse off. Thus, if there is an equilibrium for which the actors obtain a payoff 2, and another for which they obtain 4, the latter equilibrium is a Pareto improvement of the first. The outcome for which all players obtain a payoff 4 is selected as the solution on the basis of the payoff dominance criterion. If there would be two equilibria for which the payoffs are 2 for actor 1 and 4 for actor 2 in one equilibrium and the payoffs are reversed in the second equilibrium, I cannot select one of the equilibria with the payoff dominance criterion, because these equilibria cannot be compared with the Pareto criterion: in one equilibrium one actor obtains more and in the other equilibrium the other actor obtains more.

Although equilibrium selection is a rapidly expanding research field, a generally accepted selection theory that guarantees a unique solution in the games analyzed below is still lacking.[10] In this book, I will apply subgame perfectness and payoff dominance for equilibrium selection.

REPEATED GAMES

"Repeated" or "iterated" games are games in which actors have to make the same choices repeatedly. This allows them to take into account what has happened in previous periods of play and to anticipate on future play (Fudenberg and Tirole 1991: Chapter 5; Gibbons 2001). In Chapter 1, I argued that actors are hardly ever involved in isolated transactions, but that they are embedded in a social context that evolves over time. Temporal embeddedness can be modeled by assuming that a trustor and trustee do not only play one Trust Game. Instead, after each period, they play another Trust Game with probability $1 - \delta$. The parameter δ, $0 < \delta \leq 1$, is the *drop-out rate* of the trustor. In this book, it is assumed that a trustee continues to have transactions for ever, but that the trustor has an exogenously given probability of stopping a series of transactions with the trustee.[11] In this repeated game, the Trust Game Γ shown in Figure 1.1

[10] Other equilibrium refinements, such as renegotiation proofness and properness, are proposed and criticized (Van Damme 1987; Harsanyi 1995; Norde, Potters, Reijnierse, and Vermeulen 1996), but it is not necessary to discuss them here.

[11] Note that this probability does not depend on the behavior of the trustee.

is called the "constituent game." Before the repeated game can be analyzed, the payoffs of the game have to be defined. In every period, actor i obtains a payoff u_{it} related to the outcome of that period of play. Here, $t = 0, 1, 2, \ldots$ is a discrete time parameter, and $i = 1, 2$ with 1 indicating actor 1 or the trustor and 2 indicating actor 2 or the trustee. In all periods in which the actors do not play they obtain a payoff $u_{it} = 0$. I will use standard exponential discounting with discount factor w_i, $0 < w_i < 1$, to obtain the accumulated payoff over the whole game:

$$u_i = \sum_{t=0}^{\infty} w_i^t u_{it}, \tag{2.12}$$

where w_i denotes the pure time preferences of actor i and u_i the utility for actor i.

The game introduced above is the Iterated Trust Game ITG$(\Gamma, w_1, w_2, \delta)$. It is assumed that the constituent game Γ, the discount factors, and the drop-out rate are common knowledge. Folk theorems (see, for example, Abreu 1988; Kreps 1990b: Chapter 14; Fudenberg and Tirole 1991: Chapter 5; Rasmusen 1994: 124) show that in a repeated game such as the ITG, a very large number of subgame-perfect equilibria may exist. Unconditional play of the one-shot equilibrium is always an equilibrium in the repeated game. In the Trust Game, this means that the trustor never places trust and the trustee always abuses trust if trust is placed. This is an equilibrium because the trustor never has an incentive to place trust if trust is always abused, and the trustee cannot improve his payoff if the trustor never places trust. Equilibria in which trust is placed and honored can never be based on trust being placed unconditionally by the trustor. For, if there are no threats for the trustee that the trustor will change to "not placing trust," the trustee is always better off if he abuses trust. "No trust" is the only sanction the trustor has in the ITG and, therefore, equilibria in which trust is placed and honored have to be based on "conditionally cooperative" strategies in which the trustor will change to uncooperative behavior, i.e., not placing trust, if the trustee abuses trust.

Trigger strategies (Friedman 1971) are examples of such conditionally cooperative strategies. A trigger strategy for the ITG is defined as follows:

1. Trustor and trustee act cooperatively (place and honor trust) as long as the other actor acts cooperatively.

2. As soon as one actor deviates from cooperative behavior (withholds or abuses trust), the other actor changes to uncooperative behavior forever.

The ITG may have a cooperative equilibrium in *trigger strategies*. Trigger strategies are interesting because they are associated with the most severe punishment threat against the abuse of trust by the trustee (see Abreu 1988 on optimal punishment). This implies that if there exist equilibria in which trust emerges, trigger strategies are certainly in equilibrium. Furthermore, if cooperative strategies are in equilibrium the punishment threats of the trustors are credible and, therefore, the trustee will not abuse trust in equilibrium. Hence, the trustor *never* has to execute sanctions by withholding trust. Because trust is never abused in a trigger strategy equilibrium and sanctions for abusing trust need not be implemented, it is also a fact that there are no conflicts due to non-cooperative behavior in a trigger strategy equilibrium and, consequently, there is no need for conflict resolution. Trigger strategies, however, are not in equilibrium for all possible values of the parameters in the game. The following theorem states the necessary and sufficient condition for an equilibrium in trigger strategies and, hence, for the existence of a solution in which trust is always placed and never abused.

THEOREM 2.1 *Consider the* $\mathrm{ITG}(\Gamma, w_1, w_2, \delta)$. *Then, trigger strategies are a subgame-perfect equilibrium if and only if*

$$w_2(1-\delta) \geq \frac{T_2 - R_2}{T_2 - P_2}. \tag{2.13}$$

Proof. For a formal proof see Friedman (1986: 88–89). □

An intuition for the proof is the following. First, the trustor never has an incentive to deviate from the equilibrium path because obtaining R_1 is the highest payoff she can receive in every period. The trustee has an incentive to deviate if his expected payoff from receiving T_2 now and P_2 in all the remaining periods is higher than the expected payoff from receiving R_2 now as well as in all the remaining periods. The condition where this is not the case is given in the theorem. This is the formal representation of the statement that placing trust is possible for the trustor if the trustee's long-term losses from trust withheld by the trustor is larger than the short-term gains obtained by abusing trust.

Thus, if the condition for equilibrium in trigger strategies is fulfilled, there exist conditionally cooperative strategies that are in equilibrium and in which trust is always placed and is never abused. These strategies might be trigger strategies. However, it is possible that other conditionally cooperative strategies exist that form an equilibrium and that imply the same solution, namely, trust is always placed and never abused on the equilibrium path. Such an equilibrium is certainly not payoff dominated by another equilibrium because the trustor cannot obtain more than R_1 in every period.[12] The maximal payoff for the

[12] I do not know any convincing argument why this equilibrium is more realistic than other Pareto incomparable equilibria where, for example, the trustee is allowed to abuse trust in every one out of ten periods of play without "triggering" the trustor to withhold trust. The reader can check that such equilibria exist for appropriate parameter values.

trustor is reached because the trustee will never abuse trust in this equilibrium. Therefore, this equilibrium describes the situation such that the control effects for the trustor are large enough to compensate for the short-term incentive of the trustee to abuse trust. Thus, for example, if the trustor expects "enough" periods of play with the trustee in the future, she can trust the trustee.

The following hypotheses follow from this theorem about parameters in the ITG that will recur frequently throughout this book. It follows from the theorem that

- trust increases with the discount factor of the trustee (w_2),
- trust decreases with the drop-out rate (δ),
- trust decreases with the incentive of the trustee for abusing trust ($T_2 - R_2$), and
- trust increases with the loss experienced by the trustee when the trustor does not place trust ($R_2 - P_2$).[13]

The payoffs and the discount factor of the trustor do not affect the equilibrium condition. This is due to the fact that trust is never abused in equilibrium. This issue will be addressed again in Chapter 3.

Two elements that are discussed in Section 1.2 have not yet been incorporated in this game-theoretic model. First, the actors are not yet embedded in a social network. Second, because all actors have perfect information over the incentives of the partners, they do not learn about their partners. Therefore, the model presented above does not imply predictions about learning effects.

NETWORKS AND GAMES

In most game-theoretic models of repeated games, the same (two) actors are playing in every period. Some repeated games with varying opponents have been studied (see, for example, Kreps 1990a; Milgrom et al. 1990; Fudenberg and Tirole 1991: Section 5.3), but these studies do not model social networks in any detail. Also, they employ simple assumptions such as the fact that new actors in the game know what happened in the past during all periods and with all actors. Therefore, these models lead more or less to the same results as models in which the same two actors are playing all the time.

One type of model that has found a large number of successors is similar to Axelrod's (1984) computer tournament in which actors are randomly matched together to play certain games (Heckathorn 1996; Lomborg 1996). Actors in

[13]Note that $\frac{T_2-R_2}{T_2-P_2} = \frac{T_2-R_2}{(T_2-R_2)+(R_2-P_2)}$.

these games have prescribed strategies such as always abusing trust or playing Tit-for-Tat, but there is no network structure that facilitates information transmission about past periods among actors.

Raub and Weesie (1990; Weesie 1988: Chapter 5) explicitly model a network of information relations between actors playing Prisoner's Dilemmas with each other. Only one global property of the network, namely, the minimal outdegree in the network, affected the trigger strategy equilibria. There is a growing literature on models in which actors are assumed to be placed on a grid ("cellular automata"), which can be interpreted as a social network, and actors play with neighbors on the grid. However, in these models all actors have the same number of neighbors and equal probabilities of playing with each of these neighbors (Nowak, Szamrej, and Latané 1990; Messick and Liebrand 1995; Hegselmann 1996). There are some analyses in which the number of neighbors of an actor is varied. This allows predictions about differences *between* networks but not *within* networks, because all positions in the network are equivalent. In most real-world networks there are, of course, individual differences between actors. Some actors have more contacts than others and these contacts may be more intense. The models in Chapter 3 and 4 seek to make predictions about such individual differences.

Incomplete Information

Game theorists have long realized that the complete information assumption used in many models is very problematic. Harsanyi (1967–68) laid the foundation of including incomplete information in game-theoretic models. Actors may be uncertain about the payoffs of other actors, for example. This kind of uncertainty can be modeled with a random move by Nature at the beginning of the game. Imagine that there are two trustees as illustrated in Figure 2.2: a "good" trustee who has no incentive to abuse trust in any period ($T_{2,2} < R_2$) and a "bad" trustee who has payoffs equal to the ordinary Trust Game ($T_{2,1} > R_2$). Nature chooses at the start of the game with given probabilities which of the two trustees has to play with the trustor. However, the trustor is not able to observe the outcome of this move, i.e., she does not know whether the trustee is good or bad. The trustee knows his own "type," i.e., he knows whether or not he has an incentive to abuse trust. The game that starts after the move by Nature can also be repeated. During the game the trustor can adjust her beliefs about the type of trustee and maybe she can deduce from his behavior with which trustee she plays. For example, if the trustee were ever to abuse trust, he would be the bad type. Thus, *learning* becomes an issue if incomplete information is introduced. Moreover, a bad trustee can try to behave as if he is the good type, because it is more profitable for him if the trustor believes he is the good type. In other words, trustees might be concerned to maintain the reputation of being a good type of trustee (see also Kreps, Milgrom, Roberts, and Wilson 1982).

Analyses of the finitely repeated Trust Game with incomplete information yield some appealing results with respect to control and learning effects (see Dasgupta 1988).[14] The problem with the finitely repeated ordinary Trust Game Γ is the following. If the trustee has an incentive to abuse trust, this implies that the trustee will certainly abuse trust in the last period. Therefore, the trustor will not place trust in the last period. Consequently, the trustee will abuse trust in the last period but one, because in the last period he will receive P_2 anyway. This implies that the trustor also cannot place trust in the last period but one. This argument continues up to the first period, which means that the trustor can never place trust. The situation changes if there is even a slight probability that the trustee does not have an incentive to abuse trust (see Camerer and Weigelt 1988; Neral and Ochs 1992). Then, the trustor might want to test whether the trustee has an incentive to abuse trust. Therefore, "some" trust is possible if there are "enough" periods to be played in the future. An equilibrium exists that consists of three phases. In the first phase, all types of trustees honor trust and, consequently, the trustor places trust. If the end of the game is approached (the exact timing depends on the parameters of the game), the bad trustee starts to randomize between abusing and honoring trust.[15] Of course, the good trustee continues to honor trust throughout the game. As long as the trustee continues to honor trust in this randomization period, the trustor is more and more convinced that she is playing with a good trustee and, therefore, continues to trust although the end of the game comes closer and closer. As soon as the trustee abuses trust for the first time, he reveals himself as being a bad trustee and the trustor will never place trust again.

Recently, games resembling the Trust Game have been analyzed (Cripps and Thomas 1997; Levine and Martinelli 1998). In these games, one actor cannot observe the type of another actor. Levine and Martinelli consider a buyer-seller relationship as a starting point of their game. The seller has the possibility of selling high-quality or low-quality products. The seller has to make that decision in advance because he has to make an extra investment, for example in production technology, committing himself to one of the two strategies. He cannot change that decision later in the game. The buyers cannot directly observe the choice of the seller. In Levine and Martinelli's model, the probability that the seller will make the investment depends on the time he expects to be in the market with that product and the extent to which buyers are able to evaluate whether he is selling high-quality or low-quality products. Interpreting the results in terms of social networks, sellers have a larger incentive

[14]In the finitely repeated Trust Game, the first move is a move by Nature similar to the first move in Figure 2.2 and the part of that game after the move by Nature is repeated.

[15]The term "randomize" indicates that the trustee chooses abusing trust with probability p and honoring trust with probability $1 - p$, $(0 < p < 1)$.

to sell high-quality products to buyers who obtain more information about the behavior of this seller from other buyers.

The two examples of games with incomplete information discussed above indicate that such games can shed some light on the relation between control and learning. I want to stress here that (rational) actors in these models have to be forward-looking as well as backward-looking to optimize their expected payoffs. They have to be backward-looking to learn from the information obtained from past periods of play and forward-looking to take into account potential sanctions and learning effects in the future. Some recent studies (Macy 1993; Flache 1996) suggest that actors in game-theoretic models are assumed to be forward-looking only and contrast these models with backward-looking learning models. This contrast makes sense only in game-theoretic models with complete information. However, game-theoretic models with incomplete information are themselves examples of learning models in which completely rational actors optimize their future payoffs using what they learned from past periods and even trying to exploit the learning efforts of other actors. However, modeling incomplete information and detailed social networks in a game-theoretic context at the same time is beyond the scope of this book and beyond the scope of current research in general. Therefore, I limit the analysis of learning effects to modeling how fast trustors can obtain information, assuming that trustors who obtain more information learn faster. Consequently, trustors who obtain more positive information can place more trust in the trustee than other trustors. In this book, I will not model the strategic use of and search for information. Developing and analyzing a model that combines social networks with a game-theoretic model including incomplete information may well be part of future research efforts. A first model in this direction consists of two trustors who play a finitely repeated Trust Game with one trustor and can inform each other between periods about the behavior of the trustee (see Buskens 2000).

Chapter 3

A GAME-THEORETIC MODEL FOR CONTROL EFFECTS IN SOCIAL NETWORKS

3.1 INTRODUCTION

The model developed in this chapter is based on the idea that customers of a seller can trust this seller if they have "enough" possibilities for sanctioning the seller when the seller deceives his customers. For example, if a baker in a small village produces bread that is below basic quality norms, he will promptly lose many customers, because the people in the village see each other frequently and will discuss the quality of the baker's bread. More in general, a seller who deceives his buyers openly and frequently is condemned to lose many customers. Thus, if such a seller is interested in future profits, he should take his reputation seriously. In the example, it is important that there are frequent contacts between the potential customers of the bakery and that these customers are willing to communicate information about the untrustworthiness of the baker. As discussed in Chapter 1, I expect that social networks are essential for information diffusion among the customers. If the social network facilitates fast information diffusion through the network, information about untrustworthy behavior will be passed quickly to many customers. Consequently, a seller who has customers in such a dense network should be more careful about his reputation than a seller with customers who do not communicate very often. Therefore, the customers in the network with fast information diffusion possibilities can trust their seller better than customers who hardly communicate.

This basic intuition will now be captured in a game-theoretic model.[1] Control effects are modeled using a social network of trustors who have transactions with a trustee. Trustors communicate information to each other at different rates.

[1] Of course, information can also be diffused through public sources or formal institutions, but I restrict myself here to informal information diffusion in social networks.

All trustors have repeated transactions with the trustee. These transactions are modeled as Trust Games. I analyze properties of equilibria in trigger strategies of the trustors. Accordingly, trustors trust a trustee only if they do not have information about any abuse of trust by the trustee in the past *and* the short-term incentive for the trustee to abuse trust is not too large. From the model, I derive predictions indicating how the extent to which trustors are prepared to trust the trustee depends on network parameters such as density, centralization, outdegrees, and indegrees. Because a trustee will take into account the sanction possibilities of trustors, a trustor with more sanction potential can place more trust than a trustor with less sanction potential. I also derive hypotheses about the effects of non-network parameters on trust, including interaction effects between network and non-network parameters.

I want to begin by emphasizing that the model has a number of limitations. First, the model does not include learning effects. The model will be defined as a game with complete information. The payoffs, discount factors, and social network will all be common knowledge. Thus, actors cannot "learn" anything about the incentives of other actors in the game. Second, and related to the first limitation, a trustee will not abuse trust if his long-term incentive of honoring trust is larger than his short-term incentive of abusing trust. Moreover, the trustor will not place trust if the short-term incentive for the trustee of abusing trust is too large. Consequently, there will never be an occasion that the trustee abuses trust in equilibrium. As will be explained in the following section, additional assumptions are needed to reach a tractable model. However, in a first attempt to develop a game-theoretic model in which detailed network effects are included, it is reasonable to keep other elements of the model as simple as possible.

Even if I abstain from introducing complicating assumptions in respect of incomplete information, for example, the model is already rather complex and I will not be able to derive analytically many hypotheses about the effects on trust of the individual and global network parameters introduced in Section 2.1. I use two approximations methods to derive such hypotheses. The first approximation method is *linearization* of the solution of the model in the neighborhood of homogeneous networks. This analysis shows that density and outdegree are the most important network parameters. Also, density becomes relatively more important in relation to outdegree if the dyadic relations are more problematic, for example, if the costs of sanctions for the trustee decrease. To verify that these predictions hold for networks that are not "close" to homogeneous networks, a second approximation method is used. This method is a *simulation analysis* similar to Yamaguchi (1994a). The predictions about the extent to which trustors trust the trustee are numerically calculated for a sample of networks and regressed on the defined network parameters using statistical methods.

This chapter is rather technical. The main game-theoretic concepts used here have already been introduced in Section 2.2. Section 3.2 introduces the model assumptions and gives an illustration corresponding to a real-world situation that reflects the model relatively closely. Section 3.3 analyzes the mathematical properties of the model and I derive a class of equilibria. The "solution" of the game will be related to one of these equilibria. Comparative statics of the solution in the model parameters are derived in Section 3.4. Sections 3.5 and 3.6 derive additional implications from the solution using the two approximation methods. Finally, Section 3.7 summarizes the main results of this chapter, namely, a collection of hypotheses on the determinants of trust and Section 3.8 discusses some of the shortcomings of the model. Appendix A presents proofs of the theorems.

3.2 CONSTRUCTION OF THE MODEL

This section describes an analytically tractable model for predicting network effects in trust situations. To model control effects, the minimal requirement is a model with repeated games between subsets of actors who may inform other actors about their experiences. The first element needed is a constituent game that is played in the different periods of the game. The constituent game is a Heterogeneous Trust Game (HTG) Γ_F, a variant of the Trust Game modeling simple trust relations (Dasgupta 1988; Kreps 1990a). The extensive form of the HTG is shown in Figure 3.1.

THE CONSTITUENT GAME

Nature generates $\theta > 0$ randomly from a probability distribution F in the first move of Γ_F. θ is the incentive for the trustee to abuse trust placed by the trustor. For technical reasons it is assumed that F is a continuous probability distribution with full support on $[0, \infty)$. An example of such a distribution with favorable analytical properties is $F_a(\vartheta) = Pr(\theta \leq \vartheta) = \vartheta/(a + \vartheta)$ (see Raub and Weesie 1993b; Weesie et al. 1998). Here, a is the MEDIAN INCENTIVE of F_a and so a can be interpreted as the trustee's "average" incentive for opportunistic behavior.[2] In the HTG, both trustor and trustee are informed on θ. In the second move, the trustor chooses whether or not she places trust. If the trustor does not place trust, the constituent game is over and the actors receive a payoff P_i. If the trustor places trust, the constituent game continues with a third move. Here, the trustee can honor trust or abuse trust. If he honors trust, the actors receive $R_i > P_i$. If he abuses trust, the trustee receives $R_2 + \theta > R_2$ and the trustor receives $S_1 < P_1$. Clearly, the trustor will not place trust for any

[2] In this chapter and the next, the labels for the variables that are also used in the statistical analyses are set in SANS SERIF typeface.

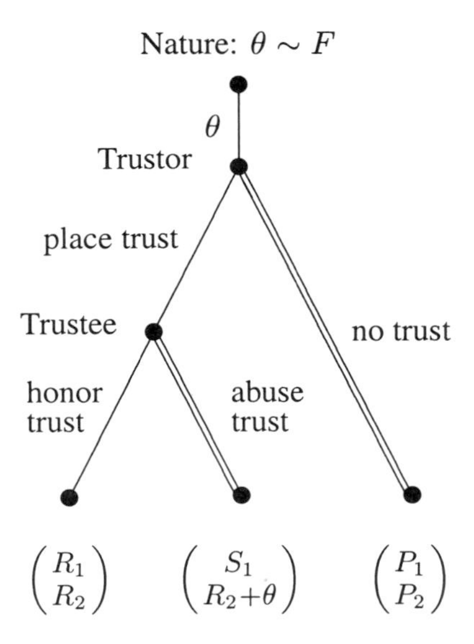

Figure 3.1. Extensive form of a Heterogeneous Trust Game Γ_F, where $R_i > P_i$, $(i = 1, 2)$, $P_1 > S_1, \theta > 0$.

$\theta > 0$ in the unique subgame-perfect equilibrium of the constituent game Γ_F.[3] The double lines in Figure 3.1 indicate the predicted move for each actor in the corresponding node of the constituent game. The equilibrium is inefficient because both actors prefer placing trust and honoring trust over the situation in which no trust is placed. The difference $R_i - P_i$ is the efficiency loss for the trustor ($i = 1$) and the trustee ($i = 2$) due to the trust problem.

Repeating the HTG in a Network

Now, I proceed with defining the Iterated Heterogeneous Trust Game (IHTG) $\Gamma(\Gamma_F, w, \boldsymbol{\delta}, \boldsymbol{\pi}, \boldsymbol{A})$. The constituent game Γ_F is played at discrete moments in time, $t = 0, 1, 2, \ldots$ between a trustee and one of the trustors in a network of n trustors $(\boldsymbol{\pi}, \boldsymbol{A})$.[4] Thus, there are two main differences between the Iterated Trust Game (ITG) introduced in Section 2.2 and the IHTG. First, the ordinary Trust Game is replaced by the HTG as the constituent game. In the discussion about the assumptions of the model below, I will explain the advantages of this modification. Second, the trustee plays with a network of n trustors $(\boldsymbol{\pi}, \boldsymbol{A})$

[3] Formally, it should be added that if the trustor would place trust, the trustee abuses trust in equilibrium.

[4] To avoid notational complexity, the homogeneity assumption is made that the payoffs of the trustee and the distribution F are independent of the trustor with whom the trustee plays. The analyses easily generalize for the case that the payoffs depend on the trustor.

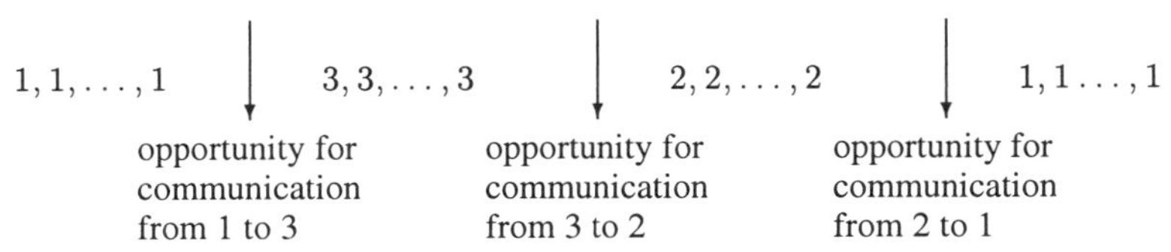

Figure 3.2. A sequence of transactions.

instead of one trustor. The vector $\boldsymbol{\pi} = (\pi_1, \ldots, \pi_n)$ reflects the normalized importance of each trustor for the trustee, with $\pi_i > 0$ and $\sum_{i=1}^{n} \pi_i = 1$, and is interpreted as the vector of probabilities for the trustors to start transactions with the trustee. The entries α_{ij} of the network matrix $\boldsymbol{A}$ are interpreted as the probabilities that trustor i transmits information to trustor j in one time period.

In the next step, I will explain how the sequences of transactions are modeled and when communication is possible. Again, in the "discussion of assumptions," I will pay attention to the reasons for these assumptions. To reduce complexity while maintaining the essential character of network information diffusion, I constructed a scenario in which the information diffusion process is somehow restricted (see also Weesie et al. 1998). The first assumption is that the trustee has transactions with trustors for ever. Trustors play series of constituent games to allow for bilateral control effects as described in Subsection 1.2.3, in addition to the control effects through the network. The second assumption is that the trustors play series of transactions with the trustee *sequentially* (see Figure 3.2). A new trustor is chosen for a next series of transactions only after a trustor drops out. A series of transactions with trustor i ends with a probability δ_i, $0 \leq \delta_i \leq 1$ that is called DROP-OUT RATE. The end of a series of transactions is stochastically independent of what happened in earlier transactions.[5] The probability that the new trustor is trustor j is π_j. Because j may be equal to i, the probability that trustor i continues a series of transactions at time t equals $1 - \delta_i + \delta_i \pi_i$.

The third assumption is that only the trustor who is involved in transactions with the trustee has information about the behavior of the trustee in the past. *Exclusively* at the moment that one trustor drops out and another trustor enters the game, can information be communicated and then *only* between the old and new trustor (see Figure 3.2). The probability that trustor i informs trustor j about the behavior of the trustee after a series of transactions equals α_{ij}. The

[5]This implies, for example, that the continuation of a relation does not depend on what happened in earlier transactions. Endogenous probabilities are used in models about exit from a relation (Schüßler 1989; Vanberg and Congleton 1992; Lahno 1995; Weesie 1996; Blumberg 1997). Introducing exit endogenously in the model would complicate the analysis considerably.

diagonal elements are defined $\alpha_{ii} = 1$, indicating that a trustor always remembers information from past transactions as long as her series of transactions continues. If a trustor informs the next trustor, she does not only communicate her own experiences with the trustor, but also all the information she obtained from trustors before her. In this way, it is still possible that information is transmitted from trustor i to j to k and so on. It is important to realize the exact assumption made above about recall of the trustors. Usually, it is assumed that actors have *perfect recall*, i.e., they remember everything that happened in all previous periods. Here, *imperfect recall* is assumed for the trustors. It is assumed that trustors remember the information they have as long as they are playing a series of transactions with the trustee until the next trustor starts a new series of transaction. This implies that at most one trustor at a time has information about the past behavior of the trustee. If this trustor i stops a series of transactions, she has a possibility of communicating the information she has to the next trustor. Thereafter, trustor i "forgets" the information. If trustor i does not communicate with trustor j, all information of previous transactions is lost and trustor j has to start her series of transactions without information about previous transactions. Furthermore, it is assumed that all information is accurate; no incentives to withhold or misrepresent information strategically are analyzed, nor does information become distorted unintentionally. Finally, it is assumed that the trustee knows whether or not the next trustor is informed by her predecessor. The argument for the last assumption will become apparent in the discussion about the trigger equilibria that will be studied.

Summarizing, three things might happen "between" time t and time $t+1$. First, the same trustor continues a series of transactions. Second, a new trustor is chosen and the old trustor informs the new trustor about the behavior of the trustee. Third, a new trustor is chosen and the old trustor does not inform the new trustor. Now, a transition matrix $\boldsymbol{T}$ can be derived, where t_{ij} is the probability that the former transaction was a transaction of the trustee with trustor i, *and* the following transaction is with trustor j, *and* trustor i communicates the information she has to trustor j. This implies that if $i \neq j$ then $t_{ij} = \delta_i \pi_j \alpha_{ij}$. For the diagonal elements holds that $t_{ii} = 1 - \delta_i + \delta_i \pi_i$, because $1 - \delta_i$ is the probability that a series of transactions of trustor i continues, and $\delta_i \pi_i$ is the probability that a series of transactions of trustor i ends and trustor i is chosen again for a new series of transactions. In matrix notation, the transition matrix is

$$\boldsymbol{T} = \begin{pmatrix} 1-\delta_1+\delta_1\pi_1 & \delta_1\pi_2\alpha_{12} & \cdots & \delta_1\pi_n\alpha_{1n} \\ \delta_2\pi_1\alpha_{21} & \ddots & \ddots & \vdots \\ \vdots & \ddots & \ddots & \delta_{n-1}\pi_n\alpha_{n-1,n} \\ \delta_n\pi_1\alpha_{n1} & \cdots & \delta_n\pi_{n-1}\alpha_{n,n-1} & 1-\delta_n+\delta_n\pi_n \end{pmatrix}. \quad (3.1)$$

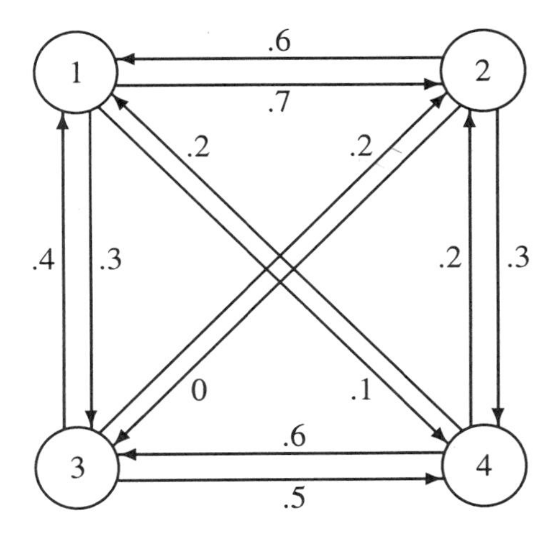

$$\pi = \begin{pmatrix} .25 \\ .3 \\ .2 \\ .25 \end{pmatrix} \quad \boldsymbol{A} = \begin{pmatrix} 1 & .7 & .3 & .1 \\ .6 & 1 & 0 & .3 \\ .4 & .2 & 1 & .5 \\ .2 & .2 & .6 & 1 \end{pmatrix} \quad \boldsymbol{\delta} = \begin{pmatrix} .4 \\ .4 \\ .4 \\ .4 \end{pmatrix}$$

$$\boldsymbol{T} = \begin{pmatrix} .7 & .084 & .024 & .01 \\ .06 & .72 & 0 & .03 \\ .04 & .024 & .68 & .05 \\ .02 & .024 & .048 & .7 \end{pmatrix}$$

Figure 3.3. Example of a network of trustors.

The rows of $\boldsymbol{T}$ do not add up to 1, and, hence, $\boldsymbol{T}$ is not a real transition matrix, because the transitions in which information is not communicated between two consecutive trustors are not included in $\boldsymbol{T}$. Figure 3.3 is an illustration of a network of trustors. With a probability $\pi_1 = 0.25$, trustor 1 is chosen for a new series of transactions with the trustee, trustor 2 with a probability $\pi_2 = 0.3$, trustor 3 with a probability $\pi_3 = 0.2$, and trustor 4 also with a probability $\pi_4 = 0.25$. All DROP-OUT RATES are 0.4. Since $\alpha_{23} = 0$, trustor 2 will never tell trustor 3 about the behavior of the trustee. Trustor 1 informs trustor 2 with a probability $\alpha_{12} = 0.7$. The transition matrix is calculated in correspondence with equation (3.1). For example, $t_{11} = 1 - 0.4 + 0.4 \times 0.25 = 0.7$ and $t_{12} = 0.4 \times 0.3 \times 0.7 = 0.084$.

PAYOFFS

The payoff function in the IHTG is defined similar to the payoff function in the ITG in Section 2.2. If a trustor is not involved in a transaction at time t, she receives a payoff 0. A trustor and trustee who are involved in the game at time t obtain the payoffs associated with the outcome of the game in that time period. Payoffs are discounted exponentially with DISCOUNT FACTOR w, $0 \leq w \leq 1$, for the trustee and all trustors.[6] The DISCOUNT FACTOR reflects pure time preferences. Thus, the total payoff of an actor i associated with a stream of payoffs $(u_{i0}, u_{i1}, \ldots)$ equals $\sum_{t=0}^{\infty} w^t u_{it}$.

DISCUSSION OF ASSUMPTIONS

First, I will discuss why the HTG instead of the ordinary Trust Game was chosen as the constituent game. In the solution of the ITG discussed in Section 2.2, the trustor always places trust or never places trust, depending on the parameters of the game. In the IHTG, trustors cannot place trust in all periods because θ can be very large, which creates "golden opportunities" for the trustee in which the incentive to abuse trust is so large that it exceeds possible long-term losses. This implies that the situation in which the trustor and the trustee always obtain R_i, cannot be reached in the IHTG. Thus, there will always be some inefficiency. The extent of inefficiency depends on how large the incentive to abuse trust might be for which trustors cannot trust the trustee anymore. It will be shown that in the solution of the IHTG the trustor will only place trust if θ is not too large. The more the trustor trusts the trustee, the larger the values θ for which the trustor still places trust, and, thus, the higher the efficiency level that is reached. While for the ITG, hypotheses can only be derived from the comparative statics of the condition for which trust can always or can never be placed by the trustors, for the IHTG, hypotheses can be derived from the comparative statics of the *extent* to which trust can be placed by the trustor. One thing that does not change in comparison with the ITG is that the trustee never abuses trust in the solution presented in the next section.

Second, I want to comment on the scenario for the order of transactions and opportunities for communication among trustors. In an "ideal" and more realistic model, trustors would have transactions with the trustee at every point in time. Between transactions, the trustors may have opportunities to communicate information about the behavior of the trustee. However, a model in which all trustors have simultaneous transactions with the trustee and communicate information is already fairly complex. In particular, it is a complex matter to determine what the optimal behavior for the trustee is *after* one abuse of trust. This can be understood as follows. Even under the assumption that trustors

[6]In the analyses, only the discount factor of the trustee is relevant. Thus, this homogeneity assumption is made only to avoid useless notational complexity.

never forget information about abused trust and the deceived trustor i transmits information about the abuse of trust as soon as possible to other trustors, it is a fairly complex task for the trustee to decide whether he should abuse trust that is placed by another trustor j. On the one hand, the trustee has to take into account that trustor j obtains the information that the trustee deceived trustor i through the network and, consequently, that trustor j might not trust the trustee anymore in the near future. Therefore, it might be profitable for the trustee to take the short-term profit from abusing trust. On the other hand, if the trustee abuses trust again, trustor j also starts to transmit information about this deceit through the network. This means that other trustors will be informed more quickly about the untrustworthiness of the trustee. Thus, the trustee has to take into account all possible information diffusion patterns amongst the trustors including his own role in this process if he should abuse trust again. Such a scenario could be studied using simulation. I do not apply such a simulation method, because there are hardly any analytic results for the effects of detailed network parameters on information diffusion in a game-theoretic context as presented here. It is then quite difficult to obtain *robust* results in a simulation study for such a complex model. Therefore, it is preferable to obtain some analytic results first, even if the model is more restrictive. After some analytic results have been obtained, the model could be extended and a simulation could be guided by the analytic results.[7]

The scenario studied in this chapter can be compared with a model of Yamaguchi (1994a) I discuss in Chapter 4 in the sense that information is transferred as a "package" from one trustor to another. This restrictive assumption on the way information is communicated among trustors seems necessary to obtain analytic results within the game-theoretic context. The advantage of this approach is that the payoffs, DISCOUNT FACTOR, DROP-OUT RATES, and the social network are included simultaneously in the analysis. Therefore, it is possible to deduce not only hypotheses about the *main effects* of these different elements of the model, but also about *interaction effects*. In Chapter 4, I will analyze a pure information diffusion model, in which only the social network is included. That model can be analyzed with less restrictive assumptions about information diffusion, and the changes in the effects of network parameters can be studied in a less restrictive information diffusion process.

[7]Note that simulations in Chapters 3 and 4 are used in a somewhat different sense as meant here. I use simulation to approximate first and second-order partial derivatives of variables in the *analytic* solution of a model. In this way the simulation is only used to interpret a complex analytic solution. Here, I contrast my approach with a simulation for which it is unclear beforehand how the simulation depends on the parameters in the model that is simulated.

Example: The Aircraft Constructor

Before starting to analyze the model, I will give an example of a situation that resembles the model. Consider an aircraft constructor who can only build one aircraft at a time. This aircraft constructor has a customer, an airline, that wants one or more airplanes. When ordering a new airplane, the airline decides to trust or not to trust the aircraft constructor. The decision will influence the amount of investments in costly monitoring of the construction process by the airline. After the delivery, the airline orders a new airplane or the series of transactions ends because the airline faces reduced demand for transportation or because the airline goes bankrupt. If the series of transactions with a given customer ends, a new airline will take over and a new series of transactions is initialized. The probability of communicating information about the performance of the constructor between the old and new customer depends on the network among the customers. It is assumed that new customers only take into account information about the constructor obtained from the last customer. New customers do not care about information about the constructor as far as they do not obtain this information from the last customer. Because transactions last a considerable time in this example, it is reasonable that information from the last costumer is more relevant than information from customers in the past. Even information from one's own experiences in the past will be considered outdated if a constructor is chosen again after a number of years.

3.3 SOLUTION OF THE MODEL

I will analyze equilibria in a particular type of strategies, namely, trigger strategies (see Friedman 1971) for $\Gamma(\Gamma_F, w, \boldsymbol{\delta}, \boldsymbol{\pi}, \boldsymbol{A})$. The constituent game can be characterized by the pair (i, θ), where i is the trustor involved and θ is the incentive for the trustee to abuse trust. Trigger strategies for trustors and trustee are defined via thresholds ϑ. In a constituent game (i, θ), a trustor i will place trust if $\theta \leq \vartheta_{i1}$ and the trustor has no information that the trustee abused trust in the past. Otherwise, the trustor does not place trust. Thus, a trustor does not place trust if the trustee's incentive for abusing trust in a particular period is too large or if she has any information that the trustee abused trust in the past. Consequently, as soon as the trustor obtains information about trust abused by the trustee, either from own experience or from another trustor, she will *never* place trust again. However, since trustors have imperfect recall, a trustor might place trust in a later series of transactions if the information about the abuse of trust by the trustee is not communicate through the network.

Similarly, the trustee uses a trigger strategy with threshold ϑ_{i2} for his decision node in the game (i, θ). That means that in a period with trustor i and incentive to abuse trust θ, the trustee will honor trust if trust is placed and $\theta \leq \vartheta_{i2}$ and

INTERMEZZO 3.1 *Interpretation of the model.*

The model is described above with *one* trustor for each node in the network. Another interpretation that leaves the results almost the same is described in an earlier working paper (Buskens and Weesie 2000a). Every node in the network is a group of equivalent trustors in the sense that trustors within a group have the same proportion of ties to trustors of the other groups. The groups are assumed to be infinitely large in order to obtain a zero probability that the same trustor has a series of transactions with the trustee again. Thus, the assumption that trustors forget the outcomes of earlier transactions after stopping a series of transactions is no longer needed. The groups of trustors are, for example, classes of students who want to buy used cars. In this case, α_{ij} is still the probability that any trustor of subgroup i, after her series of transactions ends, informs a trustor of subgroup j who is involved in the subsequent transactions with the trustee. Then α_{ij} is the density of ties from subgroup i to subgroup j of trustors. The diagonal elements are not necessarily equal to 1, but indicate the network density within subgroups. Thus, in this case the matrix $\boldsymbol{A}$ of contact probabilities represents a stochastic blockmodel (Wasserman and Faust 1994: 695). Most theorems in this chapter generalize straightforwardly to the blockmodel interpretation. Some network parameters have to be defined in a slightly different way due to the other meaning of the diagonal elements of $\boldsymbol{A}$. I refer to Buskens and Weesie (2000a) for details about the blockmodel interpretation. An advantage of using the blockmodel interpretation in an empirical case in which there are large groups of equivalent trustors is that the computational complexity can be reduced considerably by analyzing the model over the equivalence classes instead of over individuals. Note that in the case of a finite number of trustors in each subgroup a restriction on the memory of the trustors is still necessary to prevent that a trustor remembers information from an old series of transactions if she enters in a new series. The version of the model with one trustor per node is used in this book to facilitate a comparison with the model in Chapter 4.

abuse trust otherwise. Moreover, the trustee will abuse trust if the trustor has information about any abuse of trust by the trustee.[8]

Important advantages of trigger strategies are that they are analytically tractable and cognitively simple, i.e., they do not make excessive demands on the computational skills or memory of the actors. Equilibria will be found in which trust is only placed if the incentive for abusing trust is not too large. These equilibria are suboptimal because, if trust would always be placed and honored,

[8] In Appendix A, it is shown that this last addition to the strategy description of the trustee is only necessary to obtain *subgame-perfect* equilibria. In equilibrium, the trustor will never place trust if she has information about an abuse of trust. Therefore, the behavior of the trustee in such situations only guarantees equilibrium behavior in subgames that are not part of the equilibrium path.

all actors would receive a higher payoff. This is a consequence of choosing a HTG instead of an ordinary Trust Game as the constituent game, as I explained before. This leads to the favorable property of the model that the thresholds are a *measure for efficiency* that permits comparison of the trigger equilibria with the efficient situation that trust is always placed and honored. The higher the threshold ϑ, the higher the proportion of transaction $F(\vartheta)$ in which the trustor will trust the trustee, the higher the efficiency.

The following theorem states that, in a subgame-perfect equilibrium in trigger strategies, the associated thresholds for the trustee and the trustor are the same ($\vartheta_{i1} = \vartheta_{i2}$).[9] Hence, on the equilibrium path, trust is placed and honored, or trust is not placed, but it never happens that trust is placed and the trustee abuses trust. In other words, trust will not always be placed, but if trust is placed, it will never be abused in equilibrium.[10]

THEOREM 3.1 *The* IHTG $\Gamma(\Gamma_F, w, \boldsymbol{\delta}, \boldsymbol{\pi}, \boldsymbol{A})$ *has the following properties.*

i) At least one subgame-perfect equilibrium in trigger strategies exists, namely, $\vartheta_{i1} = \vartheta_{i2} = 0$ *for all* i.

ii) If a vector of trigger strategies is a subgame-perfect equilibrium, $\vartheta_{i1} = \vartheta_{i2}$ *for all* i.

Proof. The proofs of this theorem and all other theorems in this chapter can be found in Appendix A. □

As a result of this theorem, trigger strategy equilibrium vectors are denoted, with some abuse of notation, by $\boldsymbol{\vartheta} = (\vartheta_1, \ldots, \vartheta_n)$. In the following theorem, a solution of $\Gamma(\Gamma_F, w, \boldsymbol{\delta}, \boldsymbol{\pi}, \boldsymbol{A})$ is specified. First, a condition for subgame-perfect equilibrium in trigger strategies is given. Additional properties of the set of subgame-perfect equilibria in trigger strategies are found in Theorem A.1 in Appendix A. Because usually multiple equilibria in trigger strategies exist, the condition of the first part of the theorem does not provide explicit predictions

[9] Strictly speaking, as soon as a trustor does not communicate with the subsequent trustor, the game does not have proper subgames because everything that has happened before is unknown to the new trustor. Still, it is a subgame if a period starting with an uninformed new trustor is considered as the start of a new game or a collapse of all possible prior states to one new state that resembles the initial beginning of the game. For the trustor, the situation is exactly the same as in the beginning of the game. The only concern is that the trustee remembers what happened before in the game. This is not problematic because the trigger strategies of the trustee are not conditional on what happened earlier in the game, but only on what the trustor knows about past periods (see also Appendix A: page 216).

[10] There exist many equilibria that involve other strategies as follows from the Folk theorem (see, for example, Fudenberg and Tirole 1991: Section 5.1). For example, strategies in which trustors refrain from placing trust for only a finite number of time periods might be in equilibrium. However, threatening with "eternal" punishment is the most effective in my model in which actors perfectly monitor each other, because the trustee's loss after abused trust will be as large as possible. Therefore, trust of the trustor will be as large as possible using trigger strategies if there exist equilibria in these trigger strategies.

for the behavior of the actors. For example, never placing trust by the trustor is an equilibrium ($\boldsymbol{\vartheta} = \mathbf{0}$). For equilibrium selection within the class of trigger strategies I use payoff dominance (Harsanyi and Selten 1988: 80–81). The second part of the next theorem states that the payoff dominance selection criterion yields a unique subgame-perfect equilibrium in the class of trigger strategies. The $\boldsymbol{\vartheta}^*$ belonging to this subgame-perfect equilibrium is called the *solution* of the game.

THEOREM 3.2 *Consider the* IHTG $\Gamma(\Gamma_F, w, \boldsymbol{\delta}, \boldsymbol{\pi}, \boldsymbol{A})$ *with transition matrix* $\boldsymbol{T}$. *Let* $\tilde{\boldsymbol{T}}_w = (\boldsymbol{I} - w\boldsymbol{T})^{-1}$.[11]

i) The vector $\boldsymbol{\vartheta} = (\vartheta_1, \ldots, \vartheta_n)$ *of trigger strategies is a subgame-perfect equilibrium if and only if*

$$\vartheta_i \leq (R_2 - P_2)\boldsymbol{e}_i'(\tilde{\boldsymbol{T}}_w - \boldsymbol{I})F(\boldsymbol{\vartheta}) \text{ for all } i. \tag{3.2}$$

ii) There exists a unique Pareto-optimal subgame-perfect equilibrium in the class of trigger strategies, with thresholds $\boldsymbol{\vartheta}^*$. *This* solution $\boldsymbol{\vartheta}^*$ *can be characterized as the maximal solution in* $\boldsymbol{\vartheta}$ *of*

$$\vartheta_i = (R_2 - P_2)\boldsymbol{e}_i'(\tilde{\boldsymbol{T}}_w - \boldsymbol{I})F(\boldsymbol{\vartheta}) \text{ for all } i, \tag{3.3}$$

where

$\boldsymbol{e}_i$ *is the* i*-th unit vector of length* n,

$\boldsymbol{I}$ *is an identity matrix of size* n, *and*

$$F(\boldsymbol{\vartheta}) = (F(\vartheta_1), \ldots, F(\vartheta_n)).$$

The solution presented in Theorem 3.2 provides the Pareto-optimal equilibrium threshold for every trustor indicating how much the trustor can trust the trustee. I call the threshold belonging to the solution of the game the *trust threshold*. The essential property of the solution is that the trustor places trust if the incentive to abuse trust for the trustee is "compensated" by the expected number of times he will be sanctioned by the trustors, weighted by time preferences. This number depends on the "control effect" of a trustor in the network, in particular, it depends on how long the information about abuse of trust will be in the network. Therefore, the sanction potential depends on the extent to which trustor i transmits information into the network and not on the extent to which trustor i receives information out of the network. However, the exact properties of the solution are not directly clear from equation (3.3). In the following section, I elaborate on the properties of the solution.

[11] I define $\tilde{\boldsymbol{X}}_w = (\boldsymbol{I} - w\boldsymbol{X})^{-1}$. Throughout this book invertability is ensured using the theory of non-negative matrices (Berman and Plemmons 1979: 133).

3.4 PROPERTIES OF THE SOLUTION

Although equation (3.3) is a non-trivial formula, the different elements of the model are clearly separated. The first part on the right hand side contains the SANCTION COSTS for the trustee $(R_2 - P_2)\boldsymbol{e}_i'$. The second term involves the matrix $(\tilde{\boldsymbol{T}}_w - \boldsymbol{I})$. Here, the element $(\tilde{\boldsymbol{T}}_w - \boldsymbol{I})_{ij}$ is the expected discounted number of times trustor j will not place trust after the trustee has abused the trust placed by trustor i. In this expression the DISCOUNT FACTOR w is the discount factor of the trustee. The discount factors of the trustors do *not* affect the trust thresholds. Moreover, the payoffs of the trustors do *not* influence the trust thresholds. In particular, the payoff S_1 for the trustors when trust would be abused, does not affect the extent to which the trustors trust the trustee, although it can be argued that the higher the payoff for a trustor if trust would be abused, the less problematic placing trust is.[12] S_1 does not affect the solution because in the equilibria in the class of trigger strategies, trust is never abused by the trustee. Namely, if trust would be abused, the trustor would not have placed trust because she anticipates on the abuse of trust by the trustee. Consequently, the model does not provide predictions about the effects of payoffs of the trustors and the discount factors of trustors on the extent to which trustors can place trust. Finally, it can be seen from equation (3.3) that the distribution F of incentives to abuse trust is important.

SPECIAL CASES

Before the comparative statics of the trust thresholds are studied, I discuss some special cases for which the complexity of equation (3.3) is reduced considerably. First, without social network and without temporal embeddedness, $\alpha_{ij} = 0$ and $\delta_i = 1$ for all i and j, the game is a one-shot game. No information about abusing trust by the trustee is transferred to the next period. Thus, the only equilibrium is the equilibrium in which trust is never placed, $\boldsymbol{\vartheta} = \boldsymbol{0}$. Second, if $\alpha_{ij} = 0$ for all $i \neq j$, no information transfer between different trustors occurs (see also Raub and Weesie 1993b). The extent to which trust is placed, is the maximal solution in ϑ_i of

$$\vartheta_i = \frac{w(1 - \delta_i + \delta_i \pi_i)}{1 - w(1 - \delta_i + \delta_i \pi_i)} (R_2 - P_2) F(\vartheta_i) \text{ for all } i. \qquad (3.4)$$

Thus, what happens between trustor i and the trustee does not depend on the other trustors. The constructive proof of assertion *ii*) of Theorem 3.2 implies that, although the solution is only characterized implicitly, if the right hand side of (3.4) increases, the equality becomes a strict inequality and, consequently,

[12] See Snijders (1996) for experimental evidence in one-shot games.

that the new solution is a Pareto improvement of the former solution. Thus, the trust thresholds decrease in the DROP-OUT RATE δ_i, increase in the DISCOUNT FACTOR w, and increase in the SANCTION COSTS for the trustee $R_2 - P_2$.

Third, if $\alpha_{ij} = 1$ for all i and j, information of abusing trust by the trustee will be known for ever by the trustors who play the game. Therefore, trust will never be placed after the first defection of the trustee. Thus, $\boldsymbol{\delta}$ does not matter anymore. The payoff dominant subgame-perfect equilibrium in this case is given by the maximal solution in ϑ of

$$\vartheta = \frac{w}{1-w}(R_2 - P_2)F(\vartheta) \text{ for all } i, \tag{3.5}$$

which is a special case of (3.4) with $\boldsymbol{\delta} = 0$. Thus, here trust thresholds increase in the DISCOUNT FACTOR and the SANCTION COSTS.

Fourth, if $\alpha_{ij} = \alpha$ for all $i \neq j$, $\delta_i = \delta$, and $\pi_i = \frac{1}{n}$ for all i, the trust thresholds are the same for all trustors. The result associated with these parameters is similar to the result from Weesie et al. (1998) for homogeneous networks, and equals the maximal solution in ϑ of

$$\vartheta = \frac{w(\eta_1 + (n-1)\eta_2)}{1 - w(\eta_1 + (n-1)\eta_2)}(R_2 - P_2)F(\vartheta), \tag{3.6}$$

where

$$\eta_1 = 1 - \delta + \frac{\delta}{n} \quad \text{and} \quad \eta_2 = \frac{\delta\alpha}{n}. \tag{3.7}$$

This equation for homogeneous networks implies that the trust thresholds increase in DENSITY α.

The last special case is the case that $\delta_i = \delta$ and $\pi_i = \frac{1}{n}$ for all i, and all trustors have the same probability to transmit their information to the next trustor, i.e., all trustors have the same OUTDEGREE:

$$D_{out}(i) = \frac{\sum_{j \neq i} \pi_j \alpha_{ij}}{\sum_{j \neq i} \pi_j} = \alpha \text{ for all } i. \tag{3.8}$$

The following theorem states that all trust thresholds are the same if all trustors have the same $D_{out}(i)$. Thus, the following theorem implies that the structure of the network does not matter if the $D_{out}(i)$ are all the same.

THEOREM 3.3 *Assume that $\delta_i = \delta$, $\pi_i = \frac{1}{n}$, and $D_{out}(i) = \alpha$ for all i. Define $\eta_1 = 1 - \delta + \frac{\delta}{n}$ and $\eta_2 = \frac{\delta\alpha}{n}$. Then, the Pareto-optimal trust thresholds $\boldsymbol{\vartheta}^*$ in trigger strategies are the maximal solutions of*

$$\vartheta_i = \frac{w(\eta_1 + (n-1)\eta_2)}{1 - w(\eta_1 + (n-1)\eta_2)}(R_2 - P_2)F(\vartheta_i) \text{ for all } i. \tag{3.9}$$

GENERAL RESULTS

The thresholds $\boldsymbol{\vartheta}^*$ indicate the maximal incentives to abuse trust for which the trustors still trust the trustee. In this sense, $\boldsymbol{\vartheta}^*$ is an indicator for the extent to which trustors can trust the trustee. $F(\boldsymbol{\vartheta}^*) = (F(\vartheta_1^*), \ldots, F(\vartheta_n^*))$ are the proportions of transactions in which the different trustors will place trust. Because this indicator gives the expected proportion of periods a trustor expects to obtain R_1 compared to P_1, this might be an even better indicator than $\boldsymbol{\vartheta}^*$ for how efficiently trustors can arrange their transactions. The following theorem shows how $\boldsymbol{\vartheta}^*$ and $F(\boldsymbol{\vartheta}^*)$ depend on the parameters of the model.

THEOREM 3.4 *The Pareto-optimal subgame-perfect equilibrium in trigger strategies with trust thresholds $\boldsymbol{\vartheta}^*$ has the following properties.*

i) ϑ_i^* and $F(\vartheta_i^*)$ increase in the SANCTION COSTS *for the trustee $R_2 - P_2$ for all i.*

ii) ϑ_i^* and $F(\vartheta_i^*)$ increase in the DISCOUNT FACTOR *w of the trustee for all i and are independent of the discount factors of the trustors.*

iii) ϑ_i^* and $F(\vartheta_i^*)$ decrease in the DROP-OUT RATE *δ_j if and only if a path exists from trustor i to trustor j in the network $(\boldsymbol{\pi}, \boldsymbol{A})$.*[13]

iv) ϑ_i^* and $F(\vartheta_i^*)$ increase in α_{jk} if and only if a path exists from trustor i to trustor j in the network $(\boldsymbol{\pi}, \boldsymbol{A})$.

v) ϑ_i^* and $F(\vartheta_i^*)$ decrease in F in the sense of stochastic ordering.[14]

By Theorem 3.4, a trustor will trust the trustee more often and efficiency will be higher if the SANCTION COSTS for the trustee are higher. In other words, if the trustee suffers more if a trustor does not place trust, the trustor will more frequently trust the trustee. Moreover, if the future is more important to the trustee (w is larger), punishment by a trustor i will be more severe for the trustee and so the trust threshold ϑ_i^* and the efficiency $F(\vartheta_i^*)$ will be higher. If the incentives for abusing trust become smaller in the sense of stochastic ordering, the trust threshold will be higher, and the proportion of periods in which trust can be placed increases. If the trustee deals with the same trustor i for a longer time (δ_i is lower), trustor i has better punishment possibilities, and so ϑ_i^* becomes higher with temporal embeddedness. In addition, the trust thresholds of those trustors increase who, directly or indirectly, have ties to trustor i. The reason for this is that if trustor j is deceived by the trustee, there is a probability that trustor i receives information about that deceit. The corresponding punishment

[13] There exists a path between two trustors i and j if information that starts from trustor i reaches trustor j with a positive probability.

[14] $F_1 < F_2$ in the sense of stochastic ordering means that $F_1(\theta) > F_2(\theta)$ for all $\theta > 0$.

of the trustee by trustor i is expected to be larger if δ_i increases. Thus, bilateral control effects increase with a longer bilateral shadow of the future. And, control effects through the network increase with the "strength of ties" between connected trustors (α_{jk} increases) or if the shadow of the future for connected others becomes larger. The control effects imply that control is more effective if information about abused trust stays longer with trustors, not necessarily the deceived trustor, and if information is transferred with a higher probability to other trustors. In particular, it is again seen that possibilities for transmitting information to others increase trust.

The comparative statics of the model for non-network parameters are in correspondence with earlier models in which the network structure was not modeled explicitly (for example, Raub and Weesie 1993b; Weesie et al. 1998). Thus, additional assumptions made to incorporate the social network in a way that analytical tractability is maintained do not distort findings about the effects of other parameters. However, as far as network embeddedness is concerned, the only result for the new model is that trust increases with the individual tie strength α_{ij}. This is a strong result but it does not translate into predictions about network parameters. For instance, it does not even imply that trust increases with the density of the network.

It is striking that the effects of temporal and network embeddedness including the DISCOUNT FACTOR are summarized in the matrix $\tilde{\boldsymbol{T}}_w - \boldsymbol{I}$ and that elements representing the payoffs ($R_2 - P_2$ and F) just weight the elements in this matrix. Therefore, the matrix is worth studying in more detail. Realizing that this chapter is already rather technical, I do not want to introduce more mathematics than is absolutely necessary. Therefore, I will just state here that the game can be represented in terms of a Markov chain (see Appendix A for details). It is a direct consequence of the theory of Markov chains (Kemeny and Snell 1960: Theorem 3.5.4) that the sum of the elements of the ith row

$$\gamma_i = \sum_{j=1}^{n} (\tilde{\boldsymbol{T}}_w - \boldsymbol{I})_{ij} \tag{3.10}$$

is the expected discounted number of times that the trustee will obtain P_2 as a consequence of an abuse of trust placed by trustor i. Therefore, I call γ_i the *chain length* related to trustor i. I expect that if information about the abuse of trust by the trustee stays in the network of the trustors for a longer time, the consequences for the trustee are worse and, thus, the trust threshold would be higher. The following theorem states that if the network consists of more than two trustors, a trustor with a longer chain length *cannot* always place more trust in the trustee than a trustor with a shorter chain length.

THEOREM 3.5 *The Pareto-optimal trust thresholds* $\boldsymbol{\vartheta}^*$ *in trigger strategies have the following properties.*

i) If $n = 2$ *and* $\gamma_1 > \gamma_2$ *then* $\vartheta_1^* > \vartheta_2^*$.

ii) If $n > 2$, *the* ϑ_i^**'s are not necessarily increasing in* γ_i.

Assertion *ii)* of Theorem 3.5 states that there is not a perfect correspondence between the order of the trust thresholds and the order of the chain length in a network if $n > 2$ (see Appendix A for an example). This can be explained as follows. Informing a trustor with a higher trust threshold about an abuse of trust by the trustee causes a stronger sanction for the trustee than informing a trustor with a lower trust threshold, because, ceteris paribus, the trustor with the higher trust threshold would place trust more often than the trustor with the lower trust threshold if they were not informed about the abuse of trust. Nevertheless, in a numerical simulation, the correlation between ϑ_i^* and γ_i was very high and the example given in the proof of Theorem 3.5 is, in a sense, an exception. Moreover, for such exceptions the difference between the chain lengths and trust thresholds of the trustors for which the order is changed is usually small compared to differences among trust thresholds in general. Note that, on the one hand, Theorem 3.5 provides a reason for the usefulness of modeling network diffusion in a game-theoretic context. In a pure diffusion model, the chain length is the decisive factor. On the other hand, the close correspondence between chain length and trust threshold indicates that studying a pure diffusion model in which information diffusion is modeled in a more realistic way seems to be a relevant additional modeling exercise.

In an earlier paper (Buskens and Weesie 2000a), I derived two more theorems about network implications that follow from the model. These theorems characterize the network configuration under which trust thresholds are maximal, if all OUTDEGREES $D_{out}(i)$ are given. The theorems are not repeated here in detail because they mainly address the efficiency problem at the global network level and not at the level of individual trustors. The main result is that the most efficient network is centralized around the trustor with the highest OUTDEGREE. Here, trustors transmit information "as much as possible" to the trustor with the highest OUTDEGREE. If trustors have an OUTDEGREE that is "high enough," they also transmit information to the trustor who has the next highest OUTDEGREE and so forth. Thus, in an "optimal" network, everybody transmits information to the trustor with the highest OUTDEGREE, but hardly anybody to the trustor with the lowest OUTDEGREE. This structure can still be optimal even for a trustor with a low OUTDEGREE because the information a trustor receives does not influence the trust threshold of a trustor: there is no learning in the model, but only control.

Unfortunately, the analytic results do not yet answer the questions posed in Section 1.3. The results do not show whether trust thresholds increase or decrease with the OUTDEGREE of a particular trustor, or what the effect is of centralization of the network. I was not able to derive such results analytically because the trust thresholds are not easily expressed as functions of the relevant network parameters. Sections 3.5 and 3.6 describe two approximation methods, namely, linearization and simulation. Using these approximations, hypotheses are developed about the effects of the network parameters on trust thresholds as "approximate implications" of the model.

3.5 APPROXIMATION USING LINEARIZATION

Although this may seem a paradox, all exact science is dominated by the idea of approximation.

—Bertrand Russell

In Section 3.3, I characterized the trust thresholds of the trustors in the IHTG in terms of the parameters of $\Gamma(\Gamma_F, w, \boldsymbol{\delta}, \boldsymbol{\pi}, \boldsymbol{A})$. To obtain a better insight into the solution (3.3) to the IHTG, I apply linearization around parameter values where explicit expressions of the trust thresholds can be obtained. To be able to focus on the network effects on the trust thresholds, I use two additional homogeneity assumptions in the remainder of this chapter:

$$\pi_i = \frac{1}{n} \quad \text{and} \quad \delta_i = \delta \quad \text{for all } i.$$

Moreover, I use the distribution

$$F_a(\theta) = \frac{\theta}{a+\theta}, \qquad \theta \geq 0, a > 0, \tag{3.11}$$

of incentives to abuse trust for the trustee (see also Raub and Weesie 1993b; Weesie et al. 1998). This distribution is likewise used in the simulation (Section 3.6). Below, I will also use the first derivative of $F_a(\theta)$ with respect to θ:

$$f_a(\theta) = \frac{a}{(a+\theta)^2}. \tag{3.12}$$

Define $G(\boldsymbol{\vartheta}^*(\boldsymbol{x}), \boldsymbol{x})$ as the implicit function that describes $\boldsymbol{\vartheta}^*$ in terms of the other parameters $\boldsymbol{x} = (R_2 - P_2, a, w, \delta, \boldsymbol{A})$,

$$G(\boldsymbol{\vartheta}^*(\boldsymbol{x}), \boldsymbol{x}) = \boldsymbol{\vartheta}^* - (R_2 - P_2)\left((\boldsymbol{I} - w\boldsymbol{T})^{-1} - \boldsymbol{I}\right) F(\boldsymbol{\vartheta}^*) = 0. \tag{3.13}$$

Because $G(\boldsymbol{\vartheta}^*(\boldsymbol{x}), \boldsymbol{x})$ is a smooth function of $\boldsymbol{x}$ and $\left(\frac{\partial G}{\partial \boldsymbol{\vartheta}^*}\right)^{-1}$ exists almost everywhere, the implicit function theorem (Dieudonné 1960: 270–273) can be used. This implies that $\boldsymbol{\vartheta}^*$ depends smoothly on $\boldsymbol{x}$ and

$$\frac{\partial \boldsymbol{\vartheta}^*}{\partial \boldsymbol{x}} = \left(\frac{\partial G}{\partial \boldsymbol{\vartheta}^*}\right)^{-1} \frac{\partial G}{\partial \boldsymbol{x}}. \tag{3.14}$$

I linearize around a homogeneous network $\boldsymbol{A}_0$ with DENSITY α,

$$\boldsymbol{A}_0 = (1-\alpha)\boldsymbol{I} + \alpha \boldsymbol{J}, \text{ where } \boldsymbol{J} = \mathbf{1}\mathbf{1}'. \tag{3.15}$$

All OUTDEGREES of this network are equal to α. The reason for using this network is that the trust thresholds can be calculated explicitly. The transition matrix for homogeneous networks $\boldsymbol{T}_0$ equals

$$\boldsymbol{T}_0 = (1-\delta)\boldsymbol{I} + \frac{\delta}{n}\boldsymbol{A}_0 = (\eta_1 - \eta_2)\boldsymbol{I} + \eta_2 \boldsymbol{J}, \tag{3.16}$$

where $\eta_1 = 1 - \delta + \frac{\delta}{n}$ and $\eta_2 = \frac{\delta\alpha}{n}$. For $\boldsymbol{T}_0$, the payoff dominant trigger equilibrium can be easily derived explicitly. The trust thresholds are the same for all trustors and satisfy

$$\vartheta_0^* = \vartheta^*(\boldsymbol{A}_0) = \max\left(0, \frac{(R_2 - P_2)w(\eta_1 + (n-1)\eta_2)}{1 - w(\eta_1 + (n-1)\eta_2)} - a\right). \tag{3.17}$$

This equation is slightly different from (3.6) due to the fact that I incorporated the distribution F_a as given in (3.11). Generally, the original equation holds for two values of ϑ_0^*, namely, 0 and a value that depends on the parameters and can be positive or negative. A negative value implies that no trust is possible for the given parameters. Taking the maximum in (3.17) implies that in these cases the all-zero equilibrium is the solution of the game.

A first-order approximation is deduced for the trust threshold corresponding to a network matrix $\boldsymbol{A}$ in the "neighborhood" of $\boldsymbol{A}_0$ under the assumption that positive equilibria exist. The approximation symbol ($\approx$) in the Theorem 3.6 indicates that the difference between the approximation and the true value is of the order of magnitude of the difference between $\boldsymbol{A}$ and $\boldsymbol{A}_0$ (see Appendix A for details). Theorem 3.6 gives the first-order approximation of the trust thresholds $\boldsymbol{\vartheta}^*(\boldsymbol{A})$ for $\boldsymbol{A}$.

THEOREM 3.6 *Let $\boldsymbol{A} \approx \boldsymbol{A}_0 = (1-\alpha)\boldsymbol{I} + \alpha\boldsymbol{J}$ and $\vartheta_i^*(\boldsymbol{A}_0) > 0$ for all i. Then the solution of equation (3.3) for trust thresholds $\boldsymbol{\vartheta}^*$ satisfies*

$$\begin{aligned} \boldsymbol{\vartheta}^*(\boldsymbol{A}) &\approx \boldsymbol{\vartheta}^*(\boldsymbol{A}_0) + \rho_1(\boldsymbol{I} + \rho_2\boldsymbol{J})(\boldsymbol{A} - \boldsymbol{A}_0)\mathbf{1} \\ &= \boldsymbol{\vartheta}^*(\boldsymbol{A}_0) + (n-1)\rho_1\Big(\boldsymbol{D}_{out}(\boldsymbol{A}) - \boldsymbol{D}_{out}(\boldsymbol{A}_0)\Big) \\ &\quad + n(n-1)\rho_1\rho_2\Big(\Delta(\boldsymbol{A}) - \Delta(\boldsymbol{A}_0)\Big)\mathbf{1}, \end{aligned} \tag{3.18}$$

where

$$\rho_1 = \frac{\delta w(R_2 - P_2)F_a(\vartheta_0^*)}{n(1 - w(\eta_1 + (n-1)\eta_2))(1 - w(\eta_1 - \eta_2)(1+\mu))} > 0, \quad (3.19)$$

$$\rho_2 = \frac{(1 + f_a(\vartheta_0^*)(R_2 - P_2))w\eta_2}{1 - w(\eta_1 + (n-1)\eta_2)(1+\mu)} > 0, \quad (3.20)$$

$\boldsymbol{D}_{out}$ *the vector of all* OUTDEGREES, *and* (3.21)

$$\mu = f_a(\vartheta_0^*)(R_2 - P_2). \quad (3.22)$$

It follows immediately from Theorem 3.6 that $(n-1)\rho_1$ is the magnitude of the change in the trust thresholds for a change in the OUTDEGREE for a trustor, while $n(n-1)\rho_1\rho_2$ is the "weight" of a small increase in DENSITY. Because ρ_1 and ρ_2 are both positive, positive effects are predicted of OUTDEGREE and DENSITY on the trust thresholds $\boldsymbol{\vartheta}^*$. The magnitudes of the effects of OUTDEGREE and DENSITY depend on the other parameters of the model ($R_2 - P_2$, a, w, δ, and n). If ρ_1 and ρ_2 would be monotonic in some of the parameters, interaction effects could be straightforwardly derived from the theorem. However, ρ_1 is not monotonic in any of the parameters in the relevant range. Consequently, I do not find hypotheses about interaction effects between OUTDEGREE and DENSITY, and the other parameters directly from this linearization.

The linearization result also implies that the parameters in the game-theoretic model determine how large the relative size of the effect of changes in OUTDEGREE and DENSITY will be. The parameter ρ_2, or more precisely $n\rho_2$, can be interpreted as the relative effect of DENSITY compared to OUTDEGREE. Again, monotonicity of ρ_2 is not guaranteed for w and δ. However, two monotonic effects are found, namely, ρ_2 increases in a and decreases in $R_2 - P_2$.[15] Therefore, it is predicted that DENSITY becomes more important compared to OUTDEGREE if the SANCTION COSTS for the trustee ($R_2 - P_2$) decrease and if the MEDIAN INCENTIVE for the trustee to abuse trust (a) increases. These two results are interesting because they indicate that the "whole network" (DENSITY) becomes more important compared to the "ego-centered network" (OUTDEGREE) if the trust problem in the constituent game increases. This point will be addressed more extensively following the simulations in Section 3.6.

The findings based on linearization are limited to networks "close" to a homogeneous situation. They cannot be generalized to more heterogeneous

[15] These results can be seen directly from (3.20), realizing that $\mu(R_2 - P_2)f_a(\vartheta_0^*) = \frac{(R_2-P_2)a}{(\vartheta_0^*+a)^2} = \frac{a(1-w(\eta_1+(n-1)\eta_2))^2}{(R_2-P_2)w^2(\eta_1+(n-1)\eta_2)^2}$, which decreases in $R_2 - P_2$ and increases in a.

networks without further examination. For this purpose, I use a simulation method. Furthermore, I investigate effects of network parameters other than DENSITY and OUTDEGREE on trust thresholds in more heterogeneous networks.

3.6 APPROXIMATION USING SIMULATION

3.6.1 METHODS

In this section, I use a second approximation method to study the implications of the model, namely, computer simulation. The simulation is a variant of the method used in earlier studies (Yamaguchi 1994a; Buskens and Yamaguchi 1999). A considerable set of networks is selected with substantial variation in the independent variables, i.e., network and non-network parameters. I compute the game-theoretic solution and the network parameters numerically for these networks. This constitutes a simulated data set. These data will be analyzed using conventional statistical methods to approximate the comparative statics for the network parameters on the trust thresholds. The set of networks described in this chapter will be used both in the present chapter and the next chapter.

In the papers mentioned above, a set of discrete networks that consist of 7 actors and 6 to 9 ties is used. For valued networks with weighted nodes $(\boldsymbol{\pi}, \boldsymbol{A})$, I needed a different set of networks. It was not at all obvious how a set of networks could be constructed with substantial variation in the network parameters. For instance, sampling every α_{ij} from a uniform distribution from the interval $[0, 1]$ obviously results in networks with DENSITY close to $\frac{1}{2}$, and INDEGREE and OUTDEGREE will often be close to $\frac{1}{2}$. Therefore, I developed four methods to sample random networks such that acceptable variations are obtained in the network parameters as discussed in Section 2.1. Details on the network construction methods are provided in Appendix B. In the regression analyses later on, I will check whether results differ between construction methods.

SAMPLED NETWORKS

The number of trustors n varies between 2 and 10 in the sample of networks. For each value of n, 250 networks are sampled. Thus, $9 \times 250 = 2,250$ networks are sampled. This results in a data set with 13,500 cases $(250 \times (2 + 3 + \cdots + 10))$, clustered within networks. The importance of the trustors $\boldsymbol{\pi}$ within the networks is not varied, i.e., $\pi_i = \frac{1}{n}$ for all i. Networks are generated via a randomly selected construction method. Moreover, it is randomly decided whether the network is made symmetric after the construction.[16] The network parameters

[16] I chose half of the networks symmetric in order to be able to check whether systematic differences are found between symmetric and asymmetric networks. I did not find any differences between symmetric and asymmetric networks.

Table 3.1. Summary statistics and correlations of the network parameters for the constructed networks (13,500 trustors in 2,250 networks).

	Individual network parameters						*Global network parameters*				
	D_{out}	D_{in}	Q_{out}	Q_{in}	LD_{out}	LD_{in}	Δ	V_{out}	V_{in}	$V_{out,in}$	Tr
Minimum	.00	.00	−.11	−.11	.00	.00	.00	.00	.00	−.21	.00
Mean	.47	.47	.01	.01	.51	.51	.47	.02	.02	.01	.47
Maximum	1.00	1.00	.15	.13	1.00	1.00	1.00	.21	.21	.07	1.00
INDEGREE	.81										
OUTDEGREE QUALITY	.09	.10									
INDEGREE QUALITY	.10	.09	.83								
LOCAL OUTD. DENSITY	.44	.46	.34	.34							
LOCAL IND. DENSITY	.45	.44	.33	.34	.96						
DENSITY	.82	.82	.03	.03	.69	.69					
OUTDEGREE VARIANCE	.05	.05	.43	.30	.25	.33	.07				
INDEGREE VARIANCE	.06	.06	.27	.42	.33	.24	.07	.30			
OUTD.-IND. COVARIANCE	.01	.02	.67	.67	.38	.38	.01	.21	.20		
TRANSITIVITY	.65	.65	.22	.23	.88	.87	.79	.16	.18	.33	
NETWORK SIZE	−.01	−.02	.08	.08	.23	.23	−.02	−.00	−.01	.24	.29

introduced in Section 2.1 are calculated for each network and trustor in the network. These are the central "independent variables" in the analyses below. Table 3.1 presents summary statistics of the network parameters in the set of networks. OUTDEGREE, INDEGREE, LOCAL OUTDEGREE DENSITY, LOCAL INDEGREE DENSITY, DENSITY, and TRANSITIVITY vary between 0 and 1. The variances and covariances have smaller extremes. OUTDEGREE VARIANCE and INDEGREE VARIANCE have a large number of very low values.

Table 3.1 also shows the (Pearson) correlations among the network parameters of the constructed networks. If the correlations are low (in the absolute sense), effects in regression analyses are easy to separate. The higher the correlations, the more cases are needed to distinguish the effects of the different network parameters. Table 3.1 shows that not all the correlations are low. It cannot be expected that all correlations are low because some of the network parameters are related by definition. For instance, a high OUTDEGREE contributes to a high DENSITY. If all actors have a high OUTDEGREE, actors should also have a high INDEGREE, because the sum of OUTDEGREES equals the sum of INDEGREES. Furthermore, in symmetric networks all pairs of network parameters based on OUTDEGREE and INDEGREE are pairwise the same. High positive correlations are indeed found between DENSITY, OUTDEGREE, and INDEGREE. Moreover, positive correlations are found between OUTDEGREE QUALITY and INDEGREE QUALITY, and between LOCAL OUTDEGREE DENSITY and LOCAL INDEGREE DENSITY. The correlation between LOCAL OUTDEGREE DENSITY and LOCAL INDEGREE DENSITY is very high (0.96) and this is problematic for the interpretation of regression results as will be seen below. High correlations are also found among DENSITY, TRANSITIVITY, LOCAL OUTDEGREE DENSITY, and LOCAL INDEGREE DENSITY. These correlations are due to the fact that triads are, to a large extent, closed and consequently transitive in dense networks. Thus, although there are some rather high correlations among the network parameters, most of them are probably unavoidable and will occur in any set of networks, simulated or empirical.

Sampled Non-Network Parameters

Together with the network parameters $\boldsymbol{A}$, I vary the other parameters:

- The distribution of incentives to abuse trust $F_a(\theta) = \frac{\theta}{a+\theta}$ is used with a, the MEDIAN INCENTIVE of F_a, equal to 1, 2, or 3, each with probability $\frac{1}{3}$.
- The SANCTION COSTS for the trustee $R_2 - P_2$ are an integer between 2 and 7, each with probability $\frac{1}{6}$.
- The DROP-OUT RATE δ that the same trustor and trustee are not involved in another transaction is sampled from a uniform distribution on the interval $[0.25, 0.9]$ and has the same value for all trustors in each network.
- The DISCOUNT FACTOR w is sampled from a uniform distribution on the interval $[0.85, 0.95]$.

All these values for the different parameters are sampled independently (in the probabilistic sense) for each network.

Dependent Variables

Now, for each trustor in the network, the Pareto-optimal trust threshold and diffusion times (see Chapter 4) are calculated.[17] These are the "dependent variables" used in this chapter and the following chapter.

Method of Analysis

It is important to note that in the analysis below, the dependent variable is calculated in a deterministic way using the independent variables. Thus, there

[17] In an earlier paper (Buskens 1998), I calculated the trust thresholds for one randomly chosen trustor in the network to prevent dependencies between cases due to clustering within networks. Because the computation of diffusion times is a particular computer-time consuming process, I decided to use all the trustors in a network although that creates dependencies among the cases. The results from earlier simulation experiments hardly differed conditional upon whether one or all trustors in a network were included in the analyses. This implies that it does not appear to be a problem to use all trustors in a network. Moreover, statistical techniques are used that adjust standard errors for the clustering of cases within the networks (see the "method of analysis" in this section).

is *no* stochastic element in the data. Still, I will use statistical modeling to approximate the trust threshold with a "simple" function of the parameters

$$\vartheta_i^*(\boldsymbol{x}) = g(\boldsymbol{x}) + \varepsilon_i(\boldsymbol{x}), \tag{3.23}$$

where $\boldsymbol{x} = (R_2 - P_2, a, \delta, w, \boldsymbol{A})$ and g is a linear or quadratic function of the parameters including networks parameters. The residual terms indicate the extent to which the trust thresholds can be approximated by the function g. I model these residuals via stochastic variables although the residual terms are not caused by stochastic noise, but depend deterministically on the parameter values. Consequently, the assumptions of standard regression analysis that the residuals are stochastically independent is clearly violated. An elegant way to solve this problem would be to model "spatial correlation" among the residual terms, i.e., to adjust directly for the fact that residual terms in the same area of the sample space of parameters will be correlated. This can be expected because both ϑ_i^* and g are "smooth" functions of the parameters. However, only the network parameters vary among the trustors within a network and all the other parameters are the same for all the trustors in a network. Thus, the "largest" dependencies of residuals are expected between trustors within networks. Therefore, I will use Huber standard errors that are modified for clustering of the observations within networks.[18]

Another problem with the analyses is that ϑ_i^* cannot be lower than 0. The reason for this is that the trust threshold indicates the extent to which trust is possible if any trust is possible. If no trust is possible, it is unclear how large the trust problem is. Equation (3.17) gives an expression for the lack of trust in homogeneous networks with given DENSITY if maximization with 0 is disregarded. Substituting $\alpha = 0$ in this expression results in the lack of trust in case the trustors are not connected at all in a network. This is the worst case for a trustor in a given network. Thus, the maximal value (in the absolute sense) of "lack of trust" equals $\frac{(R_2-P_2)w\eta_1}{1-w\eta_1} - a$. It is not clear how much this lack of trust is decreased (in the absolute sense) by network embeddedness in a heterogeneous network. For trust thresholds equal to 0, it is only known that there is still a certain amount of lack of trust and, therefore, that the actual value of trust of the trustor is an element of the interval

$$\left[\frac{(R_2 - P_2)w\eta_1}{1 - w\eta_1} - a, 0\right]. \tag{3.24}$$

[18]Huber standard errors are consistent under heterogeneity in the residual variables. The Huber estimator of variance was "independently" discovered by Huber (1967) and White (1980) and is also called the White, sandwich, or robust estimator of variance. The estimator of variance can be generalized for clustered observations (Rogers 1993).

For analysis of data in which the dependent variable does not always have a known value, but sometimes is only known to be an element of an interval, a generalization of the *tobit* model for censored dependent variables can be used (see Tobin 1958; Amemiya 1973).[19]

3.6.2 ANALYSES FOR SIMULATED DATA

Model 1 in Table 3.2 gives results of the tobit-like regression analysis of the effects of payoffs, DISCOUNT FACTOR, DROP-OUT RATE, DENSITY, OUTDEGREE, and NETWORK SIZE on the trust thresholds. The hypotheses on the effects, as derived from the analytic and linearization results, are presented in the second column of the table.

The $\text{corr}(\vartheta^*, \hat{\vartheta^*})^2$ reported in Table 3.2 is the squared correlation between the predicted trust threshold and the actual trust threshold for the positive trust thresholds. This is an analogue to R^2 for ordinary regression. The zero-equilibria are not included in the squared correlation because the predictions are based on the assumption that trust is "negative" in these cases while the trust thresholds are 0. The values of $\text{corr}(\vartheta^*, \hat{\vartheta^*})^2$ give a measure for the extent to which adding a group of variables improves the fit of the model. Furthermore, the correlation gives an idea of the extent to which, for this set of networks at least, the trust thresholds can be approximated with the variables in the regression. I do not report the log-likelihoods of the tobit models because they are not informative for clustered regression. The tobit models assume that residual terms follow a normal distribution $N(0, \sigma^2)$. The parameter σ is estimated in the model and gives an indication of the size of the residual term.

The first analysis in Model 1 is in accordance with the comparative statics that are formally derived in Section 3.4. Of course, this is a necessary condition for the simulation data and the approximation method to make sense. Trust increases in the SANCTION COSTS for the trustee and in the DISCOUNT FACTOR of the trustee. Trust decreases in the DROP-OUT RATE of the trustor and in the MEDIAN INCENTIVE for the trustee to abuse trust.[20] Furthermore, trustors in a denser network and trustors with a higher OUTDEGREE place more trust.[21]

[19]This generalization is implemented in Stata 5.0 and higher under the name "interval regression." Ordinary tobit analysis without taking into account the lower bound of the interval for the zero-equilibria, however, gives similar results. There are 652 zero-equilibria in 88 networks.

[20]The DROP-OUT RATE is slightly adjusted. Because a trustor can be chosen again after she drops out, namely, with a probability $\frac{1}{n}$, the *actual* DROP-OUT RATE equals $\delta(1 - \frac{1}{n})$. Without this adjustment, NETWORK SIZE had an effect in the opposite direction as the DROP-OUT RATE. Clearly, an increase in NETWORK SIZE decreases the probability that a trustor is chosen again. After changing to the "actual" DROP-OUT RATE no effect of NETWORK SIZE was found.

[21]This analysis and the following analyses can also be done for the proportion of transactions in which a trustor can place trust $F(\vartheta_i^*)$ instead of the trust thresholds. Because the comparative statics of $F(\vartheta_i^*)$ resemble the comparative statics of ϑ_i^* (see Theorem 3.4), the qualitative results for these two dependent variables are the same.

Table 3.2. Tobit-like regression of the trust thresholds (13,500 trustors in 2,250 networks, 652 observations in 88 networks are censored).[a]

Independent variable	Hypothesis	Model 1	Model 2	Model 3	Model 4
NON-NETWORK PARAMETERS					
SANCTION COSTS $(R_2 - P_2)$	+	2.52	2.50	2.52	2.57
MEDIAN INCENTIVE (a)	–	−1.11	−1.00	−1.11	−1.09
DROP-OUT RATE $(\delta(1 - \frac{1}{n}))$	–	−20.40	−21.54	−21.12	−21.50
DROP-OUT RATE^2	?		37.90	35.49	32.36
DISCOUNT FACTOR (w)	+	55.13	58.59	56.84	57.87
SANCTION COSTS × DROP-OUT RATE	?		−4.34	−5.01	−5.04
SANCTION COSTS × DISCOUNT FACTOR	?		9.53	12.64	12.64
DROP-OUT RATE × DISCOUNT FACTOR	?		−105.92	−122.02	−133.17
NETWORK PARAMETERS					
OUTDEGREE	+	10.08		9.69	9.77
OUTDEGREE^2	?			−3.43	−4.30
DENSITY	+	17.74		14.53	14.56
DENSITY^2	?			28.70	28.52
DENSITY × OUTDEGREE	?			20.90	22.16
INTERACTION EFFECTS BETWEEN NETWORK AND NON-NETWORK PARAMETERS					
SANCTION COSTS × OUTDEGREE	?				2.64
SANCTION COSTS × DENSITY	?				3.39
MEDIAN INCENTIVE × OUTDEGREE	?				−.89
MEDIAN INCENTIVE × DENSITY	?				(−.21)
DROP-OUT RATE × OUTDEGREE	?				−12.99
DROP-OUT RATE × DENSITY	?				14.67
DISCOUNT FACTOR × OUTDEGREE	?				59.68
DISCOUNT FACTOR × DENSITY	?				229.26
CONSTANT		−52.38	−43.11	−54.53	−55.44
$\text{corr}(\vartheta^*, \hat{\vartheta}^*)^2$		.76	.42	.86	.94
σ (standard deviation of residuals)		4.59	6.85	3.39	2.20

[a] Except for the one in parentheses, all coefficients are "significant" at $p < 0.01$, based on Huber standard errors, modified for clustering within networks (two-sided tests).

The coefficients in the regression models can be roughly interpreted as "average" derivatives of the related parameters over the sample used in the simulation. It has to be realized that these coefficients may depend on the sampling distribution. For instance, the DISCOUNT FACTOR is only varied between 0.85 and 0.95. The effect of the DISCOUNT FACTOR is expected to accelerate toward 1, because the effect of the DISCOUNT FACTOR is more or less proportional to $\frac{w}{1-w}$ (see, for example, equation (3.5)). If the discount factor tends to 1, the trust threshold increases strongly, at least if the DROP-OUT RATE is not too high and the DENSITY is not too low. If the DISCOUNT FACTOR tends to 0, the trust threshold decreases to 0. However, because only relatively large values of the DISCOUNT FACTOR are chosen, the coefficient is rather large and the effect is approximately linear; the quadratic term for the DISCOUNT FACTOR does not have an additional effect. Moreover, "significance levels" and "explained variance" depend largely on the given sample. This is also a reason why I made a special effort to obtain high variance and low covariance among the network parameters. For example, DENSITY and OUTDEGREE vary on their complete range from 0 to 1. Moreover, by using four different methods to construct networks, I can "test" whether effects differ between different subsamples of the total set of networks.

In Models 2 to 4, I analyze a full quadratic model of the independent variables of Model 1. From equation (3.3), it can be seen that the trust thresholds are not a linear function of the parameters. Therefore, it is not surprising that a quadratic model fits the data better.[22] The "non-significant" effects are excluded from the model in so far as I do not want to discuss them specifically. In Model 2, only non-network parameters are included in the model. The squared correlation between the predicted and actual trust thresholds is 0.42. The additional non-linear effects are easy to interpret. The effect of (adjusted) DROP-OUT RATE $\delta' = \delta(1 - \frac{1}{n})$ is proportional to $\frac{1-\delta'}{\delta'}$, which decreases in δ' and decreases slower if δ' increases toward 1. Other quadratic effects are not important or significant. From equation (3.17), it could be expected that the MEDIAN INCENTIVE to abuse trust would have an additive effect, and the coefficient should be close to -1. This is indeed the case. The DISCOUNT FACTOR is more important if the sanctions of the trustors continue for a longer time. Thus, if the DROP-OUT RATE becomes lower, the transaction duration between the trustee and the same trustor increases and, therefore, the effect of the DISCOUNT FACTOR becomes larger. Also the effect of the SANCTION COSTS for the trustee becomes higher if the future is more important, i.e., the DROP-OUT RATE is lower or the DISCOUNT FACTOR is larger.

In Model 3, the main network parameters OUTDEGREE, DENSITY, and their quadratic and interactions effects are added to the non-network parameters. The squared correlation of Model 3 is $0.44 = 0.86 - 0.42$ higher than in Model 2. The effect of OUTDEGREE decreases with increasing OUTDEGREE and the effect of DENSITY increases with increasing DENSITY. Furthermore, the effects of DENSITY and OUTDEGREE strengthen each other.

Finally, Model 4 includes interactions between non-network and network parameters. First, note that the effects for the other independent variables

[22] All the quadratic and interaction terms are constructed as the product of the centered values for the different variables.

hardly change with the inclusion of these interactions. Second, the interactions add about 0.08 to the squared correlation between predicted and actual trust thresholds. A Wald test (which is appropriate with clustered observations) shows that Model 4 fits the data better than Model 3. Thus, the effort made in developing a model in which network and non-network parameters are included together shows its value here. The effects predicted from linearization are supported: the importance of DENSITY compared to OUTDEGREE increases if the SANCTION COSTS for the trustee decrease and if the MEDIAN INCENTIVE to abuse trust increases.[23] Thus, the larger the trust problem in the constituent game due to the magnitude of payoffs, the more important global network properties become for trust and the less a trustor can rely on her own ties.

The simulation suggests additional interaction effects that were not obtained from the linearization. The effect of OUTDEGREE decreases with increasing incentives to abuse trust. As could be expected, the effect of the DISCOUNT FACTOR increases if information stays longer in the network. This effect is larger for DENSITY than for OUTDEGREE. The interaction effects with DROP-OUT RATE indicate that the shorter a series of transactions with the same trustor and, thus, the less a trustor can punish the trustee herself, the more she has to rely on the global network (interaction effect with DENSITY) relative to her own ties (interaction with OUTDEGREE).

Some additional models were estimated that are not reported in the table. One can explicitly model the multi-level structure in the data: trustors are nested within networks. I estimated models with random effects at the individual as well as at the network level ignoring censoring. The implications of these multi-level models do not differ from the models presented above. To control for effects of sample methods, a regression model was estimated that includes dummy variables for network construction methods and interactions of these dummies with the other variables. Small differences are found for the effects of the network and non-network parameters for the different constructions of networks, but the changes in the effects were small compared to the sizes of the effects. Thus, the comparative statics are the same over the different subsamples of networks. Furthermore, the dummies for construction methods and their interaction effects contribute only marginally to the squared correlation between actual and predicted trust thresholds.

The main problem with the regression analyses shown above is that the controls for non-network parameters are still imperfect. While I used interactions and quadratic terms of the non-network parameters, they do not account for all

[23]It is not immediately clear that the effect of OUTDEGREE increases compared to the effect of DENSITY if SANCTION COSTS for the trustee increase. Combining the main effects of OUTDEGREE and DENSITY with the interaction effects, it can be calculated that the net effect of DENSITY is twice as large as the effect of OUTDEGREE for the lowest values of SANCTION COSTS and only 1.5 times as large for the highest value of SANCTION COSTS.

the variance due to these parameters. That could be one of the reasons why network parameters other than OUTDEGREE and DENSITY have hardly any effect in the analyses. The only consistent but small additional network effect is a positive effect of OUTDEGREE QUALITY, that is, of the extent to which trustor can reach other trustors in two steps. Because OUTDEGREE QUALITY is an extension of OUTDEGREE, this is the expected effect.

FOCUS ON NETWORK EFFECTS

To control for the non-network parameters in a more model-inspired way, I introduce the *normalized threshold* $\tilde{\vartheta}^*$. Consider the homogeneous case where $\alpha_{ij} = \alpha$ for all i and j, $i \neq j$. Then, the trust threshold is the same for every trustor. Restricting the analyses to cases where at least some trust is possible ($\vartheta^* > 0$), the trust threshold equals

$$\vartheta^* = \frac{(R_2 - P_2)(w(\eta_1 + (n-1)\eta_2)}{1 - w(\eta_1 + (n-1)\eta_2)} - a > 0, \tag{3.25}$$

which involves the network parameter α in a "complicated" role ($\eta_1 = 1 - \delta + \frac{\delta}{n}$, $\eta_2 = \frac{\delta\alpha}{n}$). Equation (3.25) suggests a possibility of controlling for effects of non-network parameters and NETWORK SIZE, because here the DENSITY effect can be explicitly isolated. Define the *normalized threshold* $\tilde{\vartheta}_i^*$ as

$$\tilde{\vartheta}_i^* = 1 - \frac{n}{n-1}\left(\frac{1}{\delta} - \frac{(\vartheta_i^* + a)}{\delta w(\vartheta_i^* + a + (R_2 - P_2))}\right). \tag{3.26}$$

Note that normalization involves all model parameters but DENSITY α. For homogeneous networks $\tilde{\vartheta}^*$ equals DENSITY α. In cases where $\vartheta_i^* = 0$, the normalized threshold can also be calculated. But as in the reasoning for ϑ_i^*, it is not known how large the lack of trust will be in these cases, and, therefore, the effect of the network is unclear. Substituting the lower and upper bound of the interval (3.24) used for the ϑ_i^* results in

$$\tilde{\vartheta}_i^* \in \left[0, 1 - \frac{n}{n-1}\left(\frac{1}{\delta} - \frac{a}{\delta w(a + (R_2 - P_2))}\right)\right] \text{ if } \vartheta_i^* = 0, \tag{3.27}$$

which corresponds exactly with the fact that the lower bound for the interval of the trust threshold was based on the situation where there was no network at all.

It is not self-evident that the transformation (3.26) "controls" adequately for non-network parameters and NETWORK SIZE in heterogeneous networks. A regression analysis with the normalized threshold as the dependent variable shows that the main effects of these parameters are negligible. Moreover, the normalized threshold depends almost entirely on the effects of network parameters and, therefore, the normalized threshold can be considered as *the* contribution to trust of the network.[24] The following task is to determine the magnitude of the network effect with the network parameters defined in Section 2.1. For this purpose, I will predict the normalized threshold $\tilde{\vartheta}^*$ with a linear combination of network parameters N_k (possibly completed with non-linear terms and interactions between network parameters):

$$\tilde{\vartheta}_i^*(\boldsymbol{A}) = \sum_k \beta_k N_{ik}(\boldsymbol{A}) + \varepsilon_i(\boldsymbol{A}), \tag{3.28}$$

where the network parameters N_k include DENSITY, OUTDEGREE, TRANSITIVITY, and ε_i is the residual term that depends on the network as well as the individual observation.[25] Note that there is no intercept in equation (3.28), because the network effect is expected to be 0 if DENSITY equals 0.[26] The coefficients in the regression analyses for the normalized thresholds can again be roughly interpreted as average derivatives on the chosen sample for the network parameters. They can be easily linked to effects with respect to the trust threshold because

$$\frac{\partial \tilde{\vartheta}_i^*}{\partial N_k} = \xi_i \frac{\partial \vartheta_i^*}{\partial N_k}, \quad \text{with} \quad \xi_i = \frac{R_2 - P_2}{\delta^2 w^2(\vartheta_i^* + a + (R_2 - P_2))^2} > 0. \tag{3.29}$$

The fact that $\xi_i > 0$ guarantees that the signs in the comparative statics for the normalized threshold are the same as those of the unnormalized trust thresholds.

Table 3.3 presents four tobit-like regression models for the normalized thresholds. The second column of the table presents the conjectures about the variables as they are described in Section 2.1.[27] Results for Model 0 show that the squared correlation between DENSITY and the normalized threshold is 0.85. Because DENSITY is a global network measure, DENSITY does not explain any variation within the networks. Multi-level models indicated that DENSITY alone accounts for nearly 99% of the variance of the network effect at the global network level.[28]

---

[24] Some interaction effects of non-network parameters and network parameters have small effects on the normalized threshold. However, because these effects are difficult to interpret in terms of the trust threshold and because they do not affect other results, I will not take them into account in the analyses.

[25] I also estimated multi-level regression models with separate residual terms for the network and the observation: $\tilde{\vartheta}^* = \sum_k \beta_k N_k + \varepsilon_{net} + \varepsilon_{net,i}$, but that did not yield substantially different results. Again "spatial correlations" of the residual terms can be expected, because the residual terms are related to the structure of the networks, but I will not model this correlation among residual terms.

[26] Including an intercept in the models shown below changes the results only marginally, and the estimated intercept is very close to 0.

[27] The conjectures for DENSITY and OUTDEGREE can already be considered to be hypotheses due to the linearization results.

[28] For the multi-level models with residual terms at the individual and global level, the standard errors are different, but the differences are not very large. The standard errors are slightly smaller than the standard errors of the models in Table 3.3 for almost all variables.

Table 3.3. Tobit-like regression of the normalized thresholds (13,500 trustors in 2,250 networks, 652 observations in 88 networks are censored).[a]

Independent variable	Conjecture	Model 0	Model 1	Model 2	Model 3
INDIVIDUAL NETWORK PARAMETERS					
OUTDEGREE	+		.52	.52	.50
OUTDEGREE^2	?			−.56	−.54
INDEGREE	0				(.00)
OUTDEGREE QUALITY	+				.53
INDEGREE QUALITY	0				(.04)
LOCAL OUTDEGREE DENSITY	−				(−.01)
LOCAL INDEGREE DENSITY	0				(.01)
GLOBAL NETWORK PARAMETERS					
DENSITY	+	1.00	.47	.50	.50
DENSITY^2	?			.18	.16
OUTDEGREE VARIANCE	−				−.12
INDEGREE VARIANCE	−				(.04)
OUTDEGREE-INDEGREE COVARIANCE	+				.32
TRANSITIVITY	−				(.01)
NETWORK SIZE	?				(−.00)
INTERACTION EFFECT					
DENSITY × OUTDEGREE	?			.34	.39
$\text{corr}(\tilde{\vartheta}^*, \hat{\tilde{\vartheta}}^*)^2$		.854	.976	.986	.992
σ (standard deviation of residuals)		.077	.033	.025	.020

[a] Except for those in parentheses, all coefficients are "significant" at $p < 0.01$, based on Huber standard errors modified for clustering within networks (two-sided tests). Note that the models do not contain a constant (see text page 83).

It was expected from the linearization that OUTDEGREE would explain most of the variance within the networks. This is confirmed by Model 1. Due to the addition of OUTDEGREE in the model, the squared correlation between the predicted normalized threshold and the actual normalized threshold increases with 0.13 to 0.98. Moreover, multi-level models show that OUTDEGREE explains 87% of the variance in the normalized thresholds within networks. Furthermore, OUTDEGREE explains more than 83% of the "real" structure, i.e., of the variance that could not be explained by DENSITY alone and, therefore, is due to the heterogeneity of the network.

Although these analyses show that the normalized threshold is almost a linear combination of DENSITY and OUTDEGREE, at least for the sampled networks, a quadratic model of DENSITY and OUTDEGREE fits the data even better. The coefficients in Model 2 indicate that the positive effect of OUTDEGREE decreases with increasing OUTDEGREE and that the positive effect of DENSITY increases with increasing DENSITY. The interaction effect suggests that a higher OUTDEGREE is more worthwhile in a high-density network. This can be understood as follows. On the one hand, if a trustor has a very low OUTDEGREE, it hardly matters whether DENSITY is high or low, since she will not inform other trustors anyway. On the other hand, if a trustor almost always communicates information to others, the impact of this information will be increased if others pass this information on to many other trustors again.[29] Note that these findings correspond with the results in Table 3.2.

In Model 3, I added the other network parameters introduced in Section 2.1. All these effects are relatively small compared to the effects of DENSITY and OUTDEGREE. Most of them are not even significant. The squared correlation between the predicted normalized threshold and the actual one increases with only a half percent. Together the additional network parameters account for about 4% of the heterogeneity in the network. As stated earlier, INDEGREE, INDEGREE QUALITY, LOCAL INDEGREE DENSITY, and INDEGREE VARIANCE are not expected to have an effect in my game-theoretic model because receiving information does not play a role in the model. The effects of INDEGREE, INDEGREE QUALITY, LOCAL INDEGREE DENSITY, and INDEGREE VARIANCE are indeed very close to 0. The expected positive effect of OUTDEGREE QUALITY is confirmed. In contradiction to the conjecture that LOCAL OUTDEGREE DENSITY inhibits efficient information transfer, LOCAL OUTDEGREE DENSITY does not have an effect on the normalized threshold.

For the global network parameters, two additional effects are found concerning the centralization of the network. The conjecture is that centralization only has a positive effect on trust if the centralization occurs around "central" actors, namely, if trustors with high INDEGREES also have high OUTDEGREES. The conjectures for OUTDEGREE VARIANCE and OUTDEGREE-INDEGREE COVARIANCE also follow from the model. The covariance between OUTDEGREES and INDEGREES does, in fact, have the expected positive effect. Additional centralization due to OUTDEGREE VARIANCE has a negative effect on the normalized threshold and, therefore, on the trust thresholds. Recall that TRANSITIVITY measures whether there are locally dense parts in the network. The expected negative effect of TRANSITIVITY is not found. This is probably due to the assumption in my model that information is given from one trustor to the other while the first trustor does not retain the information. Due to the restrictive nature of information diffusion in the model, it is not possible for a trustor to give information to another trustor while this trustor already has the information. As a consequence, redundant information transfer that is caused by the TRANSITIVITY of the network

[29]It is more than likely that these quadratic and interaction effects would also follow from an approximation analysis similar to the linearization in which second-order terms are incorporated.

cannot occur. A similar reasoning explains why no effect is found for LOCAL OUTDEGREE DENSITY. In Chapter 4, in which the information diffusion process is modeled less restrictively, the expected effect of TRANSITIVITY will be found. Finally, no effect of NETWORK SIZE (i.e., the number of actors) is found, and interactions of NETWORK SIZE with other network parameters do not have an effect on the normalized threshold. This indicates that the effects of the other network parameters do not depend on NETWORK SIZE.

Dummies for the construction methods have only very small but significant effects in the regression. Nevertheless, I cannot exclude the possibility that the residuals depend on the construction method. The following reasoning is important. The more homogeneous the networks, the better the regression model fits. The model fits perfectly for all networks in which all trustors have the same OUTDEGREE. Therefore, a construction method that produces more heterogeneous networks is expected to have larger residuals than a construction method that produces more homogeneous networks. In particular, it can be tested whether or not some observations have larger residuals than others. I estimated a multiplicative heteroscedastic regression model (ignoring censoring) in which the log-variance is modeled via dummies for the construction methods, NETWORK SIZE, and the absolute difference between the DENSITY and the OUTDEGREE of a trustor. The last variable is an explicit measure for how "deviant" a particular trustor is within a network. In this analysis, I find small differences between the construction methods: trust in networks for which every tie is randomly chosen from the interval [0,1] is comparatively better described by the network parameters than trust in the networks from other construction methods. This indicates that it was useful to use network construction methods that create more heterogeneous networks. The analysis also shows that the normalized threshold for larger networks are slightly better predicted than normalized threshold for smaller networks. Finally, "deviant" trustors are indeed deviant. Predictions for trustors who have a low OUTDEGREE in a dense network or for trustors who have a high OUTDEGREE in a sparse network have larger residuals than predictions for other trustors. This is an indication that the regression model is not able to account for all heterogeneity in the networks, although the correlation between the predicted and actual normalized threshold is so close to 1.

3.7 SUBSTANTIVE IMPLICATIONS

Detailed analyses have shown that the model in this chapter has substantive as well as methodological appeal. This section summarizes the substantive implications of the model that can be formulated in terms of testable hypotheses. The following section discusses major shortcomings of the model.

The results of the model discussed in this chapter support and extend theoretical hypotheses for trust in trust relations. In accordance with existing literature (Coleman 1990; Raub and Weesie 1993b; Weesie et al. 1998), the following results are found for non-network parameters. More trust can be placed by a trustor if the costs of sanctions for the trustee are higher. Trustors can place more trust if the incentives for the trustee to abuse trust are smaller. Moreover, trustors can place more trust if the future is more important for the trustee. Finally, trustors can place more trust if the expected duration of a series of transactions with the trustee is longer.

These outcomes of the model for non-network parameters can be translated in the following testable hypotheses:

HYPOTHESIS 3.1 *Trust increases with the costs of sanctions for the trustee.*

HYPOTHESIS 3.2 *Trust decreases with the incentives of the trustee to abuse trust.*

HYPOTHESIS 3.3 *Trust increases with the importance of the future for the trustee.*

HYPOTHESIS 3.4 *Trust of a trustor increases with the expected duration of a series of transactions between the trustor and the trustee in the future.*

HYPOTHESIS 3.5 *The positive effect of the expected duration of a series of transactions on trust increases with the costs of sanctions for the trustee and with the importance of the future for the trustee.*

HYPOTHESIS 3.6 *The positive effect of the costs of sanctions for the trustee on trust increase with the importance of the future for the trustee.*

Using the approximation methods, it was possible to deduce a number of hypotheses about control effects based on the trustors' network embeddedness, i.e., the effects of global and individual network parameters on the extent to which trustors can place trust in the trustee. I have found considerably more than just an effect of density. Trustors with a higher outdegree will trust the trustee more often, also after controlling for density. In addition, quadratic effects are found for density and outdegree, namely, the positive effect of outdegree decreases with increasing outdegree, while the positive effect of density increases with increasing density. Moreover, the positive effect of outdegree is stronger for higher density. Trust increases further if trustors are connected to others with high outdegrees. Trust increases if trustors who receive more information transmit information at a higher rate. But, trust decreases with the centralization of the network if trustors who transmit most information are *not* the trustors who receive most of the information. Consequently, trust decreases with the centralization of the network if centralization is not well-organized.

HYPOTHESIS 3.7 *Trust increases with network density and this effect increases with increasing density.*

HYPOTHESIS 3.8 *Trust of a trustor increases with the outdegree of the trustor and this effect decreases with increasing outdegree.*

HYPOTHESIS 3.9 *The positive effect of a trustor's outdegree on trust increases with density.*

HYPOTHESIS 3.10 *Trust of a trustor i increases with the outdegrees of the trustors connected to trustor i.*

HYPOTHESIS 3.11 *Trust increases with the centralization of the network if trustors with high outdegrees also have high indegrees.*

HYPOTHESIS 3.12 *Trust decreases with the centralization of the network if trustors with high outdegrees do not have high indegrees.*

The analyses of the model did not yield hypotheses for some network parameters, mainly those network parameters related to indegree. The reasons will be discussed in the next section.

In addition, several interaction effects are found between non-network parameters and network parameters (density and outdegree). The effect of outdegree on trust increases with the costs of sanctions for the trustee, with the expected duration of a series of transactions between a trustor and trustee, and with the importance of the future for the trustee. The effect of outdegree decreases with the incentives of the trustee to abuse trust. The effect of density increases with the costs of sanctions for the trustee, the importance of the future for the trustee, and decreases with the expected duration of a series of transactions between a trustor and trustee. One important insight from the interaction effects is that density becomes more important compared to outdegree if the dyadic trust relation has a more severe trust problem, i.e., the trustee has larger incentives to abuse trust or the costs of sanctions for the trustee from withholding trust by the trustors are less. These hypotheses are the explicit result of developing a model in which a network of trustors is combined with a game-theoretic context. As far as I know, this is the first model that provides not only hypotheses about global and individual network parameters on trust, but also hypotheses about non-network parameters, *and* about interaction effects between both network parameters and non-network parameters.

HYPOTHESIS 3.13 *The positive effects of outdegree and density on trust increase with the costs of sanctions for the trustee.*

HYPOTHESIS 3.14 *The positive effect of outdegree on trust decreases with the incentives for the trustee to abuse trust.*

HYPOTHESIS 3.15 *The positive effects of outdegree and density on trust increase with the importance of the future for the trustee.*

HYPOTHESIS 3.16 *The positive effect of a trustor's outdegree on trust increases and the positive effect of density on trust decreases with the expected duration of a series of transactions between the trustor and the trustee.*

HYPOTHESIS 3.17 *The relative effect of a trustor's outdegree compared to density decreases with the trustee's incentives to abuse trust and the importance of the future for the trustee, and increases with the expected duration of a series of transactions between this trustor and the trustee in the future and with the trustee's costs of sanctions.*

These hypotheses about interaction effects are certainly intuitively appealing. Network embeddedness is more effective if the costs of sanctions for the trustee in each transactions are higher and if the trustee is more concerned about his future. Moreover, if a trustor is more vulnerable, i.e., sanctions for the trustee of withholding trust are lower, the duration of a series of transactions is shorter, and the trustee has larger incentives to abuse trust, then such a trustor can rely less on his own individual ties, and is more dependent on a globally dense network to be able to trust the trustee.

3.8 DISCUSSION

Although a series of hypotheses could be derived from the model, some attention has to be paid to parameters in the model for which no hypotheses could be derived. The complete information assumption and the focus on trigger strategies led to a solution, i.e., a predicted level of trust, that does not depend on the payoffs of the trustor and the discount factor of the trustor. Nevertheless, I expect that costs of sanctions for the trustor $(R_1 - P_1)$ and the loss from abused trust $(P_1 - S_1)$ affect the choices of the trustor.[30] At the equilibrium path of the solution, trust is never abused because trustors place trust only if the trustee's short-term incentive to abuse trust is smaller than his long-term costs. Therefore, the trustor *never* executes sanctions and she never obtains a payoff S_1. This limitation might be solved by studying other equilibria, for example, equilibria in which the trustee can abuse trust sometimes without triggering the trustor to withhold trust in the following periods of play. Another option is to extend the constituent game (HTG) with a (random) possibility that the trustee unintentionally abuses trust although he "tries" to honor trust. If such a game is repeated, the extreme trigger punishment seems too strong, given that the trustor cannot observe whether an abuse of trust was intentional or not. These extensions of existing models will be the subject of further research.

Another consequence of the fact that trust is never abused in the presented solution of the game is that there will never be information in the network

[30] See Snijders (1996) for experimental support for this expectation in one-shot Trust Games.

about abuse of trust. Therefore, receiving information is not essential, because trustors will not obtain any additional information about the trustee from other trustors. The solution is entirely based on the *potential* of transmitting information through the network. Consequently, network parameters related to indegree do not affect the outcomes of analyses, and hypotheses about indegree and related network parameters do not follow from the model. Nevertheless, I am convinced that indegree plays a central role in a more "noisy" environment. If a trustor obtains information that the trustee abused trust from one trustor, and she cannot verify the information herself, the trustor might be reluctant to sanction the trustee. Only if she repeatedly obtains information about the abuse of trust, she may become sufficiently convinced that the trustee is untrustworthy, so that she may execute sanctions. In such a context, indegree and, more generally, the extent to which actors receive information will have an effect on trust. One way to extend the game-theoretic model so that predictions about indegree can be derived, is introducing incomplete information assumptions in the model. Incomplete information assumptions may involve different aspects of the model. For instance, trustors do not exactly know the incentives of the trustee, trustors cannot perfectly interpret the information they receive from other trustors, or trustors and trustees do not exactly know the structure of the trustors' network.

Another assumption that requires future attention is the way in which information is transmitted through the network. It seems rather restrictive that trustors act sequentially with the trustee and can only transmit information obtained from a series of transactions once and afterwards forget the information. I suspect that the fact that no effects of local density and transitivity were found is mainly due to this assumption. The assumption implies that only one trustor at a time has information about the behavior of the trustee. Therefore, redundant communication of information, i.e., trustors receiving information they already have, cannot occur under the given assumption.

Although only limited transmission of information is possible within the model, a considerable number of network effects are found. This chapter indicates that studying the outdegree and the overall network density should be enough to account for most of the variance in trust due to network effects. But, I suspect that the effects of network parameters other than outdegree and density will be larger if information can spread more freely throughout the network. Paying the price of losing the game-theoretic framework, I will elaborate this intuition in the next chapter.

Finally, the simulation approach used in this and the following chapter seems promising in a wide range of network studies. Simulating a large number of network structures and studying the results of these structures with conventional statistical methods can increase insights into the implications of a model and can produce hypotheses that supplement analytically obtained results (see also

Yamaguchi 1994a, 1996). One of the main problems in the simulation is how to obtain a "good" set of networks. This is important if the results from the simulation differ between subsets of networks in different "areas" of the sample space of networks. To predict effects in real-world situations, one should know the distribution of relevant networks in the world. However, it is impossible to make a reasonable estimate of such a distribution. Therefore, it is more useful to investigate the extent to which the implications of the model are constant over a large range of possible networks. Using multiple methods to sample random networks and comparing the results for different subsets of networks gives some insights into the consistency of the results over subsets of networks. The results for my game-theoretic model show that the qualitative implications are the same for the different subsets of networks. Magnitudes of different effects may change over different samples of networks, but the directions of most effects are likely to stay the same. Certainly, improvements of the method are necessary including, for example, improvements of the definitions of network parameters. Changing some of the definitions could decrease correlations between network parameters, which would make interpreting and distinguishing the effects of the parameters easier.

Chapter 4

A STOCHASTIC MODEL FOR INFORMATION DIFFUSION IN SOCIAL NETWORKS*

4.1 INTRODUCTION

In Chapter 3, I introduced a game-theoretic model to study the control effects of social networks on trust. A main conclusion was that the extent to which a trustor can trust a trustee increases with her information transmission rate through a network of trustors who are all connected to the trustee. To keep the game-theoretic model analytically tractable, only limited information transfer opportunities were modeled. In this chapter, I present a more elaborated stochastic information diffusion model. In this stochastic model, the information transfer structure can be made more complex than in the game-theoretic model. Strategic choice situations are not included in the model. In the stochastic model, trustors meet with given probabilities and communicate information accurately whenever they meet. Still, the stochastic model is interesting for various reasons.

First, predictions can be derived from the stochastic model about how fast a trustor can *receive* information that is initially obtained by another trustor. As a consequence, learning effects are explicitly derived from this theoretical model. The expected time for information initiated from other trustors to reach

*This chapter contains major parts of an article I wrote with K. Yamaguchi, in which the same model is used (Buskens and Yamaguchi 1999). There are two important differences between the article and this chapter. First, the simulated data set is different. In the original article this was a set of discrete networks with 7 actors and 6, 7, 8, or 9 ties. From the discrete networks valued networks were constructed. Our results proved to be quite sensitive to this construction—an undesirable feature indeed. Thus, in this chapter, I will use valued networks of size 2 up to 10 that are generated directly in the simulation and are not derived from discrete networks. Second, in this chapter I consider only individual diffusion times, namely, how fast an actor transmits information to other actors and how fast an actor receives information. The article considered also global and dyadic measures for diffusion, i.e., the speed with which information spreads in the network in general and how much time it takes for information to be communicated from a particular transmitter to a particular receiver.

a focal trustor will be used as a measure for how fast this trustor obtains information about the trustee's behavior and, therefore, as a measure for how fast the trustor can learn about past behavior of the trustee. Whether learning leads to more or less trust depends on the content of the information a trustor receives. More positive information about the trustee will lead to more trust of a trustor, while more negative information will lead to less trust. If a trustor receives inconsistent information, a trustor may simply become more uncertain about the characteristics of the trustee. I will not explicitly model the *content* of information in this chapter. The content of information is considered as an empirical question. Only if there is empirical data about the content of information on behavior of trustees and if the information is consistent, can predictions about learning effects on trust be derived from this model.

Second, the stochastic model provides a possibility of investigating how fast a trustor can *transmit* information through the network under less restrictive information transfer assumptions than in the game-theoretic model. The information transmission rate of a trustor to other trustors in a network is a measure for her third-party sanction potential. Consequently, the model provides predictions about *control* effects of network parameters on trust. The faster a trustor can transmit information to other trustors, the larger the sanction potential of this trustor, and the better she can control a trustee. However, I will not analyze the actual loss of a trustee through sanctions of the trustors. The link between a game-theoretic model and the stochastic diffusion model is discussed in Intermezzo 4.1 on page 102.

The stochastic model avoids the problematic assumption made in the game-theoretic model that information is handed from one trustor to another as if it is a kind of package.[1] In the game-theoretic model, *one* trustor has a "package" of information. The trustor who has the package sometimes gives the package to one of the other trustors, while she does not retain the information herself. This way of exchanging a package in a network is inconsistent with "[the] peculiar feature of information as a resource, in contradistinction to other sorts of resources ...., that it is not consumed or lost in exchange but becomes 'possessed' by both the transmitter and the receiver" (Laumann and Knoke 1987: 192). I believe that it is a crucial property of communication that the transmitter does *not* lose the information by giving it to somebody else. In the stochastic model, the information transfer assumption is changed so that it is now assumed that an actor who has obtained information will retain this information for ever, also if she transfers the information to another actor. This is, of course, another extreme situation compared to the situation that trustors immediately lose the information after an information transfer. "Intermediate" models can be found

[1] A similar assumption is made by Yamaguchi (1994a) in his information diffusion model (see Buskens and Yamaguchi 1999).

in the research on epidemics (see, for example, Bailey 1975; Bartholomew 1982). However, in relatively small networks where information spreads in a short time, the assumption that actors continue to communicate during the diffusion of information in the network seems not very problematic.

The new assumption on information transfer in the stochastic model provides a possibility to investigate the extent to which effects of network parameters on information diffusion change as a result of this new assumption. There are several reasons, why one can expect that the diffusion process differs between the game-theoretic model and the stochastic model. First, consider a locally dense area of a network with few ties to other parts of the network. If information is transmitted as a package it is likely that the information needs a long time "to find its way out" of that area of the network through the few actors that connect this part of the network with the other actors. If all actors retain the information, actors who are connected to other parts of the network will have the "continuous" possibility of passing on information after receiving the information. Second, as I argued in the previous chapter, redundant information diffusion due to the transitivity of the network cannot occur under the package assumption. In the new model, it is certainly possible for actors to receive the same information from more other actors. Thus, I expect that, while density and outdegree explain nearly the whole effect of the network on trust in Chapter 3, also other network parameters such as centrality and transitivity are more important in this chapter.

A considerable amount of research has been devoted to studying the diffusion of different kinds of goods through networks. Models of processes such as epidemics of infectious diseases (Bailey 1957, 1964, 1975; Altmann 1993), diffusion of innovations (Mahajan and Peterson 1985; Rogers 1995; Valente 1995), information diffusion (Yamaguchi 1994a, 1994b), and influence (Friedkin 1991) are based on contacts between actors in a social network.[2] Most models are related to homogeneous networks with density as the only network parameter, although there are several studies that include other network parameters in explanations of diffusion patterns. In particular, Rapoport (1951, 1953a, 1953b, 1957, 1979) analyzed contagion models and showed that network parameters such as transitivity could explain empirical diffusion patterns that could not be explained by the density of the network alone. Coleman (1964: Chapter 17) also studied diffusion in networks with subgroups. In Coleman's model, diffusion rates *within* groups are larger than diffusion rates *between* groups. In the last decade, more attention has been paid to the influence of structural aspects of social networks on the diffusion of infectious diseases as well (see, for example, Morris 1993). Most of these models, however, concern

[2]Besides contacts among actors, public sources, for example, radio, television, or publication may influence information diffusion processes. I will make only few remarks on this issue in this chapter, mainly in the concluding section.

infinitely large networks. For comparison of a stochastic diffusion model with the game-theoretic model in Chapter 3, it seems most appropriate to extend the Yamaguchi's (1994a) information diffusion model on finite and discrete networks.

Section 4.2 describes the new model for the diffusion process and presents formal definitions of the individual information diffusion times. Section 4.3 presents a number of analytic results. In Section 4.4, I turn to the simulation method, and regress network parameters on individual information diffusion times. Finally, Section 4.5 summarizes the results.

4.2 THE MODEL

4.2.1 ASSUMPTIONS AND MAIN THEOREM

I consider a valued network $(\boldsymbol{\pi}, \boldsymbol{A})$ with n actors similar to the networks used in Chapter 3 with all actors having the same weight π_i equal to $\frac{1}{n}$. Time is modeled in a discrete manner. Information diffusion happens at discrete points in time $t = 0, 1, 2, \ldots$. The $n \times n$ incidence matrix of this network is given by $\boldsymbol{A}$ with α_{ij} the probability that if actor i has information at time t, actor i transmits this information to actor j who, as a consequence, will be informed at time $t + 1$. I assume that the network associated with $\boldsymbol{A}$ is strongly connected. Consequently, the probability that information is transmitted in a finite period of time between any pair of actors is positive. For disconnected networks, the diffusion process can be solved by applying the model to the different components of the network.

Expected diffusion times can be derived from the probabilities that actors in the network transmit information to other actors in a time period. These expected diffusion times indicate how quickly an actor receives information from other actors in the network and how rapidly an actor can spread information to other actors. The information reception rate is defined as the *mean expected time* before an actor i receives information that starts from another actor. The information transmission rate is defined as the mean expected time an actor needs to transmit information to each other actor in the network.[3] The *mean transmission time* (MTT) is the expected time for information transmission from one actor to all other actors. The expected time before an actor receives information initiated from a random other actor is referred to as *mean reception time* (MRT).[4]

[3] Buskens and Yamaguchi (1999) distinguished more events and compared results from the new model with results from the earlier models of Yamaguchi (1994a, 1994b). The results of this chapter will mainly be compared with the results of Chapter 3. Due to the fact that discrete networks were used in the earlier papers, assumptions in this chapter are too far from the earlier papers for a close comparison.

[4] Other location parameters of the distribution of these diffusion times, such as the median, are analytically much less tractable.

Yamaguchi's (1994a) model and the model of Chapter 3 are based on a Markov chain (almost) directly described by $\boldsymbol{A}$. This Markov chain has n states, and each state represents one actor who is able to *give* information to other actors. The element α_{ij} is the probability that actor i will provide information to actor j while *not* retaining the information herself. Thus, the process represented by this Markov chain resembles passing a package between the actors in the network according to the probabilities in $\boldsymbol{A}$. The expected time for information to travel from one actor to another is based on the expected number of steps this package needs to travel from one actor to another, including the possibility that the package takes detours, and may even return to the original actor. The Markov property states that the state at time $t + 1$, depends on history only via the state at time t. Thus, the transition does not depend on what happened before time t. However, to predict how an information diffusion process will proceed if actors do not lose the information they transmit to someone else, one should know all actors who have been informed before. Therefore, the state space of the stochastic process needs to be the set of all subsets of actors rather than the set of all actors.

This does not imply that Markov chain theory cannot be used to describe the new diffusion model. On the contrary, it is a very useful theory if all necessary states are included in the model. In the model analyzed below, I make the following assumptions:

1. The information is initially obtained by *one* actor in the network who transmits this information to others. For example, a trustor is deceived by a trustee and communicates this to other trustors.

2. After the first actor is informed, no information enters the network from outside: there is no public source that diffuses information.[5] Also, a trustee does not deceive any other trustor who starts to inform others independently.

3. Each actor in a network is either informed (i.e., she obtained the information that entered the network at any time in the past) or not informed.

4. Nobody ever forgets information once obtained. This assumption is not necessary to define the Markov chain, but it seems a plausible assumption if information that enters the network is known to all actors in the network in relatively short time.[6]

[5] One can also assume that every actor is informed with a certain probability by a public source at each point in time, for example, because a trustee deceives more trustors after deceiving the first one. I do not expect that such a public source affects the effect of network parameters on information diffusion among the actors. One could even include such a public source as an additional actor in the network.

[6] Of course, this is not a suitable assumption in, for example, the study of epidemics in which the time that an actor is infectious is short compared to the time the disease needs to spread through the population. Including

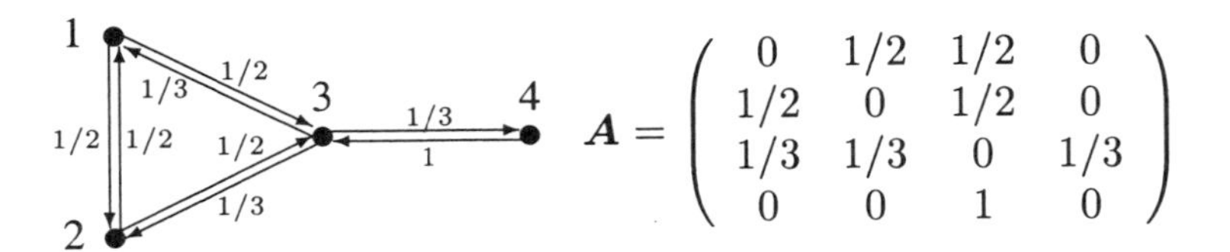

Figure 4.1. A four-person network as an example.

5. All communication of information among actors occurs (stochastically) independently within and between time periods. This implies that whether an actor informs a second actor is (stochastically) independent of whether she informs another actor in the same time period. Moreover, whether an actor is informed by one actor does not depend on whether she is informed by another actor in the same time period. Thus, time constraints for transmitting or receiving information are ignored.[7] Finally, whether an actor informs another actor does not depend on whether she informed the other actor already in an earlier time period.

The probabilities in $\boldsymbol{A}$ could be interpreted as *random contacts* rather than as outcomes of purposive searches for actors who should be informed. Now, a Markov chain can be defined in which the states are the elements of the power set of actors in the network: each (non-empty) subset of actors forms a state in the new Markov chain. Consider the example of the sample network in Figure 4.1. The power set $\mathcal{S}$ for this example has $2^4 - 1 = 15$ elements,

$$\mathcal{S} = \Big\{\{1\}, \{2\}, \{3\}, \{4\}, \{1,2\}, \{1,3\}, \{1,4\}, \{2,3\}, \{2,4\}, \{3,4\},$$
$$\{1,2,3\}, \{1,2,4\}, \{1,3,4\}, \{2,3,4\}, \{1,2,3,4\}\Big\}, \qquad (4.1)$$

where each element represents the subset of actors who are informed in this state of the Markov chain. $\mathcal{S}$ has $2^n - 1$ elements for a network with n actors. Actually, the number of states can be reduced. To start the information process, at least one actor has to be informed. The assumptions imply that the actor originally informed is always informed. Thus, I need only consider the states

---

the possibility that actors forget information or stop transmitting information is possible, but the information diffusion process would become more complex.

[7]Buskens and Yamaguchi (1999) also consider the assumption that each actor informs at most one other actor in each time period. Based on an analysis of similar network matrices, they found very little effect of this assumption on diffusion times. The assumption that an actor can only inform one other actor is included in that paper to facilitate a closer comparison with the earlier results of Yamaguchi (1994a, 1994b).

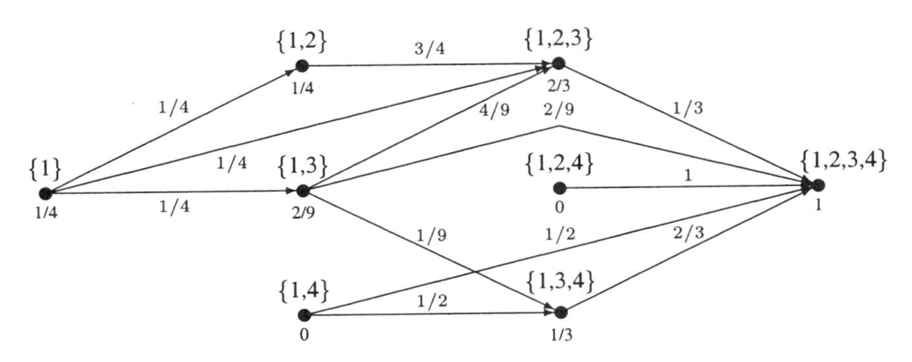

Figure 4.2. Markov chain belonging to the four-person network. At each node, the probability of staying at that node is displayed.

in which this actor is informed, which reduces the number of states to 2^{n-1}. Because the index of the actor where the information starts is only a label, this actor can always be labeled by 1 without loss of generality. In special situations the number of states can be reduced even further.[8]

Next, a transition matrix $\boldsymbol{T}$ has to be derived for the "large" set of states of the Markov chain.[9] The calculation of the transition matrix for the new Markov chain $\boldsymbol{T}$ is quite straightforward, although it becomes tedious for large networks. Consider two states S_1 and S_2, i.e., two subsets of actors. Denote the transition probability from S_1 to S_2 by $T_{S_1 S_2}$. Then, $T_{S_1 S_2} = 0$ if $S_1 \not\subset S_2$, because actors cannot forget information, which implies that the set of actors who have information can only increase. If $S_1 \subset S_2$,

$$T_{S_1 S_2} = \prod_{j \in S_2 \setminus S_1} \Big(1 - \prod_{i \in S_1} (1 - \alpha_{ij})\Big) \prod_{j \notin S_2} \Big(\prod_{i \in S_1} (1 - \alpha_{ij})\Big), \tag{4.2}$$

where $S_2 \setminus S_1$ is the set of all elements of S_2 that are not elements of S_1. Equation (4.2) is easy to understand. The first part of the right-hand side of (4.2) is the probability that, for each actor j who will be one of the newly informed actors, at least one of the already informed actors informs her. The

[8] For example, for the sample network in Figure 4.1, if the information starts from actor 1, then actor 4 can only be reached through actor 3. Therefore, the states $\{1, 4\}$ and $\{1, 2, 4\}$ will never occur during a diffusion process starting from actor 1. This implies that they do not play a role in the diffusion process and can be omitted. Furthermore, if there are groups of structurally equivalent actors, i.e., actors with identical contact probabilities to and from all other actors, only the number of these equivalent actors who are informed is important, while their identities are irrelevant. In the four-person network, actor 1 and actor 2 are structurally equivalent. This chapter does not elaborate on this issue, although it is very relevant if one wants to apply the method to larger networks.

[9] Note that the transition matrix $\boldsymbol{T}$ in this model differs from the transition matrix in Chapter 3.

second part of (4.2) expresses the probability that none of the informed actors in S_1 informs any actor not in S_2. Because all these events are independent and occur at the same time, their respective probabilities have to be multiplied. Note that the diagonal elements of $\boldsymbol{A}$ are not used to calculate $\boldsymbol{T}$. Thus, the extent to which an actor "informs herself" does not influence the diffusion process.

For the sample network in Figure 4.1, this results in the following transition matrix:

$$
\begin{array}{r} \\ \{1\} \\ \{1,2\} \\ \{1,3\} \\ \boldsymbol{T}=\{1,2,3\} \\ \{1,4\} \\ \{1,2,4\} \\ \{1,3,4\} \\ \{1,2,3,4\} \end{array}
\begin{array}{c} \{1\}\{1,2\}\{1,3\}\{1,2,3\}\{1,4\}\{1,2,4\}\{1,3,4\}\{1,2,3,4\} \\
\left(\begin{array}{cccccccc}
1/4 & 1/4 & 1/4 & 1/4 & 0 & 0 & 0 & 0 \\
0 & 1/4 & 0 & 3/4 & 0 & 0 & 0 & 0 \\
0 & 0 & 2/9 & 4/9 & 0 & 0 & 1/9 & 2/9 \\
0 & 0 & 0 & 2/3 & 0 & 0 & 0 & 1/3 \\
0 & 0 & 0 & 0 & 0 & 0 & 1/2 & 1/2 \\
0 & 0 & 0 & 0 & 0 & 0 & 0 & 1 \\
0 & 0 & 0 & 0 & 0 & 0 & 1/3 & 2/3 \\
0 & 0 & 0 & 0 & 0 & 0 & 0 & 1
\end{array}\right) \end{array} .
$$

From this transition matrix and the graph that illustrates the Markov chain associated with $\boldsymbol{T}$ (Figure 4.2), one sees that the states $\{1,4\}$ and $\{1,2,4\}$ could have been omitted since one is only interested in paths that initiate from $\{1\}$.

Markov chains constructed in this way have simple characteristics. As long as the network is connected all the states are *transient* states, except the state in which everybody is informed, which is the unique *absorbing* state. Furthermore, once the process leaves a transient state, it can never return. The theory on absorbing Markov chains (see Kemeny and Snell 1960: Theorem 3.5.4) is used to formulate the following theorem.

THEOREM 4.1 *Let $\boldsymbol{T}_m$ be the minor containing the rows and columns of $\boldsymbol{T}$ without the row and column for the absorbing state. Actor 1 is the actor who is informed first and $S_1 = \{1\}$. Then the following properties hold:*

i) $(\boldsymbol{I} - \boldsymbol{T}_m)^{-1}_{S_1 S_j}$ *is the expected time the process is in the j-th state before reaching the absorbing state.*

ii) $\sum_{S_j \in \mathcal{S}} (\boldsymbol{I} - \boldsymbol{T}_m)^{-1}_{S_1 S_j}$ *is the expected time the process needs to reach the absorbing state.*

iii) $\sum_{S_j \in \mathcal{S}, k \notin S_j} (\boldsymbol{I} - \boldsymbol{T}_m)^{-1}_{S_1 S_j}$ *is the expected time to inform actor k.*

Proof. Proofs for assertions $i)$ and $ii)$ can be found in Kemeny and Snell (1960: Theorem 3.5.4). Assertion $iii)$ is not true for absorbing chains in general, but it is true in this case because returning to any state is impossible. I do not present a formal proof here. The following intuition can be translated into a formal proof quite easily. To derive the time needed to inform actor k, one considers the set of states in which actor k is informed as new absorbing states. This implies that only a part of $(\boldsymbol{I} - \boldsymbol{T}_m)$ has to be inverted. However, because the probability of going from a state in which k is informed to a state in which k is not informed is always 0, the inverse of the suitable part of $(\boldsymbol{I} - \boldsymbol{T}_m)$ equals the corresponding part of $(\boldsymbol{I} - \boldsymbol{T}_m)^{-1}$. □

For the four-person network the first row of $(\boldsymbol{I} - \boldsymbol{T}_m)^{-1}$ becomes

$$\begin{array}{ccccccc} \{1\} & \{1,2\} & \{1,3\} & \{1,2,3\} & \{1,4\} & \{1,2,4\} & \{1,3,4\}. \\ \frac{4}{3} & \frac{4}{9} & \frac{3}{7} & \frac{18}{7} & 0 & 0 & \frac{1}{14} \end{array} \tag{4.3}$$

According to Theorem 4.1, the expected time to inform actor 2 from actor 1 equals $\frac{4}{3} + \frac{3}{7} + \frac{1}{14} = \frac{11}{6}$. The expected time to inform actor 3 from actor 1 is $\frac{4}{3} + \frac{4}{9} = \frac{16}{9}$. The expected time to inform actor 4 is $\frac{4}{3} + \frac{4}{9} + \frac{3}{7} + \frac{18}{7} = \frac{43}{9}$. And, the expected time for actor 1 to reach the absorbing state in which all other actors are informed is $\frac{4}{3} + \frac{4}{9} + \frac{3}{7} + \frac{18}{7} + \frac{1}{14} = \frac{611}{126}$.

4.2.2 DIFFUSION TIMES AND CENTRALITY MEASURES

In this subsection, I formalize the "dependent variables" used in this chapter. These dependent variables are centrality measures related to individual diffusion times for transmitting and receiving information. Conjectures for the effects of the independent variables are described in Section 2.1. The faster a trustor can spread information in a network of trustors, the larger her "transmitter centrality," *and* the more she trusts the trustee. Moreover, the faster a trustor receives information, the larger her "receiver centrality" *and*, as long as information is positive, the more she trusts the trustee.

The expected time it takes to transmit information starting from actor i to actor j is the *dyadic mean transmission time* (MTT_{ij}). MTT_{ij} is a measure of the distance from actor i to actor j in a network and a building block for the individual dependent variables defined below. Note that MTT_{ij} is not symmetric and, hence, not a real distance. How MTT_{ij} has to be calculated is shown in Theorem 4.1. This dyadic mean transmission time is a suitable building block for constructing individual diffusion times, because individual diffusion times will be based on what happens with information if it starts from one actor.

For an actor i, one can average MTT_{ij} over all other actors j. This is called *individual mean transmission time*:

$$\mathrm{MTT}_i = \frac{1}{n-1}\sum_{j\neq i}\mathrm{MTT}_{ij}. \tag{4.4}$$

A straightforward alternative to this diffusion measure is the expected time needed for information to reach the absorbing state in which everyone is informed, when information starts from some actor. The disadvantage of this alternative measure is that one cannot determine whether many actors are in-

INTERMEZZO 4.1 *Linking the game-theoretic model and the diffusion model.*

I want to look back for a moment at the model discussed in Chapter 3 in which a trustee plays the Iterated Heterogeneous Trust Game with a network of trustors. Using the model of this chapter, the trustors in such a setting can calculate how many transactions a trustee can expect with trustors who do not know about an abuse of trust by the trustee after the trustee deceived a particular trustor in the network. The trustee has to decide whether he prefers abusing trust and receiving a payoff $R_2 + \theta$ now, some R_2 or $R_2 + \theta$ thereafter, followed by all P_2, or honoring trust and remaining to receive R_2 in all cases where θ is small enough. I would again assume that trustors never place trust if they know about some deceit committed by the trustee. In fact, under the assumption that trustors never forget information, the trustee has to optimize an end-game to decide whether he abuses or honors trust. Of course, if the trustee is able to do this and the trustors have the same information as the trustee, they will do the calculations for him and they will never place trust if the trustee is known to abuse trust. The optimization is especially complex because in every new encounter with a trustor who places trust, the trustee has to decide whether an acceleration of the diffusion process by a new deceit is better or worse than honoring trust in such a new event. It is questionable whether the trustee knows which other trustors know about an earlier deceit. However, I do not expect that the observability of information states by the trustee has a real effect on the solution of the game. The fact that the trustee, for his first deceit, has to calculate all the expected times of information and transactions beforehand and that in equilibrium no deceit will occur, implies that trustors in equilibrium never have information about abused trust. The described process optimization procedure can be analyzed using linear programming methods or by "policy iteration" methods in Markov Decision Theory (Bellman 1957). My expectation is that predictions for the main effects of network parameters on the extent to which trustors can place trust in the solution of such a model resemble closely the effects of network parameters on the time an actor needs to spread information among the other actors in a network as predicted by the stochastic diffusion model.

formed early in the diffusion process and few at the end or the other way round. I would like my measure to be sensitive to this, so that individual mean transmission time is "shorter" for an actor who informs many actors early in the diffusion process. For example, when a trustee deceives a trustor, it is better for the trustee if many trustors remain innocent about this abuse of trust for a longer time than if most trustors are quickly informed about his abuse of trust. This requirement can be accomplished by weighting a period of time before absorption with the expected number of actors not informed in that time period. Thus, an alternative definition of individual mean transmission time would be:

$$\widehat{\mathrm{MTT}}_i = \frac{1}{n-1} \sum_{S_k \in \mathcal{S}} (n - |S_k|)(\boldsymbol{I} - \boldsymbol{T}_m)^{-1}_{S_1 S_k}, \tag{4.5}$$

where $S_1 = \{i\}$ and $|S_k|$ is the number of elements in S_k, the set of informed actors corresponding to the k-th column in the matrix $\boldsymbol{T}_m$. However, it can be proven that this alternative definition is equivalent to the first definition, i.e., $\mathrm{MTT}_i = \widehat{\mathrm{MTT}}_i$. The reason is that

$$\begin{aligned} \sum_{j \neq i} \mathrm{MTT}_{ij} &= \sum_{j \neq i} \sum_{S_k \in \mathcal{S}, j \notin S_k} (\boldsymbol{I} - \boldsymbol{T}_m)^{-1}_{S_1 S_k} \\ &= \sum_{S_k \in \mathcal{S}} (n - |S_k|)(\boldsymbol{I} - \boldsymbol{T}_m)^{-1}_{S_1 S_k}. \end{aligned} \tag{4.6}$$

In the following, I usually apply (4.4).[10]

Because $\boldsymbol{A}$ is not symmetric, the expected time for transmitting information to other actors is not equal to the expected time for receiving information from other actors. The "mirror" concept of individual mean transmission time is *individual mean reception time* and is defined as

$$\mathrm{MRT}_i = \frac{1}{n-1} \sum_{j=1}^{n} \mathrm{MTT}_{ji}. \tag{4.7}$$

Individual mean reception time is the expected time before an actor receives information obtained by some actor in the network if the other actors obtain the

[10] To use this diffusion model in a game-theoretic context comparable to the situation described in Chapter 3, one could easily include the importance of trustors for the trustee $\boldsymbol{\pi}$ and a discount factor w in the formula. Then, the expression

$$\mathrm{MTT}_{w,i} = \frac{1}{1-\pi_i} \sum_{S_k \in \mathcal{S}} (1 - \sum_{j \in S_k} \pi_j)(\boldsymbol{I} - w\boldsymbol{T}_m)^{-1}_{S_1 S_k}$$

gives the expected discounted number of transactions the trustee will have with uninformed trustors after a single abuse of trust by the trustee against trustor i. Because I only want to study the effects of network parameters on information diffusion, these aspects are not included in this chapter.

information with equal probabilities.[11] Individual mean transmission time and individual mean reception time are measures of an actor's ability to transmit and receive information quickly through the network. I use these measures directly to introduce the related centrality measures: TRANSMITTER CENTRALITY

$$\mathrm{TC}_i = \frac{1}{\mathrm{MTT}_i}, \tag{4.8}$$

and RECEIVER CENTRALITY

$$\mathrm{RC}_i = \frac{1}{\mathrm{MRT}_i}. \tag{4.9}$$

These centrality measures will be analyzed in the simulation discussed below. Both centrality measures are closely related to closeness centrality as defined by Freeman (1979) and immediate effects centrality as introduced by Friedkin (1991).[12]

In considering information transfer in a network from the actor's point of view, there are actually three things that matter. Not only is it important how quickly an actor transmits information throughout a network or how long it takes before the information reaches the focal actor. The importance of an actor for diffusion of information in a network also depends on the extent to which others need her to communicate information between them. The importance of an actor for transmitting information between other actors can be measured using "betweenness centrality" (see Freeman 1979). Buskens and Yamaguchi (1999) analyze betweenness centrality. In the models in this book, communication is costless and communication is profitable for everybody in the network as is discussed before. This implies that trustors will not exploit their betweenness centrality in a network. Therefore, I will not discuss betweenness centrality here. Betweenness as a measure of the extent to which trustors control information communication among other actors may be of major importance especially in situations where information is used strategically.

4.3 ANALYTIC RESULTS FOR DIFFUSION TIMES

To obtain relations between diffusion times and simple network parameters, an initial attempt is made to derive these relations analytically. First, a logical relation between TRANSMITTER CENTRALITY and RECEIVER CENTRALITY is shown.

[11] That these probabilities are equal is a rather arbitrary assumption. Again, in a game-theoretic context the dyadic transmission times could be weighted, for example, with the importance of the trustors for the trustee π.

[12] The new closeness centrality measures are generalizations of Freeman's closeness centrality (1979), because TC_i and RC_i reduce exactly to Freeman's measure if $\boldsymbol{A} = \boldsymbol{N}$, where $\boldsymbol{N}$ is the incidence matrix for a discrete network. Note that Freeman defines his closeness measure only for symmetric networks. TC_i and RC_i are identical in that case.

Second, I give some illustrations to demonstrate that analytic results are complex and hard to interpret even for small networks, unless a very particular network structure is imposed. Third, analytic results for homogeneous networks are presented that are useful in guiding the simulation portrayed in the following section.

RELATION BETWEEN TRANSMITTER AND RECEIVER CENTRALITY. Consider the matrix $\boldsymbol{A}'$, which is the transpose of $\boldsymbol{A}$, i.e., $\alpha'_{ij} = \alpha_{ji}$ for all i and j. The definition of the dyadic mean transmission time implies that the expected time needed for information to be transmitted from actor i to actor j in a network represented by $\boldsymbol{A}$ is the same as the expected time for information to be transmitted from j to i in a network represented by $\boldsymbol{A}'$. Formally,

$$\mathrm{MTT}_{ij}(\boldsymbol{A}) = \mathrm{MTT}_{ji}(\boldsymbol{A}'). \tag{4.10}$$

Obviously,

$$\begin{aligned}\mathrm{MTT}_{i}(\boldsymbol{A}) &= \frac{1}{n-1}\sum_{j=1}^{n}\mathrm{MTT}_{ij}(\boldsymbol{A}) \\ &= \frac{1}{n-1}\sum_{j=1}^{n}\mathrm{MTT}_{ji}(\boldsymbol{A}') = \mathrm{MRT}_{i}(\boldsymbol{A}'), \end{aligned} \tag{4.11}$$

and, consequently,

$$\mathrm{TC}_{i}(\boldsymbol{A}) = \mathrm{RC}_{i}(\boldsymbol{A}'). \tag{4.12}$$

Therefore, there is a straightforward relation between transmission times and reception times. All network parameters that are introduced in Chapter 2 exist in pairs that are either each others "mirror" concept with respect to transposing the network matrix, or they are invariant under transposing the network matrix. For degrees, degree qualities, local densities, and degree variances, it holds that

$$\begin{aligned} &D_{out}(\boldsymbol{A}) = D_{in}(\boldsymbol{A}'), Q_{out}(\boldsymbol{A}) = Q_{in}(\boldsymbol{A}'), \\ &LD_{out}(\boldsymbol{A}) = LD_{in}(\boldsymbol{A}'), \text{ and } V_{out}(\boldsymbol{A}) = V_{in}(\boldsymbol{A}'). \end{aligned} \tag{4.13}$$

DENSITY, OUTDEGREE-INDEGREE COVARIANCE, and TRANSITIVITY are invariant under transposing the network matrix:

$$\Delta(\boldsymbol{A}) = \Delta(\boldsymbol{A}'), V_{out,in}(\boldsymbol{A}) = V_{out,in}(\boldsymbol{A}'), \text{ and } Tr(\boldsymbol{A}) = Tr(\boldsymbol{A}'). \tag{4.14}$$

These properties imply that the analyses about the centrality measures need not be performed for both TRANSMITTER CENTRALITY and RECEIVER CENTRALITY. It is a logical consequence that, for example, a relation that is derived between TRANSMITTER CENTRALITY and OUTDEGREE can be derived in exactly the same way as a relation between RECEIVER CENTRALITY and INDEGREE. Of course, this does not mean that the two centrality measures are the same, but only that the implications that follow from the analyses of TRANSMITTER CENTRALITY can be *translated* directly into implications for RECEIVER CENTRALITY. Consequently, I will only analyze TRANSMITTER CENTRALITY in detail and derive the results for RECEIVER CENTRALITY from the analyses of TRANSMITTER CENTRALITY. These last results will be described in the conclusion to this chapter.

SMALL NETWORKS

A symmetric *tree* is a connected network with n actors and $2(n-1)$ directed ties with no cycles of length greater than 2 (see, for example, Harary et al. 1965: 260–262). Dyadic transmission time can be calculated easily for symmetric trees. In a symmetric tree, only $2(n-1)$ off-diagonal elements of $\boldsymbol{A}$ are positive, the others are 0. In a symmetric tree $\boldsymbol{A}$, information can travel from one actor i to actor j only via one possible path. Paths in which information goes back and forth between actors can be disregarded because those do not occur in the information diffusion process as defined in the model. If actor i and actor j would be connected by a tie, $\alpha_{ij} > 0$, and actor i is informed, the expected time before actor j is informed equals $\frac{1}{\alpha_{ij}}$. The expected time needed for information to be transferred from actor i and j does not depend on which other actors are or have been informed during the diffusion process. Therefore, the expected time needed to traverse a path in $\boldsymbol{A}$ is the sum of the expected times for each tie on that path. Consequently, the mean transmission time needed for information to travel from actor i to actor j in a symmetric tree equals

$$\text{MTT}_{ij} = \frac{1}{\alpha_{ik_1}} + \frac{1}{\alpha_{k_1 k_2}} + \cdots + \frac{1}{\alpha_{k_t j}}, \qquad (4.15)$$

where $k_1, \ldots, k_t$ are the actors that necessarily have to be passed to reach j from i.[13] This is an appealing result because it closely fits the intuition that the diffusion process is straightforward if there is only one path for information diffusion. Furthermore, the result implies that in a two-person network, which is by definition a symmetric tree, the expected diffusion time from actor 1 to actor 2 equals $\frac{1}{\alpha_{12}}$, which is the inverse of the OUTDEGREE of actor 1. Results are not this simple for models in which information is transferred as a package

[13]This implies that if I would approximate diffusion time for $\boldsymbol{A}$ in a "neighborhood" of $\boldsymbol{I}$ using linearization, I obtain similar expressions using the shortest paths, because probabilities of longer paths tend to 0. Note also that these expressions do not hold if information may start with more than one actor at the same time.

because in these models information can go back and forth, even in symmetric trees.

Analytic expressions become fairly complex for networks more complicated than trees. For a general three-actor network in which information starts from actor 1, the expected time to reach actor 2 is

$$\begin{aligned} \mathrm{MTT}_{12} &= \frac{1}{1-(1-\alpha_{12})(1-\alpha_{13})} \\ &+ \frac{\alpha_{13}(1-\alpha_{12})}{(1-(1-\alpha_{12})(1-\alpha_{13}))(1-(1-\alpha_{12})(1-\alpha_{32}))}. \end{aligned} \quad (4.16)$$

These analytic results enable calculation of the expected diffusion times for the sample network in Figure 4.1. For example, because the only way for information to reach actor 4 is through actor 3, mean transmission time from actor 1 to actor 4 equals mean transmission time from actor 1 to actor 3 plus the time needed for information to go from actor 3 to actor 4. The Markov property implies that the mean transmission time from actor 1 to actor 4 in the four-person network of Figure 4.1 equals

$$\begin{aligned} \mathrm{MTT}_{14} &= \frac{1}{1-(1-\alpha_{12})(1-\alpha_{13})} \\ &+ \frac{\alpha_{12}(1-\alpha_{13})}{(1-(1-\alpha_{12})(1-\alpha_{13}))(1-(1-\alpha_{13})(1-\alpha_{23}))} + \frac{1}{\alpha_{34}}. \end{aligned} \quad (4.17)$$

Thus, for networks without cycles with length greater than 3, diffusion times can be calculated analytically. However, for a cycle with four actors the situation is complex enough to refrain from presenting it here. For a complete four-actor network, the expression exceeds one printed page (results were obtained by a Maple-script), and is not interpretable.

Homogeneous Networks

It may seem that the homogeneous case, $\alpha_{ij} = \alpha$ for all ties, can be analyzed easily. Of course, this case is much less complex than the general case, but the complexity is still surprising. Note that all actors have the same TRANSMITTER CENTRALITY and that the differences of TRANSMITTER CENTRALITY among networks only depend on DENSITY and NETWORK SIZE for homogeneous networks. The Markov chain for a homogeneous network can be reduced to n states in which S_i is the state in which i actors in the network have some information. The transition probability for information from a state in which j actors have the information to one in which k actors have the information ($j \leq k$) equals

$$T_{S_j S_k} = \binom{n-j}{n-k}\left(1-(1-\alpha)^j\right)^{k-j}(1-\alpha)^{j(n-k)}, \quad (4.18)$$

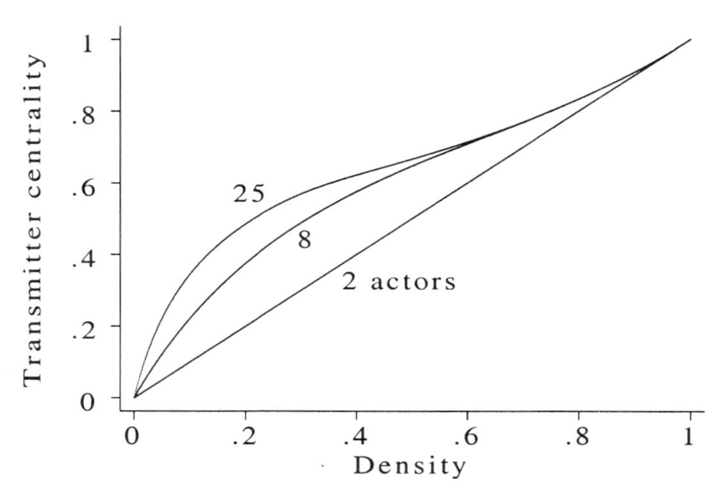

Figure 4.3. TRANSMITTER CENTRALITY for homogeneous networks with 2, 8, and 25 actors.

which can be derived straightforwardly from (4.2). Still, I did not succeed in deriving a simple formula in n and α for the TRANSMITTER CENTRALITY in homogeneous networks. Using a Maple script and (4.18), it was possible to derive analytic expressions for TRANSMITTER CENTRALITY for small networks. Trivially, for $n = 2$, TRANSMITTER CENTRALITY is α. I calculated TRANSMITTER CENTRALITY numerically for varying values of DENSITY for larger networks (up to $n = 25$). In Figure 4.3, the graphs are shown for networks with 2, 8, or 25 actors. The graphs for all intermediate values of NETWORK SIZE are in between these graphs. The graphs show that TRANSMITTER CENTRALITY increase in DENSITY and that this increase is larger if DENSITY is close to 0. The effect of DENSITY decreases in the middle part of the DENSITY range, and increases again if DENSITY approaches 1. This implies that a polynomial approximation of TRANSMITTER CENTRALITY requires at least a cubic term in DENSITY to allow for the non-monotonous changes in the effect of DENSITY.

The "average" effect of DENSITY is 1 for each NETWORK SIZE because TRANSMITTER CENTRALITY increases from 0 to 1 while DENSITY increase from 0 to 1. Therefore, no effect is expected from the interaction between NETWORK SIZE and DENSITY. However, the *changes* in the effect of DENSITY are larger for larger networks. Initially, the increase in the effect of DENSITY is larger for large networks than for small networks, and, later, the increase in the effect is smaller for large networks. Therefore, a negative interaction effect is expected from NETWORK SIZE and squared DENSITY.

Another effect that can be derived from Figure 4.3 is that TRANSMITTER CENTRALITY is larger for larger networks and that this effect decreases with increasing NETWORK SIZE. The graphs for larger networks are above the graphs for smaller networks, and the graph for size 8 is relatively close to the one for size 25. In networks with more than 20 actors, the graphs for TRANSMITTER CENTRALITY hardly change. Of course, the relative change in NETWORK SIZE of an additional actor is larger for small networks than large networks. Thus, a quadratic polynomial in NETWORK SIZE is needed to account for the effect of NETWORK SIZE. It turns out that TRANSMITTER CENTRALITY can be approximated quite closely with a polynomial of the first three powers of DENSITY, a linear and quadratic term of NETWORK SIZE, and interactions of size with the first two powers of DENSITY. This result will be used as a base line for the analyses in the following section.

4.4 THE SIMULATION

4.4.1 METHODS

SAMPLED NETWORKS

As discussed in Section 4.2, it does not seem feasible to obtain relations between diffusion times and network parameters analytically in more general cases. Therefore, I use the same simulation method as used in Chapter 3. More specifically, the same set of networks is used although networks with NETWORK SIZE equal to 2 are excluded. Because I am especially interested in the more complex network parameters in this chapter and because some of these parameters such as TRANSITIVITY are not well-defined for networks of size 2, networks of size 2 are excluded from the analyses here. The data set contains information about 2,000 networks with NETWORK SIZE 3 to 10. There are 250 networks of each size. Every actor in each network is an observation in the data set. Consequently, the data set contains $(3+4+\cdots+10)\times 250 = 13,000$ observations. I used several methods to construct the networks and refer to Subsection 3.6.1 for the motivations. The description of the construction methods can be found in Appendix B. TRANSMITTER CENTRALITY and RECEIVER CENTRALITY are calculated for all the networks using Theorem 4.1. For networks of size 2, TRANSMITTER CENTRALITY equals the OUTDEGREE of the transmitter and RECEIVER CENTRALITY equals the INDEGREE of the receiver.

METHOD OF ANALYSIS

The analyses in this chapter suffer from the same type of shortcomings as the analyses in Chapter 3. I am modeling a dependent variable that is "deterministically" calculated on the basis of the social network with a linear combination of network parameters. This implies that there is no randomness in the data. The residuals in the analysis depend on the networks and will be larger for some types of networks and smaller for others. Consequently, "significance levels" and "explained variance" are hard to interpret in this context.

Because the information diffusion process of the model in this chapter is more complex than for the game-theoretic model, the construction methods appear to play a more important role for the centrality measures than for the trust thresholds. If all networks are pooled in an ordinary regression analysis, the variance of the residuals depends strongly on the construction method. This implies that one of the basic assumptions of ordinary linear regression is not fulfilled, namely a homoscedastic distribution of residuals. Although the robust standard errors applied in the analyses below are consistent for heteroscedastic distributed residuals, efficiency in estimation can be increased by using regression that explicitly models heteroscedasticity. I employ the model with multiplicative heteroscedasticity (see Harvey 1976; Greene 1993: 405–407). This method estimates a regression equation and, simultaneously, an equation in which the log-variance of the residuals is explicitly modeled with covariates:

$$\mathrm{TC}_i = \mu_i + \sigma_i \varepsilon_i \tag{4.19}$$

where

$$\mu_i = \boldsymbol{x}_i' \boldsymbol{\beta} \quad \text{and} \quad \sigma_i^2 = \exp(\boldsymbol{z}_i' \boldsymbol{\gamma}). \tag{4.20}$$

In these equations, μ_i is the mean and σ_i^2 the conditional variance of the dependent variable TC_i. The residuals ε_i are assumed to be standard normally distributed. The vectors $\boldsymbol{x}_i$ and $\boldsymbol{z}_i$ are vectors of covariates predicting the mean and the log-variance of TC_i respectively. The vectors of coefficients $\boldsymbol{\beta}$ and $\boldsymbol{\gamma}$ will be estimated. In the tables, the vector $\boldsymbol{\beta}$ are the coefficients for the network parameters and the vector $\boldsymbol{\gamma}$ the coefficients related to what I call the "variance components," although they are not additive but multiplicative. The standard errors in these analyses are modified for clustering of the observations within networks (Rogers 1993). Similar to the analyses in Chapter 3, I use the squared correlation between the predicted and actual centrality measures $\mathrm{corr}(\mathrm{TC}, \hat{\mathrm{TC}})^2$ to indicate how well the centrality measures are approximated by a linear (or higher-order) combination of network parameters. The variance weighted least squares (VWLS) R^2 is also presented for models with multiplicative heteroscedasticity. This is a measure of the model fit that weights residuals less for observations for which the predicted variance is larger than residuals for observations for which the predicted variance is smaller.

It follows from the analysis of homogeneous networks that at least a third-order polynomial in DENSITY is needed to fit TRANSMITTER CENTRALITY adequately. However, DENSITY, OUTDEGREE, and INDEGREE cannot be distinguished for homogeneous networks. It appears that a third-order polynomial in DENSITY as well as OUTDEGREE is needed to fit TRANSMITTER CENTRALITY well. INDEGREE is less important in transmitting information. Therefore, only a linear effect of INDEGREE is used. The signs of the effects of the higher-order terms of DENSITY and OUTDEGREE cannot be predicted using the analysis of homogeneous networks because these effects cannot be disentangled from the results for homogeneous networks. A quadratic polynomial in NETWORK SIZE is also required in correspondence with the homogeneous case. OUTDEGREE has the largest effect for the interaction between NETWORK SIZE and the network parameters. Therefore, two interaction terms with NETWORK SIZE are included in the analyses, namely, interactions with the linear and quadratic term of OUTDEGREE.

In linear regression analysis, the "effect" of an independent variable x is the coefficient associated with this variable. If higher-order terms of independent variables or interactions are included in the analysis, the term "effect" is used in a generalized way as the partial derivative of the expected value of the dependent variable y with respect to the independent variable x:

$$\text{effect}(x) = \frac{dEy(x)}{dx}. \tag{4.21}$$

If interaction terms are included in the analysis for a variable x, the size of the effect of x depends on the values of the other variables in the interaction terms. If in such cases the effect of x is discussed, I always consider the effect evaluated in the average value of the variables for which interactions are included.

Related to the problem of the non-linear relations between dependent and independent variables is that TRANSMITTER CENTRALITY has a value between 0 and 1. In the regression analysis, these restrictions on TRANSMITTER CENTRALITY are not implied by the model. Therefore, it can be expected that a suitable transformation of TRANSMITTER CENTRALITY can be better modeled by a linear model than TRANSMITTER CENTRALITY itself. A Box-Cox analysis (Box and Cox 1964) shows that a transformation of centrality with an exponent 2.5 could be better fitted by a third-order polynomial in OUTDEGREE and DENSITY than the untransformed TRANSMITTER CENTRALITY.[14] Because, I do not have hypotheses about the specific functional form of the relation between TRANSMITTER CENTRALITY and the network parameters and certainly not for heterogeneous networks, the best fitting transformation is used. This transformation does not solve the problem that TRANSMITTER CENTRALITY is bounded between 0 and 1. However, the predicted values for TRANSMITTER CENTRALITY are hardly ever smaller than 1 or larger than 0 in the analyses. Thus, I do not consider this to be a real problem. Note that if the transformed TRANSMITTER CENTRALITY increases in a network parameter, this implies that the untransformed TRANSMITTER CENTRALITY also increases in this parameter.

---

[14] I also tried transformations that transform TRANSMITTER CENTRALITY to a variable that varies between $-\infty$ and ∞, but I did not succeed in finding a transformation that fitted the data better than the Box-Cox transformation.

Selecting a well-fitting model proved to be very complicated and was only partially successful. A good model would describe sets of networks sampled by different construction methods equally well. However, effects of network parameters are not very constant over the different subsets. The analyses for the different subsets will be presented to allow investigation of the consistency of effects and for comparisons with the overall analyses. Using the subsets of networks based on a construction method can be considered as the selection of the weights of the networks in the analyses, because certain networks have a higher probability of being included in the sample than others, depending on the sampling method. Some parts of the "sample space" are even explicitly excluded for certain construction methods, as can be seen from the description of the construction methods in Appendix B. Still, if the assumptions of linear regression would be met, the results do not depend on the sampling method.

4.4.2 ANALYSES FOR SIMULATED DATA

Table 4.1 presents the results for five models. In all models, the (transformed) expected value of TRANSMITTER CENTRALITY is predicted with OUTDEGREE, DENSITY, INDEGREE, and NETWORK SIZE. All interaction effects, squared and cubic effects are constructed from the centralized versions of the original variables. In the first model, all the networks are analyzed and the log-variance is modeled with dummy variables for the construction models. This results in separate estimates for the residual variance for each of the construction methods. In the other models, TRANSMITTER CENTRALITY is analyzed separately for each construction method. I will not go into the details of the construction methods here, but the numbers correspond with those used in Appendix B.

In correspondence with the analyses of the game-theoretic model in Chapter 3, OUTDEGREE and DENSITY are important "predictors" for TRANSMITTER CENTRALITY. However, the higher-order terms are much more important for predicting TRANSMITTER CENTRALITY than for predicting trust thresholds. The effect of OUTDEGREE is presented in Figure 4.4 for all five models.[15] The thick line indicates the effect in the model estimated on all networks. The thin lines represent the effects of OUTDEGREE for the models estimated on the networks within one construction method. Note that the extreme values for OUTDEGREE that occur for each construction method are not the same. Overall, it is certainly true that TRANSMITTER CENTRALITY increases in OUTDEGREE because the effect of OUTDEGREE is always positive. The graphs demonstrate that the effect of OUTDEGREE decreases if OUTDEGREE is low and starts to increase at about an OUTDEGREE

[15]The effects in Figures 4.4 through 4.6 are the effects on the transformed TRANSMITTER CENTRALITY, which is also the dependent variable in the analyses. Because the transformation is a monotone transformation and the main function of the figures is a comparison of effects for the construction methods, I present the effects on the transformed TRANSMITTER CENTRALITY.

Table 4.1. Linear regression of (transformed) TRANSMITTER CENTRALITY with ordinary least squares for the separate construction methods (CM) and with multiplicative heteroscedasticity for all observations.[a]

Independent variable	Conjecture	All	CM 1	CM 2	CM 3	CM 4
INDIVIDUAL NETWORK PARAMETERS						
OUTDEGREE	+	.69	.68	.54	.71	.64
OUTDEGREE^2	?	.63	.53	1.07	.60	.70
OUTDEGREE^3	?	.57	.89	1.25	.31	.82
INDEGREE	0	−.048	−.052	−.14	−.040	−.069
GLOBAL NETWORK PARAMETERS						
DENSITY	+	.26	.30	.64	.24	.36
DENSITY^2	?	−.20	(.04)	.43	−.26	−.23
DENSITY^3	?	−.50	(−.47)	−2.25	−.69	−.91
NETWORK SIZE	+	.014	.014	(−.004)	.013	.017
NETWORK SIZE^2	−	−.002	−.003	(−.001)	−.002	−.001
INTERACTION EFFECTS						
OUTDEGREE × NETWORK SIZE	0	−.005	(−.002)	(.001)	−.004	(.000)
OUTDEGREE^2 × NETWORK SIZE	−	−.082	−.087	(.024)	−.062	−.095
CONSTANT		−.23	−.24	−.32	−.23	−.26
VARIANCE COMPONENTS						
Construction method 2	?	3.73				
Construction method 3	?	−.85				
Construction method 4	?	(.27)				
CONSTANT		−7.90				
$\text{corr}(\text{TC}, \hat{\text{TC}})^2$		.92	.97	.94	.99	.98
VWLS R^2		.98				
Number of actors		13,000	3,255	3,277	3,152	3,316
Number of networks		2,000	504	506	484	506

[a] Except for those in parentheses, all coefficient are "significant" at $p < 0.01$, based on Huber standard errors modified for clustering within networks (two-sided tests).

of 0.2. The pattern of the changes in the effect is similar for the analyses on the subsets of networks. This could also be seen from the coefficients for the OUTDEGREE terms in Table 4.1. The most prominent deviation from the average pattern is the sharper increase in the effect of OUTDEGREE for the second construction method. The small coefficient of the cubic term of OUTDEGREE for the third construction method means that the effect of OUTDEGREE does not decrease for this subset of networks if OUTDEGREE is low.

Figure 4.5 presents the effect of DENSITY for the five models in Table 4.1. Again, the overall pattern of the effect has considerable resemblance for all

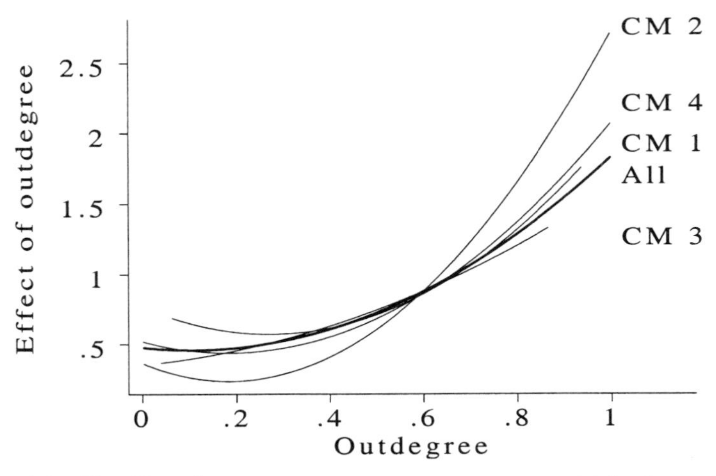

Figure 4.4. The effect of OUTDEGREE on TRANSMITTER CENTRALITY for the models in Table 4.1. The thin lines represent the effects for networks within construction methods (CM), the thick line for all networks.

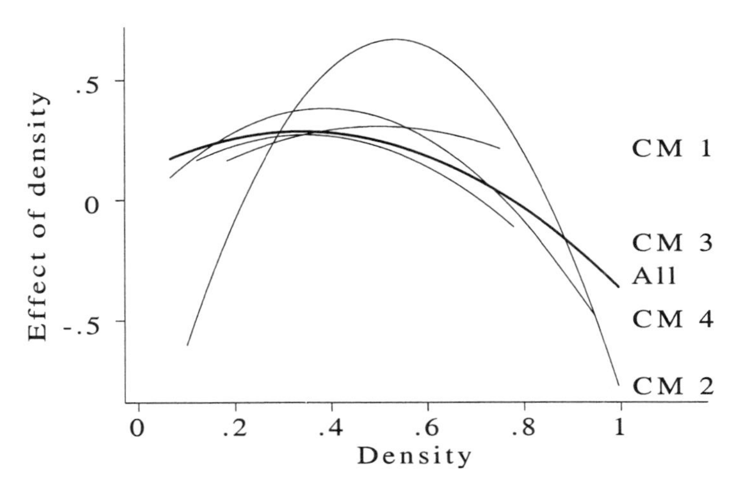

Figure 4.5. The effect of DENSITY on TRANSMITTER CENTRALITY for the models in Table 4.1. The thin lines represent the effects for networks within construction methods (CM), the thick line for all networks.

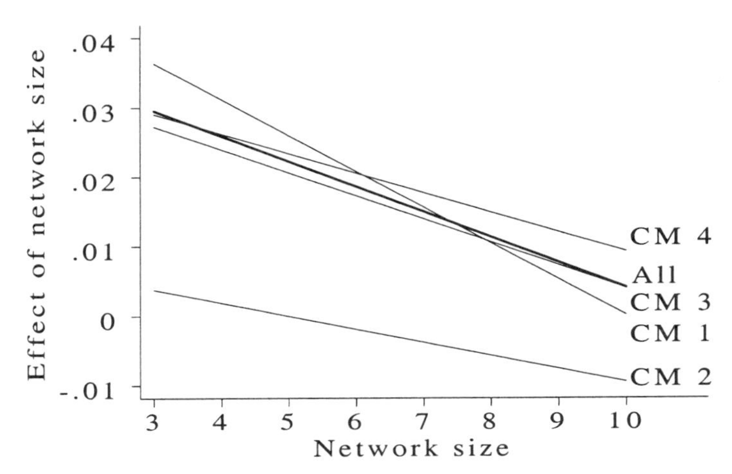

Figure 4.6. The effect of NETWORK SIZE on TRANSMITTER CENTRALITY for the models in Table 4.1. The thin lines represent the effects for networks within construction methods (CM), the thick line for all networks.

construction methods. Initially, there is an increase in the effect of DENSITY and, later, the effect of DENSITY decreases. However, for the second construction method, the effect of DENSITY is *negative* for low values of DENSITY as well as high values of DENSITY, while for the other construction methods the effect of DENSITY is only negative if DENSITY is close to 1. The reason that the effect of DENSITY is sometimes negative is probably due to the interdependence between OUTDEGREE and DENSITY. The effect of OUTDEGREE is, namely, larger than 1 if OUTDEGREE is lower than 0.8. The results for homogeneous networks suggest that the combined effect of DENSITY and OUTDEGREE should be close to 1 if DENSITY is close to 1. However, this cannot explain the large negative effect of DENSITY for networks with low DENSITY sampled with the second construction method. It is notable that the sum of the effect of the linear terms for DENSITY and OUTDEGREE is close to 1 in all analyses. This is indeed what would be expected from the formal analysis of the homogeneous networks. Moreover, the "average" effect of DENSITY on TRANSMITTER CENTRALITY is certainly positive, which can be seen from the effect of the linear term.

The effects of NETWORK SIZE and the interactions of NETWORK SIZE with OUTDEGREE are in correspondence with the expectations from homogeneous networks with the exception, again, of the analysis for the second construction method (see Figure 4.6). NETWORK SIZE has a positive effect on TRANSMITTER CENTRALITY and this effect decreases if NETWORK SIZE increases. Moreover, the interaction of NETWORK SIZE with squared OUTDEGREE has an effect in the expected direction. The interaction between the linear term of OUTDEGREE and NETWORK SIZE does in fact have a very small effect.

A negative effect of INDEGREE on TRANSMITTER CENTRALITY is found. In Chapter 2, I argued that INDEGREE should not have an effect on TRANSMITTER CENTRALITY. However, DENSITY is the mean of all indegrees, and the higher INDEGREE of the initial transmitter of information, the larger the part of the DENSITY that cannot be "used" to transmit information to the other actors in the network. Thus, the effect of INDEGREE on TRANSMITTER CENTRALITY is probably due to the fact that DENSITY among the other actors is lower compared to the total DENSITY if the focal actor's INDEGREE is higher. Some additional analyses demonstrated that the INDEGREE effect indeed can be attributed to the "overlap" of DENSITY with INDEGREE. Instead of DENSITY of the whole network, density of the network with exclusion of the focal actor was included in the analysis. With this change, the effect of INDEGREE disappears.

The analyses for the second construction method are quite distinct from those used for the other construction methods, which might suggest that these networks are the most heterogeneous and that there is more unexplained structure in these networks. One indication for this is that the variance in the residuals for the second construction method is considerably larger than for the other construction methods. Another indication would be that the differences between the second construction method and the others decrease if additional, more detailed network parameters are added to the analyses.

The addition of the other network parameters as independent variables to "explain" centralities does not add very much to the squared correlation between the actual and predicted TRANSMITTER CENTRALITY. The increase is largest for the second construction method, which is indeed an indication that these networks are more heterogeneous than the networks generated with the other construction methods. All the substantive results that followed from Table 4.1 follow again from Table 4.2. The non-linear effects of OUTDEGREE, DENSITY, and NETWORK SIZE are similar to the ones displayed in the figures before. The only difference is that the effects for the second construction method are more similar to those for the other construction methods. In the table, this can be seen, for example, from the smaller coefficient (in absolute sense) of the cubic term in DENSITY for the second construction method and from the effects of NETWORK SIZE that are now more in correspondence with the coefficients for the other construction methods.

Other effects that are expected *and* consistently found are the positive effect of OUTDEGREE QUALITY and the negative effects of OUTDEGREE VARIANCE, INDEGREE VARIANCE, and TRANSITIVITY on TRANSMITTER CENTRALITY. OUTDEGREE QUALITY, which is an extension of OUTDEGREE, indeed facilitates information transmission in the network. The negative effects of OUTDEGREE VARIANCE and

Table 4.2. Linear regression of (transformed) TRANSMITTER CENTRALITY including detailed network parameters with ordinary least squares for the separate construction methods (CM) and with multiplicative heteroscedasticity for all observations.[a]

Independent variable	Conjecture	All	CM 1	CM 2	CM 3	CM 4
INDIVIDUAL NETWORK PARAMETERS						
OUTDEGREE	+	.70	.68	.57	.72	.67
OUTDEGREE^2	?	.68	.63	.80	.60	.79
OUTDEGREE^3	?	.64	.93	1.12	.44	.71
INDEGREE	0	−.032	−.032	−.082	−.010	−.056
OUTDEGREE QUALITY	+	.42	.59	.50	.36	.54
INDEGREE QUALITY	0	−.47	−.48	−1.33	−.66	−.35
LOCAL OUTDEGREE DENSITY	−	(−.006)	−.067	−.14	(−.013)	(.020)
LOCAL INDEGREE DENSITY	0	.059	.13	.19	.097	(.021)
GLOBAL NETWORK PARAMETERS						
DENSITY	+	.24	.30	.63	.15	.32
DENSITY^2	?	−.30	−.31	(.002)	−.29	−.33
DENSITY^3	?	−.48	−.87	−1.42	−.74	−.92
NETWORK SIZE	+	.014	.013	.006	.013	.016
NETWORK SIZE^2	−	−.002	−.002	−.002	−.002	−.001
OUTDEGREE VARIANCE	−	−.23	−.61	−.46	(−.12)	−.30
INDEGREE VARIANCE	−	−.75	−.60	−1.44	−.59	−.69
OUTD.-IND. COVARIANCE	+	(−.090)	−.27	.68	.46	(.10)
TRANSITIVITY	−	−.056	−.067	−.24	(−.032)	(.000)
INTERACTION EFFECTS						
OUTDEGREE × NETWORK SIZE	0	−.007	−.006	−.014	−.007	(−.001)
OUTDEGREE^2 × NETWORK SIZE	−	−.082	−.097	(.011)	−.071	−.092
CONSTANT		−.22	−.22	−.18	−.22	−.27
VARIANCE COMPONENTS						
Construction method 2	?	3.69				
Construction method 3	?	−.75				
Construction method 4	?	(.39)				
CONSTANT		−8.26				
$\text{corr}(\text{TC}, \hat{\text{TC}})^2$		.95	.98	.97	.996	.98
VWLS R^2		.99				
Number of actors		13,000	3,255	3,277	3,152	3,316
Number of networks		2,000	504	506	484	506

[a] Except for those in parentheses, all coefficients are "significant" at $p < 0.01$, based on Huber standard errors modified for clustering within networks (two-sided tests).

INDEGREE VARIANCE are as expected. The effect demonstrates that the actors with low degrees have a relatively larger influence on the average TRANSMITTER CENTRALITY in a network than the actors with the high degrees. Because no effect of OUTDEGREE-INDEGREE COVARIANCE is found, I conclude that, in general, *centralization* of the network decreases the TRANSMITTER CENTRALITY of all actors in a network. The negative effect of TRANSITIVITY is not found for all construction methods. A plausible reason why the effect is only found for the first and second construction method is that the correlation of TRANSITIVITY with DENSITY for the first two construction methods is considerable lower (below 0.8) than for the last two construction methods (above 0.9).

The conjecture for the positive effect of OUTDEGREE-INDEGREE COVARIANCE is that actors who have high OUTDEGREE as well as high INDEGREE contribute to fast diffusion of information in a network. Probably, the effect of the covariance between outdegrees and indegrees is not found because this covariance can also be caused by actors who have *low* outdegrees and indegrees and, these actors will not have a positive effect on information diffusion. Thus, it can be expected that the effect of OUTDEGREE-INDEGREE COVARIANCE depends on other variables such as DENSITY. Because interpretation of interaction effects without theoretical arguments will be difficult, I do not consider such interaction effects.

The variables for LOCAL OUTDEGREE DENSITY and LOCAL INDEGREE DENSITY do not have consistent effects. The effects are always small. Whether the effects are positive or negative depends on the other variables included in the model and on which subgroup of networks is considered. In many analyses, the effects cannot be distinguished from 0. Thus, I do not find predictions for the effects of local density from these analyses. One reason for this is, again, that LOCAL OUTDEGREE DENSITY and LOCAL INDEGREE DENSITY are highly correlated with each other and with DENSITY and TRANSITIVITY.

To summarize, it can be said that the results indicate that *additional* network parameters (next to OUTDEGREE and DENSITY) are important to predict TRANSMITTER CENTRALITY in the stochastic diffusion model, while for the game-theoretic model these two variables predict almost all variance that could be attributed to the network for the trust thresholds. Moreover, correlations among the variables cause some instability of the coefficients if different subsets of networks are analyzed. Still, for several network parameters, the intuitive conjectures can be translated into hypotheses about the effects of network parameters on TRANSMITTER CENTRALITY. The results confirm the positive effects of DENSITY and OUTDEGREE on TRANSMITTER CENTRALITY. In addition, the positive effect of OUTDEGREE QUALITY and the negative effects of OUTDEGREE VARIANCE, INDEGREE VARIANCE, and TRANSITIVITY are in accordance with the conjectures.

4.5 SUBSTANTIVE IMPLICATIONS RELATED TO TRUST

This chapter discussed a stochastic model for information diffusion in heterogeneous networks. The substantive implications of this model include hypotheses about information diffusion rates in social network and do not directly concern trust in social networks. In this section, I explain how the findings for information diffusion relate to hypotheses about trust and, thereafter, I formulate these hypotheses explicitly. I compare network effects for the stochastic diffusion model with the network effects derived from the game-theoretic model in Chapter 3. In the diffusion model, the information transfer opportunities are modeled more realistically than in the game-theoretic model in which information is given from one actor to another as a package. In the diffusion model, every actor who obtained information keeps the information for ever, and continues transferring the information to others.

TRANSMITTER CENTRALITY

From the game-theoretic model the implication is derived that trustors who can inform many other trustors in a short time about an abuse of trust by the trustee can place more trust in the trustee than trustors who need more time to inform others. Thus, the control effects of the trustor are larger if she can inform other trustors earlier. Although the diffusion model does not incorporate transactions between trustors and trustees, I expect that trustors with a larger TRANSMITTER CENTRALITY can place more trust in a trustee than trustors with a smaller TRANSMITTER CENTRALITY and, thus, that trustors with a larger TRANSMITTER CENTRALITY can control a trustee better. The results for the diffusion model are consistent with the results from the game-theoretic model. DENSITY and OUTDEGREE are the most important predictors for trust. One difference is that due to the more complex and realistic information diffusion process in the diffusion model, more effects of network parameters could be found. However, because no transactions are modeled in this chapter, no hypotheses about interaction effects between network parameters and non-network parameters could be derived from this model, while such hypotheses could be derived from the game-theoretic model. Now, I state the hypotheses about TRANSMITTER CENTRALITY that follow from this chapter in terms of trust.

HYPOTHESIS 4.1 *Trust increases with* OUTDEGREE *of a trustor.*

HYPOTHESIS 4.2 *Trust increases with the outdegrees of the contacts of a focal trustor (*OUTDEGREE QUALITY*).*

HYPOTHESIS 4.3 *Trust increases with* DENSITY *of a network.*

HYPOTHESIS 4.4 *Trust decreases with centralization of a network (*OUTDEGREE VARIANCE *and* INDEGREE VARIANCE*).*

HYPOTHESIS 4.5 *Trust decreases with* TRANSITIVITY *of a network.*

The hypotheses about DENSITY, OUTDEGREE, and OUTDEGREE QUALITY already followed from the game-theoretic model. The effects of centralization and TRANSITIVITY are new.

The effects of NETWORK SIZE, INDEGREE, and INDEGREE QUALITY that are found for TRANSMITTER CENTRALITY can hardly be interpreted in terms of control effects. These effects probably result from the correlation of these network parameters with other network parameters such as OUTDEGREE and DENSITY. The effects are not due to the particular properties of the network parameters itself.

RECEIVER CENTRALITY

The game-theoretic model only provided hypotheses about effects that are related to transmitting information to other actors and, hence, to the possibilities for the trustor to sanction abuse of trust. Hypotheses about *learning effects* can be deduced from the results of RECEIVER CENTRALITY. It is known from the analytic results in Section 4.3 that the results for TRANSMITTER CENTRALITY can be related directly to results for RECEIVER CENTRALITY by changing the roles of OUTDEGREE and INDEGREE. Thus, RECEIVER CENTRALITY increases in DENSITY and INDEGREE, although not in a linear way, and RECEIVER CENTRALITY decreases in OUTDEGREE. Moreover, RECEIVER CENTRALITY increases in INDEGREE QUALITY and decreases in OUTDEGREE QUALITY. Finally, it is expected that RECEIVER CENTRALITY decreases in the centralization and TRANSITIVITY of a network.

As was stated in Chapter 1, learning effects are always conditional on the type of information. If the information is mainly positive, trustors with a larger RECEIVER CENTRALITY will obtain more positive information about the trustee, and these trustors are expected to place more trust in the trustee. If information is mainly negative, trustors with a larger RECEIVER CENTRALITY will place less trust in the trustee. If information is not consistent, it is not clear whether trustors with a larger RECEIVER CENTRALITY will trust the trustee more or less. The content of information is not modeled explicitly in this chapter, and I consider the content of information as an empirical issue. The model provides hypotheses about learning effects only if information is consistent. Below, I present *new* hypotheses for trust based on the results for RECEIVER CENTRALITY.

HYPOTHESIS 4.6 *Trust increases with* INDEGREE *of a trustee if information in the network about the trustee is positive.*

HYPOTHESIS 4.7 *Trust decreases with* INDEGREE *of a trustee if information in the network about the trustee is negative.*

HYPOTHESIS 4.8 *Trust increases with the indegrees of the contacts of a focal trustor (*INDEGREE QUALITY*) if information in the network about the trustee is positive.*

HYPOTHESIS 4.9 *Trust decreases with the indegrees of the contacts of a focal trustor (*INDEGREE QUALITY*) if information in the network about the trustee is negative.*

The effects of OUTDEGREE and OUTDEGREE QUALITY are not included in the hypotheses because the effects depend on the relations between the network parameters rather than the particular properties of these network parameters themselves. Also the hypotheses based on RECEIVER CENTRALITY with respect to DENSITY, centralization, and TRANSITIVITY are not repeated here, because they are exactly the same as the hypotheses that followed from TRANSMITTER CENTRALITY if information about the trustee is positive. It is important to realize that for empirical effects of network parameters that are symmetric with respect to the "global" direction of ties, such as DENSITY or TRANSITIVITY, it is impossible to disentangle whether such an effect is a control effect or a learning effect. Moreover, if information about the trustee is negative, the direction of the total effect of DENSITY, centralization, and TRANSITIVITY is unclear because learning effects and control effects are in opposite directions.

4.6 DISCUSSION

The most prominent problem that occurred in analyzing the diffusion model was that the regression analyses apparently failed to fit the data accurately. Although the variables in the analyses explained most of the variance in TRANSMITTER CENTRALITY, the analyses of the different subsets of networks demonstrated that exact statements about the size of coefficients cannot be made. Nevertheless, I believe that the results are robust enough to justify statements about some comparative statics as presented in the hypotheses in the foregoing section. It would be preferable if the model could be understood better. Therefore, the analytic results need to be extended. With an explicit expression for diffusion times for some particular type of networks, linearization analyses in the neighborhood of such networks would be possible similar to those given in Chapter 3. However, I did not succeed in finding such an expression even for homogeneous networks.

Notwithstanding the problems with the results of the diffusion model, I cannot resist the "temptation" to sketch some extensions that could make the model more realistic. There are two straightforward extensions that do not make the model substantially more complex. First, one could add a possibility that actors forget information during a time period or stop transferring information. If forgetting information does not depend on time, a probability for forgetting information could be included, while the number of states in the Markov chain remains at most 2^n. This model is only slightly more complex because the diffusion process does not move to a state in which everybody is informed. If actors forget information, the absorbing state is the state in which everybody has forgotten the information. If actors transmit information relatively more frequently than they forget information, it can take a long time before the absorbing state is reached.

Second, one could add a public source that transmits information to all actors. A public source is a very common element in diffusion studies and, therefore, a useful extension of the model. A public source could be modeled as an additional actor who transmits information to all actors, though not necessarily with the same probability. The public source could be the "actor" who starts the diffusion process. Another property of a public source should be that it does not receive information from the actors in the network. Thus, for the introduction of a public source, the network matrix $\boldsymbol{A}$ has to be extended with one column and one row. The column contains zeros only and the row contains the probabilities that the actors receive information from the public source in a certain time period. The definitions about the mean transmission time and centrality measures have to be changed accordingly.

Two assumptions of the model that are less easily replaced are the purely stochastic and accurate nature of information transmission. Social psychological experiments (for example, Parry 1967: Part 2; Gilovich 1987) indicate that *noise* cannot be disregarded even for relatively simple messages and that first-hand information differs considerably from second-hand information. Although the actor who transmits the information is willing to transmit accurate information, the receiver will not "understand" the information as it is transmitted. After information is transmitted over a number of links between actors, information can be heavily distorted. Taking into account that a certain amount of noise is added to a message with every transmission of information would be a relevant extension to the model. However, such a model should incorporate how actors treat inconsistent information while they, for example, do not know how far away they are from the source of information. This is, probably, a non-trivial issue both from a theoretical as well as from a modelling perspective.

While unintentional distortions of information can be described with a purely stochastic model, it is plausible that actors have reasons for distorting information intentionally. A buyer who obtained a computer that does not suit her demands may blame the supplier for selling the wrong machine when discussing the subject with another customer. However, she may conceal that she actually did not inform the supplier well enough about the computer she wanted. In such a situation, the other customer obtains a negative image of the supplier although the actual reason for the problem is a lack of communication between buyer and supplier. Another reason for intentional misrepresentation of information among customers may be that the customers are competitors and that a customer does not want to disclose her failures to her competitors. A model of intentional distortion of information should include the incentives for transmission of accurate or distorted information and the information actors have about each others incentives for transmitting information.

As another form of goal-oriented behavior, actors can *choose* the actors to whom they want to transmit information. In the current model, all the occurrences of information transmission are stochastically determined in the model. However, if an actor has transmitted information to an actor today, it is highly improbable that she will again transmit the same information to that actor tomorrow. Moreover, actors may be aware that certain of their contacts are more interested in some information than others. For example, an actor discovers that a certain used-car dealer is highly untrustworthy and she has a friend who is looking for a used car. This actor will probably make an effort to inform her friend about the untrustworthy car dealer, although she does not meet that friend frequently.

Adding some kind of intentional behavior to the model asks for a game-theoretic context in which the model should be placed. Such extensions are beyond the scope of this book. Furthermore, before theoretical extensions are explored, it is useful to test the hypotheses developed so far in some empirical settings.

Chapter 5

CONTRACTING IN INFORMATION TECHNOLOGY TRANSACTIONS: A SURVEY

Mathematical theorems are tautologies. They cannot be false because they do not say anything substantive. They merely spell out the implications of how things have been defined.

—Binmore (1994: 95–96)

5.1 INTRODUCTION

In terms of Binmore, as far as the mathematics of Chapters 3 and 4 are concerned, the statements made in those chapters are true—with the obvious exception of logical or mathematical errors. In this chapter, I will put the models to a first empirical test based on survey data. An experimental test follows in Chapter 6. The empirical data used in this chapter were collected from small and medium-sized Dutch firms that bought information technology (IT) products. They gave information about how they searched for and negotiated the purchase of these products. The products include software packages, personal computers, computer networks, and computer-controlled machines. Details of the survey are given in Section 5.2.

Transactions and not firms are the *units of analysis* here. The most important argument for why IT transactions are trust problems is that the supplier is usually better informed about the quality of a product than the buyer (see Chapter 1). The buyer has to trust that the supplier will deliver a product that fulfills the specifications they have agreed upon. In the survey, the buyers are small and medium-sized firms, often with only limited IT experience. This makes the asymmetric information argument even more plausible. In contrast with the examples drawn from densely connected societies such as Jewish diamond merchants (Wechsberg 1966: 81–86), buyers of IT products are not expected to be embedded in dense social networks. Rather, it can be expected that network embeddedness varies among buyers of IT products depending on the individual (firm) characteristics of a buyer or characteristics of organizations, such as sector organizations, of which the buyer is a member. Such differences may mean that one buyer has more ties than another or is embedded in a denser network.

Following the reasoning developed in this book, a trust problem is regarded as a one-sided problem for the buyer. Opportunities and incentives for opportunistic behavior by the buyer, such as delayed payments, are neglected. This is not the only simplifying assumption needed to apply the game-theoretic model of repeated Trust Games in empirical research on IT transactions. Two additional aspects are particularly important. First, I address the way trust of a buyer is measured in an IT transaction. Second, I discuss the relationship of Trust Game payoffs to the properties of an IT transaction.

From "Lack of Trust" to Contracts

In the Trust Game, the choice of the trustor (in this case, the buyer) is restricted to two options: "trust" or "no trust." In reality, buyers have many other options. They can buy a product without making any agreement about what will happen if the product is defective. They can make a verbal agreement with the supplier or they can write contracts varying in length and elaboration (Macaulay 1963). Therefore, for empirical tests, I consider qualitative implications of the model rather than exact predictions. As shown in Chapter 3, the game-theoretic model of repeated Trust Games predicts the *extent* to which the trustor trusts the trustee. Contracts provide safeguards that mitigate opportunistic behavior by the supplier as well as compensate the buyer if the supplier behaves opportunistically (see, for example, Raub 1998). However, contractual safeguards come at a price, in this case negotiation and bargaining costs. Hence, I assume that the less the buyer trusts the supplier, the more contractual safeguards the buyer will include in the contract. This argument is consistent with principal-agent theory (see, for example, Kreps 1990b: Chapter 16) and transaction cost theory (Williamson 1985: Chapter 3). Moreover, the larger the trust problem for the buyer, the more the buyer will demand safeguards that decrease the seller's incentive to abuse trust and that decrease the buyer's loss in case of abused trust. A buyer's willingness to contract can be expressed in terms of *effort* (time and money) invested in the process of contracting or in the *safeguards* the buyer wants to include in the contract. Because the predictions of the game-theoretic model are mainly based on the incentives of the supplier to abuse trust, I am more interested in the type and number of safeguards than in the effort invested by the buyer. This differs from Batenburg et al. (2002) who mainly study the amount of investments of the buyers in contractual management of the transaction using the same data. Hence, I have studied the number of safeguards in a contract (SAFEGUARDS) as a measure of the "lack of trust" of buyers.[1]

Four remarks are in order with respect to SAFEGUARDS as a "dependent variable." First, because there are costs involved in writing a contract, the longer the contract, the more costs have to be made in designing the contract. Therefore, the number of safeguards still contains an indication for the effort the buyer wants to invest in formal management. Second, costs of contracts are not the same for all buyers. For buyers with more law expertise, writing contracts is expected to be less costly than for buyers with hardly any expertise in contracting. In the following section, some variables are discussed that may influence the costs of contracting for the buyer, and thereby the number of safeguards included. Third, a contract serves more functions than simply preventing actors from behaving opportunistically. For example, the contract will also address coordination problems specifying the product desired by the buyer and the timing of certain activities in a transaction (Macaulay 1963; Milgrom and Roberts 1992: Chapter 4). I assume that specifications of technical details, such as the desired size of internal memory of a personal computer, are typically included in such contracts to solve coordination problems, while legal and financial issues are more important for mitigating opportunistic behavior. For example, a strict agreement on the delivery time of the product is a typical safeguard against opportunistic behavior by the supplier. Hence, SAFEGUARDS is restricted to legal and financial issues included in the contract. Fourth, measuring lack of trust with the number of safeguards is somewhat problematic because including more safeguards in a contract does not necessarily imply that the contract is more "complete" (Hart 1987). For a more complex transaction, a "complete" contract needs to be much more extensive than for a relatively standard transaction. Thus, if more safeguards are included in the contract of a complex transaction, the opportunities for the supplier to behave opportunistically are not necessarily less than for a standard transaction with a contract that includes less safeguards. Consequently, the remaining trust problem may be larger for a large transaction with a contract that includes many safeguards than for a small transaction with a contract that includes few safeguards. As will be discussed below, this implies that contracts are expected to have more safeguards when designed for more complex transactions.

From a Trust Game to an IT Transaction

Testing the implications of the game-theoretic model with survey data on IT transactions requires that the payoffs in a Heterogeneous Trust Game (HTG) can be related to characteristics of IT transactions (see Figure 3.1). A general

[1] While in the foregoing chapters the theoretical variables were set in SANS SERIF typeface, in this chapter and the following chapter, labels of empirical variables are set in SANS SERIF typeface.

and important point is that, in the game-theoretic model, trust is based on the incentive of the trustee to abuse trust in the *ongoing* game and the possibilities of the trustor to sanction the trustee in *future* games. In a similar way, a rational buyer of IT products will base her choice on what the supplier can gain from abusing trust in the current transaction surveyed in the questionnaire (and probably also what the buyer will lose herself if trust is abused), compared to the possibilities she has of sanctioning the trustee in future transactions. Therefore, I relate the characteristics of the current transaction to payoff differences that occur in the HTG *after* trust is placed. These payoff differences are the incentive to abuse trust for the supplier ($\theta = R_2 + \theta - R_2$) and the buyer's loss if trust is abused ($R_1 - S_1$).

Now, I discuss five transaction characteristics that can be operationalized with the available data and I discuss the relation of these transaction characteristics with the payoffs in the HTG defined in Chapter 3. The financial volume of a transaction, i.e., the amount of money the buyer has to pay for the product, is an overall measure for the size of the payoffs, and, in particular, the payoffs related to the outcomes that can occur if trust is placed in the current transaction. Therefore, it is a measure for the incentive of the supplier to abuse trust (θ) as well as for the loss for the buyer if trust is abused ($R_1 - S_1$). Both the supplier's incentive to abuse trust and the buyer's loss if trust is abused are expected to increase with the financial volume.

The second and third transaction characteristics are the number of components of the product and the complexity of the product. The number of components, in addition to financial volume, is an indication for the "size" of the transaction. Therefore, I consider this also as a measure for the incentive of the supplier to abuse trust and the loss for the buyer if trust is abused. More complex products require more effort on the part of the supplier to produce a good product. In addition, complex products leave more opportunities for "hidden" defects. Thus, the incentive to abuse trust for the supplier is expected to increase with the complexity of the product.

The fourth characteristic of the transaction is the dependence of the buyer on (the trustworthiness of) the supplier. The more the buyer depends on the supplier, the larger will be the costs for the buyer if trust is abused ($R_1 - S_1$). This corresponds with Williamson's (1985) argument that in transactions with more one-sided specific investments the partners need more formal management due to the increased dependency of the investing partner on the other actor's cooperative behavior.

The last transaction characteristic I discuss here are the monitoring problems of the buyer. If it is difficult for a buyer to evaluate the quality of an IT product, it is easier and, therefore, less costly for the supplier to deliver an inferior product. This corresponds with Williamson's (1985) reasoning that if more aspects of a transaction are uncertain, there is more room for opportunistic behavior. Consequently, the incentive for the supplier to abuse trust (θ) is expected to increase with monitoring problems for the buyer.

It follows from the game-theoretic model that the larger the incentive to abuse trust, the larger the probability that the buyer will not trust the supplier. The analysis of the game-theoretic model did not yield hypotheses about the effects of the payoffs of the trustor on the extent of trust. The reason for this is that, in equilibrium, trust will never be abused by the trustee and the buyer will never obtain the "sucker" payoff S_1. This is mainly a result of complete information assumptions. However, the buyer is certainly not completely informed about all incentives and characteristics of the supplier in an IT transaction. Therefore, even in equilibrium, it cannot be excluded that the supplier ever delivers an inferior product. In game-theoretic models in which incomplete information is included, the payoffs of the trustor have effects on trust (see, for example, Camerer and Weigelt 1988; Snijders 1996: Section 2.4; Raub 1998; Buskens 2000). It follows from such models that trust decreases with the loss for the trustor if trust is abused ($R_1 - S_1$). Consequently, it follows from the arguments above that the number of safeguards increases with the financial volume of the transaction, the number of components of the product, the complexity of the product, the dependence of the buyer on the supplier, and monitoring problems of the buyer.

The costs of the trustor if she does not trust are $R_1 - P_1$. Because lack of trust is interpreted in terms of the number of safeguards in the contract, these costs are the costs of contracting for the trustor.[2] It is expected that the number of safeguards decreases with the costs of contracting for the trustor (see Raub 1998).

It follows from the model that trust increases in the costs of sanctions for the supplier ($R_2 - P_2$). As discussed above, these are the costs of sanctions for the supplier in future transactions *after* a focal transaction in which the supplier abused trust. This implies that the costs of sanctions for the trustee do not only depend on the expected frequency of future transactions, but also the expected volume of future transactions. It is expected that the larger future transactions will be, the larger the costs will be for the supplier if the buyer sanctions the supplier in these subsequent transactions and, consequently, fewer safeguards need to be included in the contract. As discussed in Chapter 1, sanctions imposed by the buyer can include ending the relation with the supplier after a serious abuse of trust and searching for another supplier for subsequent transactions, or asking for extensive safeguards in subsequent transactions.

---

[2] As discussed in Subsection 1.2.4, lack of trust of the trustor can also imply that the trustor searches for another partner. The costs of such a choice are included in the dependence of the buyer.

THE REMAINDER OF THIS CHAPTER

Section 5.2 describes the data. Thereafter, the operationalizations of variables and the hypotheses to be tested are presented. Appendix C contains the main questions from the survey used in the operationalizations and analyses. The theoretical variables representing temporal and networks embeddedness will be operationalized in a straightforward way in Subsection 5.2.2. Table 5.6 offers an overview of testable hypotheses in terms of the "empirical" variables and references to corresponding theoretical hypotheses. After a brief discussion of the statistical issues involved in the analyses, Section 5.3 presents straightforward tests of hypotheses. The section concludes with some additional analyses concerning network effects that take into account some of the shortcomings of the models and the data. Ways of improving the model and improving future data collection are outlined. Section 5.4 discusses the most important findings of this chapter.

5.2 DATA AND HYPOTHESES

5.2.1 DESCRIPTION OF THE DATA

The data set results from the survey "The External Management of Automation 1995" (MAT95; Batenburg and Raub 1995; Batenburg 1995/7a). This survey is a multi-purpose survey on the management of interfirm relations. Effects of network embeddedness are one of the topics, but certainly not the only one. In the survey, questions were asked about the management of buyers of their IT transactions. The main topics in the survey address searching a supplier of IT products, the negotiations for the transaction, and the transaction itself. Respondents were employees (mostly IT managers) of buyers of IT products that were selected by a stratified sample of Dutch small and medium-sized enterprises (SMEs).[3] The sampling frame was the Directview[4] database of Dutch SMEs that contained information about the characteristics of these SMEs with respect to automation. About 80% of all Dutch firms with more than five employees were included in the database. The database could be considered as representative for the Dutch population (see Batenburg 1995/7a). Three criteria were used for stratification. First, the sample was stratified by the number of automation specialists employed by the firm. Three groups were distinguished: firms with no specialist, firms that had only part-time specialists, and firms with one or more full-time automation specialists. Second, the sector of industry was used to obtain a stratification criterion related to network embeddedness. Business experts were asked about the strength of interfirm relations within certain sectors of industry. Their judgement was

[3]The Dutch definition of SMEs is used that comprises firms with between 5 and 200 employees.

[4]A Dutch firm specialized in IT marketing data of Dutch organizations.

based on how often firms meet informally and how many activities within the sector were organized to bring firms together. Using these expert judgements, sectors were divided in three groups: sectors with weak, medium, and strong interfirm relations. The third stratification criterion was the type of IT products bought by a firm. This criterion distinguished four groups: standard hardware, complex hardware, standard software, and complex software. These three stratification criteria were used because they represent three important theoretical dimensions, namely, the expertise of the buyer, her network embeddedness, and the complexity of the transaction. The three stratification criteria resulted in a sampling design with $3 \times 3 \times 4 = 36$ cells. Randomization procedures for sampling transactions were used until at least 15 cases were collected for each cell. Respondents were first interviewed briefly by a structured Computer Assisted Telephone Interview (CATI). In this interview, the interviewer and respondent selected an IT transaction randomly from all IT transactions of the firm in the last ten years, while taking into account that the product should meet the third stratification criterion. Here, randomization was used to prevent oversampling of transactions with or without conflicts between buyer and supplier.

Following this sampling procedure, a main sample of 547 IT transactions was obtained. Thereafter, the data set was extended with an additional sample. This additional sample was collected in order to obtain more observations on innovative and complex IT products. The additional sample was stratified using only the criterion related to the automation specialists in the buyer's firm. Because trust problems are expected to be more prevalent in complex transactions, I will include both samples in my analyses.[5] Another 241 questionnaires were collected within this additional sample.

While the questionnaire was designed to be self-administrated, most respondents were visited by an interviewer. About 25% of the respondents did not agree with this procedure. In these cases, the questionnaire was sent by mail. After finishing the questionnaire, respondents were asked to fill out another questionnaire for a second IT transaction. About 20% of the respondents agreed to do this. These questionnaires were left at the site and returned by mail. A total of 183 questionnaires on a second IT transaction were collected. This brings the total number of transactions in the data set to $547 + 241 + 183 = 971$.

Most of the fieldwork was done between January and June 1995. The response rate of the telephone interview was 67%.[6] From all the firms that promised to cooperate during the CATI questionnaire, 87% actually completed a questionnaire. This led to a total response rate of 59%, which is relatively

---

[5] In contrast with the main stratified sample, the additional sample is not representative for Dutch SMEs. However, representativity of results for Dutch SMEs is not an issue in this book.

[6] Nearly 26% of the firms that were telephoned were "not suitable," because there was no suitable respondent, no IT investments or IT products used in the firm, the firm did not exist anymore, or the firm was too large or too small. From the firms that were suitable 33% refused to cooperate.

high for surveys among organizations. Overall, the quality of the data is high due to considerable "care intensity" during approaching and interviewing the respondents. Non-response analyses have shown no indication for selectivity in non-response. Likewise, partial non-response is low and limited to a few "difficult" questions (see Batenburg 1995/7b). As a result, 893 cases can be included in the analyses of this chapter. For the 78 cases that are not included in the analyses, 60 respondents did not answer the question about the content of the contract. For the remaining 18 cases, there are missings at essential independent variables that are difficult to impute.

The questionnaire consisted of six sections. The transaction for which the questionnaire was completed is called the "focal" transaction and the respondent's firm is called the "buyer." In the first section, questions were asked about transaction characteristics including the financial volume of the transaction and the different components making up the product. Furthermore, questions were posed about the importance of the product for the buyer and the difficulty for the buyer in judging the quality of the product. The second section of the questionnaire involved the effort invested by the buyer in searching and selecting a suitable product and supplier. The third section contained questions about the relation of the respondent's firm and the supplier *before* the transaction. Questions were included about the frequency and size of transactions with the same IT supplier prior to the focal transaction. One question was included on the extent to which the buyer expected future transactions with the same IT supplier at the time of the focal transaction. Questions were also asked about partners or other customers of the supplier who were known to the buyer. Using the questions in the first three sections of the questionnaire, the variables for transaction characteristics, temporal embeddedness, and network embeddedness are constructed. The fourth section asked for the activities of the respondent's firm in negotiating and contracting with the supplier. The content of the contract was also addressed. Using these questions, the number of safeguards in the contract is estimated. The fifth section focused on the execution of the transaction and the period after the transaction had been completed. It contained questions about problems that occurred, problem regulation, and the development of the relation between the buyer and supplier after the focal transaction. This section of the questionnaire will not be analyzed here but is used for related research on problems and problem regulation in interfirm relations (Rooks 2002). Finally, general questions about the respondent's firm and the respondent were asked in the sixth section of the questionnaire. The questions used in this chapter are presented in Appendix C.

5.2.2 OPERATIONALIZATIONS

In this subsection, I discuss the operationalizations of the theoretical concepts. References are given to questions of the survey questionnaire (see Appendix C). I start with the dependent variable. Thereafter, I discuss operationalizations of temporal and network embeddedness and go on to describe transaction characteristics, variables reflecting the costs of contracting for the buyer, and firm characteristics.

NUMBER OF SAFEGUARDS IN THE CONTRACT

The questionnaire contained a list of 24 financial and legal issues that can be included in a contract of an IT transaction. For every issue, questions were asked whether agreement had been reached verbally, had been arranged by written contract, or had not been arranged at all (question 4.14). An issue that was not arranged at all is coded 0; an issue that was agreed verbally is coded 1; and an issue that was arranged in a written contract is coded 2. The values indicate that an agreement that is verified in a contract leaves less room for deviation than a verbal arrangement. Issues that were not answered are coded 0 assuming that respondents considered such an issue to be irrelevant and made no arrangements for it.

A Mokken scale analysis for polytomous items is used to check whether there is a scale underlying the contract issues (Mokken 1970).[7] The analysis shows that all issues are scalable within one scale with a lower bound of Loevinger's H equal to 0.30. The overall scale coefficient equals 0.43, which indicates a scale of medium strength. This scale analysis justifies a construction of the variable for SAFEGUARDS as the sum of the scores at all 24 contract issues (see Table 5.1).

It has to be noted that some issues may not be relevant in certain transactions. For example, if standard software was bought, it is not likely that there were arrangements about availability of spare parts. However, it is difficult to determine what the relevant issues are for each transaction separately. Therefore, more issues will be relevant in complex transactions compared to standard transactions. This provides an additional argument as to why SAFEGUARDS is expected to increase with the complexity of the transaction. Moreover, it could be argued that because trust is considered to be a one-sided problem for the buyer, only those issues are relevant that decrease incentives for opportunistic behavior on the part of the trustee or that compensate the buyer when the supplier is opportunistic. Arguments can be found in the case of many issues that they are safeguards for the supplier, for the buyer, or for both. Therefore, I have decided to restrict myself to the *number* of safeguards in the contract and leave investigations that take into account the specific contents of certain issues in the contract for later research.

[7] See Molenaar (1982) for the generalization to polytomous items.

Table 5.1. Frequencies and Mokken scale analysis of the 24 issues relating to the contract (893 transactions).

	Response frequencies			
Issue	Not arranged	Verbally arranged	Arranged in contract	Loevinger's H
Non-disclosure	696	75	122	0.50
Reservation spare-parts	652	95	146	0.41
Calculation R&D costs	653	82	158	0.45
Insurance supplier	621	67	205	0.46
Sanctions on late payment	623	46	224	0.39
Arbitration	595	68	230	0.46
Termination	557	63	273	0.48
Protection against privacy	501	145	247	0.44
Force majeure	505	110	278	0.45
Restrictions on product use	493	127	273	0.43
Joint management transaction	394	316	183	0.40
Price changes	422	143	328	0.33
Quality (norms)	399	174	320	0.39
Intellectual property	409	53	431	0.43
Updating	368	131	394	0.42
Liability supplier	299	119	475	0.49
Duration maintenance	270	70	553	0.46
Technical specifications	195	96	602	0.43
Duration service	158	96	639	0.52
Delivery time	96	180	617	0.40
Payment terms	132	64	697	0.36
Warranties supplier	120	79	694	0.53
Price determination	79	124	690	0.36
Price level	49	75	769	0.40
Scale coefficient H				0.43

Temporal Embeddedness

The *past* of a transaction refers to previous transactions between the focal buyer and the supplier. During these past transactions the buyer has had opportunities to obtain information about the incentives and characteristics of the supplier. A first question concerned whether a past relationship between the buyer and the supplier existed at the time of the focal transaction (question 3.6). About 50% of the buyers had had previous transactions with the supplier. Using a five-point scale, these buyers were asked how frequently the firm had transactions with the supplier before the focal transaction (question 3.8). Three other questions were asked about past transactions with the supplier. These referred to the length of the past relation, the volume of past business, and the buyer's satisfaction with past business conducted with the supplier (questions 3.7, 3.9, and 3.10). All these variables are coded 0 for the cases for which no past relationship existed and are coded 1 to 5 for the categories of the five-point scale. With the exception of 14 buyers, all buyers reported to be quite satisfied, satisfied, or very satisfied with past transactions. A probable explanation for this is that unsatisfactory relations dissolve. As a consequence, past relations between buyer and supplier are considered to be positive in the sense that a negative effect is expected of (positive) past experiences on SAFEGUARDS.[8] I consider the *frequency* of past transactions the best measure of the amount of learning in the past. The length of the relation does not give information about the number and volume of transactions during this relation. I do not have very convincing arguments to choose between volume and frequency of past transaction as the independent variable for "past." The frequency of past transactions gives the most direct indication of how many "learning experiences" the buyer has had in transactions with the supplier.[9] The resulting variable PAST has a value 0 for about 50% of the transactions without a past and a value of between 1 and 5 for transactions with a past depending on the frequency of the past transactions.

In measuring opportunities for *control* within the dyadic relation, there was only one question on the expectation of the respondent about the frequency and volume of business with the supplier in the *future* at the time of the focal transaction (question 3.13). There are at least two problems as far as this question is concerned. First, the answer categories combined two dimensions: frequency and volume. As a consequence, this question also gives an indication of the costs to the supplier if the buyer does not trust him in subsequent transactions, because sanctions on the part of the buyer can be more extensive for larger transactions. Second, the respondent had to recall a probably vague expectation from a number of years ago.[10] The accuracy of answers to such a

[8]Some additional analyses are done to test whether results in the following section change if the 14 transactions with a "negative" past are treated differently from the other transactions, for example, by coding the past variable negatively. Given the very small number of transactions with a negative past, such a modification could hardly be expected to affect the results and, indeed, does not affect the results.

[9]The variables for volume and frequency of past transactions are highly correlated (0.92; 0.60 for the non-zero cases only) and the effects of the two variables on SAFEGUARDS are similar. However, in terms of explained variance with respect to SAFEGUARDS, frequency of past transactions is the better candidate. Moreover, the effect of frequency is approximately linear over all categories including the zero-category that contains the cases for which no past exists. Frequency of past transactions predicts SAFEGUARDS slightly better compared to a dummy variable that only indicates whether a past relation exists. The volume of past transactions is a worse predictor of SAFEGUARDS than such a dummy variable.

[10]The year of purchase for the focal transactions varies between 1978 and 1995. About 800 transactions are completed between 1988 and 1994, while the survey is done in 1995. If necessary, errors in variables could be modeled assuming that the variance increases with the delay. However, I will not use such models in the analyses below.

retrospective question is doubtful (Bernard, Killworth, Kronenfeld, and Sailer 1985). Still, I could not come up with a better measure for expected future transactions from this questionnaire. Therefore, this question with answers on a five-point scale is used as the FUTURE variable.

Network Embeddedness

Network embeddedness is multi-dimensional. As discussed in Chapters 3 and 4, global and individual network parameters account for different aspects of the network. The social network considered in the models as well as in this chapter is the network of customers of the same supplier. Theoretically, density and outdegree turned out to be the most important network parameters that determine control effects of the network of customers. Density and indegree are the most important parameters that determine learning effects via the network. Density is the only global network parameter considered in this chapter. Indegree and outdegree are the individual network parameters discussed here.

In MAT95, two methods for measuring networks were applied. First, the ego-centered network of the buyer and other customers of the supplier was measured. Second, questions about the "network activities" of the buyer were asked such as whether employees of the buyer go to congresses or fairs related to IT products.

The extensive question about the *ego-centered* network of customers known by the buyer started with a question about how many customers of the supplier the buyer knew at the time of the transaction (question 3.19). About 52% of the respondents reported that their firm did not know any of the supplier's other customers, while 9% knew one or two other customers. The number of other customers mentioned (truncated at 7) is used as the DEGREE variable.[11] More detailed information was asked for up to four other customers to allow more detailed network parameters to be operationalized. If the buyer knew more than four other customers, the most important customers were chosen. For these other customers, questions were asked about

- the automation experience of the other customers compared to the automation experience of the buyer,
- the importance of the other customers for the supplier compared to the importance of the buyer,
- the frequency of contacts between employees of the buyer and employees of the other customers, and
- the frequency of contacts between employees of the other customers.

---

[11] Some respondents mentioned very large numbers of other customers, namely, up to 50. Truncation at seven customers is done to prevent outlier effects of these extreme observations. I experimented with different values for truncation (between 5 at 10), but there were no major differences between the analyses with the degree variable truncated at other values around 7.

Although the automation experience of the other customers does not say so much about the amount of information the customers can provide about the behavior of the supplier, it does at least give an indication of the value of information obtained from these customers. Therefore, a variable for INDEGREE is constructed by summing the automation experience of the other customers, weighted by the frequency of contacts between the buyer and the other customers. The importance of the other customers gives an indication of the potential sanctions for the supplier if such customers would be informed by the buyer about untrustworthiness of the supplier. The OUTDEGREE variable is constructed by summing over the importance of the other customers, again weighted by the contact frequency between the buyer and the other customers.[12] Because information about the contact frequencies among the other customers is available, outdegrees and indegrees can be calculated for the other customers as well.[13] Theoretically, density is the average of all outdegrees or all indegrees and these two averages should be the same. However, due to the fact that the variables for outdegree and indegree as proposed here are not reciprocal concepts, the average of the values for both variables over all customers are not the same. I use the average of the outdegrees of all customers and the buyer as a variable for DENSITY because the outdegrees are more related to the communication and sanction opportunities among the customers than the indegrees, which are more related to automation experience. For buyers who did not know any other customers, INDEGREE, OUTDEGREE, and DENSITY are defined as 0. An additional variable NETWORK DUMMY is used for the analyses. NETWORK DUMMY is 0 if buyers did not know any other customer of the supplier and 1 if they did.

There are various problems with the variables INDEGREE, OUTDEGREE, and DENSITY. First, only about half the buyers reported knowing the supplier's other customers and only about 10% completed a whole network with four other customers. Therefore, the network effects have to be tested in addition to the effect of whether the respondent knew any other customer at all. This does not need to be a problem but it reduces the number of cases for testing an effect of the extent of network embeddedness drastically. Second, INDEGREE, OUTDEGREE, and DENSITY are highly correlated (above 0.82) even if only the cases with a network are included. Third, DENSITY is especially problematic because it is well-known that most actors in a network do not have an accurate view of their ego-centered network (see, for example, Bernard, Killworth, and Sailer 1981). Systematic biases have been found in individual views of networks (Freeman 1992; Kumbasar, Romney, and Batchelder 1994). For example, actors often consider themselves

[12]Of course, more important customers can also provide more information about the behavior of the supplier. Thus, indegree and outdegree are again not strictly disentangled.

[13]Note that for these other customers, the ego-centered network of the buyer does not suffice to obtain reliable measures.

to be more central in a network than is, in fact, the case. Still, knowledge about such biases is limited and it is almost impossible to obtain reliable network data from one individual observation. Moreover, in this case one respondent answers a network question about the contacts of a whole firm, which will be even more problematic. Finally, for an accurate density measure one should not only know the supplier's customers known by the buyer, but also the supplier's customers who are linked through indirect paths to the buyer, and again all the ties between those customers. These data are not available. However, it may be that *perceptions* of buyers about their network have an effect on behavior (Krackhardt 1987) rather than their *actual* networks. Because the proposed measure is the best density measure I could derive directly from the questionnaire, I will test whether DENSITY has the predicted negative effect on SAFEGUARDS. The measurement problems are probably even larger for other network parameters such as transitivity and centralization. Since effects of these network parameters are also much smaller theoretically, I do not operationalize them.

Given these measurement problems, I construct two additional indicators for the density of the network of the buyer and the supplier. The first indicator is SECTOR DENSITY of the buyer's sector of industry. In the description of the stratification criteria in MAT95, I have already mentioned that experts were asked to rate the sectors of industry with respect to interfirm relations and the extent to which sector-specific meetings were organized in which the employees and managers of firms within the sector meet each other. About 20 experts estimated the network density of sectors at a scale from 1 to 10. The average of these estimates was used as a density measure.[14] Unfortunately, the variance in the experts' estimates was considerable and some experts indicated that networks within sectors sometimes cannot be considered as homogeneous. Moreover, SECTOR DENSITY does not include contacts of buyers between different sectors. Therefore, I will not consider SECTOR DENSITY as a very precise measure for density. There are only 20 missing values at this variable. For these cases the variable is given a value 6, which is about the average value.

The second indicator for density is an estimate of the geographical DISTANCE between municipalities in which the buyer and the supplier are located.[15] The use of DISTANCE as an indicator for the density of a network among firms is based on the assumption that there is a higher probability for firms located closer together to have ties to common third parties and, also, that these third

[14]Alternatively, the average of the z-scores of the experts per sector could be used, assuming that comparisons between experts might be similar although their scales differ. Moreover, I checked whether some experts gave estimates that differed much from other experts and whether these, therefore, should be left out. In this way, some alternative measures were obtained, but results with these alternative measures did hardly differ from the results presented here.

[15]For suppliers outside the Netherlands (14 cases), DISTANCE is given a value equal to the maximal value obtained for suppliers in the Netherlands.

parties have more contacts among each other. Nohria (1992, see page 26 above) argues that partners in close proximity to each other are often preferred partners, especially because of the embeddedness argument.[16] Only 39 missings occur for this variable. For those cases, the variable is given a value 3, which is slightly above the average for this variable.

TRANSACTION CHARACTERISTICS

I use five variables constructed from the questionnaire to operationalize the transaction characteristics distinguished in the introduction of this chapter: financial volume of the transaction, number of components included in the product, complexity of the product, dependence of the buyer on the supplier, and monitoring problems of the buyer. Some of these variables are also used by Batenburg et al. (2002).

One question measured the financial volume of the transaction using a five-point scale (question 1.4). The answer categories consisted of price classes for the amount of money the buyer paid the supplier for the transaction. The logarithm of the midpoints of the price classes of the five categories is used as the actual variable VOLUME (divided by NLG 100,000). An estimate has to be made for the last category, because this category does not have an upperbound on the money paid for the transaction. Consequently, the first category obtains a value $\log(0.125)$, and the following categories $\log(0.375)$, $\log(0.75)$, $\log(1.5)$, and $\log(3.5)$, respectively. The logarithm is taken because it is assumed that an additional unit of money is less important given that the amount of money is larger.

The variables for the number of components and complexity of the product are both derived from a question about the components that were included in the product are indicated (question 1.2). Eighteen possible components could be selected, including the kind of software, the kind of hardware, and the additional services that were delivered by the supplier. A principal components analysis of these eighteen variables results in two well-interpretable dimensions, namely, a first dimension with positive factor loadings for all variables indicating the number of components included in the product (COMPONENTS), and a second dimension with negative factor loadings for standard components and positive factor loadings for more complex components (COMPLEXITY). Table 5.2 presents the results of the principal components analysis.

A combination of questions measuring the importance for the buyer of obtaining a well-functioning product is used for the operationalization of the dependence of the buyer on the supplier (questions 1.6a, 1.6b, 1.10, 1.12a–1.12c, and 1.13a–1.13d). The categories of all questions are coded from 1 to 5. As

[16] It might be questioned whether the assumption of more mutual contacts still holds if both firms are situated in large cities such as Amsterdam. However, in additional analyses, I did not find indications that the effects found differ for firms located in large cities.

Table 5.2. Principal components analysis for COMPONENTS and COMPLEXITY (893 transactions).

Variable[a]	COMPONENTS	COMPLEXITY
Standard software	0.10	−0.15
Adjusted software	0.16	0.13
Tailor-made software	0.19	0.18
Sector-specific software	0.15	0.14
Personal computers	0.03	−0.50
Workstation	0.26	−0.22
Network configuration	0.20	−0.41
Mini computer	0.18	0.19
Mainframe	0.11	0.05
Computer-controlled machines	0.05	0.15
Side equipment	0.28	−0.32
Cabling	0.30	−0.38
Design	0.22	0.12
Training	0.29	0.19
Instruction	0.33	0.18
Consultation	0.32	0.03
Documentation	0.32	0.21
Support	0.37	0.10
Fraction of total variance	0.21	0.09

[a] These variables do not include any missings.

the variable DEPENDENCE, I use the first component in a principal components analysis that includes all answers, also from cases that have missings at some of the variables (see Table 5.3). The analysis suggests that there is one major component underlying the variables used.

The variable MONITORING PROBLEMS is operationalized in a similar way as DEPENDENCE. MONITORING PROBLEMS consists of two sub-components. First, the ability of the buyer to judge the product and compare it with other products (questions 1.7, 2.8, 2.9, and 2.10). The second sub-component comprises the buyer's automation experience and availability of automation employees within the firm (questions 1.8, 1.15, 6.3aa, and 6.3ab). Because not all variables in the principal components analysis are at the same scale, the standardized values for the variables are included in a principal components analysis. The principal components analysis suggests that one major component underlies these variables (see Table 5.4). The variables related to automation experience of the buyer have negative factor loadings because an increase in experience decreases monitoring problems.

Table 5.3. Principal components analysis for DEPENDENCE (893 transactions).

Variable	Question	Loading	Missing[a]
Importance			
of product for automation of buyer	1.6a	0.21	0
of product for profitability of buyer	1.6b	0.22	29
of timely delivery	1.10	0.25	2
of durability of product	1.12a	0.15	1
of support by supplier	1.12b	0.22	5
of compatibility product	1.12c	0.12	4
Damage from malfunctioning in terms of			
investment costs	1.13a	0.43	3
costs of training personnel	1.13b	0.40	5
costs of data entry	1.13c	0.47	6
costs of idle production	1.13d	0.45	12
Fraction of total variance explained by first factor		0.37	

[a] Principal components analysis is applied here using the Expectation-Maximization algorithm to avoid deletion of observations with missing values (Weesie and Van Houwelingen 1983). Factor scores are obtained for all observations for which at least one variable is not missing.

Table 5.4. Principal components analysis for MONITORING PROBLEMS (893 transactions).

Variable	Question	Loading	Missing[a]
Difficulty of judging quality product	1.7	0.43	1
Experience buyer with automation	1.8	−0.28	4
Buyer's possibility of making or adapt product	1.15	−0.03	1
Difficulty of comparing tenders	2.8	0.48	258
Difficulty of comparing product and alternatives	2.9	0.50	14
Difficulty of comparing price-quality relation	2.10	0.49	15
Automation employees/division of the buyer[b]	6.3ab, bb	−0.10	0
Fraction of total variance explained by first factor		0.42	

[a] Principal components analysis is applied here using the Expectation-Maximization algorithm to avoid deletion of observations with missing values (Weesie and Van Houwelingen 1983). Factor scores are obtained for all observations for which at least one variable is not missing.

[b] This variable is coded 1 if the buyer has automation specialists in the firm, coded 2 if the buyer has a specialized automation division, and coded 0 otherwise.

COSTS OF CONTRACTING FOR THE BUYER

Three variables are used as indicators for the costs of contracting for the buyer. The first variable indicates the extent to which negotiating and contracting procedures are standardized by the buyer (question 4.20). On the one hand, standardization could increase efficiency in contracting procedures and, therefore, decrease the costs of contracting. On the other hand, standardization could cause unnecessary clauses to be part of the contract only because they are part of the procedures. Both arguments suggest that SAFEGUARDS increases with STANDARDIZATION. The 44 missings for this variable are given a value 2, which is slightly below the average value for this variable. The second variable is based on two questions about the legal expertise of the buyer (question 6.3ac,bc). The variable is operationalized as a dummy variable that is coded 1 if the buyer has employees with legal expertise or a specialized division on legal issues and 0 otherwise. If the buyer has legal expertise, writing contracts will be less costly than in the situation where the buyer does not have legal expertise because experts do not need to be hired from outside the firm. Therefore, SAFEGUARDS is expected to increase with LEGAL EXPERTISE. The third variable is a dummy variable that indicates whether the contract is a modified form of a previous contract or not. A previous contract could contain issues that are not directly relevant for the new transaction, but can be kept in the new contract without additional costs. Thus, I expect that modified versions of a previous contract contain more SAFEGUARDS. Missings at PREVIOUS CONTRACT are set to 0 assuming that if a respondent does not say anything about a previous contract there will be no previous contract.

FIRM CHARACTERISTICS

Finally, two firm characteristics are included in the analyses that could have an influence on SAFEGUARDS. These are the size of the supplier and the size of the buyer. I do not have direct hypotheses based on the theory developed in the earlier chapters for these variables. Respondents were asked to estimate the size of the supplier in terms of the number of employees using a five-point scale (question 3.2). This five-point scale is directly used as the variable SIZE SUPPLIER. Missings are imputed using a question about whether the supplier is a retailer, part of an international concern or another description that gives an indication for the size of the supplier. The logarithm of the number of employees at the time of the transaction reported by the respondent (question 6.1b) is used for SIZE BUYER. Missings are imputed using the logarithm of the number of employees at the time of the questionnaire (question 6.1a).

5.2.3 SUMMARY STATISTICS OF THE VARIABLES

Before the explanatory analyses, I present summary statistics of the variables used. This makes the interpretation of effects in the following section easier and allows the effects to be compared. It should be noted that COMPONENTS, COMPLEXITY, DEPENDENCE, and MONITORING PROBLEMS are standardized factor scores. The 893 cases that are used in the analyses are included in the overview of the summary statistics. The correlations among the network vari-

Table 5.5. Summary statistics of the key variables (893 observations, all missing values imputed).

Variable	Mean	Standard deviation	Minimum	Maximum
SAFEGUARDS	24.29	11.12	0	48
PAST	1.65	1.85	0	5
FUTURE	2.79	1.38	1	5
OUTDEGREE	2.86	3.41	0	18.91
INDEGREE	1.44	2.16	0	13.73
DENSITY	2.84	3.30	0	16.81
DEGREE	1.34	1.34	0	7
SECTOR DENSITY	6.15	0.74	4.20	8
DISTANCE	2.61	1.32	0	4.84
VOLUME	−0.72	1.21	−2.08	1.25
COMPONENTS[a]	0	1	−1.29	2.98
COMPLEXITY[a]	0	1	−2.60	2.82
DEPENDENCE[a]	0	1	−2.56	2.58
MONITORING PROBLEMS[a]	0	1	−2.42	2.93
STANDARDIZATION	2.49	1.16	1	5
LEGAL EXPERTISE	0.20	0.40	0	1
PREVIOUS CONTRACT	0.19	0.39	0	1
SIZE SUPPLIER	3.34	1.43	1	5
SIZE BUYER	3.66	1.04	0	7.82

[a] These variables are standardized factor scores.

ables DENSITY, INDEGREE, and OUTDEGREE are all very high (0.88, 0.99, and 0.92). Other correlations between independent variables are generally low (always below 0.5). Relatively large correlations occur between the transaction characteristics. Also PAST and FUTURE are quite highly correlated (0.45), which could indicate that expectations of the future are largely based on past transactions.

5.2.4 HYPOTHESES

In Chapters 3 and 4, hypotheses about trust have been formulated in terms of theoretical variables. Here, I repeat the hypotheses that will be tested in the next section in terms of the empirical variables used to operationalize the theoretical variables. In Table 5.6, the hypotheses about the effects of the independent variables on SAFEGUARDS are presented. References are provided to the theoretical hypotheses and the pages where the main reasoning underlying a hypothesis or the theoretical deduction of an effect can be found.

The interaction effects of FUTURE and the network variables are somewhat problematic because FUTURE is a combination of the expected duration of the relation between buyer and supplier and the costs of sanctions for the trustee. Because the theoretical hypotheses on interaction effects of expected duration and costs of sanctions with (OUT)DEGREE are both positive, the interaction effect of FUTURE with (OUT)DEGREE is expected to be positive. Since the interaction effects with density are in opposite directions, however, the hypotheses about the interaction effects of (SECTOR) DENSITY and DISTANCE with FUTURE are uncertain. An indication about the most suitable interpretation of FUTURE can be obtained if an interaction effect with (SECTOR) DENSITY or DISTANCE is found. If this interaction effect is negative, the interpretation of FUTURE related to the duration of the relation is more plausible, while a positive interaction effect would make the sanction interpretation more plausible.

There are a few hypotheses that could not be derived from the models in Chapters 3 and 4, because they are related to "incomplete information" assumptions that are not included in the game-theoretic model and because they do not address network effects. Of course, the effect of a (positive) PAST with a supplier is similar to the effect of INDEGREE. If positive information about the supplier is obtained, SAFEGUARDS is expected to decrease, regardless of whether the information is obtained from own experiences with the supplier or from the experiences of other customers in the network. It is known from the data that the effect of PAST on SAFEGUARDS can be expected to be negative because only a very few buyers report negative experiences with their suppliers. Similarly, a negative effect is expected from INDEGREE because almost all buyers reported that the supplier had a positive reputation at the time of the focal transaction.

I argued in the introduction to this chapter that if there is a possibility that a supplier ever delivers an inferior product, it is plausible that DEPENDENCE has a positive effect on SAFEGUARDS. Moreover, if the costs of contracting would be zero, I would have no argument as to why not all possible safeguards are used if trust between buyer and supplier is limited. Consequently, the larger the costs of contracting for the buyer, the smaller the optimal number of safeguards will be. Additional theory on contracting in transactions with incomplete information suggests that the negative effect of FUTURE will not be found in a first transaction between a buyer and a supplier, but mainly in later transactions (see Batenburg et al. 2002; Raub 1998). To test this hypothesis, the interaction effect between PAST and FUTURE is included. In the discussion section, I will treat this hypothesis more elaborately.

In principle, the hypothesis that the relative effect of OUTDEGREE compared to DENSITY decreases with the incentive to abuse trust and increases with future (Hypothesis 3.17) can be tested. However, the somewhat disappointing results for the main effects and interaction effects of the network variables shown below make testing these even more complex hypotheses superfluous.

Table 5.6. Hypotheses on effects on SAFEGUARDS.

Independent variable	Sign related to hypothesis	Theoretical hypothesis[a]	Page reference[b]
TEMPORAL EMBEDDEDNESS			
PAST	−	see text	10
FUTURE	−	3.4	68
NETWORK EMBEDDEDNESS			
(OUT)DEGREE	−	3.8, 4.1	79, 113
(IN)DEGREE	−	4.6	120
(SECTOR) DENSITY	−	3.7, 4.3	79, 113
DISTANCE	+	3.7, 4.3	79, 113
TRANSACTION CHARACTERISTICS			
VOLUME	+	3.2	68
COMPONENTS	+	3.2	68
COMPLEXITY	+	3.2	68
DEPENDENCE	+	see text	9
MONITORING PROBLEMS	+	3.1	68
COSTS OF CONTRACTS FOR THE BUYER			
STANDARDIZATION	+	see text	129
LEGAL EXPERTISE	+	see text	129
PREVIOUS CONTRACT	+	see text	129
INTERACTION EFFECTS			
PAST × FUTURE	−	see text	13
FUTURE × (OUT)DEGREE	+	3.13, 3.16	79
FUTURE × (SECTOR) DENSITY	?	3.13, 3.16	79
FUTURE × DISTANCE	?	3.13, 3.16	79
(OUT)DEGREE × (SECTOR) DENSITY	−	3.9	79
(OUT)DEGREE × DISTANCE	+	3.9	79
(OUT)DEGREE × VOLUME	+	3.14	79
(OUT)DEGREE × COMPONENTS	+	3.14	79
(OUT)DEGREE × COMPLEXITY	+	3.14	79
(OUT)DEGREE × MONITORING	+	3.14	79

[a] The hypotheses can be found in the concluding sections of Chapters 3 and 4.

[b] Page references are to tables or theorems. If hypotheses are only discussed in the text, references are to the appropriate discussions.

5.3 ANALYSES

5.3.1 METHODS

The analyses shown below are all linear regression models with Huber standard errors that are modified for clustering of transactions within buyers (Huber 1967; Rogers 1993). The adjustment for clustering is necessary because some buyers answered the questionnaire for two transactions. Another option to account for clustering of observations would be to model the multi-level structure explicitly by including residual terms both at the level of the transaction and at the level of the buyer. Multi-level models demonstrate that about the same amount of variance in SAFEGUARDS can be attributed to the buyers as to the transactions. However, the substantive results from the multi-level models are not different from the regression models as far as the effects of the independent variables are concerned. Therefore, I do not present the multi-level analyses below. Strictly speaking, there is also clustering of transactions within suppliers, because some buyers are customers of the same supplier. Because only the name and municipality of the supplier are known, it is not always self-evident which suppliers can be considered the same. For example, if a respondent only mentions IBM in Amsterdam as the supplier, it can be that she did business with IBM headquarters or she bought an IBM computer from a retailer. If I consider suppliers whose name and municipality are the same to be the same supplier, it appears that a relatively small number of suppliers occur more than once in the data, and a couple of suppliers occur more than ten times in the data.[17] A multi-level model based on clustering of transactions within suppliers results in a zero estimate for the variance of the residual term at the supplier level. Moreover, the effects for the independent variables do not change when compared to the straightforward regression model.[18]

A number of specification tests are performed for the regression models. First, tests on heteroscedasticity of residuals give only slight indications that the size of residuals depends on independent variables. A weak relation is found between the density of the sector of the buyers and the variance in the residuals. However, in a regression model with multiplicative heteroscedasticity (see Section 4.4), in which the log-variance of the residuals is modeled with SECTOR DENSITY, the effect of SECTOR DENSITY on the log-variance is not significant. Second, a Box-Cox analysis demonstrates that a transformation of the dependent variable fits the data slightly better than the linear model. The substantial interpretation of the regression on the transformed dependent variable resembles the results of the regression on the untransformed dependent vari-

[17] In 893 transactions, 517 suppliers occur only once in the data set, 80 suppliers occur twice, 23 occur three times, 20 occur between four and ten times, and 3 occur more than ten times.

[18] Because the discussed multi-level analyses did not change substantive results, I did not perform "cross-classified" analyses that simultaneously account for clustering among buyers and suppliers.

able, indicating that the transformation is not necessary. Third, non-linearities in the effects of the independent variables are checked using quadratic terms of variables at an interval scale and dummies for each value of ordinal variables. Only two small deviations from linearity are found. Namely, for MONITORING PROBLEMS, a small second-order effect is found and, for STANDARDIZATION, the effect of one value deviates from a linear trend over the different values. Again, controlling for these small deviations from linearity does not change the results substantively. Therefore, only the linear effects are shown below. Fourth, several diagnostic tests are performed to check whether there are influential cases or outliers. Special attention was given to cases (45 cases in the set of 893 cases) where some variables are imputed in a rather ad-hoc manner such as SECTOR DENSITY, DISTANCE, and STANDARDIZATION. However, there are no indications that cases have to be removed from the data to prevent undesirable influences or outlier effects.

5.3.2 TESTS OF THE HYPOTHESES

From earlier analyses of Batenburg et al. (2002) on the same data, it is known that transaction characteristics are the main predictors for *investments* in pre-contractual negotiations and contracting. I expect that the transaction characteristics are important predictors for SAFEGUARDS as well. Model 1 of Table 5.7 contains only the transaction characteristics, variables for costs of contracting for the buyer, and firm characteristics. In this way, an indication is obtained about the additional contribution of temporal and network embeddedness to the explanation of SAFEGUARDS in the subsequent models.

The results for Model 1 demonstrate that VOLUME, COMPONENTS, COMPLEXITY, DEPENDENCE, and MONITORING PROBLEMS have positive effects on SAFEGUARDS. Thus, the hypotheses about the transaction characteristics are supported. Moreover, SAFEGUARDS increases with STANDARDIZATION. Thus, the hypothesis about STANDARDIZATION is supported. A weak effect is found for LEGAL EXPERTISE and no effect is found for PREVIOUS CONTRACT. Consequently, the hypothesis for LEGAL EXPERTISE is weakly supported and the hypothesis for PREVIOUS CONTRACT is not supported. SIZE BUYER does not have an effect on SAFEGUARDS and SIZE SUPPLIER has a positive effect on SAFEGUARDS. I do not have a straightforward explanation for this effect. One reason could be that large suppliers probably have considerable legal expertise in their firm, and they propose relatively long contracts to their customers.

In Model 2, the two variables representing future and past aspects of temporal embeddedness are added to the analyses. PAST has a significant effect in the expected direction. Because almost all buyers who had past experiences with the supplier had positive experiences, this effect can be interpreted as a learning effect: buyers who have experienced themselves that their supplier is trustworthy trust the supplier more than buyers who do not have such experiences. Thus,

Table 5.7. Linear regression of SAFEGUARDS (893 transactions for 734 buyers).

Independent variable	Hyp.	Model 1	Model 2	Model 3	Model 4	Model 5
TEMPORAL EMBEDDEDNESS						
PAST	−		−0.92**	−0.90**	−0.91**	−0.83**
FUTURE	−		0.18	0.17	0.12	0.04
NETWORK EMBEDDEDNESS						
NETWORK DUMMY	−			2.17		
OUTDEGREE	−			−0.89		
INDEGREE	−			0.46		
DENSITY	−			0.49		
DEGREE	−				0.38*	0.47**
SECTOR DENSITY	−				−0.81	−0.72
DISTANCE	+				0.47˜	0.45˜
TRANSACTION CHARACTERISTICS						
VOLUME	+	1.67**	1.66**	1.58**	1.61**	1.66**
COMPONENTS	+	2.48**	2.51**	2.46**	2.42**	2.44**
COMPLEXITY	+	1.68**	1.57**	1.54**	1.37**	1.44**
DEPENDENCE	+	1.56**	1.49**	1.50**	1.39**	1.35**
MONITORING PROBLEMS	+	1.02**	0.75*	0.72*	0.73*	0.65˜
COSTS OF CONTRACTING FOR THE BUYER						
STANDARDIZATION	+	0.92**	0.99**	0.95**	1.00**	1.04**
LEGAL EXPERTISE	+	1.34˜	1.45˜	1.40˜	1.42*	1.31˜
PREVIOUS CONTRACT	+	0.26	1.28	1.16	1.01	1.27
FIRM CHARACTERISTICS						
SIZE SUPPLIER	?	0.89**	1.04**	1.01**	0.94**	0.93**
SIZE BUYER	?	−0.31	−0.22	−0.23	−0.33	−0.32
INTERACTION EFFECTS						
PAST × FUTURE	−					−0.19
FUTURE × DEGREE	+					−0.03
FUTURE × SECTOR DENSITY	?					−0.37
FUTURE × DISTANCE	?					0.06
DEGREE × SECTOR DENSITY	−					0.02
DEGREE × DISTANCE	+					0.08
DEGREE × VOLUME	+					−0.12
DEGREE × COMPONENTS	+					−0.12
DEGREE × COMPLEXITY	+					−0.18
DEGREE × MONITORING	+					0.10
CONSTANT		21.04	20.80	20.46	24.93	24.65
R^2		0.31	0.32	0.33	0.33	0.34

**, *, and ˜ represent two-sided significance at respectively $p < 0.01$, $p < 0.05$, and $p < 0.10$ based on Huber standard errors modified for clustering.

the hypothesis for PAST is supported. It should be noted that the effect of PAST is more than an effect of the difference between "no past" and a "positive past." The effect of PAST is almost linear indicating that "more" past induces more trust. This suggests that more (positive) information about a supplier indeed induces more trust in the supplier, which is an assumption that I used to relate the results for receiver centrality in Chapter 4 to hypotheses about trust. Contrary to my expectation, there is no support for the hypothesis on control effects of FUTURE. I have already mentioned that there are several problems with the measurement of FUTURE in the discussion of the operationalization (see page 135). Except for the obvious possibility that the theory is wrong, this could be one reason why the effect is not found. A more theoretical argument why the effect is not found is given below in the discussion of the interaction effects. PAST adds about 1.6% to the explained variance compared to Model 1. Although temporal embeddedness seems less important for explaining the SAFEGUARDS than the transaction characteristics, the significance level of the PAST effect is comparable to the effects of the transaction characteristics ($p < 0.001$) with the exception of MONITORING PROBLEMS, which has a slightly lower significance level.

In Model 3, the network variables based on the network of at most four other customers of the supplier are added. A dummy variable that indicates whether a buyer knew any other customers is included. The other network variables are also equal to 0 for all the cases where the buyer did not know any other customer. Consequently, the network variables in this model are highly correlated. By adding the dummy variable, the other network variables measure the additional effect of a certain structural property of the network on top of the effect that the buyer knows any other customers. The hypotheses for OUTDEGREE, INDEGREE, and DENSITY are not supported. Even if the variables are added one by one to the analysis of Model 2, no effects are found. However, as I already discussed in the operationalization section, the manner in which the network was measured in the questionnaire is not unproblematic. This could be an important reason why the hypotheses about these network variables are not supported.

Model 4 shows the effects of three other network variables, namely, DEGREE, SECTOR DENSITY, and DISTANCE. Although the effect of the global network variable SECTOR DENSITY is in the expected direction and close to the 5% significance level in a one-sided test, the effect is small and does not provide real support for the density hypothesis. The effect of the other global network variable DISTANCE is stronger and in the expected direction. The most important problem with DISTANCE is that it is not only interpretable as a network effect. It might be argued that it is easier to solve a problem with a supplier who is a neighbor than with a supplier whose residence is far away. Thus, it will be less costly to have a problem with a neighbor. This reasoning implies that trust does not increase with DISTANCE, but that the costs for the buyer if trust is abused increase with DISTANCE. This last explanation is certainly not an explanation based on network embeddedness.[19] Even if the network explanation is accepted, it cannot be said whether this is a control or a learning effect. A buyer can have more information about a supplier in the neighborhood. But, also, a supplier in the neighborhood can be easier and more effectively sanctioned than a supplier who resides further away. The network variable DEGREE is the only individual network variable in Model 4. DEGREE has a significant effect, but in the opposite direction to the one expected. Therefore, it seems as if the hypotheses about indegree and outdegree are rejected. Below, I will investigate this effect more carefully and show that this conclusion is somewhat premature. The effects of the network variables are all relatively small compared to the effects of transaction characteristics and PAST. Moreover, the DEGREE effect is in the wrong direction. Consequently, the network effects hardly explain any variation in the contracts in addition to the other variables included in the model.

To reach Model 4, I have added groups of variables to the model sequentially. However, this is not a "fair" comparison for comparing the predictive power of different groups of variables, if the groups of variables are not orthogonal. The same parts of the variance in SAFEGUARDS may be explained by different groups of independent variables. Using the method of sequentially adding groups of variables, the groups of variables added last have a "disadvantage," because a part of the variance they explain may already be explained by a group of variables that has been added earlier. Furthermore, significant effects that reject the theory should not be included in comparing the predictive power of (groups of) variables, because the theory clearly does not have any predictive power for these variables.

To obtain an additional indication of the predictive power of the different groups of variables in Model 4, I first remove DEGREE from the model. Thereafter, I remove all the groups of variables from the analysis separately and compare the decrease in explained variance due to the omission of each group of variables. Simultaneously, I test whether removing a group of variables causes a significant reduction in the explanatory power of the model. The explained variance decreases with 1.6% if PAST and FUTURE are removed from the analyses. These variables contribute significantly to the model. This contribution is mainly due to the PAST effect. The explained variance decreases with 0.6% if the network variables DISTANCE and SECTOR DENSITY are removed. The contribution of these variables is hardly significant ($p = 0.051$). The

[19]Other studies have also found negative effects of geographical distance on trust. Lorenz (1988: 207) finds in a more qualitative manner that geographical distance has a negative effect on trust, but he presents an alternative explanation: "Invariably interviewees stressed the need for personal contact, and a number of firms stated that geographical proximity was desirable because it facilitated this." Lyons (1994) finds a positive effect of geographical distance between a subcontractor and his customer in the engineering industry on the probability that they govern their relationship with a formal contract.

transaction characteristics are clearly the most important variables to explain SAFEGUARDS. If they are removed, the explained variance decreases with 18.2%. The variables for costs of contracting for the buyer and the firm characteristics do not add considerably to the explained variance. Removing these two groups of variables decreases the explained variance with 1.7% and 1.1% respectively. However, both groups of variables contribute significantly to the model.[20]

Finally, the interaction effects are added in Model 5. The results are not very encouraging. The interaction effects together do not make any significant improvement to the model. None of the interaction effects with network variables are significant and, therefore, all the related hypotheses are not supported. The indirect measurement for network embeddedness via SECTOR DENSITY and DISTANCE might be one reason for this. The fact that the main effect of DEGREE is in the wrong direction demonstrates that this variable needs further investigation. This will be done in the next section.

I do not find a negative interaction effect between past and future as was found by Batenburg et al. (2002). The theoretical argument for this effect (see also Raub 1996, 1998) is as follows. Investments in the management of transactions can be used in more transactions if more future transactions are expected. Therefore, investments in managing the focal transaction are more attractive if more future transactions are expected. Together with the control argument for future transactions, the total effect of future transactions is then indeterminate. However, if a positive past exists in a relation between buyer and supplier, the initial investments in management have already been made in previous transactions and, therefore, the need for safeguards is decreased. This implies that only the control argument for future transactions remains after positive past experiences. These arguments predict a negative interaction effect between PAST and FUTURE. Although these arguments provide an explanation why I do not find a main effect of FUTURE, it is still questionable why no effect of FUTURE is found for the transactions with a positive past. In addition to the problematic measurement of FUTURE mentioned before, a reason can be that buyers are more concerned with their own outcomes than with the outcomes of the supplier (see Snijders 1996: 99). I find that buyers are concerned with the incentive for the supplier to abuse trust in the focal transactions. This can be seen from the effects of the transaction characteristics. However, as far as *future* sanction opportunities are concerned, the effects are not found. One interaction effect is found that is not hypothesized, namely, an interaction between FUTURE and DEPENDENCE. This interaction has a negative effect, indicating that the

[20] Of course, the importance of effects for the explained variance does not only depend on the "theoretical" importance of groups of variables, but also on the quality of the measurement of variables. The measurement problems mentioned for FUTURE and the network variables are expected to explain to some extent the large difference between the predictive power of transaction characteristics and embeddedness variables.

buyers are less concerned about their dependence and, thus, about their potential loss if trust would be abused, if they expect more transactions in the future. If DEPENDENCE could also be considered as a measure for the expected duration of the relation of the buyer with the supplier, this interaction effect may be interpreted as support for Hypothesis 3.5 and, more specifically, for the interaction effect between expected duration of the relation and costs of sanctions for the trustee.

5.3.3 INTERPRETATION OF THE NETWORK EFFECTS

In this subsection, I discuss some explanations for the limited support for the network hypotheses. The main emphasis will be on the unexpected positive effect of DEGREE on SAFEGUARDS, but some arguments are certainly applicable to other network effects as well. Using additional arguments based on restrictions of the theory, the data, and the statistical models, I try to demonstrate that the evidence in the foregoing section is certainly not strong enough to reject my theory. The arguments given in this subsection will be translated in hypotheses and some of them can be tested with the available data. It has to be clear that the main aim of the arguments presented here is *not* to "save" the theory, but to give suggestions for improvements of the theory, for alternative statistical models, and for improvements of future data collections. The arguments address the following topics:

- the endogeneity of DEGREE,
- unmeasured variance in the trust problem that may correlate with DEGREE,
- selectivity of the set of transactions in the sample compared to the set of potential transactions, and
- the concern of suppliers with respect to well-embedded customers.

ENDOGENEITY OF DEGREE

One reason why the relation between DEGREE and SAFEGUARDS is positive could be that degree, and network ties in general, are not static but change over time. If a buyer wants to buy a product, she will search for information about this product and possible suppliers for the product. As a by-product of this process, she gets acquainted with other buyers of the product. This effect is expected to increase with the size or importance of the product.[21] The data indeed show a positive correlation between VOLUME and the time buyers spent in finding a suitable product. Furthermore, investments in this search are positively related to DEGREE. Also, other variables are related to the number of the supplier's customers a buyer knows. If a buyer knows the supplier from earlier transactions,

[21] Blumberg (1997: Section 2.3) presents a theoretical framework for the explanation of investments in search activities.

Table 5.8. Linear regression of DEGREE (893 transactions for 734 buyers).

Independent variable	Conjecture	Model 1	Model 2
PAST	+	0.18**	0.18**
SIZE SUPPLIER	+	0.16**	0.11*
SIZE BUYER	?	0.05	0.05
NETWORK ACTIVITIES	+	0.16**	0.16**
TIME SPENT IN SEARCH	+	0.21**	0.12˜
FORMAL SEARCH	0	−0.17	−0.30
INFORMAL SEARCH	+	1.46**	1.49**
EXTENSIVE SEARCH	?	−0.03	0.00
INTENSIVE SEARCH	0	0.14**	0.13*
VOLUME	?		0.07
COMPONENTS	?		0.11
COMPLEXITY	?		0.14*
DEPENDENCE	?		0.07
MONITORING PROBLEMS	?		−0.02
CONSTANT		−0.31	0.05
R^2		0.14	0.16

**, *, and˜represent two-sided significance at respectively $p < 0.01$, $p < 0.05$, and $p < 0.10$, based on Huber standard errors modified for clustering.

she tends to know more other customers of the supplier. And, if the supplier is larger, he probably has more customers, which increases the probability that a buyer knows some of these customers.

Table 5.8 shows a linear regression of the discussed variables on DEGREE. There are some new variables in the analyses. NETWORK ACTIVITIES is a measure for the time employees of a buyer spend on fairs, seminars, congresses, meetings, the Lions or Rotary Club, associations, and so on. TIME SPENT IN SEARCH is the number of men-days the buyer spent in searching and selecting a product and supplier. FORMAL SEARCH is a count of search activities including search through data-bases, fairs, congresses, and sector associations. INFORMAL SEARCH refers to a number of different search activities involving colleagues, friends, family, for example. EXTENSIVE SEARCH is an indication of the number of suppliers a buyer approached to select one supplier. INTENSIVE SEARCH is a measure for the specificity and detail of the tenders the buyer received from potential suppliers. The different search activities are distinguished because a relation with DEGREE is expected especially for INFORMAL SEARCH and to a lesser extent for the TIME SPENT IN SEARCH and for EXTENSIVE SEARCH. No effects are expected of FORMAL SEARCH and INTENSIVE SEARCH on DEGREE.

Model 1 in Table 5.8 shows that a buyer who has done business more frequently with the supplier knows more other customers of this supplier. Moreover, buyers tend to know more other customers of larger suppliers. As could be expected, a buyer who is more active in network activities knows more of her supplier's customers. Buyers who spent more time in searching and selecting a product and supplier know more other customers of the chosen supplier. In particular, buyers who search for the supplier through informal channels know more other customers. FORMAL SEARCH and EXTENSIVE SEARCH are not related to the number of customers the buyer knows. The most surprising result of this analysis is the result for INTENSIVE SEARCH. Buyers who obtained more explicit and detailed tenders know more other customers of the chosen supplier. It is clear that this is not a direct causal effect. However, it suggests that the buyer makes sure that she knows other customers in transactions in which she carefully selects her supplier. Therefore, it could be the case that the coefficient for INTENSIVE SEARCH becomes smaller if I would control for transaction characteristics. However, Model 2 demonstrates that the effect of INTENSIVE SEARCH is hardly affected by the addition of the five transaction characteristics to Model 1, and only COMPLEXITY has a significant effect on DEGREE.

The analyses reported in Table 5.8 clearly show that some variables that have an influence on SAFEGUARDS are correlated with DEGREE. Of course, this need not explain the positive DEGREE effect. However, networks change over time and they change while buyers are searching for the product they want to buy. This implies that a model about the effect of DEGREE on trust or SAFEGUARDS should simultaneously reflect the effects of other variables on the network and the effects on the contract. This could be done, for example, with structural equation models or simultaneous regression models. In such a model, at least three (types of) endogenous variables should be included. First, SAFEGUARDS as a dependent variable is explained by transaction characteristics, temporal embeddedness, and network embeddedness. Second, search as a dependent variable is explained by temporal embeddedness and transaction characteristics. Third, network embeddedness as a dependent variable is explained by temporal embeddedness and search activities. Firm characteristics may be added as explanatory variables for all dependent variables. Unfortunately, the theory developed in this book does not suffice to provide predictions for such a structural equation model. A rigorous theory about the relations in the model is necessary before strong statements can be made on the basis of such a model. In general, it is not a problem to find a structural equation model for which the data fit fairly well. However, interpreting the associations in such a model as causal relations demands a convincing theory (see, for example, Bollen 1989: Chapter 3). Such extended theoretical investigations are beyond the scope of this book.

UNMEASURED VARIANCE IN THE TRUST PROBLEM

The explanation of the positive effect of INTENSIVE SEARCH on DEGREE suggests a second argument for the DEGREE effect. The explicitness of tenders is a straightforward measure of how detailed the buyer's search has been. The relation between INTENSIVE SEARCH and DEGREE indicates that DEGREE is related to the extent to which a partner searches for a good product. Because this effect is still strong after controlling for transaction characteristics, I suspect that DEGREE measures a part of the trust problem that has not yet been measured by the transaction characteristics. It is indeed true that if INTENSIVE SEARCH is added to Model 4 in Table 5.7, the coefficient for DEGREE decreases from 0.38 to 0.33 and the significance level falls below the 5% level. Thus, although no support is found for the hypotheses about outdegree and indegree, this additional analysis indicates that the hypotheses should not be rejected outright.

The problem addressed above may be related to the research design. The stratification criterion on complexity of the product caused considerable variance in the type of products and the related trust problems within the data set. Of course, this is important in finding effects of transaction characteristics on trust. The results for transaction characteristics confirm that this aim is attained. However, network embeddedness is a much more problematic stratification criterion, because the expert ratings of sectors of industry did not provide a clear division in high-density and low-density sectors. Moreover, SECTOR DENSITY is a variable at the level of the sector and not a characteristic of the buyer. The correlation between SECTOR DENSITY and DEGREE is limited though significant (0.069, $p = 0.038$). It suggests that stratification on the embeddedness criterion is far from perfect. Moreover, 67% of the buyers do not know more than one of the supplier's other customers and there are relatively few buyers that are indeed well-embedded in a network with their supplier. In a setting in which most buyers are relatively unimportant for the supplier and buyers know few other buyers of the supplier, control effects can be expected to be small, because the sanction potential of these buyers via network embeddedness is limited. For future research in which the main aim is to find effects of variables related to temporal and network embeddedness, it may be preferable to limit variation in the transactions, for example, by choosing a limited number of well-comparable products. Such a design will prevent unmeasured variance in transaction characteristics obscuring embeddedness effects. Increasing variation in embeddedness variables may be difficult in a survey, although one could search for settings in which certain groups of actors are more densely organized in social networks. Experimental research is, of course, well-suited for determining beforehand the variation in independent variables. Chapter 6 describes an experiment in which embeddedness variables are the principal variables varied.

SELECTIVITY OF THE SAMPLE OF TRANSACTIONS

A third problem can be addressed, which is related to the search process. The Trust Game as discussed in Chapter 3 is a simplified representation of a transaction. As demonstrated by the brief analysis of the search process, a transaction cannot simply be represented by writing a contract with a supplier, while the number of safeguards depends on the characteristics of the trust problem. Two steps can be distinguished in a transaction. First, the buyer selects a supplier and, second, the contract is written with the chosen supplier. Many potential suppliers are *not* chosen as a partner. One reason for this may be that the basis for trust with these suppliers is too small or smaller than that with the chosen supplier. I expect that factors involving trust do not only have an effect on the contract but also on the probability that a certain supplier is chosen as a partner. Moreover, I expect that this effect increases with the size and importance of a transaction, because buyers invest a larger amount of effort in searching for larger transactions. Assuming that third-party ties with the supplier promote trust, this is an alternative explanation for the bivariate correlation between DEGREE and SAFEGUARDS in the contract(cf. Buskens et al. 2002). Furthermore, because SAFEGUARDS does not decrease with third-party ties, it seems that the presence of third-party relations, as a basis for trust, has a more important effect on the selection of a partner than on the number of safeguards in the contract.

As an illustration, Figure 5.1 shows a hypothetical situation in which embeddedness, number of safeguards in the contract, and size of a transaction are varied for a group of potential transactions. It is assumed that embeddedness partly solves the trust problem. Therefore, transactions at the right side require fewer safeguards than the corresponding transactions at the left side. Now, it is expected that, especially where large transactions are concerned, the buyer will search for partners with whom she is well-embedded. Moreover, for some potential transactions the trust problem due to the size of transaction characteristics *and* a lack of embeddedness may be simply too large to be covered by safeguards in a contract. Therefore, the probability that potential suppliers are actually chosen for a transaction is relatively small in transactions indicated by the dashed box when compared to the other boxes. This implies that in an analysis of actual transactions, which mainly includes transactions in the solid boxes, the effect of embeddedness will be underestimated if the analysis is not adjusted for selectivity of actual transactions compared to the whole set of potential transactions.[22]

In principle, biases of estimates in regression models due to selection related to the dependent variable can be addressed with sample selection models

[22]It should be noted that the same argument can be applied to all independent variables that are used to predict SAFEGUARDS. However, for variables with relatively small effects, the problem is most severe because these effects can become insignificant although they are only slightly underestimated.

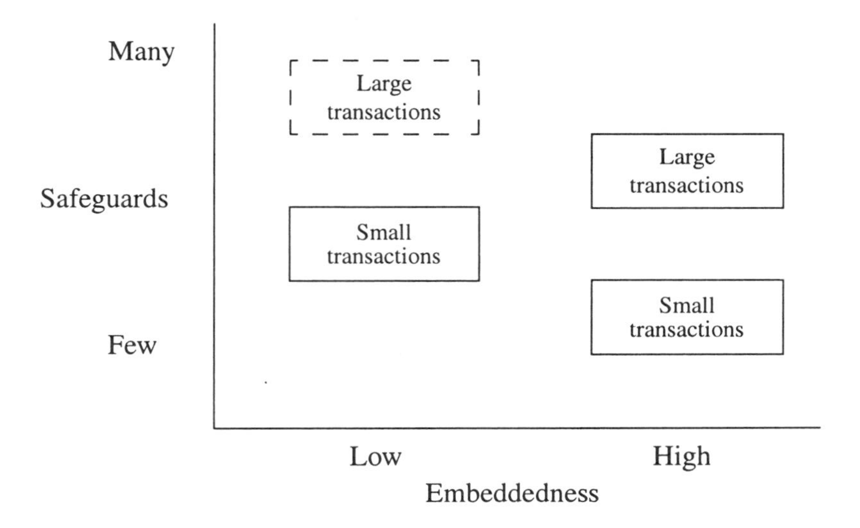

Figure 5.1. Selectivity in the sample of transactions.

(Maddala 1983: Chapter 9). However, because I do not have any information about potential transactions that did not occur and I do not have good predictors for the probability that a certain transaction is included in the model or not (except for the predictors of SAFEGUARDS), sample selection models cannot be reasonably used here. Results would depend quite strongly on the parametric form that lacks a sound theoretical basis. Still, the effect of INTENSIVE SEARCH on DEGREE is an indication that buyers prefer suppliers with whom they already have some third-party contacts. Other empirical research (Nohria 1992; Gulati 1995a, 1995b) confirms that the presence of third-party relationships increases the probability that two firms cooperate. In future research, it can be useful to obtain more information about suppliers that are not selected for a transaction. With data about such suppliers and the relation between these suppliers and the buyer, it may be possible to apply sample selection models.

The Position of the Supplier

Another explanation for the effect of DEGREE could be that suppliers want to write a longer contract with a well-embedded buyer. One reason for this is that the supplier realizes that his reputation can be negatively affected by a well-embedded buyer if he delivers an inferior product. The supplier cannot rule out the possibility that he fails to deliver a high-quality product due to unexpected circumstances. Such a failure is especially problematic if it has the potential to affect other customers. Thus, the supplier may require a contract with a well-embedded buyer that includes enough safeguards to prevent the buyer having strong reasons for believing that the failure is intentional. There are possibilities in the data that allow this hypothesis to be tested. It was asked in the questionnaire whether the supplier or the buyer wrote the contract. Under the assumption that it is really the supplier who causes the positive relation between DEGREE and SAFEGUARDS, it seems plausible that the effect is stronger if the contract is explicitly drafted by the supplier. Models are analyzed that included an interaction effect of DEGREE and a dummy variable indicating whether the contract was written by the supplier. The interaction effect is almost significant ($p < 0.1$), but negative, suggesting that the unexpected DEGREE effect is only found for contracts that were written by the buyer.[23] Thus, the idea that the supplier has a large impact on the contract, which is indicated by the DEGREE effect cannot be confirmed. In a sense, however, this is a fortunate finding because if such an effect had been found, this would be a major problem for considering an IT transaction as a one-sided trust problem on the buyer's part.

Although I do not find a direct indication that arguments about the supplier are important in explaining the DEGREE effect, it is certainly the case that relatively limited attention is paid to the position of the supplier in my theory and in the collection of the data. More than 80% of the contracts in the data are designed by the supplier. Of course, this does not imply that the buyer does not have any influence on these contracts, but it indicates that the considerations of the supplier also determine the contents of the contract. Moreover, the effect of SIZE SUPPLIER on SAFEGUARDS cannot be explained because no information is available about more specific properties of the supplier that might cause this effect. It cannot be denied that the supplier is confronted with a trust problem in a transaction. For example, he has to trust that the buyer will pay in time and, for example, that she does not make illegal copies of a software program. The theory should be changed considerably for treating transactions as two-sided trust problems, and exact implications of such changes are far from self-evident. For example, sanctions of buyers can be much more severe if buyers are not restricted to sanctioning the supplier by withholding trust and are allowed to abuse trust of the supplier themselves. Moreover, in order to test such a theory, data should be collected from the buyer *and* from the supplier in a transaction.

5.4 CONCLUSIONS AND DISCUSSION

This chapter has evaluated effects of temporal and network embeddedness on the number of safeguards in contracts of IT transactions. The findings for the transaction characteristics demonstrate that the number of safeguards increases with the financial volume of the product, the number of components included in the product, the complexity of the product, the dependence of the buyer on

[23] Separate analyses of cases with a contract written by the supplier and cases with a contract written by the buyer also indicate that the DEGREE effect is found only for the cases in which the buyer wrote the contract.

the supplier, and monitoring problems of the buyer. Buyers for whom writing contracts involves less costs drafted longer contracts with their suppliers. This effect is found mainly for buyers who use more standardization procedures while searching for and negotiating with suppliers.

The explanatory power of embeddedness variables turned out to be smaller than the explanatory power of transaction characteristics. The most important effect, in addition to the effects of transaction characteristics and costs of contracting, is a learning effect of (positive) prior transactions with the same supplier. Almost all buyers who had done business earlier with the same supplier had a positive past with their supplier and the number of safeguards in the contract decreases with the frequency of these positive past experiences. No control effect of temporal embeddedness is found. The expected frequency and volume of future transactions of the buyer with the same supplier are measured simultaneously in one question. And, although more frequent and more extensive future transactions should both increase trust, such an effect is not found. Additional theory on trust in situations with incomplete information suggests that the control effect will only be found in transactions for which the buyer has had positive experiences with the supplier in the past. However, the control effect is also not found for transactions with such a positive past.

Concerning network effects, I have found one (global) network effect for buyers and suppliers who are located close to each other. The fact that two partners reside close together induces more trust in these transactions, which is expressed in shorter contracts. However, whether this effect is a control or a learning effect is unclear. Buyers are expected to have more information about suppliers who are located nearby. But suppliers in the neighborhood will also be easier to punish through sanctions affecting the supplier's reputation. Of course, the distance between the locations of the buyer and the supplier is a rather indirect measure of network density and this variable is certainly subject to alternative interpretations. Unfortunately, I have not found any indication for network effects from more direct network variables. In Subsection 1.2.4, I have already discussed why control through social networks may be problematic and, consequently, why it is not self-evident that control effects through social networks are found. However, learning effects would be still plausible, certainly because the learning effect from own past experiences is fairly strong. Several explanations for the absence of this effect are provided in this chapter. I consider a combination of two factors plausible. First, I found indications that the number of other customers known by the buyer (degree) correlates with unobserved heterogeneity in the size of the trust problem due to the transaction characteristics. Initially, I found a positive effect of the degree of the buyer on the number of safeguards in the contract. That result would have rejected the degree hypothesis. However, adding a variable for the specificity of tenders received by the buyer reduced the degree effect considerably. Thus, it seems that degree correlates with how carefully the buyer has searched and selected an appropriate product and supplier. Second, selection of a supplier from a group of potential suppliers probably affects the degree effect. One reason for this is that potential suppliers that are hardly embedded with the buyer are less likely to be selected for large transactions because the trust problem becomes too large to be covered by safeguards in a contract. Finally, networks of customers of IT products seem to be rather sparse. Few customers know more than one of their supplier's other customers. Because the customers are SMEs and the transactions are relatively small, most customers are not of considerable importance for their suppliers. In such a context, control effects cannot be expected to be very strong.

Because main effects of the network variables are hardly found, it is not surprising that no support is found for interaction effects. However, this does not imply that everything the models predicted has to be immediately rejected. One lesson may be that the game-theoretic model as it was tested here, may have a closer relationship to more densely connected groups and societies in which a basic level of trust is present. In fact, the model does not give predictions for situations in which "enough" trust is difficult to obtain. Given that complete contracts are impossible to write or are prohibitively costly, the Iterated Heterogeneous Trust Game (IHTG) does not provide straightforward predictions if there is no base for trust and a transaction does not occur.[24] Many of the transactions analyzed in this chapter seem to approximate circumstances in which buyers who really needed a certain transaction searched for a suitable partner about whom they obtained information from third parties.

Moreover, the effect of past transactions suggests that learning effects cannot be neglected. Hence, game-theoretic models based on complete information assumptions are unsatisfactory. Therefore, a major task of subsequent modeling will be to shift attention from pure control issues to issues of uncertainty and information also in a game-theoretic context and not only in a stochastic context as in Chapter 4. Considerable additional insights can be obtained by studying why certain partners are chosen, and not only how actual transactions evolve. This gives more insights into the influence of potential transactions that are in fact not executed. If it is true that third parties create trust but that this effect is mainly found in the choice for a supplier, then my model should be interpreted differently, namely, the extent to which a buyer trusts a supplier is a measure for the probability that a transaction will occur between the buyer and supplier. A second step is needed in the model to predict the safeguards in the contract. The number of safeguards is then predicted given that a certain buyer

[24]The hypotheses derived from the game-theoretic model are all based on comparative statics for the extent to which trust is possible *given* that there is some trust possible.

is chosen. Such an extended model could enlarge insights into the mechanisms of buyer-supplier relations.

However, I think that the results of this chapter are not strong enough to begin immediately with an extensive study of new models. There are two reason why the analyses in this chapter are particularly difficult and fairly tentative. First, the measurement of network embeddedness is rather problematic. The data provide mainly indirect measures for density and only one measure for degree. Indegree and outdegree could not be distinguished. As a consequence, learning and control effects could not be disentangled. Second, degree seems to be rather endogenous and is more an indication for search activity than for an established network among the buyers. To overcome some of these problems, Chapter 6 discusses a vignette experiment in which I make an explicit effort to disentangle control and learning effects and to obtain exogenous measures for network variables. In this way, I try to acquire additional and more specific indications about the merits and shortcomings of the models discussed in this book.

Chapter 6

BUYING A USED CAR: AN EXPERIMENT

6.1 INTRODUCTION

Chapter 5 has provided empirical evidence for embeddedness effects on trust. The data show a learning effect of temporal embeddedness on trust. I did not find a control effect of temporal embeddedness on trust. One specific effect of network embeddedness was found. Buyers and suppliers who reside in each others' neighborhood include fewer safeguards against opportunistic behavior in their contracts than buyers and suppliers who are located further away from each other, indicating a positive effect of global network density on trust. It is not clear whether this is a learning effect or a control effect. I have not found effects of individual network parameters on trust. Various tentative explanations have been discussed as to why some hypotheses about the effects of network parameters on trust are not supported. These explanations include measurement problems for network parameters, endogeneity of the network of buyers as a result of search efforts of buyers to find a supplier, and unexplained variance in transaction characteristics that correlates with network parameters. Moreover, control effects may be small because individual buyers are relatively unimportant for a supplier and buyers do not know many other buyers of the supplier so that potential sanctions of the buyers are limited. The explanations suggest that the survey data on IT transactions are less than optimally suited for testing hypotheses about network effects. Moreover, the survey data violate various assumptions of the theoretical models used for deriving the hypotheses on the effects of network embeddedness on trust. Therefore, I am not willing to give up my hypotheses only on the basis of the evidence from the survey. This chapter offers a further test of the hypotheses using experimental data on transactions. Compared to the survey in Chapter 5, the disadvantage of these data is that they do not come from "real-life" transactions and as such are not interesting per se. The advantages, however, are that an experiment can provide a better approximation of assumptions underlying my theoretical models and more control over the values, variances, and covariances of the core independent variables is achievable.

In an experiment, the conditions in which subjects enter the experiment can be better controlled than the conditions for respondents in a survey. Random assignment of conditions to subjects strengthens the interpretation that effects are causal effects rather than, for example, the result of self-selection (see also Lieberson 1985: 14–15). Moreover, random assignment of subjects to conditions eliminates bias in parameter estimates due to the influence of *omitted* variables such as subject characteristics. Furthermore, experiments are useful in disentangling the effects of variables that are often highly correlated in real-life situations such as the indegree and outdegree of an actor, because conditions in the experiment can be chosen so that variables are not highly correlated. Finally, variation in variables can be chosen in a range of the variables where effects are theoretically expected.

As a result of using an experimental method in this chapter, some of the problems that occurred in the survey can be avoided. First, the networks of buyers do not change as a result of a transaction in the experiment. This solves the problem of network endogeneity. Second, the variance in embeddedness variables and transaction characteristics is controlled within the experiment. Therefore, unmeasured variance in transaction characteristics is not a problem. Third, the variation in the network parameters can be chosen in such a way that control and learning via network embeddedness is expected to be substantial.

Testing hypotheses about learning and control requires that variables on temporal embeddedness and network embeddedness are varied in the experiment. Variables that induce "learning" and "control" are incorporated for both temporal and network embeddedness. Consequently, the design includes variables for earlier transactions of the buyer with the supplier, expected future transactions of the buyer with the supplier, indegree of the buyer, and outdegree of the buyer. Furthermore, density is varied to allow for a comparison of global and individual network parameters. In an earlier experiment (Rooks, Raub, Selten, and Tazelaar 2000), it was found that transaction characteristics such as financial volume of a transaction, complexity of the product, and the difficulties a buyer had in judging the quality of the product are all important variables affecting trust. Because these effects of transaction characteristics have also been found in Chapter 5 and are not the main focus of this book, the corresponding hypotheses do not need to be tested extensively in this experiment. Therefore, only one transaction characteristic, namely, the financial volume of a transaction is included to allow the hypotheses concerning the interaction effects between embeddedness variables and transaction characteristics to be tested (see Chapter 3).

A first step in the design of the experiment is the choice between an "abstract" experiment and an experiment based on "real-life" transactions. An *abstract* experiment could for instance comprise a setting in which subjects occupy positions in a network of trustors and play Trust Games with a trustee. Communication between trustors should be possible only within the constraints of a given network structure. The task for the subjects in such an abstract experiment would be rather difficult and it would be questionable whether subjects have any idea about the merits of the network structure. Because I was unable to come up with an appropriate design, I have chosen to present *concrete* transactions to the subjects instead of abstract games. Network parameters are described in qualitative terms in these transactions. Subjects can be expected to make sensible choices in the experiment if the choices they have to make resemble choices they have to make in daily life. Therefore, it is important that the transactions selected for the experiment have a resemblance to transactions made by the subjects in everyday life. A disadvantage of using real-life transactions is that the operationalization of embeddedness variables via properties of a real-life transaction may be ambiguous both for the subjects and for the researcher, such that multiple interpretations of the embeddedness variables are possible. I will discuss such alternative interpretations of the variable operationalizations, especially with respect to future and outdegree.

A second decision in designing the experiment is whether the subjects have to make "real" or "hypothetical" decisions. If subjects make *real* decisions, they get actual payments related to their decisions. This would be a feasible option if subjects play abstract games. However, I could not think of a straightforward way to link payments to choices made in virtual transactions. Thus, the subjects will have to make hypothetical decisions in the experiment that do not have direct monetary consequences for them. There are some objections to this method (Faia 1980).[1] For instance, subjects may have difficulties in relating the choices they have to make in the experiment to real-life transactions. Still, I will assume that subjects act *as if* the transactions are real.[2]

An experiment in which subjects are asked questions about hypothetical real-life situations is often called a *vignette experiment*. Inspired by Lazarsfeld (Rossi 1979), the use of vignettes in sociology was developed by Rossi and his colleagues (Rossi, Sampson, Bose, Jasso, and Passel 1974). Topics of early studies were social standing of families (Sampson and Rossi 1975; Nock and Rossi 1978, 1979) and social justice of income distributions (Jasso and Rossi 1977; Alves and Rossi 1978; Hermkens 1983). An overview of this

[1] See also the discussion on the role of financial motivation of subjects in the experimental economics literature (for example, Wallis and Friedman 1942; Camerer 1995: 634–635; Roth 1995: 5–8).

[2] The subjects are asked whether they considered the transactions as realistic. It will be tested whether subjects who had difficulties in relating their choices to decisions in real-life transactions made different choices compared to other subjects.

early research was presented by Rossi and Nock (1982). Recently, vignette experiments were used to study contracting in buyer-seller relations (Rooks et al. 2000). This seems an appropriate experimental method that can be used here.

The remainder of the chapter is structured as follows. Section 6.2 describes the vignette experiment itself, the properties of the vignettes, and how vignettes are selected for each subject. Section 6.3 provides details about the data collection. Section 6.4 discusses the statistical methods used to analyze the data and reports tests of hypotheses that followed from the game-theoretic model and the stochastic diffusion model. Section 6.5 discusses the extent to which the experimental results confirm the predictions of the models. Suggestions for further model building and data collection conclude the chapter.

6.2 THE VIGNETTE EXPERIMENT

6.2.1 THE SETTING

The first and crucial decision in the design of the vignette experiment concerns an appropriate setting. The setting should be a context in which trust is a serious issue. Moreover, it should be plausible that social networks can play a role in terms of "control" as well as "learning." Furthermore, the setting should be realistic for the subjects and related to their own experiences. A transaction in which a buyer buys a used car from a professional car dealer seems to satisfy these conditions, certainly if the buyer is not a car expert and the dealer is not a member of a sector association that provides guarantees for the quality of its members' cars. As illustrated in Example 2 in Chapter 1, information asymmetry between the buyer and dealer induces a trust problem in such a transaction. The buyer has to trust that the dealer gives accurate information about the quality of the car. In this example, I explained that repeated transactions of buyers with the same used-car dealer may be less probable than, for example, in IT transactions. Therefore, I expect that learning and control through social networks are more important for buying used cars than in IT transactions. DiMaggio and Louch (1998) demonstrate that a considerable proportion of buyers prefers a relative as a dealer for buying used cars to a dealer with whom they do not have a social relationship.[3] This indicates that social networks indeed play an important role in these transactions. I used mainly American and Dutch students as subjects wanting to buy used cars. I assume that many students have experience with buying used products, and maybe even used cars. At least, they can probably imagine the relevant considerations in such a transaction from others' experiences. In general, students are not car experts and they cannot

[3]However, the discussion of the operationalization of outdegree in this chapter gives an argument why some buyers may *not* prefer a relative as their used-car dealer.

be expected to resolve their information deficiency on the quality of the car through careful inspection before the transaction.[4]

To make sure that subjects understand that they have to make decisions in trust situations, some elements of the setting are emphasized in the instruction for the subjects. Subjects are told to imagine that they had enough money to pay for the car, but that the amount of money is relatively large compared to their budget. Consequently, it is important for them to use the money carefully. Furthermore, subjects are instructed to imagine that they are not car experts and have difficulties in judging the quality of the car. Moreover, the car dealer is introduced as a professional dealer who is not a member of an organization that guarantees quality. It is explicitly mentioned that there are car dealers who try to sell "lemons" for high prices. These instructions should make the trust problem realistic. Finally, it is explicitly stated that buyers cannot ask for warranties that could compensate their loss if they would buy an inferior car.

6.2.2 INDEPENDENT VARIABLES

A vignette describes six attributes corresponding to the six independent variables that are varied in the experiment: VOLUME, PAST, FUTURE, DENSITY, INDEGREE, and OUTDEGREE. Adding variables for more detailed network parameters would have complicated the experiment considerably not only for the subjects but also for myself, because complex network parameters are difficult to describe informally. Below, I discuss the arguments for the descriptions of the different values of the variables, while the exact formulations are shown in Table 6.1. I assume that a vignette with attributes $\boldsymbol{x}$ represents a certain utility for a subject $u(\boldsymbol{x})$. Since the instruction does not contain a specific description of the car, the utility or attractiveness of a vignette reflects the judgement of a subject whether she will obtain a good car, i.e., the extent to which the subject *trusts* the dealer. Another interpretation of the attractiveness is that if the buyer would have the possibility of writing a contract with the dealer, how incomplete and "open" would such a formal arrangement be. The attractiveness of the vignettes is the main dependent variable in this chapter.

VOLUME of the transaction is operationalized as the price of the car to be bought. The possible prices are $1000 (NLG 2000) or $4000 (NLG 8000). Similar to the reasoning for IT transactions (see Section 5.1), I assume that incentives to abuse trust for the dealer are larger for a more expensive car, and the loss for the buyer is larger if trust is abused in a transaction of a more expensive car.

PAST indicates whether the buyer has bought a car from the dealer before and was satisfied, or did never buy a car from the dealer. I only study the difference

[4] In the last part of the experiment, subjects were asked whether they were able to judge the quality of a car. Less than 20% of the subjects said that they could make such a judgement.

Table 6.1. Description of the variables in the vignette experiment.

Variable	Value	Text
VOLUME	0	You can buy a car for about $1000.
	1	You can buy a car for about $4000.
PAST	0	You never bought a car from The Autoshop before.
	1	You bought a car from The Autoshop before and you were satisfied.
FUTURE	0	You will move to the other side of the country in a few weeks.
	1	You do not expect to move out of town soon.
DENSITY	0	The Autoshop is an unknown garage in your neighborhood.
	1	The Autoshop is a well-known garage and has many customers in your neighborhood.
INDEGREE	0	As far as you know, none of your friends have bought a car from The Autoshop before.
	1	You have friends who bought a car from The Autoshop before and they were satisfied.
OUTDEGREE	0	You do not have a close social link with the owner of The Autoshop.
	1	The owner of the garage and you are members of the same football team.[a]

[a] For the English version of the experiment, the typical American sport football is chosen, while for the Dutch version the typical Dutch sport soccer is chosen. In the discussion of the experiment, I use the general term "sports club."

between *no* information and *positive* information from past experiences with the dealer, disregarding negative or mixed information. I expect that a vignette in which the buyer had positive experiences with the dealer is more attractive than a vignette in which the buyer had no positive experiences with the dealer. The effect of negative information from earlier experiences on the attractiveness of a vignette is expected to be in the opposite direction to the effect of positive information. The data analyzed in Chapter 5 contained only a few cases of transactions with partners with whom the buyer had negative experiences. This suggests that a buyer seldom returns to a dealer who sells her a lemon ("exit").

FUTURE indicates whether or not the buyer expects to move to the other side of the country soon.[5] Control is more difficult for a buyer if she moves to the

[5] In a pre-test, FUTURE was formulated in terms of whether or not the dealer had close-out sales. This formulation was changed because close-out sales appeared to have negative connotations that were not

other side of the country. Moreover, the probability that the buyer has future transactions with the dealer is smaller if the buyer moves away. Therefore, it is expected that a vignette is more attractive if the buyer does not expect to move than if the buyer expects to move. One problem with the operationalization is that, theoretically, the effect of FUTURE is based on the sanctions of the buyer *anticipated by the dealer*. Therefore, strictly speaking, FUTURE can be expected to affect the behavior of the buyer only if the dealer is informed about the buyer's plans to move. Another problem is that if a buyer moves, the possibilities of control through the network also becomes smaller. I will come back to this issue in the discussion of OUTDEGREE.

DENSITY differentiates between a dealer whose garage is or is not well-known in the neighborhood of the buyer. As should be the case for the operationalization of a global network variable, this distinction does not directly address the relationship between the buyer and the dealer. If more potential customers in the neighborhood know the dealer, the buyer probably knows more other customers and it is likely that there are more ties among these other customers. Therefore, control of a well-known garage through the network of customers can be more effective than control of a garage that is not well-known. It is not explicitly indicated in the description of DENSITY whether the garage has a good or a bad reputation. Still, I suppose that "well-known" is mostly interpreted as a *positive* reputation. Such an interpretation induces a learning effect of DENSITY. Therefore, it is expected that the attractiveness of a vignette increases with DENSITY although it cannot be distinguished whether this is a learning or control effect.

INDEGREE indicates whether or not the buyer has information from friends about transactions of these friends with the garage. As argued before, only positive information is included, because I focus on the difference between *no* and *positive* information rather than the effect of negative or mixed information. INDEGREE is clearly related to the information received by the buyer. Therefore, INDEGREE is expected to have a positive (learning) effect on the attractiveness of a vignette.

OUTDEGREE indicates whether or not both the buyer and the dealer are members of the same sports club. This is a measure for OUTDEGREE, because the number of acquaintances the buyer and dealer have in common is expected to be larger if the buyer and dealer are members of the same sports team. Common membership provides the buyer with possibilities of controlling the dealer through reputational sanctions both in his business and as a team member. These sanctions can include discouraging others to buy from the dealer, but also social sanctions during activities at the sports club. A rational dealer should be con-

related to the possibility of repeated transactions in the future. For example, reasons for closing the garage could be related to the quality of the products sold.

cerned about these sanction opportunities of the buyer. Therefore, OUTDEGREE is expected to have a positive (control) effect on the attractiveness of a vignette. This effect of common membership may be smaller if the buyer expects to move to the other side of the country (FUTURE). In the formulation for OUTDEGREE, there is no indication about the direct relation between the buyer and dealer to prevent the effect being interpreted as a learning effect. An advantage of this formulation of OUTDEGREE is that the theoretical assumption of "common knowledge about the network" is unlikely to be violated because the buyer and the dealer know that they are members of the sports team. Although DiMaggio and Louch (1998) demonstrate that many buyers prefer a relative as a dealer for a used car rather than a dealer with whom they have no social relationship, a problem with this operationalization is that there may also be a group of buyers who are reluctant to buy a car from a team member. The relationship between the team members may be spoilt if the car happens to have a defect. Moreover, if it is not very obvious that an acquaintance has acted untrustworthy, it is questionable whether a buyer will actually execute sanctions against this acquaintance because the costs of sanctions for the buyer herself are probably relatively high. Obviously, this alternative interpretation of OUTDEGREE would make a dealer *less* attractive if he is a team member, and would therefore reduce the theoretically predicted OUTDEGREE effect.

All the vignette characteristics are "dummy" variables. In most vignette studies, variables with more than two values are included. I restricted myself to binary variables for two reasons. First, for most variables, it is difficult to find clearly distinctive formulations for more than two values. For example, for outdegree one could try to distinguish different social relations via a varying number of common acquaintances between the buyer and the dealer. This is hard to do convincingly. Second, in the vignette experiment by Rooks et al. (2000) in a similar context, the authors tried to distinguish three values for similar variables, but found that, empirically, the effect of the medium value coincided with the effect of the lower or upper value for most variables.

Table 6.2 summarizes the hypotheses on effects of temporal and network embeddedness on the attractiveness of a vignette and, hence, on trust, and provides references to the corresponding theoretical hypotheses. In addition, I test the hypothesis that the relative effect of OUTDEGREE compared to DENSITY decreases with VOLUME and increases with FUTURE (Hypothesis 3.17). For reasons discussed in the next subsection, the hypothesis about the main effect of VOLUME is not tested.

6.2.3 METHOD OF PAIRED COMPARISON

Measuring trust or the attractiveness of a vignette can be done in different ways. Rooks et al. (2000) have shown that it is possible to obtain direct measures of trust in vignette experiments using the number of contractual clauses buyers

Table 6.2. Hypotheses on effects on the attractiveness of a vignette.

Independent variable	Sign related to hypothesis	Theoretical hypothesis[a]	Page reference[b]
TEMPORAL EMBEDDEDNESS			
PAST	+	see text	10
FUTURE	+	3.4	68
NETWORK EMBEDDEDNESS			
DENSITY	+	3.7, 4.3	79, 113
INDEGREE	+	4.6	120
OUTDEGREE	+	3.8, 4.1	79, 113
INTERACTION EFFECTS			
PAST × FUTURE	+	see text	13
FUTURE × OUTDEGREE	+	3.16	79
FUTURE × DENSITY	−	3.16	79
OUTDEGREE × DENSITY	+	3.9	79
OUTDEGREE × VOLUME	−	3.14	79

[a] The hypotheses can be found in the concluding sections of Chapters 3 and 4.

[b] Page references are to tables or theorems. If hypotheses are only discussed in the text, references are to the appropriate discussions.

would prefer for certain transactions. Chapter 5 has demonstrated that a similar measurement can be used in a survey. However, the vignettes of Rooks et al. (2000) consisted of a combination of quantitative and some more qualitative attributes. In my experiment, vignettes contain almost exclusively qualitative attributes. I think that it is difficult for subjects to *quantify* the effects of the qualitative independent variables about temporal and network embeddedness in terms of a dependent variable such as the amount of contracting (see also David 1963: 9). Moreover, I asked subjects in a pre-test how much cheaper the car for the vignette that was not preferred should be such that they would be indifferent between the two vignettes. Debriefing the subjects, I concluded that they found it very difficult to *quantify* the effects of the independent variables in terms of money. Furthermore, because the effects of temporal and network embeddedness on trust may be relatively small, it may be difficult for subjects to distinguish certain vignettes if they cannot be judged simultaneously. Consequently, I decided not to measure the attractiveness of a vignette directly by asking subjects in one way or the other to rate the attractiveness of a vignette. Rather, I expected that subjects would find it easier to compare and rank vignettes in terms of which vignette they find more attractive. In principle, it is possible to ask subjects to rank more than two vignettes. However, comparing

1	2
- You can buy a car for about $4000. - You bought a car from The Autoshop before and you were satisfied. - You do not expect to move out of town soon. - The Autoshop is a well-known garage and has many customers in your neighborhood. - As far as you know, none of your friends have bought a car from The Autoshop before. - You do not have a close social link with the owner of The Autoshop.	- You can buy a car for about $4000. - You never bought a car from The Autoshop before. - You will move to the other side of the country in a few weeks. - The Autoshop is a well-known garage and has many customers in your neighborhood. - You have friends who bought a car from The Autoshop before and they were satisfied. - The owner of the garage and you are members of the same football team.

If you prefer situation 1, press "1".
If you prefer situation 2, press "2".

If your preference for situation X is far from clear, press "1".
If your preference for situation X is rather clear, press "2".
If your preference for situation X is clear, press "3".
If your preference for situation X is very clear, press "4".

Figure 6.1. Example of a pair of vignettes (X indicates the appropriate number).

more than two vignettes would complicate the tasks for the subjects considerably. Thus, subjects are asked to compare pairs of vignettes.[6,7] Trying to obtain a slightly more quantitative measurement, a simple indicator of the extent to which the subjects consider one vignette more attractive than the other is included. Figure 6.1 shows an example of a pair of vignettes with the two questions asked for each pair.

Because the method of paired comparison is used, the variable VOLUME requires some additional discussion. In fact, it is not a relevant question whether a buyer prefers a cheap car to an expensive one because no detailed description of the car is given. Of course, if these cars were indistinguishable, a buyer is expected to prefer the cheaper car. However, because VOLUME is only included

[6] According to David (1963: 16), the method of paired comparisons goes back at least to Fechner (1860). It was made popular by Thurstone (1927a, 1927b).

[7] Subjects have to choose between one of the vignettes of each pair because there is no other way to continue the experiment. I assume that subjects choose according to the attractiveness of the vignettes. Random choices are expected for pairs of vignettes between which subjects are indifferent. The statistical model discussed below exactly reflects the indifference.

to test interaction effects with embeddedness variables, it is necessary to vary VOLUME between pairs of vignettes, but VOLUME need not be varied within pairs of vignettes.

The random utility model discussed in Section 6.4 demonstrates that the results of the paired comparison can be used to estimate the attractiveness of individual vignettes. The choices of the subjects also resemble the selection of one dealer over another. In Chapter 5, I have already mentioned that selection and contracting can be seen as two distinct mechanisms for the governance of a transaction and that, presumably, effects of embeddedness are more important for selection than for contracting. Transactions with suppliers with whom the buyer is socially embedded are preferred to transactions with other suppliers, in particular, for large and complex transactions. Therefore, embeddedness effects found in this chapter also provide support for the suggestion in Subsection 5.3.3 that the set of transactions studied in Chapter 5 is possibly a selective subset of the set of potential transactions.

6.2.4 VIGNETTE SELECTION

In this rather technical subsection, I discuss the procedure for assigning vignettes to subjects. First, for practical reasons, I decided to limit the number of comparisons to *ten* per subject. A pre-test showed that ten pairs could be handled by the subjects, but that concentration was hard to maintain until the end. Thus, presenting more than ten pairs was not advisable. Presenting multiple vignettes to each subject is cost-effective, although a correction has to be made in the statistical analyses because the observations for a subject are not independent. Moreover, the fact that there are multiple observations for each subject allows for some investigation as to whether subject characteristics affect the attractiveness of vignettes and, hence, the choices of subjects. Second, it is necessary to check whether all combinations of values of variables can co-occur on a vignette without creating unrealistic combinations. I think that there are no such "improbable" combinations in this experiment. Third, it has to be decided which pairs of vignettes are to be compared by the subjects. As will be seen below, not all pairs of vignettes seem to be equally interesting. Fourth, pairs of vignettes have to be chosen for each subject from the feasible set of pairs that is used.[8] These last two considerations are now discussed in detail.

---

[8]There is extensive statistical literature on the design of optimal experiments in general (see, for example, Fedorov 1972; Pukelsheim 1993) and for paired comparisons in particular (David 1963; Van Berkum 1985). These designs select combinations of comparisons to optimize the power of tests of hypotheses, given the number of observations. However, these methods hardly consider designs in which subjects obtain multiple vignettes. Moreover, I had practical difficulties in implementing these methods. Therefore, I use my own design, paying the price of losing some (statistical) efficiency, but with considerable attention for the variation in pairs of vignettes for each subject.

Because a vignette consists of 6 variables with 2 different values each, there are $2^6 = 64$ different vignettes, and there are $64 \times 63/2 = 2016$ different unordered pairs of vignettes. There are a number of substantive arguments why a full factorial design is not desirable. First, I disregard the main effect of VOLUME. Hence, VOLUME does not vary within a pair of vignettes, but only between pairs. Then, $2 \times (32 \times 31)/2 = 992$ unordered pairs are left.

A vignette can be represented by a vector $\boldsymbol{x}' = (x_1, x_2, x_3, x_4, x_5, x_6)$ with x_i the value of the ith variable at the vignette. The variable x_1 represents VOLUME, x_2 represents PAST, and so on, $x_i = 0, 1$ for $i = 1, \ldots, 6$. Since VOLUME does not vary within a pair $(\boldsymbol{x}, \boldsymbol{y})$ of vignettes, $x_1 = y_1$ for all pairs of vignettes in the experiment. A partial (Pareto) ordering can be defined on the set of vignettes: $\boldsymbol{x} \leq \boldsymbol{y}$ if and only if $x_i \leq y_i$ for $i = 1, \ldots, 6$. Furthermore, $\boldsymbol{x} < \boldsymbol{y}$ if and only if $\boldsymbol{x} \leq \boldsymbol{y}$ and $x_i \neq y_i$ for at least one value of $i = 1, \ldots, 6$. Only pairs of vignettes that are *not* ordered by this ordering will be included in the experiment. The reason for this is that I am rather convinced that the main effects are in the expected direction. As a consequence, vignettes that are larger in the sense of this ordering are very likely to be chosen. Namely, if $\boldsymbol{x} < \boldsymbol{y}$, then for $\boldsymbol{y}$ the buyer is "better" embedded with the dealer than for $\boldsymbol{x}$. For example, if all variables at the two vignettes have the same values except for PAST, the only choice the subject has to make is whether a dealer with whom the buyer has positive experiences is more attractive than a dealer with whom the buyer has no experiences. Consequently, the choice for the vignette with more embeddedness will almost certainly be made by the subjects even if the attractiveness increases very little with a certain embeddedness variable. By excluding ordered pairs, I avoid that the effects for embeddedness variables are found purely based on such "trivial" choices. In this way, I try to obtain a more severe test for my hypotheses. For pairs of vignettes that cannot be ordered with the given ordering, the advantages of one vignette have to be compared to advantages of the other vignette. Therefore, observing choices between unordered alternatives is more informative. Using unordered pairs of vignettes also prevents subjects having to make choices they consider to be "trivial" choices, which may reduce the motivation of subjects.

The condition that only unordered pairs of vignettes are chosen implies that pairs of vignettes that are compared should differ in at least 2 variables. I expect that comparing vignettes becomes more difficult the larger the number of differences. Comparisons of vignettes that differ in all 5 variables (except VOLUME) may be too complex and are thus excluded.

The remaining number of different pairs of vignettes used in the experiment can be counted. Pairs of vignettes that differ in 2 variables and are unordered allow for comparing 2 specific embeddedness variables while the values of the other 4 variables (including VOLUME) can vary between the pairs of vignettes. One can choose 2 variables out of 5 embeddedness variables in $\binom{5}{2} = 10$

VOLUME	$= x_1$	VOLUME	$= x_1$
PAST	$= 0$	PAST	$= 1$
FUTURE	$= 1$	FUTURE	$= 0$
DENSITY	$= x_4$	DENSITY	$= y_4$
INDEGREE	$= x_5$	INDEGREE	$= y_5$
OUTDEGREE	$= x_6$	OUTDEGREE	$= y_6$

The condition for "2-pairs" is that the two vignettes differ in exactly 2 variable and, therefore, that all variables except for PAST and FUTURE obtain the same value for the two vignettes.

The condition for "3,4-pairs" is that the two vignettes differ in 3 or 4 variables and, therefore, that 1 or 2 of the variables DENSITY, INDEGREE, and OUTDEGREE also obtain different values for the two vignettes.

Figure 6.2. Example of a pair of vignettes comparing PAST and FUTURE including conditions for 2-pairs and 3,4-pairs.

different ways. There is no choice for the values of these 2 variables. The number of possible combinations of values for the other variables is $2^4 = 16$. Thus, there are $16 \times 10 = 160$ pairs of vignettes that differ in 2 variables. By a similar calculation, there are $8 \times 10 \times 3 = 240$ pairs of vignettes that differ in 3 variables and $4 \times 5 \times (4+3) = 140$ pairs that differ in 4 variables. Altogether, there are 540 unordered pairs of vignettes that satisfy the restrictions.

All subjects obtain 5 pairs of vignettes in which exactly 2 variables have different values within the pair of vignettes. I call these pairs of vignettes the "2-pairs." The other 5 pairs of vignettes for each subject have different values for 3 or 4 variables. I call these pairs of vignettes the "3,4-pairs." In Figure 6.2, a pair of vignettes is shown in which a subject has to compare the advantage of having positive experiences with the dealer (PAST) with the advantage of "not moving" (FUTURE). Moreover, the conditions for 2-pairs and 3,4-pairs are given. For 3,4-pairs, more differences between the vignettes than those of PAST and FUTURE occur.

The 2-pairs for each subject are selected in such a way that each embeddedness variable is varied exactly twice in a comparison *and* the subjects have to make 5 different comparisons. An example of 5 comparisons that fulfills the two properties given above contains comparisons of variable 2 with 3, 3 with 4, 4 with 5, 5 with 6, and 6 with 2. Here, again, the variables are numbered according the enumeration in Subsection 6.2.2, i.e., VOLUME is variable 1, PAST

Table 6.3. The 6 possible divisions of 10 pairs of variables in 2 disjunct cycles of 5 pairs.

Division 1	(2 3)(3 4)(4 5)(5 6)(6 2)	(2 4)(4 6)(6 3)(3 5)(5 2)
Division 2	(2 3)(3 4)(4 6)(6 5)(5 2)	(2 4)(4 5)(5 3)(3 6)(6 2)
Division 3	(2 3)(3 5)(5 4)(4 6)(6 2)	(2 4)(4 3)(3 6)(6 5)(5 2)
Division 4	(2 3)(3 5)(5 6)(6 4)(4 2)	(2 5)(5 4)(4 3)(3 6)(6 2)
Division 5	(2 3)(3 6)(6 5)(5 4)(4 2)	(2 5)(5 3)(3 4)(4 6)(6 2)
Division 6	(2 3)(3 6)(6 4)(4 5)(5 2)	(2 4)(4 3)(3 5)(5 6)(6 2)

is variable 2, and so on. Note again that VOLUME does not vary within a pair of vignettes. Five comparisons can only fulfill the given properties if they can be ordered in a cycle as in this example. The 12 possible cycles are shown in Table 6.3. In Table 6.3, "(2 3)" indicates that in such a pair of vignettes, at least, variables 2 and 3, i.e., PAST and FUTURE have to be compared. These 12 cycles can again be divided in 6 couples of 2 such that exactly all 10 possible comparisons of 2 variables that can be chosen from 5 variables are in one of the cycles in each couple of 2 cycles. I call such a couple of 2 cycles a "division" (see Table 6.3). For each subject, the 10 pairs of vignettes should include all 10 comparisons in a division. Thus, one division is selected for each subject. For one cycle of 5 pairs in the division, the subjects obtain pairs of vignettes that are 2-pairs, the other cycle is selected for the 3,4-pairs. For the 2-pairs, VOLUME always has the same value. The values of the variables that are constant within a pair of vignettes are selected at random. In the example displayed in Figure 6.2, the values for x_4, x_5, and x_6 are selected randomly. Then, the values of y_4, y_5, and y_6 are determined as well. For the 3,4-pairs, at most 2 additional variables that vary within a pair of vignettes are randomly selected. Thereafter, the appropriate values for all embeddedness variables are assigned to the vignettes, using equi-probable randomization for the values of variables that are constant within the vignettes. For the additional variables for which the values differ within a pair of vignettes, it is randomly decided which of the vignettes obtains the value 0 and which the value 1. For the 3,4-pairs, VOLUME has the value that is not used for the 2-pairs. Finally, within a pair of vignettes, one vignette is randomly selected to be displayed at the right side, and the order of all 10 pairs is randomized.

Given the procedure described above, three choices have to be made for each subject. First, a division has to be selected from Table 6.3. Second, one out of two cycles of 5 comparisons has to be selected from this division for the 2-pairs. Third, one of the cycles of comparisons has to be associated with the high price for a car and the other with the low price. Together there are 24 possibilities to make these selections. For each subject, one of the 24 possibilities is selected using a pseudo-randomization method that ensures that each of the 24 possibilities is used (about) equally often.

6.2.5 SUBJECT CHARACTERISTICS

Although my theory in Chapters 1 through 4 does not analyze how subject characteristics affect trust, it can hardly be expected that vignettes with the same attributes are equally attractive to all subjects. Because I could study some effects of subject characteristics without much additional costs, I will pay some attention to this topic in this chapter. Snijders and Keren (2001) present a more extensive overview and additional results on the effects of subject characteristics on trust. Snijders and Keren's main empirical result is that subject characteristics are much less important than payoffs in explaining trust in isolated trust relations. Snijders and Keren use abstract games. I want to study whether a similar conclusion is reached for hypothetical transactions.

Some questions are included at the end of the experiment to obtain data about subject characteristics. The variables resulting from this part of the experiment can be used to test whether some attributes of the vignette are more attractive to some "types" of subjects than to other "types" of subjects. First, for each of ten statements, subjects have to state whether they agree or disagree on a five-point scale. The statements concern

- the extent to which the subject cares about third-party information,
- the extent to which the subject cares about certain attributes of the dealer,
- how realistic the vignettes are for the subject,
- the experience of the subject with buying used cars or other used products, and
- the extent to which the subject thinks that others care about third-party information.

Finally, questions about standard "control" variables such as sex, age, field of study, and size of a subject's place of residence are included. These variables are often treated in other studies related to social dilemmas. For example, Scott (1983) finds differences in trust for men and women, while other studies do not find such differences (Orbell, Dawes, and Schwartz-Shea 1994). Frank, Gilovich, and Regan (1993) find differences in trust for subjects studying economics compared to those studying in other fields. Probably, subjects living in small villages are more used to being members of densely connected networks than subjects living in large cities. Therefore, attractiveness of network embeddedness may be different for subjects coming from small villages than for subjects from large cities.

6.3 DATA COLLECTION

The data are collected using a computer program that selects the vignettes and presents the instructions and vignettes to the subjects. First, the general setting is presented to the subjects. Second, the ten pairs of vignettes have to be evaluated. The variables are always presented in the same order at the vignettes (see Figure 6.1). Variables that are constant within a pair of vignettes are presented at the vignette to allow for interaction effects among embeddedness variables. For example, the effect of OUTDEGREE may differ depending on whether or not the buyer expects to move, even if FUTURE does not vary within a pair of vignettes. Third, some additional questions are asked. The exact text of the setting, the vignettes, and the additional questions of the experiment are shown in Appendix D in English and Dutch. The program is meant to be completely self-explanatory. The subjects can answer all questions interactively. The data are immediately stored after the experiment is finished. After a pre-test with Ph.D. students from the Department of Sociology of Utrecht University, three sessions of data collection were held.

The first session was held in March 1997 at the University of Chicago among graduate and undergraduate students from sociology and related fields contacted by visiting classes. The students were supplied with the program and were asked to complete the experiment at their own computer. Thus, the students were not supervised during the experiment. However, the program registered time delays during the experiment for the whole experiment and for each response task. After the subjects finished the experiment, I collected the disks with the answers. Two subjects had to be deleted from the data set because it was obvious that they did not take the task seriously. In this session, 40 subjects completed the experiment in such a way that they could be included in the data set.

A second session of data collection was held in October 1997 with undergraduate students at Utrecht University. In Utrecht, subjects were recruited using posters. During the experiment, subjects were located in a computer room and supervised by the experimenter. Completing the vignette experiment took about twenty minutes. During one day, seven groups of subjects completed the experiment, resulting in a total of 72 students. The subjects in the Utrecht experiment came mainly from mathematics, physics, physical geography, and sociology. One major change in the program was made compared to the experiment in Chicago: the formulation of OUTDEGREE was made somewhat stronger.[9] In the Chicago experiment, a social link between the subject and the owner of the garage was described through the father of the subject: "The owner of the

[9] An additional minor change was that the right-hand vignette that was originally displayed on a flashy green background was now displayed on a more neutral dark grey background, because in the Chicago experiment subjects seemed to choose more often for the right-hand vignette in spite of the randomization of which vignette should appear at the right-hand side.

garage and your father are members of the same football club."[10] During the Utrecht experiment the description was changed so that the subject had a *direct* social link with the owner of the garage: "The owner of the garage and you are members of the same football club." The indirect formulation in the Chicago session addresses "outdegree quality" rather than outdegree. Therefore, this change improved the experiment given that I primarily want to study the effect of outdegree. Moreover, as shown in Chapter 3, the effect of outdegree is expected to be larger than the effect of outdegree quality.

Finally, a session was held at a conference on "Gaming and Simulation" in Tilburg in July 1997. Thirteen researchers attended the session. One person in this session completed only nine of the ten pairs of vignettes. Thus, in total $40 + 72 + 13 = 125$ subjects participated in the different sessions of the experiment, providing answers to $400 + 720 + 129 = 1249$ pairs of vignettes.

6.4 ANALYSES

6.4.1 METHODS

There are two well-known models for the statistical analysis of paired comparisons: the Bradley-Terry model (Bradley and Terry 1952) and the Thurstone-Mosteller model (Thurstone 1927a, 1927b; Mosteller 1951).[11] The Thurstone-Mosteller model, generalized to multiple choice situations in the random utility model (McFadden 1973), is straightforwardly applicable here.

As indicated before, a subject assigns a certain utility $u(\boldsymbol{z})$ to a vignette with attributes $\boldsymbol{z}$ that is related to the attractiveness of the vignette. Now, assume that the utility depends in a linear manner on $\boldsymbol{z}$,

$$u(\boldsymbol{z}) = \boldsymbol{z}'\boldsymbol{\beta} + \varepsilon, \tag{6.1}$$

where $\boldsymbol{z}$ may include both vignette and subject related attributes, and $\varepsilon \sim N(0, \sigma^2)$ is a residual term that indicates the random variation related to the subject and the vignette. The residual term accounts for the part of the utility that cannot be "explained" by the deterministic linear function of the attributes and is included to obtain a probabilistic model.[12] A subject prefers a vignette with attributes $\boldsymbol{z}_2$ to a vignette with attributes $\boldsymbol{z}_1$ if $u(\boldsymbol{z}_2) > u(\boldsymbol{z}_1)$. As a result of the random residual term in the utility of a vignette, it is not strictly known from the $\boldsymbol{z}$-vectors and the utility weights $\boldsymbol{\beta}$ what subjects will do. However,

[10] This formulation was chosen because it seemed more realistic that students have fathers who know car dealers than that students know car dealers themselves.

[11] There is evidence from analyses on simulated and empirical data sets that these models are virtually equivalent (see Stern 1992).

[12] A strong assumption is that $\boldsymbol{\beta}$ is constant over all individuals. This assumption can be relaxed by using random effect models. In fact, I fitted some of these models without new substantial results, and so I present the simpler case here.

the *probability* that a vignette with attributes $\boldsymbol{z}_2$ is preferred to a vignette with attributes $\boldsymbol{z}_1$ is well-defined and equals

$$Pr\Big(u(\boldsymbol{z}_2) > u(\boldsymbol{z}_1)\Big|\boldsymbol{z}_1, \boldsymbol{z}_2, \boldsymbol{\beta}\Big) = Pr\Big((\boldsymbol{z}_2 - \boldsymbol{z}_1)'\boldsymbol{\beta} > \varepsilon_1 - \varepsilon_2\Big) \quad (6.2)$$

$$= \Phi\left(\frac{(\boldsymbol{z}_2 - \boldsymbol{z}_1)'\boldsymbol{\beta}}{\sigma_{12}}\right), \quad (6.3)$$

where Φ is the standard normal cumulative distribution function and $\sigma_{12}^2 = 2\sigma^2 - \mathrm{cov}(\varepsilon_1, \varepsilon_2)$ is the variance of $\varepsilon_1 - \varepsilon_2$, which is also normally distributed. Here, it is assumed that σ^2 and $\mathrm{cov}(\varepsilon_1, \varepsilon_2)$ are constant over persons. For identification of the model, I assume that $\sigma_{12}^2 = 1$. The $\boldsymbol{\beta}$ coefficients can be compared, but their absolute sizes are in a sense arbitrary.

In practical terms, this derivation means that a *probit* model can be applied for the probability that one vignette is preferred to the other. The *differences* between the values of the variables for the two vignettes are used as independent variables. The utility weights $\boldsymbol{\beta}$ measure the effects of the independent variables on the attractiveness of a vignette. Furthermore, the statistical model implies that main effects for variables that are always constant within a pair of vignettes such as VOLUME and subject characteristics are not identified. Such variables can only be used in interaction effects with variables that may vary within a pair of vignettes. Finally, it follows from (6.3) that interaction effects are defined as the differences of the products of the values for the variables on each vignette rather than the product of the differences.[13] Moreover, I would like to stress that the model does not include a constant.[14]

The statistical analyses should take into account that observations are clustered within subjects. I use the robust but somewhat inefficient parameter estimates from "independent" probit analyses with robust (Huber) standard errors modified for clustering (Rogers 1993). Log-likelihoods will not be reported, because they are not meaningful with this method for dealing with clustering. Consequently, comparing nested models with log-likelihood ratio tests is not appropriate. However, Wald tests can still be used to test whether variables added to a model represent a significant improvement in the model. Results of these analyses are reported below for all sessions together as well as separately for the Chicago, Utrecht, and Tilburg sessions.

[13] Values for dummy variables are directly used in the multiplications to calculate interaction effects. Only for interaction effects with non-dummy variables, which are related to subject characteristics obtained from the third part of the experiment, variables are centralized to calculate interaction effects.

[14] A constant in a model would reflect the possibility that subjects have an "intrinsic" preference for left-hand or right-hand vignettes. This issue will be discussed in the analyses of presentation effects.

Table 6.4. Probit analyses of the choice of vignettes.[a]

Independent variable	Hypothesis	All	Chicago	Utrecht	Tilburg
PAST	+	1.09**	0.99**	1.11**	1.39**
FUTURE	+	0.57**	0.61**	0.61**	0.30
DENSITY	+	0.71**	0.67**	0.73**	0.73**
INDEGREE	+	0.83**	0.77**	0.89**	0.86**
OUTDEGREE	+	0.26**	0.18	0.28*	0.51*
Number of subjects		125	40	72	13
Number of observations		1249	400	720	129

[a] The effect sizes are proportional to the parameter estimates and, hence, not reported.

** and * represent two-sided significance at respectively $p < 0.01$ and $p < 0.05$ based on Huber standard errors modified for clustering.

6.4.2 TESTS OF THE HYPOTHESES

MAIN EFFECTS

Table 6.4 presents the results of probit analyses with the five "main" effects for all observations and for the observations in each of the sessions individually. First, I discuss the results of the analysis including all observations. Later, I compare the results for the separate sessions. Before the effects in the analysis are interpreted, I test the goodness-of-fit of the linear model for the attractiveness of a vignette. This can be tested by comparing the linear model with a "saturated" model including coefficients for all 2^6 different combinations of attributes on the vignettes.[15] A Wald test shows that the linear model fits the data reasonably well (Wald $= 94.40$, $p = 0.0004$, based on $\chi^2_{53\text{df}}$). A quadratic model fits the data even better (Wald $= 54.93$, $p = 0.037$, based on $\chi^2_{38\text{df}}$). Thus, the interaction effects are also well interpretable.

The random utility model described in the previous subsection implies that a positive coefficient in the analyses shows that the attractiveness (utility) of a vignette increases with the variable for which the coefficient is positive. Consequently, I conclude that all types of embeddedness contribute positively to the attractiveness of a vignette and so all the hypotheses for the main effects in Table 6.2 are supported. The attractiveness of a vignette increases with PAST. This is a learning effect of temporal embeddedness. The attractiveness of a vignette increases with INDEGREE, which is a learning effect of network embeddedness. Then, the attractiveness of a vignette increases with FUTURE. This is a control effect of temporal embeddedness. The attractiveness of a vignette increases

[15] The actual number of degrees of freedom for the saturated model is not 64 but 58, because 4 combinations of attributes are excluded in the design and because of two linear dependencies due to the design. Thus, the degrees of freedom of the Wald test are 58 − 5 = 53.

Table 6.5. Comparison of choices for pairs of vignettes that differ in exactly two variables (proportions of pairs for which subjects prefer the advantage related to the "column" variable to the advantage related to the "row" variable are presented in the cells, the number of observations for each cell is shown in parentheses).

	PAST	FUTURE	DENSITY	INDEGREE
		is more important than		
FUTURE	0.65 (68)			
DENSITY	0.74 (61)	0.30 (64)		
INDEGREE	0.71 (63)	0.41 (58)	0.33 (61)	
OUTDEGREE	0.81 (58)	0.67 (60)	0.72 (64)	0.82 (68)

with OUTDEGREE, which indicates a control effect of network embeddedness. Finally, the attractiveness of a vignette increases with DENSITY. It cannot be decided whether this is a learning or a control effect of network embeddedness.

The *order* in size of the coefficients in Table 6.4 is theoretically appealing. This order is also reflected in the choices subjects made for 2-pairs. In Table 6.5, only pairs of vignettes that differ in exactly two variables are considered. For these 2-pairs, I now disregard the values of the variables that are constant within the pairs, and investigate only the two variables that differ within these pairs of vignettes. Now, the cell belonging to the column "PAST" and the row "FUTURE" indicates that for the 68 cases in which subjects had to choose for the advantage of having positive experiences with the dealer or the advantage of not moving away, they chose for having positive experiences with the dealer in 65% of the cases. This corresponds with the fact that the coefficient of PAST is larger than the coefficient of FUTURE in Table 6.4. Similarly, the advantage of having positive experiences with the dealer is in 71% of the cases more important than the advantage of having friends who have positive experiences with the dealer. Again, this corresponds with the coefficient for PAST being larger than the coefficient for INDEGREE. The reader can check that, for every pair of variables, it holds that if subjects chose for the advantage related to one variable more often than for the advantage related to another variable in Table 6.5, then it is also the case that the coefficient for the first variable is larger than the coefficient for the second variable in Table 6.4.

It is very tempting to interpret the comparisons of the sizes of the coefficients as an indication that learning is more important than control and temporal embeddedness is more important than network embeddedness. Namely, PAST has a larger effect than FUTURE and INDEGREE. The effect of INDEGREE is larger than the effect of OUTDEGREE. And, the effect of FUTURE is larger than the effect of OUTDEGREE. In the statistical sense, all these differences are significant if all observations for the three sessions are included. However, comparing the coefficients in such a strict manner is almost the same as comparing apples and oranges, because one cannot compare one "unit" of PAST with one "unit" of FUTURE in the way these variables are formulated in the experiment.[16] It would be relatively easy to find a very strong formulation for PAST and an even more ambiguous formulation for FUTURE to obtain a larger difference between the coefficients for PAST and for FUTURE. The formulation of the variables may partly explain the difference in the coefficients as I argued in the operationalization of the variables. The variables for learning could be described more directly and straightforwardly compared to the variables for control. Moreover, the variables for control are to a larger extent subject to alternative explanations than the variables for learning.

Nevertheless, I think that the indirect descriptions of the variables for control resemble to some extent the theoretical uncertainties related to these variables. As I discussed in Chapter 1, control through social networks is heavily based on the willingness of others in the social network to sanction. And, the costs of sanctions for a dealer depend on characteristics of the dealer of which the buyer probably has a vague notion at best. Moreover, learning through third-party information is also subject to uncertainties about the accuracy of the information from third parties. This may be a reason why PAST has a larger effect than INDEGREE. Thus, one can think about theoretical arguments why learning is more important than control and why temporal embeddedness is more important than network embeddedness. For example, it can be expected that the difference between the importance of control and learning depends on the extent to which control is uncertain. However, another experiment is necessary to test these hypotheses properly. Such an experiment should contain explicit manipulation of uncertainties with respect to control, and then interaction effects of variables related to control and learning with these uncertainties should be investigated.

After this discussion of the results based on the data of all the sessions combined, I compare the results for the separate sessions. The similarity of the results for the Chicago and Utrecht data is remarkable. The order of the sizes of the effects remains the same for these two analyses. Although there are only 13 respondents in the Tilburg session, the main results of this session are also similar.[17] The largest difference between the Chicago and Utrecht sessions is that the effect of OUTDEGREE is not significant in the Chicago session, while it is significant in the Utrecht session. As mentioned before, it is expected that the effect of OUTDEGREE is smaller in the Chicago experiment because the formulation of this variable was made slightly stronger in the experiment in Utrecht.

[16] Note that standardization of the variables cannot solve this problem. Standardization will change the scales of the embeddedness variables in a similar way because the variables have similar distributions and the scales will not become comparable any better.

[17] A Wald test shows that parameter estimates do not differ significantly between the sessions (Wald $= 14.09$, $p = 0.12$, based on $\chi^2_{9\text{df}}$).

Table 6.6. Probit analyses of the choice of vignettes including interaction effects.[a]

Independent variable	Hypothesis	All	Chicago	Utrecht	Tilburg
MAIN EFFECTS					
PAST	+	1.05**	0.92**	1.12**	1.30**
FUTURE	+	0.45**	0.44~	0.52**	0.20
DENSITY	+	0.74**	0.73**	0.73**	0.94*
INDEGREE	+	0.83**	0.76**	0.89**	1.00**
OUTDEGREE	+	0.46**	0.34	0.40**	1.27**
INTERACTION EFFECTS					
PAST × FUTURE	+	0.11	0.19	−0.00	0.53
FUTURE × OUTDEGREE	+	−0.04	0.07	−0.06	−0.15
FUTURE × DENSITY	−	0.19~	0.09	0.24~	0.16
OUTDEGREE × DENSITY	+	−0.21~	−0.18	−0.22	−0.38
OUTDEGREE × VOLUME	−	−0.13	−0.19	0.03	0.75*
Number of subjects		125	40	72	13
Number of observations		1249	400	720	129

[a] The effect sizes are proportional to the parameter estimates and, hence, not reported.

**, *, and ~ represent two-sided significance at respectively $p < 0.01$, $p < 0.05$, and $p < 0.10$ based on Huber standard errors modified for clustering.

Similar analyses are performed for the extent to which subjects preferred the chosen vignette to the other vignette. For this dependent variable, ordinary linear regression and an ordered probit version of the random utility model are used, both with robust standard errors modified for clustering. The substantial results of these analyses are the same as for the dichotomous dependent variable. Also, the relative size of the effects and the order of the size of effects are the same as in the analyses shown above. Therefore, details are not presented here.

INTERACTION EFFECTS

Table 6.6 presents the results for the interaction effects for which hypotheses have been derived in the theoretical chapters (see Table 6.2). These results are not very encouraging. I discuss the results for the analysis that includes all observations. The hypothesis concerning an interaction effect between PAST and FUTURE is not supported. As I explained more extensively in Chapter 5, the reasoning underlying this interaction effect is based on the effect of investments (for example, concerning contract development) in earlier transactions of a long-term relationship on investing in management for the present transaction. It is questionable whether such an investment effect can be expected at all between buyers and dealers of used cars. The interaction effects between FUTURE and OUTDEGREE, between OUTDEGREE and DENSITY, and between OUTDEGREE and VOLUME are also not supported. The interaction effect for OUTDEGREE and DENSITY is almost significant (two-sided test) but the effect is in the opposite direction to the one hypothesized. Also the interaction effect between FUTURE and DENSITY is in the opposite direction to the one hypothesized. If this interaction effect is added to the model in Table 6.4 as the only interaction effect, the effect is significant. Although the interaction effect is positive in all the analyses for the different sessions, it is only significant for the Utrecht session. The positive interaction effect has the reasonable interpretation that having a well-known garage in the neighborhood is more worthwhile if the buyer remains in that neighborhood. Finally, I have tested whether the relative effect of OUTDEGREE compared to DENSITY increases with FUTURE or decreases with VOLUME. Both hypotheses for the change in the relative effects are not supported.

6.4.3 PRESENTATION EFFECTS

Some additional analyses are performed to analyze whether aspects of the presentation of the vignettes have an influence on the behavior of subjects. In a first analysis, I compare the fairly simple 2-pairs with the more complex 3,4-pairs. It turns out that the OUTDEGREE effect is found only for 3,4-pairs. This result arises from the fact that the car dealer, being a team member of the buyer, is never more important in the 2-pairs than any of the advantages related to one of the other embeddedness variables. However, the positive effect of OUTDEGREE demonstrates that the attractiveness of a vignette increases if advantages of other embeddedness variables are combined with the dealer being a team member.

A second analysis is performed to test whether earlier choices differ from the later choices in the experiment. It could be expected that later choices will contain more "noise" because subjects become tired and, probably, focus on one or two variables instead of on vignettes as a whole. Wald tests show that the coefficients for the embeddedness variables do not change (in a linear way) with the order in the experiment (Wald $= 7.36, p = 0.20$, based on $\chi^2_{5\text{df}}$). Moreover, the variance in the residuals ε does not vary with the order of the choices.[18] The model for analyzing the variance in residuals ε can also be interpreted as a model in which the β coefficients vary all at the same rate with the order of the vignettes.

If subjects spend less time making choices, it can be expected that these choices are made less carefully and reflect more noise. The data indicate that subjects indeed need less time to make the decisions for the pairs of vignettes

[18]For estimating the variance in the residuals, a multiplicative heteroscedastic probit model is used in which the log-variance is modeled with a variable for the order of pairs of vignettes. The methods section of Chapter 4 offers a more extensive discussion of analyses with multiplicative heteroscedastic models of variance. Unfortunately, I did not have a version of heteroscedastic probit analysis that corrected for clustering. The log-likelihood ratio test of the "ordinary" heteroscedastic probit analysis is far from significant (LR $= 0.53$, $p = 0.77$, df $= 2$).

later on in the experiment compared to the earlier ones. However, the time subjects spent on making choices does not affect the main effects of the variables on the vignette (Wald $= 7.84$, $p = 0.17$, based on $\chi^2_{5\mathrm{df}}$). Also the variance in the residuals does not depend on the time subjects spent deciding which vignette in a pair is preferred.[19]

One curious effect for which I do not have a real explanation occurred in the Chicago session. In this session, subjects displayed a preference for the right-hand vignette although the order of presentation was randomized. This effect is highly significant ($p = 0.003$). Subjects may simply prefer anything that is on the right-hand side for no particular reason. A more down-to-earth explanation is that the flashy green color of the right-hand vignette drew more attention than the more neutral blue color of the left-hand vignette. To be able to reject at least one of these two "hunches," I changed the color of the right-hand vignette to gray in the Utrecht and Tilburg sessions. It turned out that subjects no longer showed a preference for the right-hand vignette in these sessions, and so the hypothesis that subjects simply prefer the right-hand side is rejected.[20]

6.4.4 SUBJECT EFFECTS

Now, I test whether preferences for types of embeddedness vary between subjects. All these tests are done with Wald tests in a model in which all the interactions of the embeddedness variables with one variable for a subject characteristic are included. I have not found significant differences in effects for men and women. No effects have been found for age, the fields studied, or the size of the subjects' place of residence. Furthermore, car experts and subjects who were experienced in buying used products made choices in a similar way to other subjects. Given the limited number of subjects and the limited variation in these "background variables" between the subjects (most subjects were students of a similar age, studied social sciences, and lived in a city), I do not consider these tests as providing much evidence that such effects do not exist. Note, however, that Snijders (1996: 99), who had more subjects in his data, also did not find effects of field of study, sex, and age on trustfulness in abstract Trust Games.

There are 16 subjects who expressed disagreement with the statement that the choices they had to make in the experiment were similar to choices they have to make in real life (see the first statement at Screen 27 in Appendix D). However, there are no significant differences between these subjects and other subjects.

[19] Again, I could only test this with a log-likelihood ratio test that is not corrected for clustering (LR = 0.11, $p = 0.94$, df $= 2$).

[20] Of course, it cannot be excluded that (social science) students of the University of Chicago simply prefer the right.

Using responses on the statements at the end of the experiment, I want to test whether network embeddedness is relatively more important than temporal embeddedness for subjects who are more concerned about the reputation of the dealer. The average of the answers for the statements 3, 4, 5, 9, and 10 (see Screens 26 and 27 in Appendix D) is used to test interaction effects with the embeddedness variables. All these statements address aspects of embeddedness. The statements concern the importance for the subject that she (3) or her friends (4) know the dealer, whether she informs acquaintances about a bad performance of a dealer (5), whether she thinks that others want to know their dealer (9), and her expectation about other people communicating information about the performance of dealers (10). It turns out that the contribution of OUTDEGREE to the attractiveness of a vignette is larger for subjects who are more concerned about the reputation of the dealer and who think that buyers communicate information about experiences with dealers. In other respects, subjects who were more concerned about the reputation of the dealer made choices similar to those made by other subjects.

Finally, the subjects in the Utrecht experiment were asked whether or not they were acquainted with game theory. It appears that subjects with knowledge of game theory are slightly more concerned with control effects than subjects who do not have this knowledge. The interaction effect with FUTURE is significant ($p = 0.016$) and the interaction effect with OUTDEGREE is positive, though not significant. Probably, subjects with knowledge of game theory are more forward-looking than other subjects and, therefore, value control aspects of embeddedness more than other subjects.

To summarize, I do not find important effects of subject characteristics on the main effects for the embeddedness variables. Similar to Snijders and Keren (2001), the effects of situational characteristics (mainly embeddedness in my case) seem to be more important in explaining trust than the effects of subject characteristics.

6.5 CONCLUSIONS AND DISCUSSION

The vignette experiment described in this chapter provides support for my hypotheses about the embeddedness effects on trust. In the experiment, subjects have to compare vignettes that describe transactions and relations with a used-car dealer. Primarily, temporal and network embeddedness of the buyer and dealer are varied between vignettes. For all five embeddedness variables, the hypotheses are supported. These effects can be interpreted in terms of trust. Subjects' choices reflect their judgement of whether they will obtain a car that is worth the price asked for it. The attractiveness of a vignette increases with the trust of a subject in the dealer's good performance. First, positive past experiences of buyers with the dealer have a positive learning effect on the attractiveness of a vignette. This effect has also been found in Chapter 5 for

IT transactions. Second, positive past experiences with the dealer from third parties known by the buyer have a positive learning effect on the attractiveness of a vignette. This is an effect of information flowing to the buyer from her network, and, therefore, can be interpreted as an effect of indegree. Third, the dealer's garage being well-known in the neighborhood of the buyer has a positive effect on the attractiveness of a vignette. This is interpreted as an effect of the density of the network between the buyer and the dealer. Fourth, a positive effect on the attractiveness of a vignette is found if the buyer does not move away fairly soon. This is interpreted as a control effect of the expected future relation between the buyer and the dealer: if the buyer moves away, the probability for new transactions with the dealer is very small. Fifth and finally, common membership of the buyer and dealer in the same sports club has a positive effect on the attractiveness of a vignette. This is interpreted as an effect of outdegree, because the buyer and dealer who are in the same sports club are expected to have more acquaintances in common, which provides the buyer with opportunities to control the dealer.

Furthermore, the experiment suggests that learning is more important than control for the explanation of a buyer's trust in a dealer. In this chapter, I have already mentioned that a reliable comparison of the strength of effects is not possible. Nevertheless, the experiment clearly demonstrates the importance of learning. Moreover, also in the vignette experiment of Rooks et al. (2000) the effect of positive past experiences with a supplier on contracting seems stronger than the effects of future transactions and network embeddedness. Thus, it is indeed problematic that learning effects have not been included explicitly in the game-theoretic model, and that they are derived more informally from the stochastic diffusion model. The importance of learning suggests that uncertainty about the characteristics of a trustee in a trust relation influences the choices of trustors. Trustors value information about the trustee and adapt their behavior as a result of such information. This indicates that introducing uncertainty in the game-theoretic model in terms of incomplete information, for example about characteristics of the trustee, seems a promising extension (cf. Buskens 2000).

The importance of learning and, in particular, of positive information about the trustee also relates to some of the results on IT transactions in Chapter 5. First, because trustors value third-party information, it can be expected that trustors will search for information about the trustee before a transaction. The search can be expected to be more extensive for transactions for which trust is more problematic (see Blumberg 1997: Section 2.3). Thus, the network of the buyers of IT products is, to a certain extent, the product of search. Second, because the choices in the experiment are related to partner selection, the experiment indicates that buyers prefer well-embedded dealers to others (see Buskens et al. 2002 for similar evidence in IT transactions). Although the experiment does not confirm that buyers prefer well-embedded partners especially for large transactions, the experiment provides indirect evidence for my suggestion in Chapter 5 that the set of actual transactions could be a selective subsample of the set of potential transactions.

No hypothesis is supported in the experiment as far as interaction effects are concerned. A problem with interaction effects, at least with respect to VOLUME, in this experiment is that subjects are likely to focus primarily on *differences* between the two vignettes. To obtain interaction effects with VOLUME, subjects should value certain types of embeddedness more for expensive cars than for cheap cars. However, if subjects focus on differences and disregard variables that are constant within a comparison, hypotheses about interaction effects will not be supported. A theoretical problem related to the interaction effect with volume is that it can be questioned whether predictions about interaction effects resulting from the game-theoretic model will be robust if the assumptions of the game-theoretic model are modified, such as including incomplete information assumptions in the model. I will elaborate on this issue in Chapter 7.

The most important objection to the vignette experiment probably concerns the interpretation of the variables, especially the "future" and "outdegree" variables. I have already discussed some of these objections. If a buyer moves to the other side of the country, it has more consequences than simply the loss of possibilities for sanctioning the dealer in the future. Similarly, next to sanction possibilities, other arguments may play a role in the decision whether a team member is more attractive as a used-car dealer than a dealer with whom the buyer does not have a social relationship. For example, a buyer does not want to risk spoiling the good atmosphere within a sports team because of a problematic transaction involving a used car. I have elaborated on these alternative interpretations in the operationalization of the variables.

An additional objection could be that the different effects of network variables need not to be due to the fact that the variables address different aspects of the *structure* of the network (as they are also distinguished theoretically in the models), but that the subjects relate each variable to different *parts* of the network or different *types* of relations. For example, third parties within a sports club may not be the same persons who provided the subject with information about a used-car dealer. Consequently, the network variables as operationalized within the experiment may be only imperfect measures of an actor's network. Therefore, the strong structural interpretation of these variables may be somewhat overemphasized. They could alternatively be interpreted as different components of something more general that could be called "social capital" (Flap 1988; Coleman 1990: Chapter 12). Still, I maintain that there is multidimensionality among the network variables in the experiment that is related to my theoretical distinction between *global* and *individual* network parameters. Namely, DENSITY is a *global* network variable because it is not directly related to the buyer or the dealer, while the *individual* network variables INDEGREE and OUTDEGREE address directly the network position of the buyer.

The problems related to the interpretation of the variables could be addressed via an abstract repeated-play experiment instead of a vignette experiment. In such an experiment, subjects could be instructed on the social network and future probabilities of transactions. Camerer and Weigelt (1988) have shown that such experiments are feasible for repeated Trust Games without a network context. In their experiment, subjects played repeated Trust Games with incomplete information after being allowed to obtain some experience with the game. However, the task becomes considerably more complex if a communication network is added to the setting. The experiment should be designed so that different positions in the network are actually related to restrictions on communication. It should not be the case that communication among trustors can occur more frequently than transactions between trustors and trustees because too frequent communication among trustors would provide even those trustors who are far from the center of the network with enough time to inform other trustors about an abuse of trust between two transactions of the trustee. Although I have not yet come up with a feasible design of an abstract experiment, exploring how such an experiment can be implemented in an appropriate and understandable way is a challenging task for further research.

Chapter 7

SUMMARY AND NEW PERSPECTIVES

This concluding chapter summarizes those parts of the "social networks and trust" puzzle that have been solved. Then, I will address problems in putting some other pieces of the puzzle together and indicate ways to solve these problems in the future. This chapter consists of three sections. In Section 7.1, I survey the main theoretical and empirical results of this book. Section 7.2 focuses on shortcomings of the theoretical models and empirical tests. In both sections, the different chapters will be explicitly linked to demonstrate how shortcomings in one chapter are compensated by the results of another chapter and to show which problems remain for further research. Section 7.3 offers suggestions for such new research. Findings from the empirical chapters indicate new research problems, while the theoretical program employed in this book provides guidance on where and how solutions might be found. The suggestions for further research include improvements of theoretical models, guidelines for data collection, and appropriate empirical tests of new predictions.

7.1 RESULTS

Chapter 1 presented an introduction to the main problem studied in this book. The chapter highlights the effects of *temporal* and, primarily, *network embeddedness* on trust. Trust is defined in a way similar to Coleman (1990: Chapter 5): A trustor trusts a trustee in a transaction if she transfers resources to the trustee taking the risk that the trustee may use these resources for his own profit, but hoping that the trustee will apply them for their mutual benefit. This book contributes to research on trust by searching for a *more structural* explanation of trust through social networks. Namely, I focus on how trust depends on different structural properties of social networks such as density, outdegree, indegree, and centralization. At the same time, other aspects of the trust problem are taken into account such as transaction characteristics and characteristics of the dyadic relationship.

Two types of effects of temporal and network embeddedness are distinguished in Chapter 1: *learning* effects and *control* effects. Learning effects emerge when a trustor receives information about the incentives and the abilities of a trustee from transactions in the past and modifies her expectations and behavior accordingly. The more transactions a trustor has engaged in with the trustee or the more information she received from other trustors who have had transactions with the trustee, the better her position is to assess the incentives and abilities of the trustee and, thereby, the better she is able to predict how the trustee will perform in future transactions. If a trustor has positive experiences with a trustee or she has information from others about trustworthy behavior of a trustee, the trustor can be expected to trust the trustee more. Control effects are related to the possibilities open to the trustor for sanctioning an abuse of trust by the trustee. A trustor with more sanction opportunities can be expected to trust the trustee more. Given temporal embeddedness in the sense of expected future transactions between the same trustor and trustee, the trustor can sanction the trustee by withholding trust after the trustee abused trust. This can deter the trustee from abusing trust in the first place. The more transactions a trustor expects to have with the trustee in the future, the more costly the potential sanctions of the trustor are for the trustee. With respect to network embeddedness, the more ties a deceived trustor has to other trustors, the more other trustors she can inform about the untrustworthiness of the trustee. Together, all these trustors can execute even more severe sanctions against the trustee than one trustor can alone by withholding trust in future transactions.

In this book, I focus on networks of trustors who have transactions with one trustee. *Individual* and *global* network parameters have been distinguished to explain learning effects and control effects through social networks of trustors. Individual network parameters describe the position of an individual trustor in a network such as the number of ties going from one actor to other actors (outdegree). Global network parameters describe properties of the network as a whole such as the total number of ties in a network (density) or the centralization of a network. Via individual network parameters one can explain differences in trust between trustors *within* one network. Global network parameters are useful in explaining differences in trust *between* different networks of trustors. In Chapter 2, formal definitions of network parameters have been provided for networks represented by valued directed graphs (Wasserman and Faust 1994: Section 4.5).

Theoretical Results

In the theoretical investigations, I wanted to include three elements. I tried to model *learning* and *control* in trust relations within social networks and the effects of social networks should be based on a model in which actors make *rational decisions* on trust in series of transactions. However, when I started this research, combining all the three elements into a single model seemed to be too complex. Therefore, I have developed two complementary models including two of the three elements in each model. The game-theoretic model in Chapter 3 consists of actors making rational decisions in series of transactions. This model makes predictions about control effects. The stochastic diffusion model in Chapter 4 makes predictions about control as well as learning effects in social networks, while the link to trust is informal and not explicitly based on rational actions of the trustors and trustees.

The game-theoretic model consists of a repeated Trust Game with one trustee and a network of trustors who communicate about the behavior of the trustee. I show how to include detailed social structure in a game-theoretic model. The analyses are based on the idea that trustors sanction the trustee if the trustee abuses trust (see, for example, Kreps 1990a). Sanctions can include the fact that the trustor herself refuses to place trust in the future. In addition, the trustor can inform other trustors about the abuse of trust by the trustee and induce other trustors to stop trusting the trustee. Trustors who are better embedded in a network can inform other trustors in a shorter time. Therefore, better embedded trustors have a higher sanction potential. Because a rational trustee has to take the sanction potential of a trustor into account in his decision whether or not to honor trust, trustors with more sanction potential can trust the trustee more. For this model, I study equilibria in conditionally cooperative strategies in which trustors never place trust if they have information about an abuse of trust by the trustee in the past (trigger strategies). Moreover, trustors do not place trust if the incentive to abuse trust for the trustee in a particular transaction is too large, i.e., if the incentive is larger than the expected costs of sanctions from the trustors withholding trust as long as they have information about the abuse of trust. I derive *trust thresholds* indicating a maximal value of the trustee's incentive to abuse trust for which trustors can trust the trustee. The trust thresholds depend on the parameters of the model, including network parameters, and can differ between trustors in the network, depending on their network position. The equilibrium related to the maximal trust thresholds reproduces results from earlier studies for similar models (Raub and Weesie 1993b; Weesie et al. 1998), namely, that trust

- increases with the costs of sanctions for the trustee,
- decreases with the incentives for the trustee to abuse trust,
- increases with the importance of future transactions for the trustee,
- increases with the expected duration of the future series of transactions between a trustor and the trustee, and
- increases with the individual strength of ties between trustors.

Except for the effect of individual tie strengths, no hypotheses about network parameters follow from straightforward comparative statics of the trust thresholds. Therefore, in the second part of Chapter 3, two approximation methods are applied: *linearization* and *simulation*. Linearization shows that density and outdegree are the most important network parameters to describe network effects on trust in the "neighborhood" of homogeneous networks. Trust increases with the outdegree of an individual trustor and with the global density of the network of trustors.

In the simulation, the trust thresholds of the game are calculated for a large number of networks (see also Yamaguchi 1994a; Buskens 1998). Statistical regression methods are used to analyze how the trust thresholds depend on network parameters. The regression analyses of the trust thresholds could be improved by using the analytic results for homogeneous networks to correct for effects of non-network parameters. Although this methodology needs to be developed further in terms of sampling networks and statistical analyses, it provides an appropriate tool for deriving "approximate hypotheses" about network effects from a complex model for which it is impossible to derive analytically the effects of network parameters.

The simulation confirms that density and outdegree are the most important network parameters for predicting the trust thresholds. Smaller effects are found for other network parameters. Moreover, trust increases with the outdegrees of the contacts of a focal trustor. Trust thresholds increase with centralization only if trustors with high outdegrees also have high indegrees, i.e, trustors who receive more information transmit this information again to more others.

An advantage of the game-theoretic model is that network parameters are combined in one model with other parameters that characterize a trust problem. Thus, hypotheses can be deduced about interaction effects between network and non-network parameters. Non-network parameters include transaction characteristics as well as a parameter for the duration of the relation. A major finding from the theoretical analysis is that the importance of global network parameters compared to individual network parameters tends to increase if dyadic trust problems are larger, i.e., if the trustee's long-term costs of sanctions are smaller and if the incentives to abuse trust are larger for the trustee.

Chapter 4 presented a stochastic information diffusion model. In this model, actors transmit and receive information according to given probabilities at discrete periods in time. Although the decision to trust is not explicitly modeled, the results can be used to derive predictions about the trust of a trustor in a trustee. The faster trustors can transmit information through the network, the more severe the sanctions of these trustors can be against an untrustworthy trustee and, therefore, the more these trustors can trust the trustee. On the other hand, the more information trustors receive from other trustors in the network, the more these trustors can learn about the incentives and abilities of the trustee. Whether more information implies that the trustor will trust a trustee more, however, depends on the *content* of the information. If the information is mainly positive, more information is expected to induce more trust.

Hypotheses about effects of network parameters are derived from the stochastic information diffusion model with the same simulation method as used in Chapter 3. Similar to the results of Chapter 3, density and outdegree are the most important determinants for the time needed to transmit information in a network. Actors with higher outdegrees and actors in a network with higher density transmit information faster and are, therefore, expected to place more trust in a trustee based on control. Smaller effects are found for other network parameters such as degree quality and centralization. These other network parameters are, however, more important in this stochastic information diffusion model than in the game-theoretic model.

Density and indegree are the most important network parameters for describing how fast actors receive information. Actors with a higher indegree and actors in networks with a higher density receive more information. These actors are expected to place more trust based on learning if they receive mainly positive information about the trustee and they are expected to place less trust if they receive mainly negative information. Other network parameters play a less important role in describing learning effects than density and indegree. Since only network parameters are included in the stochastic information diffusion model, no hypotheses about interaction effects between network and non-network parameters can be derived.

These theoretical results suggest that the simulation method used in the two theoretical chapters is quite effective. In most simulation studies, knowledge about the relation between the outcomes of the simulation and the parameters in the simulation is limited. This makes statements about comparative statics in the parameters problematic. Here, however, the simulation is closely linked to analytic results. For example, comparative statics of some parameters in the game-theoretic model follow directly from the analytic results. Moreover, additional analytic results for special cases, such as for homogeneous networks, provide insights into the outcomes of models that can be used for analyzing the data of the simulation. Consequently, the strong analytic foundation of the simulation allows for solid "approximate hypotheses" based on this simulation method.

Empirical Results

Data should ideally meet the following three criteria for testing the hypotheses derived from the theoretical models. First, behavior of actors in real-life trust situations should be considered. Second, the data should include accurate measures of the main independent variables such as network parameters of the networks among relevant actors. Third, I would like to distinguish learning and control effects of social networks. However, it is difficult to fulfill all three criteria within one data set. Therefore, two empirical studies are included in this book, each with specific strengths and weaknesses. Chapter 5 presented a survey of IT transactions in which the behavior of firms in real-life trust situations is studied. In this survey, it appears to be difficult to obtain sufficiently accurate measures for some independent variables, including network parameters. Moreover, indegree and outdegree, the main network parameters related to learning and control, cannot be clearly disentangled in the survey. Thus, Chapter 6 offers a vignette experiment as a complementary empirical study. This experiment provides better measures for some network parameters. Also, indegree and outdegree can be disentangled. The disadvantage of the experiment is that the data are judgements for hypothetical trust situations.

In the survey discussed in Chapter 5, about 800 buyers of IT products were interviewed about one or two transactions with an IT supplier. "Lack of trust" is measured indirectly in the survey as the number of safeguards included in the contract between the buyer and supplier. In order to test the game-theoretic model, the transaction characteristics of IT transactions have to be related to the payoffs in a Trust Game. The hypotheses about the effects of transaction characteristics on contracting are all supported. The number of safeguards in the contract increases with the financial volume of a transactions, with the number of components of the product, with the complexity of the product, with the dependence of the buyer on the supplier, and with the monitoring problems of the buyer. These findings confirm results from earlier research (Batenburg et al. 2002; Blumberg 1997). Furthermore, renewed support is obtained for a learning effect of positive experiences in prior transactions (see also Batenburg et al. 2002; Rooks et al. 2000). Buyers who have positive experiences include less safeguards in the contracts with their suppliers. The hypothesis for the control effect of expected future transactions with the same supplier is not supported. As far as network embeddedness is concerned, a positive effect of the geographical distance between buyer and supplier on the number of safeguards in the contract is found. This is an indication for a density effect, because buyers and suppliers who are located closer to each other are expected to have more mutual contacts, and these contacts are expected to have more contacts among each other. It is an open question whether this is a learning or a control effect. Hypotheses about indegree, outdegree, and more detailed network parameters are not supported. Also, no support is obtained for hypotheses about interaction effects between network and non-network parameters.

Chapter 6 described a vignette experiment. In this experiment, subjects are asked to choose between two hypothetical transactions in which they can buy a used car from a used-car dealer. The price of the car is not varied within pairs of transactions but only between pairs of transactions. Variation in the price between pairs of transactions allows for analyzing interaction effects of embeddedness variables with the volume of the transaction. Furthermore, the transactions vary in five embeddedness variables. Two variables address learning and control effects of temporal embeddedness. The first of these two variables indicates whether or not the buyer has positive experiences with the used-car dealer. The second variable indicates whether or not the buyer expects to move to the other side of the country. Moving should imply that no more transactions with the dealer are expected in the future. Three variables address network embeddedness. One variable indicates whether the dealer's garage is a well-known garage in the neighborhood of the buyer (density). The second variable related to learning indicates whether or not the buyer has friends who have positive experiences with the dealer (indegree). The third network variable indicates whether or not the dealer and the buyer are members of the same sports club, thereby varying whether the buyer in such a transaction has opportunities to sanction the dealer through third parties (outdegree) if the dealer would sell a car of inferior quality.

Data from the vignette experiment support both the hypotheses for the control effect and the learning effect of temporal embeddedness. A dealer with whom the buyer has positive past experiences is more attractive than a dealer with whom the buyer does not have such experiences. A transaction after which the buyer does not expect to move is more attractive than a transaction after which the buyer does expect to move. Moreover, the hypotheses on network effects, i.e., effects of indegree, outdegree, and density are supported. Subjects consider a dealer more attractive about whom they have positive information from friends on prior transactions with that dealer. Subjects prefer to buy from a team member rather than from somebody with whom they do not have a social relationship and subjects prefer to buy from a well-known garage. The indegree effect provides evidence for a learning effect through social networks, while the outdegree effect supports the related hypothesis on a control effect through social networks. It is not clear whether the effect of density is a control or a learning effect. The density effect certainly indicates that the reputation of the dealer affects the choice of the buyer. Although a comparison of the strength of the different effects in the vignette experiment is problematic, the results suggest that learning is more important than control. The importance of learning indicates that the assumption of complete information of the buyer about the dealer and the product is problematic. The results also suggest that effects of temporal embeddedness are larger than effects of network embeddedness. Again, this might be explained by an uncertainty argument. Namely, own experiences of a buyer and the sanctions a buyer can impose herself are under the control of the buyer herself, while for the effectiveness of sanctions through third parties and the information actors receive through third parties, the buyer has to rely on these third parties. Only one hypothesis about an interaction effect is supported, namely, the interaction between density and the transactions expected in the future. The interaction effect suggests that the reputation of the dealer is more important if the buyer does not move out of the neighborhood in which the dealer is well-known.

RESEARCH QUESTIONS AND ANSWERS

Now, I review the theoretical and empirical results in the light of the research questions presented on page 29:

1. What are the effects of *learning* through social networks on trust of trustors in a trustee, and how are these effects related to individual and global parameters of the social network of trustors?

2. What are the effects of *control* through social networks on trust of trustors in a trustee, and how are these effects related to individual and global parameters of the social network of trustors?

3. How important are *individual compared to global network parameters* for the description of various network effects on trust?

In the theoretical chapters, hypothetical answers for the research questions are deduced. In Chapter 3, theory about the control effects of social networks is developed, while Chapter 4 addresses control as well as learning effects. Both models provide hypotheses for effects of global and individual network parameters. The theoretical chapters show that indegree, outdegree, and density are the most important network parameters for learning and control effects. For control effects, I am able to derive hypotheses about interaction effects that give indications for the relative importance of global network parameters (mainly density) compared to individual network parameters (outdegree) depending on non-network parameters.

The survey provides limited empirical support for the hypotheses. In an indirect manner, the hypothesis about network density is supported indicating that trust increases with network density. The vignette experiment, however, provides empirical evidence for learning as well as control effects on trust not only via temporal embeddedness, but also via network embeddedness. Because hardly any hypotheses about interaction effects between network and non-network parameters are supported, there are no indications for changes of the relative effects of global compared to individual network parameters for different contexts.

7.2 DISCUSSION

THEORETICAL SHORTCOMINGS

The game-theoretic model has two important shortcomings. *First*, complete information assumptions are employed. These assumptions imply that trustors know the incentives, farsightedness, and abilities of the trustee. Moreover, the assumptions imply that the trustee and all trustors exactly know the network of trustors and the incentives of all trustors. Consequently, trustors can deduce what a rational trustee will do after they place trust. Therefore, they will never place trust if the trustee will abuse trust, because they are always better off not placing trust than being deceived. Moreover, because trustors are completely informed about the trustee, there is nothing to learn about the trustee. This implies that the model cannot yield predictions about learning effects on trust. In fact, the empirical tests demonstrate that the complete information assumptions should be rejected. The buyers of IT products search for information about products and suppliers, indicating that they are far from completely informed about all alternatives and incentives of suppliers. In the vignette experiment, subjects indicate that a used-car dealer about whom they have positive information from earlier transactions is more attractive than a dealer about whom they have no such information. This again suggests that actors' behavior is to some extent determined by their desire to decrease uncertainties in transactions. *Second*, in the game-theoretic model, trustors act only sequentially with the trustee. A related aspect of the interaction structure is that only one trustor at a time has information about the behavior of the trustee in the past, namely, the trustor who has transactions with the trustee at that moment. This implies that information about the trustee is transferred as a kind of package among trustors together with the "right" to have transactions with the trustee. It is questionable whether network parameters have the same effects if a more complex way of information transfer is allowed. One example is the effect of transitivity of a network. Transitivity is expected to hinder fast information transmission in a network, because redundancy in information the actors receive is larger if the transitivity of a network increases. However, under the restricted information transfer possibilities of the game-theoretic model, redundant information transfer cannot occur. The reason is that a trustor can never give redundant information about the trustee to another trustor, because only one trustor has information about the trustee (see also Buskens and Yamaguchi 1999).

The stochastic information diffusion model addresses both problems of the game-theoretic model to a certain extent. *First*, the information diffusion model provides hypotheses about learning effects by investigating how fast actors receive information that enters the network. However, the link from information diffusion to trust is rather informal. Also, the content of information is not an explicit element of the model. Predictions can only be derived for "consistent" information about a trustee, i.e., for situations such that trustors receive either almost always positive or almost always negative information. The model does not yield predictions for effects of ambiguous information on trust. *Second*, the information diffusion process is modeled in a more complex manner in the stochastic information diffusion model than in the game-theoretic model.

Actors continue to transmit all the information they have received, even if they are no longer transacting with the trustee. And, as long as there are some actors who do not have some information, all the informed actors can inform others if the network structure allows communication. Unbounded continuation of information transfer is an extreme assumption, but relaxing this assumption is a straightforward and feasible extension of the model. The inclusion of public sources of information is another straightforward and feasible extension. It is a more severe problem that transactions are not modeled explicitly. As a consequence, interaction effects between network and non-network parameters cannot be derived from this model. Including choice behavior in transactions in the model is certainly not a trivial task, because determining rational behavior for a trustee who has transactions with trustors communicating according to the assumptions of the stochastic model is a rather complex exercise.

Another problem that remains unsolved affects both models. In both models, the *content* of the information is assumed to be unproblematic in the sense that information transfer is always costless and accurate. However, information can be expected to be intentionally or unintentionally distorted. Thus, information from third parties is much more difficult to interpret than information from own experiences of an actor. Noise can dramatically change the content of transferred information. This may be a reason why, empirically, the learning effect of temporal embeddedness is seemingly larger than the learning effect of network embeddedness. Moreover, distortions of information can cause inconsistencies of information from different sources. This also reduces the learning effects of network embeddedness. Finally, actors may have incentives for not disclosing all information to other actors or even to lie to other actors. Buyers of the same supplier who are competitors of one another are an example.[1] If one buyer is deceived by the supplier, she "will get even" if the other buyers are deceived as well. Then, this buyer may not disclose information to the other buyers and this will undermine the sanction effects of social networks.

Finally, one reason why only limited support for hypotheses about interaction effects is obtained may be related to the theoretical shortcomings. A question that should be addressed with respect to the interaction effects is whether these effects can be expected given that complete information assumptions are violated. Almost all the hypotheses about interaction effects are derived from the game-theoretic model. As argued above, game-theoretic models in which uncertainty is incorporated seem to be more appropriate here. Then, it has to be questioned to what extent hypotheses derived from the game-theoretic model in Chapter 3 are robust with respect to such adaptations of the model. My expectation is that the hypotheses about main effects will be less sensitive to

[1] See also Lorenz (1988), Williamson (1996: 153–155), Blumberg (1997: 208–210), and the related discussion in Chapter 1.

such adaptations than the hypotheses about interaction effects. One reason for this is that most hypotheses about main effects do not only follow from this specific model but from a series of similar models as well. The hypotheses about interaction effects, however, are more unique for this model. On the one hand, yielding these hypotheses is one of the merits of the game-theoretic model. On the other hand, it needs further investigation whether the hypotheses about interaction effects are robust with respect to modifications of the model, such as relaxing the complete information assumptions.

Empirical Shortcomings

There are some features of the survey on IT transactions that can explain—at least partially—the limited support for the hypotheses developed in the theoretical chapters. First, the survey contains only one question about the expected future transactions of the buyer with the supplier at the time of transaction. This question addresses both expected volume and frequency of future transactions. However, these are two separate theoretical dimensions in the game-theoretic model. As a consequence, these two theoretical dimensions cannot be distinguished empirically. Furthermore, recall of such a, probably vague, expectation may be limited and may be highly affected by the actual number of transactions after the focal transaction. This may explain why no effects of expected future transactions of the buyers with their supplier are found.

Social networks among buyers of IT products appear to be sparse. Although the sample frame is stratified with respect to the network embeddedness of sectors of the buyer's industry, it turns out that most buyers know at most one other customer of their supplier. Moreover, because the buyers are small or medium-sized firms and most transactions are relatively small, most buyers may not be important individually to the suppliers. In such sparse networks, control effects will be small and, therefore, difficult to find. Moreover, the density of the sectors is hardly related to the number of customers known to the buyer (degree), which indicates that the stratification is not very effective in obtaining high variation in the network embeddedness of buyers.

Further investigation of the network effects demonstrates that the variable indicating degree is especially problematic for some other reasons. The number of other customers known by the buyer is related to the size and complexity of the transaction with the supplier. Initially, it seemed that the number of safeguards increases with the degree of the buyer. It is shown that this unexpected effect of degree becomes insignificant if additional variables that account for how problematic and important the transaction is for the buyer are added to the analyses. Furthermore, the degree of a buyer varies with the search effort of the buyer to find a suitable supplier. For example, buyers who collect information about potential suppliers via colleagues and other firms know more other customers of the supplier at the time of the transactions than a buyer who does not search through informal circuits. Thus, the degree of buyers seems to be an endogenous variable. For larger transactions, buyers employ more search activities and, consequently, these buyers happen to know more other customers of the supplier. Therefore, transaction characteristics do not only affect the number of safeguards in the contract, but also the degree of the buyers as a consequence of search activities. The endogeneity of degree suggests that simultaneous equation models should be used to obtain better insight into the effect of degree on the number of safeguards in the contract. However, testing such models should be preceded by the development of new and non-trivial theory about the relations to be included in the models.

Another problem with the survey is that the actual transactions are likely to be a selective subset of the potential transactions. A positive correlation between size of a transaction and the degree of the buyers may result if buyers prefer to have transactions with suppliers with whom they are well embedded in a social network. This may be particularly so in the case of large and complex transactions. This implies that relatively few transactions are implemented for which embeddedness between the partners is low and the transactions are large and complex. In Chapter 5, I demonstrate why this can imply an underestimation of the effects of embeddedness variables and effects of transaction characteristics. Particularly in the case of small effects, such as those from network embeddedness in sparse networks, an underestimation can easily result in an effect becoming insignificant.

The vignette experiment addresses some of the problems that arose in the survey. First, the variation of transaction characteristics is predetermined within the experiment. Moreover, within the choices made by subjects there is no variation in transaction characteristics. Thus, unexplained variance of transaction characteristics is not a problem within the experiment. Second, the network variables are likewise determined exogenously in the experiment and (hypothetical) networks of buyers do not change as a result of a transaction of the buyer with the used-car dealer. Third, because the variation in properties of the transactions is controlled by the experimenter, selectivity of transactions included in the experiment could be prevented beforehand.

Of course, the vignette experiment has its own shortcomings. As always in a vignette experiment, subjects are questioned about hypothetical situations. Thus, it might not be clear whether subjects are able to imagine what they would do "in reality." The careful choice of the setting for the experiment and the fact that most subjects considered the task to be related to their real-life experience convince me that this is not a serious problem. The interpretation of some variables is much more problematic. In particular, this involves the two variables for expected transactions in the future and the outdegree of the buyer. "Moving to the other side of the country" is the operationalization of a low probability of future transactions with the same supplier. Moving reduces the possibilities for sanctioning untrustworthy behavior of the dealer in the future. However, moving also implies that a buyer has to invest in searching for another garage to repair the car whatever the cause of a defect on the car may be. Consequently, it may be the costs of moving rather than the benefits of staying that causes the effect of moving to the other side of the country. Moreover, a dealer can anticipate on limited sanction possibilities by the buyer only if he knows that the buyer will move in the near future. Outdegree of the buyer is operationalized as being a team member of the used-car dealer. Sanctioning a team member through common network contacts is certainly not inconceivable. However, if a team member is a good friend, a buyer may not want to get involved with a friend in a business-like relationship. Problems with the transaction, for whatever reason, can easily lead to a deterioration in the friendship, and buyers may refrain from buying used cars from friends because they foresee and want to avoid such problems. Although the results indicate that this is not the main reasoning employed by most subjects, the relatively small effect of outdegree may be due to this problem.

Evaluation of the Research Questions

This book shows that learning as well as control are important elements in determining trust, in addition to characteristics of the trust problem per se. Also, the distinction between global and individual network parameters is essential if one wants to consider the "level" of social organizations necessary for solving a certain trust problem. Control through social networks depends primarily on the perceptions actors have of their social network, because control depends largely on the sanctions anticipated by the actors. If actors have only a rough indication of how their networks appear, it is questionable whether detailed network parameters such as transitivity or centralization do in fact induce control effects, even if they can be measured accurately. For learning effects, however, the actual network structure is of greater importance than for control effects, because the amount of information an actor will receive depends directly on who communicates with whom. Thus, if control is of major importance for trust but networks are not very visible, it would not be very promising to use network parameters that are more detailed than density, outdegree, and indegree. If learning becomes more important, other network parameters may also become essential. This distinction demonstrates that research on the factors determining the relative importance of learning and control may be of considerable interest.

Network parameters are the main independent variables in this book. Obviously, social networks can have many other effects besides the learning and control effects studied here. I have focused on network effects that result from information about characteristics or behavior of a trustee. However, other effects of networks may be important as well. For example, if the selection of a supplier or exit opportunities of buyers are considered, social networks are relevant in which not only buyers but also suppliers are included. Moreover, networks of buyers may not only provide opportunities for buyers to communicate information on the behavior of the supplier. Buyers, for example, may also learn from each other how they should manage transactions with suppliers, or they may imitate each other by writing similar contracts although they have transactions with different suppliers.

7.3 SUGGESTIONS FOR FURTHER RESEARCH

After summarizing the results and shortcomings of the research presented in this book, the task remains of sketching avenues for further research. The theoretical and empirical results show that learning and control affect trust through temporal as well as network embeddedness. Theoretically, hypotheses are derived about the relative impact of some network parameters, but only limited empirical evidence is obtained to compare the strength of the effects of network parameters. This is mainly due to the measurement of networks that do not allow for operationalizing detailed network parameters. The vignette experiment suggests that learning is more important than control in predicting trust. However, the models in this book do not provide predictions about the relative impact of learning compared to control. Moreover, although it is possible in the experiment to treat networks in an exogenous manner, an analysis of the survey suggests that social networks change over time and that insights into the dynamics of social networks can improve understanding of effects of network parameters. Therefore, three extensions of the research presented in this book are almost obvious. First, models should be improved to allow for comparisons to be made of the effects of learning and control. Preferably, they should provide predictions about how the relative effects of learning and control depend on other variables such as transaction characteristics or uncertainties about the network structure. It seems a plausible hunch that the more difficult it is for actors to observe the network structure among relevant actors, the less probable it is that they will rely on third-party sanctions. Consequently, I postulate that learning through social networks will become relatively more important than control if it is more difficult for trustors to observe their network. Second, for a better understanding of the search for information about potential partners in trust relations and the effects of search on the networks among actors, more dynamic modelling of networks is needed. Third, subsequent tests of these models should allow for a better measurement of social networks in order to obtain more insight into the relative effects of different network parameters such as outdegree, indegree, density, and, preferably, also more complex network parameters such as centralization and transitivity. For testing models about the dynamics of networks, *longitudinal network data* would be preferable.

Improving Theoretical Models

Assumptions about incomplete or other forms of imperfect information should be included in the game-theoretic model so that it allows for learning. Incomplete information can account for uncertainties experienced by the trustor about characteristics of the trustee. Moreover, there are strong indications that trustors have difficulties in assessing the extent to which other trustors are willing to sanction a trustee and that trustors have limited knowledge about the structure of the network in which they are placed. Thus, assuming incomplete information about the structure of the network and incentives of other trustors can also improve the models presented in this book. Extensions about other forms of imperfect information can include forms of bounded rationality such as imperfect recall or imperfect abilities to foresee future contingencies (for example, Rubinstein 1998). Learning itself can be addressed in a completely rational manner using Bayesian updating (see Harsanyi 1967–68), but also in a boundedly rational way using evolutionary game theory (Weibull 1995; Samuelson 1997; Fudenberg and Levine 1998).

Complexity should be added to the models in a gradual and stepwise fashion. To keep models manageable, one has to refrain from adding too much complexity at one time. This is an important reason for using a core theory at the individual level that is relatively simple, namely, that actors are purposive utility maximizers (see Coleman 1990: 18–19). The assumptions that have to be made more complex are, first, the bridge assumptions linking the macro to the micro level. Only later, assumptions about individual behavior should be made more complex (Lindenberg 1992). In terms of the models in this book, information assumptions, i.e., bridge assumptions on asymmetric information availability *within* a trust relation, are a good starting point for increasing the complexity and "realism" of the game-theoretic model. In the two empirical applications, it is clear that asymmetric information is the main argument as to why buyers of IT products and used cars confront trust problems with their supplier or dealer. Consequently, it is assumed that the buyer has difficulties in judging the quality of the product she wants to buy, but that she knows exactly the incentives for the supplier or dealer. Often, such an assumption will be less than plausible and, hence, explicitly modeling incomplete and asymmetric information in the sense that the buyers do not exactly know the incentives of the supplier seems reasonable (Buskens 2000). Second, for such extensions one can choose the way in which learning is treated. For two-actor models, analytic results will be obtainable using Bayesian learning. These models can form a baseline for more complex models with more actors.

The theory of learning in games can be used to obtain results related to evolutionary learning processes for models with one trustee and a network of trustors or other multi-actor models. In the economics literature, the emphasis is placed on the stability of evolutionary processes, investigating whether learning processes lead to Nash equilibria and whether these evolutionary processes can provide suggestions for refinements of Nash equilibria (for example, Fudenberg and Levine 1998). I think that an important step has to be made, namely, linking these more general results to more specific models that are studied in sociology. Many studies in sociological literature discuss simulations with "realistic" interpretations. In these studies, it is investigated how populations in such simulations evolve over time (see, for example, Macy 1990; Liebrand and Messick 1995; Flache and Macy 1996). Except for rather simple models (see Buskens and Snijders 1997), analytic solutions for such simulations are hardly feasible. Therefore, these models require a careful investigation of the outcomes of the simulations for variations in model parameters. Moreover, the set of feasible strategies for actors assumed within such simulations and the exact assumptions about the setting of the experiment can have a considerable impact on outcomes as can be seen from the discussion on Axelrod's (Axelrod 1984) iterated Prisoner's Dilemma tournament (see also Binmore 1998). Nowak and Sigmund (1993) have shown that a strategy called Win-Stay, Loose-Shift could surpass Tit-for-Tat, the strategy that won Axelrod's tournament, in a noisy setting.[2] Then, Wu and Axelrod (1995) have demonstrated that even in a noisy setting Tit-for-Tat could still win a tournament with a pool of strategies that differs from the pool of strategies in the simulation of Nowak and Sigmund. This shows that outcomes in these simulations strongly depend on variations such as the initial pool of strategies.

To overcome the problem that the outcomes of a simulation depend largely on the pool of strategies chosen by the researchers in a rather ad hoc way, one can use *genetic algorithms* (Goldberg 1989). Genetic algorithms are used to model how new strategies evolve from the strategies that are defined at the beginning of the simulation (see, for example, Axelrod 1986; Macy 1996; Macy and Skvoretz 1998). However, for such complex extensions, it will be more difficult to analyze the process as a whole and to produce statements about the evolutionary stability of the process and its dependence on particular parameters in the model. Therefore, I maintain that adding complexity to the model gradually and in a stepwise fashion is a precondition for understanding the impact of adding new parameters. Moreover, analytic results about equilibria and the stability of these equilibria in evolutionary games, even in very specific conditions, can provide significant improvements to the understanding of simulations.

Another group of bridge assumptions that can be made more complex involve those related to communication among trustors. In this book, information transfer is always stochastic, costless, and accurate. Moreover, the ties through

[2]Win-Stay, Loose-Shift starts with cooperation in a Prisoner's Dilemma. Thereafter, Win-Stay, Loose-Shift always repeats its former move after a cooperative move of the other player and changes to the other move after a defective move of the other player.

which communication is made possible are given and do not change within the models. One of the most straightforward extensions of the existing models would be to introduce random noise to the communication process (see, for example, Fudenberg and Maskin 1990; Wu and Axelrod 1995). This would imply, for example, that trustors should be careful about how they react to information about an abuse of trust by a trustee, because never trusting the trustee again may be a too severe sanction if the trustor is not completely sure about the accuracy of the information. Namely, if information is not accurate it may seem as though the trustee has abused trust even if the trustee never really did. Nevertheless, to prevent a trustee from abusing trust, the trustor should employ sanctions against the trustee. However, because these sanctions are also costly for the trustor, it is better for the trustor to refrain from trusting the trustee only for a period of time that is just long enough to withhold the trustee from intentionally abusing trust, rather than never trusting the trustee again. This issue is analyzed, for example, in the literature on "optimal punishment" (see Porter 1983; Green and Porter 1984). Other forms of uncertainty that are relevant with respect to the communication of information and that may be introduced in new models are uncertainties about the structure of the network among other trustors. Moreover, because control is based on the anticipation of the trustee of sanctions imposed by trustors in future, one might in fact add another "level" of uncertainty for the trustors, namely, uncertainty about how the trustee perceives the network of trustors.

More complicated extensions address intentional and strategic communication activities of actors. Such extensions can address with whom actors want to communicate, which information they are willing to disclose, as well as strategic information distortion. One can think about these questions in terms of social exchange models (see Blau [1964] 1996; Coleman 1972, 1973, 1990: Chapter 6) and, in particular, models in which network structure is explicitly modeled.[3] Two problems arise if communication of information is itself considered as an exchange. First, communication likewise resembles a trust problem. If the information should be used to solve another trust problem, the interdependence between relations becomes very complicated. Second, as argued in Chapter 4, information cannot be exchanged in the sense that the information is actually given away by the sender. The sender will still have the information after the "exchange."

More dynamic models about networks will also be useful, for example, models of buyers searching for information about potential suppliers. The buyers'

[3]For example, Cook and Emerson (1978), Markovsky, Willer, and Patton (1988), Yamaguchi (1996), and Bienenstock and Bonacich (1997) have provided important contributions to this rapidly extending literature in sociology. In the economics literature, Gilles (1990) developed models of socially structured economies using general equilibrium theory, and Van den Brink (1994) modeled power of economic agents in hierarchically structured organizations.

search for information creates network ties among customers of suppliers. In addition, buyers who have unsatisfactory experiences with a supplier can be expected to be more active in informing others about these experiences, as part of their retaliation against the supplier. Models have been developed to investigate the emergence of networks using game theory (Bala and Goyal 2000) as well as for specific empirical applications such as policy networks (Stokman and Zeggelink 1996) and friendship networks (Zeggelink, Stokman, and Van der Bunt 1996). Snijders (2001) has developed statistical models to analyze such longitudinal network data. In these models, it is assumed that actors try to realize "goals" and the extent to which they can realize these goals depends on the properties of the other actors with whom they make policy arrangements or with whom they become friends. The investments of actors in establishing relations with other actors depend on the characteristics of these other actors and the existing structure of the network. In Chapter 5, it seems that networks of buyers of IT products change as a result of buyers' efforts to collect information about IT suppliers. Buyers try to obtain a high-quality product for a low price, preferably without costly management of the relation with the supplier. The more important a product is for a buyer, the more incentives she has to invest in searching other customers who have experience with IT suppliers. The more these buyers succeed in receiving useful information about suppliers and the more other customers of a certain supplier they know after the search for information, the smaller the trust problem remaining to be settled. Although these models could provide predictions about how much buyers are willing to invest in search, which other customers they want to contact, and the extent to which they can be expected to be successful in reaching their goals, the models rely heavily on the assumption that important characteristics of all relevant actors are common knowledge. In testing these models, it is even more important than in testing the models in this book that complete networks in relatively closed settings are studied. This will be the first point to be addressed when dealing with the improvement of empirical applications.

Improving Empirical Research

At least three problems suggest that the survey data of the IT transactions are not perfectly appropriate for testing the hypotheses derived in the theoretical chapters. Networks are extremely difficult to measure in the "open" setting of small and medium-sized enterprises in the Netherlands. In such settings, all network data relate to the ego-centered networks of the buyers who are included in the sample. There will hardly be any overlap among networks of different buyers and the overlaps cannot be reconstructed from the data. Thus, the data do not allow to construct a complete network of (a group of) firms, which implies that global network parameters are difficult to estimate. Moreover, self-reports of the individual network positions are often inaccurate (see Bernard et al. 1981). Therefore, it is more appropriate to test hypotheses about the effects of detailed network parameters by studying settings that are more "closed." Such settings are networks *within* firms (see, for example, Burt 1992; Krackhardt 1992; Lazega and Van Duijn 1997; Van der Bunt 1997; Wittek 1999), which have also been studied with respect to trust (Burt and Knez 1995a, 1995b; Wittek 2001). Another setting that seems appropriate may concern networks within classes of (undergraduate) students (Zeggelink, Hiramatsu, Stokman, Van Duijn, and Wasseur 1998). These classes provide suitable opportunities to follow actors over time and for obtaining longitudinal data that can be used to test hypotheses about dynamics in social networks, for example, as a result of information search or characteristics of partners (see also Leenders 1995).[4] Different trust problems can occur among students in such classes, for example, related to cooperation in joint projects. Both problems about network data mentioned above are less problematic in such closed settings. If most of the actors in the network participate in a study, an estimate of the whole network within the group can be obtained and global network parameters can be derived. Of course, for testing hypotheses about effects of global network parameters, multiple networks should be compared. Moreover, if most actors in the network provide information about the network, repeated information for each tie is obtained and this provides possibilities for estimating individual network parameters of actors in the network from reports by other actors in the network, which are expected to be more accurate than self-reports of actors (for example, Krackhardt 1987).

Another problem with the data in Chapter 5 is the huge variation in transaction characteristics. This is not problematic as such. However, the transaction characteristics turn out to have stronger effects on the number of safeguards in the contract than the network parameters. Moreover, the number of other customers of a supplier known to the buyer seems to be correlated with unexplained variance in the transaction characteristics. As a consequence, it is difficult to determine the effect of the number of other customers known by the buyer. Therefore, I think that these tests of network hypotheses can be improved if variation in transactions characteristics is limited, for example, by choosing only complex software transactions. If other circumstances are held constant, effects of networks will be isolated more easily, which may result in a stronger test of hypotheses.

The problems with the vignette experiment are mainly due to the interpretation of the setting and the variables. Moreover, within the experiment it is almost impossible to vary more complex network parameters than indegree, out-

[4] Studying these classes starting from the entrance at the university also has the advantage that there are hardly any network ties in the beginning and that there will be considerable changes in the network over time.

degree, and density. Both problems can be solved if more abstract experiments could be designed in which abstract games are played and network structure is included.[5] The main problem is to design games in such a way that subjects can understand them. Network structure, which is manipulated by the experimenter, should be clearly visible to the subjects. Moreover, subjects should have time to experience the game and develop appropriate strategies. Camerer and Weigelt (1988) have demonstrated that subjects need such a learning phase to develop strategies in a repeated Trust Game with incomplete information. Subjects will certainly need time to experience the possible effects of the network.[6]

A computer network can provide an important tool in facilitating such experiments. It is important that circumstances for individuals are comparable if the behavior of individuals is to be compared. To prevent complex interplay between a number of individuals who all behave and communicate in very different ways, it seems useful to structure communication possibilities. For example, a useful design feature of an experiment may be that subjects can only send a given number of key messages covering the most important types of information needed within the experiment. Moreover, one could program a whole network of simulated actors, such that only one subject is a real actor in a network and, consequently, that all subjects meet exactly the same "opponents." In this way, it is also possible to obtain information about a larger number of networks than in experiments in which every position in a network is occupied by a "real" subject, which makes testing hypotheses about global networks less costly.

SUMMING UP

The research in this book highlights the interplay between the development of sociological theory and testing the theory in empirical situations. I started from theory and have shown in the early chapters that it is possible to deduce hypotheses from rational choice models about core sociological problems such as the effects of social networks on trust. The survey of IT transactions demonstrates that it is also possible to relate abstract theory to an empirical setting. The survey shows that incentives in the transactions largely determine the trust problem between buyer and supplier and that this is reflected in the number of safeguards in the contract between buyer and supplier. Moreover, it has been shown that positive experiences between a buyer and supplier in past transactions diminish the trust problem. However, effects of social networks on trust are scarcely apparent from the survey. A major problem seems to be that the measurement of networks is difficult within this empirical setting. Thus, the setting seems less than optimal for testing the effects of networks. The experi-

[5] See Flache (1996) for an example with limited variation in network structure.

[6] Modeling the exact process of learning in such games may require research related to evolutionary games.

ment related to the purchase of used cars demonstrates that network hypotheses receive more support in a setting in which testing network hypotheses is a primary goal and that comes closer to the assumptions on network properties that are presupposed in the theoretical models.

Both empirical studies demonstrate that learning is quite crucial for trust. Buyers trust suppliers more if they have positive information about the performance of the suppliers in prior transactions. This indicates that buyers' expectations about the behavior of suppliers change as a result of the information they receive about suppliers. Consequently, complete information assumptions on the buyers' knowledge about incentives and abilities of the supplier are unrealistic and cannot account for the learning effects of social networks on trust. Game theory provides tools for relaxing complete information assumptions. Thus, theory can guide the construction of new models of network effects on trust that are compatible with the empirical findings described in this book and will, hopefully, generate new predictions, for example, about the relative impact of learning and control via network embeddedness.

Appendix A
Mathematical Details

In this appendix, I prove the theorems presented in Chapter 3 and an additional theorem on the properties of the set of equilibria in trigger strategies of the IHTG.

Proof of Theorem 3.1 (page 64). If all actors play the one-shot equilibrium strategies D_i all the time, this constitutes a subgame-perfect equilibrium. This proves assertion *i)*. Now consider a strategy vector $(\vartheta_{11}, \ldots, \vartheta_{n1}, \vartheta_{12}, \ldots, \vartheta_{n2})$. First, assume $\vartheta_{i1} < \vartheta_{i2}$ for at least one i. Then, trustor i does not maximize her payoff. If she chooses $\vartheta_{i1} = \vartheta_{i2}$, her payoff increases with $R_1 - P_1$ every time that $\vartheta_{i1} < \theta < \vartheta_{i2}$. This occurs with positive probability since F has full support. In all other cases the payoff is the same. On the other hand, assume $\vartheta_{i1} > \vartheta_{i2}$ for at least one i. In this case, trustor i does not maximize her payoff, because the trustee will play D_2 if $\vartheta_{i1} > \theta > \vartheta_{i2}$. The trustee will receive $R_2 + \theta$, while trustor i receives S_1 and in all the following games trustor i plays D_1 and receives a payoff P_1. However, if trustor i would have chosen $\vartheta_{i1} = \vartheta_{i2}$, she would have received P_1 in the game mentioned and R_1 or P_1 in all the following games, which is more than she receives now. Thus, if $\vartheta_{i1} \neq \vartheta_{i2}$, trustor i increases her payoff by moving her threshold toward the threshold of the trustee. Therefore, if $\vartheta_{i1} \neq \vartheta_{i2}$ trustor i does not use a best reply. This shows that the trustor's threshold and the trustee's threshold with respect to this trustor are the same in equilibrium. □

Proof of Theorem 3.2 (page 65). First, I prove the equilibrium condition in assertion *i)*. The game analyzed here is a repeated game with infinite horizon and exponential discounting. Hence, I can apply a well-known result of dynamic programming theory, namely, Bellman's optimality principle (Bellman 1957; Kreps 1990b). Optimality on the equilibrium path is guaranteed if one-step deviations from the prescribed path in any decision node do not increase the payoff. Therefore, it has to be proven that if an actor makes a one-step deviation from the equilibrium path, the actor's payoff will not increase. Without loss of generality, consider deviations at time $t = 0$. The involved trustor is trustor i. First, consider $\theta > \vartheta_i$. Then, both actors defect, and, therefore, no one has an incentive to deviate. Now, consider $\theta \leq \vartheta_i$. Again the trustor has no incentive to deviate, because on the equilibrium path she receives her maximal payoff R_1. The trustee should play D_2 if he can obtain a short-term gain that is higher than the long-term loss due to the punishment by the trustors. Thus, it has to be proven that the restriction in Theorem 3.2 is exactly the condition that the long-term loss for the trustee will not be smaller than the short-term gain, if he plays D_2 and $\theta \leq \vartheta_i$. In other words, I will show that also the trustee has no incentive to deviate from the equilibrium path.

Let $EU_2(C_2, \theta; \boldsymbol{\vartheta})$ be the expected payoff for the trustee if both actors follow the trigger strategy. In equilibrium, no trustor is ever informed about deviations from the equilibrium path by the trustee. The expected payoff of the trustee can be expressed in terms of a matrix with probabilities indicating which trustor will be involved in subsequent games. The information exchange opportunities are not relevant in this case. The probability matrix equals

$$\boldsymbol{\Pi} = \begin{pmatrix} 1-\delta_1+\delta_1\pi_1 & \delta_1\pi_2 & \cdots & \delta_1\pi_n \\ \delta_2\pi_1 & \ddots & \ddots & \vdots \\ \vdots & \ddots & \ddots & \delta_{n-1}\pi_n \\ \delta_n\pi_1 & \cdots & \delta_n\pi_{n-1} & 1-\delta_n+\delta_n\pi_n \end{pmatrix}, \tag{A.1}$$

where the diagonal elements are the probabilities that the same trustor continues a series of transactions or stops and is chosen again as the new trustor. The other elements are the probabilities that one trustor stops and another trustor starts a series of transactions.

The trustee's payoff with any trustor j he encounters in the future equals P_2 with probability $Pr(\theta > \vartheta_j) = 1 - F(\vartheta_j)$ and R_2 with probability $F(\vartheta_j)$. The trustee's expected payoff for the equilibrium path, given that he starts transactions with trustor i and $\theta < \vartheta_i$, equals

$$EU_2(C_2, \theta; \boldsymbol{\vartheta}) = R_2 + \sum_{t=1}^{\infty} w^t \boldsymbol{e}_i' \boldsymbol{\Pi}^t \boldsymbol{\mu} = R_2 + \boldsymbol{e}_i'(\tilde{\boldsymbol{\Pi}}_w - \boldsymbol{I})\boldsymbol{\mu}, \tag{A.2}$$

where $\boldsymbol{\mu}$ is a n-vector with $\mu_i = F(\vartheta_i)R_2 + (1 - F(\vartheta_i))P_2$.

Now, the trustee deviates from the equilibrium path and abuses trust (D_2). The necessary condition for subgame-perfect equilibrium is $EU_2(C_2, \theta; \boldsymbol{\vartheta}) \geq EU_2(D_2, \theta; \boldsymbol{\vartheta})$ for all $\theta \leq \vartheta_i$. The involved trustor of course knows that trust has been abused. The probabilities whether or not the following trustors will have the information about the abuse of trust are given in

$$Q = \begin{matrix} S_{inf} \\ S_{noinf} \end{matrix} \overset{\begin{matrix} S_{inf} & S_{noinf} \end{matrix}}{\left(\begin{array}{c|c} \boldsymbol{T} & \boldsymbol{\Pi} - \boldsymbol{T} \\ \hline \boldsymbol{0} & \boldsymbol{\Pi} \end{array} \right)}, \tag{A.3}$$

where $\boldsymbol{T}$ denotes the probabilities that a trustor who has information about abused trust communicates this to the trustor in the following game (see equation (3.1) in Chapter 3). $\boldsymbol{\Pi} - \boldsymbol{T}$ are the probabilities that a trustor with information about abused trust does not communicate this to the next trustor. $\boldsymbol{\Pi}$ are the probabilities that one trustor will follow another trustor. These probabilities are relevant again after the information about abused trust is lost.[1]

The payoff for the trustee is $R_2 + \theta$ in the game in which he abuses trust; his payoff will be P_2 as long as the trustee encounters trustors who know about this deceit. As soon as information is not transmitted to the following trustor, the payoffs are as if no trustor was ever deceived. This is the consequence of the fact that information is lost among the trustors as soon as a new trustor who starts a series of transactions does not receive information from the previous trustor, and the trustee knows that the trustors do not know anymore about his abuse of trust. Thus,

$$\begin{aligned} EU_2(D_2, \theta; \vartheta) &= R_2 + \theta + \sum_{t=1}^{\infty} w^t \, (\boldsymbol{e}_i' \ \ \boldsymbol{0}') \, \boldsymbol{Q}^t \begin{pmatrix} P_2 \boldsymbol{1} \\ \boldsymbol{\mu} \end{pmatrix} \\ &= R_2 + \theta + (\boldsymbol{e}_i' \ \ \boldsymbol{0}') \, (\tilde{\boldsymbol{Q}}_w - \boldsymbol{I}) \begin{pmatrix} P_2 \boldsymbol{1} \\ \boldsymbol{\mu} \end{pmatrix}. \end{aligned} \tag{A.4}$$

Using $w\boldsymbol{T}\tilde{\boldsymbol{T}}_w = \tilde{\boldsymbol{T}}_w - \boldsymbol{I}$ and, $w\boldsymbol{\Pi}\tilde{\boldsymbol{\Pi}}_w = \tilde{\boldsymbol{\Pi}}_w - \boldsymbol{I}$, it follows by straightforward computation that

$$\begin{aligned} \tilde{\boldsymbol{Q}}_w - \boldsymbol{I} &= \begin{pmatrix} \boldsymbol{I} - w\boldsymbol{T} & -w(\boldsymbol{\Pi} - \boldsymbol{T}) \\ \boldsymbol{0} & \boldsymbol{I} - w\boldsymbol{\Pi} \end{pmatrix}^{-1} - \boldsymbol{I} \\ &= \begin{pmatrix} \tilde{\boldsymbol{T}}_w & w\tilde{\boldsymbol{T}}_w(\boldsymbol{\Pi} - \boldsymbol{T})\tilde{\boldsymbol{\Pi}}_w \\ \boldsymbol{0} & \tilde{\boldsymbol{\Pi}}_w \end{pmatrix} - \boldsymbol{I} \\ &= \begin{pmatrix} \tilde{\boldsymbol{T}}_w & \tilde{\boldsymbol{\Pi}}_w - \tilde{\boldsymbol{T}}_w \\ \boldsymbol{0} & \tilde{\boldsymbol{\Pi}}_w \end{pmatrix} - \boldsymbol{I} \end{aligned}$$

[1] The stochastic matrix $\boldsymbol{Q}$ is a transition matrix of a Markov chain with $2n$ states in which the states are defined by the identity of the trustor who has transactions with the trustee and whether or not this trustor has information about trust abused by the trustee.

$$= \begin{pmatrix} \tilde{\boldsymbol{T}}_w - \boldsymbol{I} & \tilde{\boldsymbol{\Pi}}_w - \tilde{\boldsymbol{T}}_w \\ \boldsymbol{0} & \tilde{\boldsymbol{\Pi}}_w - \boldsymbol{I} \end{pmatrix}. \quad \text{(A.5)}$$

By substituting (A.4) in (A.3):

$$\begin{aligned} EU_2(D_2, \theta; \boldsymbol{\vartheta}) &= R_2 + \theta + \boldsymbol{e}_i'(\tilde{\boldsymbol{T}}_w - \boldsymbol{I})P_2\boldsymbol{1} + \boldsymbol{e}_i'(\tilde{\boldsymbol{\Pi}}_w - \tilde{\boldsymbol{T}}_w)\boldsymbol{\mu} \quad \text{(A.6)} \\ &= R_2 + \theta + \boldsymbol{e}_i'(\tilde{\boldsymbol{T}}_w - \boldsymbol{I})(P_2\boldsymbol{1} - \boldsymbol{\mu}) + \boldsymbol{e}_i'(\tilde{\boldsymbol{\Pi}}_w - \boldsymbol{I})\boldsymbol{\mu}. \end{aligned}$$

Hence, $EU_2(C_2, \theta; \boldsymbol{\vartheta}) \geq EU_2(D_2, \theta; \boldsymbol{\vartheta})$ is equivalent to

$$\begin{aligned} \theta &\leq \boldsymbol{e}_i'(\tilde{\boldsymbol{T}}_w - \boldsymbol{I})(\boldsymbol{\mu} - P_2\boldsymbol{1}) \\ &= \boldsymbol{e}_i'(\tilde{\boldsymbol{T}}_w - \boldsymbol{I}) \begin{pmatrix} (R_2 - P_2)F(\vartheta_1) \\ \vdots \\ (R_2 - P_2)F(\vartheta_n) \end{pmatrix} \\ &= (R_2 - P_2)\boldsymbol{e}_i'(\tilde{\boldsymbol{T}}_w - \boldsymbol{I})F(\boldsymbol{\vartheta}). \quad \text{(A.7)} \end{aligned}$$

In equilibrium, equation (A.7) should hold for all $\theta \leq \vartheta_i$: $EU_2(C_2, \theta; \boldsymbol{\vartheta}) \geq EU_2(D_2, \theta; \boldsymbol{\vartheta})$; clearly, $\theta = (R_2 - P_2)\boldsymbol{e}_i'(\tilde{\boldsymbol{T}}_w - \boldsymbol{I})F(\boldsymbol{\vartheta})$ is the most restrictive θ for which the trustee has no incentive to abuse trust placed by trustor i. Consequently, the threshold of trustor i should be smaller or equal to this value, i.e.,

$$\vartheta_i \leq (R_2 - P_2)\boldsymbol{e}_i'(\tilde{\boldsymbol{T}}_w - \boldsymbol{I})F(\boldsymbol{\vartheta}) \quad \text{(A.8)}$$

to ensure that the trustee never abuses trust. Because this holds for all i, the trigger strategies are in equilibrium.

Remark. There is a minor technical problem with "subgame perfectness" in this game. As long as trustors communicate information when a new trustor enters the game, subgame perfectness is well-defined. In that case, the trigger equilibrium is subgame perfect, because the actors act according the equilibrium in the constituent game after leaving the equilibrium path, and this is also an equilibrium of the repeated game. Note that to ensure subgame perfectness here, it was necessary to assume that the trustee will continue to abuse trust after abusing trust once as long as the trustors know about the abuse of trust, and, thus, that the trustee knows whether trustors communicate information about the behavior of the trustee. If a trustor enters the game and does not receive information from her predecessor, this trustor does not know anything about what happened in the game before. She even does not know how many rounds have been played before. Thus, strictly speaking, the node in which this trustor starts, and all nodes thereafter, cannot be considered as subgames because there is a large set of nodes that the game could have reached and that are all in the same information set for the new trustor. On the other hand, the trustor cannot distinguish her situation from the first round in the game and, therefore, from the viewpoint of the trustor the whole information set can be "collapsed" to one node. The only problem is that the trustee knows what happened in previous rounds. But, because the trustee does not use his experiences in previous rounds, I consider the round that starts with a trustor who is not informed about the behavior of the trustee in earlier rounds as the start of a new game. For this new game, the trigger equilibria are subgame-perfect equilibria. This concludes the proof of the equilibrium condition.[2] $\triangle$

Now, I continue the proof of Theorem 3.2. Assertion *ii)* states that there exists a unique Pareto optimal equilibrium in trigger strategies. First, I show that if inequality (A.8) is strict for a certain threshold, there exists a Pareto superior equilibrium in which equality holds. The second step to prove assertion *ii)* consists of a construction that shows that two Pareto not-comparable equilibria thresholds are always Pareto dominated by another equilibrium threshold. Suppose there exists a subgame-perfect equilibrium with $\vartheta_i < (R_2 - P_2)\sum_{j=1}^{n}(\tilde{\boldsymbol{T}}_w - \boldsymbol{I})_{ij}F(\vartheta_j)$ for at least one i. Then, ϑ_i can be increased until $\hat{\vartheta}_i = (R_2 - P_2)\sum_{j=1}^{n}(\tilde{\boldsymbol{T}}_w - \boldsymbol{I})_{ij}F(\vartheta_j)$ because the right side is bounded above by $\frac{(R_2-P_2)w}{1-w}$ and monotonous increasing in ϑ_i, while ϑ_i is not bounded above. The other inequalities for $j \neq i$ still hold because the right sides increase with ϑ_i. In the next step, it has to be checked whether $\vartheta_{i+1} = (R_2 - P_2)\sum_{j=1}^{n}(\tilde{\boldsymbol{T}}_w - \boldsymbol{I})_{i+1j}F(\vartheta_j)$, otherwise ϑ_{i+1} can be increased until $\hat{\vartheta}_{i+1} = (R_2 - P_2)\sum_{j=1}^{n}(\tilde{\boldsymbol{T}}_w - \boldsymbol{I})_{ij}F(\vartheta_j)$. Continue this procedure until ϑ_n and start again from ϑ_1 and so on. This gives an increasing sequence of vectors $\boldsymbol{\vartheta}$ associated with equilibria in trigger strategies, which is bounded because $\vartheta_i \leq \frac{(R_2-P_2)w}{1-w}$. By the convergence theorem that bounded increasing sequences converge (Akkermans and Van Lint 1970: 217), the sequence converges to a limit $\boldsymbol{\vartheta}$ where $\vartheta_i = (R_2 - P_2)\sum_{j=1}^{n}(\tilde{\boldsymbol{T}}_w - \boldsymbol{I})_{ij}F(\vartheta_j)$ for all i and the equilibrium associated with the limit is a Pareto improvement of all equilibria in the sequence.

At this moment, it has to be shown that there exists a *unique* $\boldsymbol{\vartheta}^*$ that Pareto dominates all other equilibria in trigger strategies. Suppose that there are two Pareto dominant equilibria $\boldsymbol{\vartheta}$ and $\hat{\boldsymbol{\vartheta}}$. Then, there exists, possibly after relabeling, an l such that

[2] Note that the discussion about *subgame perfectness* of the trigger equilibria is a discussion about "subgames" and not about "perfectness." A reader who does not want to consider a round starting with an uninformed trustor as the start of a new game should introduce beliefs for the new trustor about the situation in which she enters the game. The only way to introduce beliefs that are consistent with the strategies is that the game has followed an equilibrium path. This implies that the trustor is convinced that trust is never abused and, therefore, she will act as if she starts a new game.

$$\vartheta_i \geq \hat{\vartheta}_i \text{ for } 1 \leq i \leq l \text{ and } \vartheta_i < \hat{\vartheta}_i \text{ for } l < i \leq n. \tag{A.9}$$

Define $G_i(\boldsymbol{\vartheta}) = \vartheta_i - (R_2 - P_2)\sum_{j=1}^{n}(\tilde{\boldsymbol{T}}_w - \boldsymbol{I})_{ij}F(\vartheta_j)$. Because F is a strictly increasing function, $R_2 - P_2 > 0$, and all matrix elements of $(\tilde{\boldsymbol{T}}_w - \boldsymbol{I})$ are positive, $\partial G_i/\partial\vartheta_j < 0$ if $i \neq j$. Then,

$$\begin{aligned} G_i(\vartheta_1, \ldots, \vartheta_l, \hat{\vartheta}_{l+1}, \ldots \hat{\vartheta}_n) &< G_i(\vartheta_1, \ldots, \vartheta_n) = 0, \ 1 \leq i \leq l; \quad \text{(A.10)} \\ G_i(\vartheta_1, \ldots, \vartheta_l, \hat{\vartheta}_{l+1}, \ldots \hat{\vartheta}_n) &\leq G_i(\hat{\vartheta}_1, \ldots, \hat{\vartheta}_n) = 0, \ l < i \leq n. \quad \text{(A.11)} \end{aligned}$$

Therefore, $(\vartheta_1, \ldots, \vartheta_l, \hat{\vartheta}_{l+1}, \ldots \hat{\vartheta}_n)$ is a subgame-perfect equilibrium. This equilibrium Pareto dominates the equilibria considered before. Thus, from two Pareto non-comparable equilibria, it is possible to construct a subgame-perfect equilibrium that is a Pareto improvement of these two equilibria, contradicting that $\boldsymbol{\vartheta}$ and $\hat{\boldsymbol{\vartheta}}$ were payoff dominant equilibria. Thus, it is impossible that different payoff dominant equilibria can exist, which proves uniqueness. □

In Theorem 3.2, the set thresholds associated with subgame-perfect equilibria in trigger strategies of the IHTG equals

$$\Theta = \{\boldsymbol{\vartheta} \mid 0 \leq \vartheta_i \leq (R_2 - P_2)\boldsymbol{e}_i(\tilde{\boldsymbol{T}}_w - \boldsymbol{I})F(\boldsymbol{\vartheta}) \text{ for all } i\}. \tag{A.12}$$

The following theorem specifies some properties of this set of equilibrium thresholds.

THEOREM A.1 *The set Θ, defined in (A.12), has the following properties.*

i) The set Θ is not empty: $\mathbf{0} \in \Theta$.

ii) $\Theta \subset [0, \frac{(R_2 - P_2)w}{1-w}]^n$.

iii) The set Θ is closed.

iv) A sufficient condition for the existence of another subgame-perfect equilibrium than $\mathbf{0}$ is that there exists an $S \subset \{1, \ldots, n\}$, for which

$$(R_2 - P_2)f(0)\sum_{j \in S}(\tilde{\boldsymbol{T}}_w - \boldsymbol{I})_{ij} > 1 \textit{ for all } i \in S. \tag{A.13}$$

v) If F is concave, Θ convex.

Proof. Assertion *i)* has already been shown in Theorem 3.1. Assertion *ii)* follows from the fact that if $\theta \geq \frac{w}{1-w}(R_2 - P_2)$, the incentive for abusing trust in that particular game is larger than the maximal amount that can be earned by cooperative behavior in all the following games. Assertion *iii)* holds because F is continuous. To prove assertion *iv)* assume that (A.13) holds for some S. Then, $\varepsilon > 0$ exists such that for all i

$$\begin{aligned} \varepsilon &< (R_2 - P_2)(F(\varepsilon) - F(0)) \sum_{j \in S} (\tilde{\boldsymbol{T}}_w - \boldsymbol{I})_{ij} \\ &= (R_2 - P_2) F(\varepsilon) \sum_{j \in S} (\tilde{\boldsymbol{T}}_w - \boldsymbol{I})_{ij}. \end{aligned} \tag{A.14}$$

Therefore, $\boldsymbol{\vartheta}$ with $\vartheta_j = \varepsilon$ if $j \in S$ and $\vartheta_j = 0$ if $j \notin S$ is a subgame-perfect equilibrium. Convexity of Θ follows by substitution of a convex combination of two equilibria in the inequalities. Namely, assume that $\boldsymbol{\vartheta}, \hat{\boldsymbol{\vartheta}} \in \Theta$. Then, for any $0 < \varepsilon < 1$,

$$\begin{aligned} \varepsilon\vartheta_i + (1-\varepsilon)\hat{\vartheta}_i &\leq (R_2 - P_2)\boldsymbol{e}_i'(\tilde{\boldsymbol{T}}_w - \boldsymbol{I})) \left(\varepsilon F(\boldsymbol{\vartheta}) + (1-\varepsilon) F(\hat{\boldsymbol{\vartheta}})\right) \\ &< (R_2 - P_2)\boldsymbol{e}_i'(\tilde{\boldsymbol{T}}_w - \boldsymbol{I})) \left(F(\varepsilon\boldsymbol{\vartheta} + (1-\varepsilon)\hat{\boldsymbol{\vartheta}})\right) \end{aligned}$$

because F is concave. Thus, $\varepsilon\boldsymbol{\vartheta} + (1-\varepsilon)\hat{\boldsymbol{\vartheta}} \in \Theta$ for any $0 < \varepsilon < 1$. □

Proof of Theorem 3.3 (page 67). At every period at which a new trustor starts a series of transactions with the trustee, she receives with a probability α information about the behavior of the trustee. Furthermore, the probability that the same trustor continues is the same for all trustors: $1 - \delta + \frac{\delta}{n}$. Thus, the expected time that information about defection stays among the trustors is the same for all trustors and equals

$$\sum_{j=1}^{n} (\tilde{\boldsymbol{T}}_w - I)_{ij} = \frac{w(\eta_1 + (n-1)\eta_2)}{1 - w(\eta_1 + (n-1)\eta_2)} \text{ for all } i. \tag{A.15}$$

Consequently, $\boldsymbol{\vartheta} = (\vartheta, \ldots, \vartheta)$ is a subgame-perfect equilibrium if and only if

$$\vartheta \leq \frac{w(\eta_1 + (n-1)\eta_2)}{1 - w(\eta_1 + (n-1)\eta_2)} (R_2 - P_2) F(\vartheta). \tag{A.16}$$

Furthermore, if $\boldsymbol{\vartheta}$ is not the Pareto optimal subgame-perfect equilibrium, all ϑ_i can be increased with the same amount until the Pareto optimum is obtained in which equalities hold. □

Proof of Theorem 3.4 (page 68). The iterative argument in the proof of Theorem 3.2 implies that if, for a certain change in the parameters, a ϑ_i can be increased, it is possible to construct a new subgame-perfect equilibrium that is a Pareto improvement of the original equilibria. Consequently, if one of the right sides of the equations in (A.8) increases, it is possible to increase the corresponding ϑ_i. This implies that there exists a Pareto superior equilibrium. Therefore, the comparative statics of ϑ_i can be derived from the following equation directly by studying whether the right-hand side of equation (A.17) increases or decreases in a certain parameter, although ϑ_i is only implicitly given in the equation

$$\vartheta_i^* = (R_2 - P_2) \sum_{j=1}^{n} (\tilde{\boldsymbol{T}}_w - \boldsymbol{I})_{ij} F(\vartheta_j^*). \tag{A.17}$$

Define $H_i = (R_2 - P_2) \sum_{j=1}^{n} (\tilde{\boldsymbol{T}}_w - \boldsymbol{I})_{ij} F(\vartheta_j)$. To prove *i)*, note that $F(\theta) \geq 0$ and all matrix elements of $\tilde{\boldsymbol{T}}_w - \boldsymbol{I}$ are positive, so $\frac{\partial H_i}{\partial(R_2 - P_2)} > 0$. This implies that the right-hand side of (A.17) increases in $R_2 - P_2$. As argued before, this implies assertion *i)*. Assertion *ii)* follows because $\frac{\partial \tilde{\boldsymbol{T}}_w}{\partial w} = -\tilde{\boldsymbol{T}}_w \frac{\partial(\boldsymbol{I} - w\boldsymbol{T})}{\partial w} \tilde{\boldsymbol{T}}_w > 0$ element-wise and, therefore, $\frac{\partial H_i}{\partial w} > 0$. To prove *iii)*, note that if $(\tilde{\boldsymbol{T}}_w)_{ij} > 0$ then $\frac{\partial}{\partial \delta_j} \sum_{l=1}^{n} (\tilde{\boldsymbol{T}}_w)_{il} > 0$ and, therefore, $\frac{\partial H_i}{\partial \delta_j} > 0$. This is exactly the case if a path exists from trustor i to trustor j. The argument for *iv)* is similar to the argument for *iii)*. Again, if a path exists from trustor i to trustor j, it holds that $(\tilde{\boldsymbol{T}}_w)_{ij} > 0$, which implies that $\frac{\partial}{\partial \alpha_{jn}} \sum_{l=1}^{n} (\tilde{\boldsymbol{T}}_w)_{il} > 0$; and, therefore, $\frac{\partial H_i}{\partial \alpha_{jn}} > 0$. To prove *v)*, define F_1 and F_2 to be two probability distributions for which $F_1 > F_2$ in the sense of stochastic ordering. Note that $R_2 - P_2 > 0$ and all matrix elements of $\tilde{\boldsymbol{T}}_w - \boldsymbol{I}$ are positive. Consequently, H_i increases for all i changing from F_1 to F_2 and, Moreover, the proportion of games in which trust will be placed increases because $F_1(\vartheta_{1,i}^*) < F_2(\vartheta_{1,i}^*) < F_2(\vartheta_{2,i}^*)$ for all i, where $\vartheta_{j,i}^*$ is the solution for trustor i and F_j. □

Proof of Theorem 3.5 (page 70). To prove assertion *i)*, assume $\vartheta_1 \leq \vartheta_2$. Then,

$$\begin{aligned} \vartheta_2 &= (R_2 - P_2) \sum_{j=1}^{2} (\tilde{\boldsymbol{T}}_w - \boldsymbol{I})_{2j} F(\vartheta_j) \\ &\leq (R_2 - P_2) F(\vartheta_2) \sum_{j=1}^{2} (\tilde{\boldsymbol{T}}_w - \boldsymbol{I})_{2j} \\ &< (R_2 - P_2) F(\vartheta_2) \sum_{j=1}^{2} (\tilde{\boldsymbol{T}}_w - \boldsymbol{I})_{1j}. \end{aligned} \tag{A.18}$$

The last strict inequality follows directly from $\gamma_1 < \gamma_2$. Therefore, $(\vartheta_2, \vartheta_2)$ is a feasible solution of the inequalities of Theorem 3.2 and, using Theorem 3.2, I conclude that there is a subgame-perfect equilibrium that is a Pareto improvement of the equilibrium $(\vartheta_2, \vartheta_2)$, which is already a Pareto improvement of

$(\vartheta_1, \vartheta_2)$. Moreover, it still can be improved because (A.18) is a strict inequality. This is in contradiction with the fact that $\boldsymbol{\vartheta}$ was the Pareto optimal solution. As a consequence, $\vartheta_1 > \vartheta_2$.

To prove assertion *ii)*, it is sufficient to give an example. Choose $n = 3$, $w = 0.9$, $R_2 - P_2 = 2$, $\delta_i = 1$ for all i, $F(\theta) = \frac{\theta}{1+\theta}$, and

$$\boldsymbol{T} = \begin{pmatrix} 1 & 0.05 & 0.05 \\ 0.1 & 1 & 0.95 \\ 0.95 & 0.6 & 1 \end{pmatrix}. \tag{A.19}$$

Then,

$$\begin{pmatrix} \sum_{j=1}^{3}(\tilde{\boldsymbol{T}}_w - \boldsymbol{I})_{1j} \\ \sum_{j=1}^{3}(\tilde{\boldsymbol{T}}_w - \boldsymbol{I})_{2j} \\ \sum_{j=1}^{3}(\tilde{\boldsymbol{T}}_w - \boldsymbol{I})_{3j} \end{pmatrix} = \begin{pmatrix} 0.54 \\ 1.60 \\ 1.73 \end{pmatrix}, \text{while } \begin{pmatrix} \vartheta_1^* \\ \vartheta_2^* \\ \vartheta_3^* \end{pmatrix} = \begin{pmatrix} 0.35 \\ 1.78 \\ 1.68 \end{pmatrix}.$$

Thus, it holds that $\gamma_2 < \gamma_3$ and $\vartheta_2^* > \vartheta_3^*$, which proves this assertion for $n = 3$. For larger n, examples can be constructed that are the same as for $n = 3$ for the relations among the first three trustors, while the additional trustors do not have any relation with these three trustors. □

Proof of Theorem 3.6 (page 72). Denote $\boldsymbol{\vartheta}^*(\boldsymbol{A}) = \boldsymbol{\vartheta}^*$ and $\boldsymbol{\vartheta}^*(\boldsymbol{A}_0) = \boldsymbol{\vartheta}_0^* = (\vartheta_0^*, \ldots, \vartheta_0^*)$ by symmetry of the game in $\boldsymbol{A}_0$. Furthermore, I define $F(\boldsymbol{\vartheta}^*) = F(\vartheta_0^*)\mathbf{1}$ and the scalar $\mu = (R_2 - P_2)f(\vartheta_0^*)$. Using the implicit function theorem, the first-order approximation of (3.3) is

$$\begin{aligned}
\boldsymbol{\vartheta}^* &= (R_2 - P_2)\Big((\boldsymbol{I} - w\boldsymbol{T})^{-1} - \boldsymbol{I}\Big)F(\boldsymbol{\vartheta}^*) \\
&= (R_2 - P_2)\Big(\tilde{\boldsymbol{T}}_0 - \boldsymbol{I} + w\tilde{\boldsymbol{T}}_0(\boldsymbol{T} - \boldsymbol{T}_0)\tilde{\boldsymbol{T}}_0\Big)\Big(F(\vartheta_0^*)\mathbf{1} + f(\vartheta_0^*)(\boldsymbol{\vartheta}^* - \boldsymbol{\vartheta}_0^*)\Big) \\
&\quad + \varepsilon \\
&= \boldsymbol{\vartheta}_0^* + \mu(\tilde{\boldsymbol{T}}_0 - \boldsymbol{I})(\boldsymbol{\vartheta}^* - \boldsymbol{\vartheta}_0^*) + w(R_2 - P_2)F(\vartheta_0^*)\tilde{\boldsymbol{T}}_0(\boldsymbol{T} - \boldsymbol{T}_0)\tilde{\boldsymbol{T}}_0\mathbf{1} \\
&\quad + \varepsilon,
\end{aligned} \tag{A.20}$$

where $\varepsilon = O(\boldsymbol{A} - \boldsymbol{A}_0)$ is "small" if the difference between $\boldsymbol{A}$ and $\boldsymbol{A}_0$ is "small." By straightforward multiplication, it can be verified that if $x \neq \frac{1}{n}$

$$(\boldsymbol{I} - x\boldsymbol{J})^{-1} = \boldsymbol{I} + \frac{x}{1 - nx}\boldsymbol{J}, \tag{A.21}$$

where n is the number of trustors. Therefore,

$$\begin{aligned}
\tilde{\boldsymbol{T}}_0 &= (\boldsymbol{I} - w\boldsymbol{T}_0)^{-1} = \frac{1}{1 - w(\eta_1 - \eta_2)}\left(\boldsymbol{I} - \frac{w\eta_2}{1 - w(\eta_1 - \eta_2)}\boldsymbol{J}\right)^{-1} \\
&= \frac{1}{1 - w(\eta_1 - \eta_2)}\left(\boldsymbol{I} + \frac{w\eta_2}{1 - w(\eta_1 + (n-1)\eta_2)}\boldsymbol{J}\right)
\end{aligned}$$

$$= \frac{1}{1-\zeta_1}\left(\boldsymbol{I} + \frac{w\eta_2}{1-\zeta_2}\boldsymbol{J}\right), \tag{A.22}$$

where $\zeta_1 = w(\eta_1 - \eta_2)$ and $\zeta_2 = w(\eta_1 + (n-1)\eta_2)$. Note that $\zeta_1 + nw\eta_2 = \zeta_2$. Substituting (A.22) and $\left(\boldsymbol{I} + \frac{w\eta_2}{1-\zeta_2}\boldsymbol{J}\right)\mathbf{1} = \frac{1-\zeta_1}{1-\zeta_2}\mathbf{1}$ in (A.20) results in

$$\begin{aligned} \boldsymbol{\vartheta}^* &= \boldsymbol{\vartheta}_0^* + \mu(\tilde{\boldsymbol{T}}_0 - \boldsymbol{I})(\boldsymbol{\vartheta}^* - \boldsymbol{\vartheta}_0^*) \\ &\quad + \frac{(R_2 - P_2)wF(\vartheta_0^*)}{(1-\zeta_1)(1-\zeta_2)}\left(\boldsymbol{I} + \frac{w\eta_2}{(1-\zeta_2)}\boldsymbol{J}\right)(\boldsymbol{T} - \boldsymbol{T}_0)\mathbf{1} + \varepsilon. \end{aligned}$$

Using $\boldsymbol{\vartheta}_0^* = \mu(\tilde{\boldsymbol{T}}_0 - \boldsymbol{I})\boldsymbol{\vartheta}_0^*$ and under the assumption that the inverse of $\boldsymbol{I} - \mu(\tilde{\boldsymbol{T}}_0 - \boldsymbol{I})$ exists, it holds that

$$\boldsymbol{\vartheta}^* = \frac{(R_2 - P_2)wF(\vartheta_0^*)}{(1-\zeta_1)(1-\zeta_2)}\left(\boldsymbol{I} - \mu(\tilde{\boldsymbol{T}}_0 - \boldsymbol{I})\right)^{-1}\left(\boldsymbol{I} + \frac{w\eta_2}{(1-\zeta_2)}\boldsymbol{J}\right)(\boldsymbol{T} - \boldsymbol{T}_0)\mathbf{1} + \varepsilon. \tag{A.23}$$

Using (A.21) and (A.22) and more "tedious but straightforward calculation," it follows that

$$\begin{aligned} \left(\boldsymbol{I} - \mu(\tilde{\boldsymbol{T}}_0 - \boldsymbol{I})\right)^{-1} &= \left(\boldsymbol{I} - \mu\left(\frac{1}{1-\zeta_1}\left(\boldsymbol{I} + \frac{w\eta_2}{1-\zeta_2}\boldsymbol{J}\right) - \boldsymbol{I}\right)\right)^{-1} \\ &= \frac{1-\zeta_1}{1-\zeta_1(1+\mu)}\left(\boldsymbol{I} - \frac{\mu w\eta_2}{(1-\zeta_1(1+\mu))(1-\zeta_2)}\boldsymbol{J}\right)^{-1} \\ &= \frac{1-\zeta_1}{1-\zeta_1(1+\mu)}\left(\boldsymbol{I} + \frac{\mu w\eta_2}{(1-\zeta_1))(1-\zeta_2(1+\mu))}\boldsymbol{J}\right). \end{aligned} \tag{A.24}$$

Because this inverse matrix exists, the existence of $\left(\frac{\partial G}{\partial \boldsymbol{\vartheta}^*}\right)^{-1}$ is guaranteed, which ensures that I indeed could apply the implicit function theorem. Furthermore, it follows from the definitions of $\boldsymbol{T}$ and $\boldsymbol{T}_0$ that

$$\begin{aligned} (\boldsymbol{T} - \boldsymbol{T}_0)\mathbf{1} &= \left(\left((1-\delta)\boldsymbol{I} + \frac{\delta}{n}\boldsymbol{A}\right) - \left((1-\delta)\boldsymbol{I} + \frac{\delta}{n}\boldsymbol{A}_0\right)\right)\mathbf{1} \\ &= \frac{\delta}{n}(\boldsymbol{A} - \boldsymbol{A}_0)\mathbf{1} \\ &= \frac{\delta(n-1)}{n}\left(\boldsymbol{D}_{out}(\boldsymbol{A}) - \boldsymbol{D}_{out}(\boldsymbol{A}_0)\right). \end{aligned} \tag{A.25}$$

By substituting (A.24) and (A.25) in (A.23), the expression for ρ_1 as defined in the theorem follows directly:

$$\rho_1 = \frac{\delta w(R_2 - P_2)F(\vartheta_0^*)}{n(1-\zeta_1)(1-\zeta_2(1+\mu))}. \tag{A.26}$$

Using the same equations and some more calculus leads to

$$\rho_2 = \frac{(1+\mu)w\eta_2}{1-\zeta_2(1+\mu)}. \tag{A.27}$$

The expression in terms of the outdegrees and density follow immediately from (A.25) and the fact that $n\Delta = \sum_{i=1}^{n} D_{out}(i)$.

According to the definition of the transition matrix, $0 < \zeta_1 < \zeta_2 < 1$. Because all other parts of ρ_1 and ρ_2 are clearly positive, the signs of ρ_1 and ρ_2 depend on the magnitude of $f(\vartheta_0^*)(R_2 - P_2)$. The assumption that the distribution F is concave and (3.17) ensures that

$$\mu = f(\vartheta_0^*)(R_2 - P_2) < \frac{F(\vartheta_0^*)(R_2 - P_2)}{\vartheta_0^*} = \frac{1-\zeta_2}{\zeta_2}. \tag{A.28}$$

Consequently, it holds that $0 < \zeta_2(1+\mu) < 1$, which implies that ρ_1 and ρ_2 are positive. □

Appendix B
Network Construction Methods for Valued Networks

This appendix describes the construction methods for the networks $(\boldsymbol{\pi}, \boldsymbol{A})$ used in Chapters 3 and 4. Because I only use networks in which all actors are equally important, i.e., $\pi_i = \frac{1}{n}$ for all i, where n is the number of actors in the network, the construction methods only have to sample network matrices $\boldsymbol{A}$.

Consider the set of networks $\mathcal{A} = \{\boldsymbol{A} \mid 0 \leq \alpha_{ij} \leq 1\}$ with n actors and $\alpha_{ii} = 1$ for all i, which is isomorphic with $[0, 1]^{n(n-1)}$. Formally, a construction method is a probability distribution on $\mathcal{A}$.[1] A "naive" method would sample every directed tie α_{ij} uniformly from $[0, 1]$. This results in a set of networks that has a low variation in density and degrees. If the size of the network is n, the number of ties equals $n(n-1)$. The average weight of these ties will be close to $\frac{1}{2}$ and, therefore, the density will often be close to $\frac{1}{2}$.[2] Even the degree for each actor will be close to $\frac{1}{2}$ if n is not too small. Because I want "much" variation and limited covariation among a number of network parameters $N_k(\boldsymbol{A})$, I developed several construction methods that mainly try to increase the variation and reduce the covariation of specific network parameters. The extent to which I succeed in keeping covariances low is shown in Subsection 3.6.1. Probably, it is possible to improve my methods with methods for "optimal experimental designs" (see, for example, Fedorov 1972; Pukelsheim 1993).

One advantage of using multiple construction methods is that I can compare the results of analyses for different construction methods. The network parameters are independent variables in models that explain trust and information

---

[1] Similar construction methods can be used to sample blockmodels.

[2] With this simple method, the distribution of density Δ is the sum of $n(n-1)$ uniform distributions on $[0, 1]$. Therefore, the mean μ of this distribution is $\frac{1}{2}$ and the variance $\sigma^2 = \frac{1}{12n(n-1)}$. With Chebyshev's inequality (Feller 1950), it follows that $Pr(|\Delta - \frac{1}{2}| > \frac{1}{10}) \leq \frac{100}{12n(n-1)}$. Thus, the expected proportion of networks with $|\Delta - \frac{1}{2}| > \frac{1}{10}$ is less than 1% for networks with more than 5 actors.

diffusion in Chapters 3 and 4. The construction methods can be interpreted as different weightings of the networks in the whole sample space. Comparison of the construction methods can reveal whether effects of network parameters on a dependent variable are similar for different samples of networks. Ideally, results do not depend on the samples of networks. Below, I discuss the different construction methods.[3]

1. Random Networks

The first method to construct networks is the one that was already presented as naive and undesirable, namely, assign to every directed tie a value uniformly generated from [0,1]. I included this procedure to enable comparison of this method with the more complex methods.

2. Networks with Given Density

Network density Δ is generated uniformly from $[0.3, 1]$ for the second construction method.[4] The aim that is directly realized using this method is to obtain more extreme values of density and a more even distribution over the interval $[0.3, 1]$.

To obtain variation also in the outdegrees and indegrees, I choose a special method to fill the incidence matrix. First, the outdegrees $D_{out}(i)$ or indegrees $D_{in}(i)$ are determined. The choice between these two is made equi-probable. Assuming that the outdegrees are generated first, $D_{out}(1)$ is generated uniformly from the interval that has a lower bound equal to Δ and an upper bound equal to the maximal value allowed, which equals 1 or the value for which the density of the whole network is reached immediately. Note that the density equals the average of all outdegree. This implies that $D_{out}(1)$ is larger than the average outdegree. The average of the other outdegrees has to be lower. This average is calculated and the $D_{out}(2)$ is generated uniformly from the interval with a lower bound equal to the new average and an upper bound that equals the maximal value allowed. This procedure is continued until $D_{out}(n)$. It is not a problem that actors with lower numbers have higher outdegrees, because actors in any network can be relabeled such that the degrees are decreasing.

I use a similar procedure to generate the α_{ij}. Assume again that the outdegrees were generated in the first part of the procedure, then α_{i1} is generated uniformly from the interval with a lower bound $D_{out}(i)$ and an upper bound that equals the maximal value allowed. Note that $D_{out}(i)$ equals the average

[3]The Pascal code of the implementation of these methods for valued networks as well as blockmodels is available from the author.

[4]Of course, this interval can be changed easily and the specific choice is rather arbitrary. I exclude very small densities, because the networks are used to study trust in a game-theoretic model, and I am mainly interested in situations where at least some level of trust was possible. If network density is too low, there do not exist trigger strategies for which the trustor ever places trust.

of all the α_{ij} for $j = 1, \ldots, n$ and, therefore, the first α_{ij} will be larger than the later α_{ij}. The subsequent α_{ij} are generated from the interval with a lower bound that is the average value of the α_{ij} that still have to be generated and an upper bound equal to the maximal value allowed.

I start sometimes with indegrees and sometimes with outdegrees to obtain similar variations for the indegrees and outdegrees and to prevent that more or specific variation occurred in one of the two.

3. Degree Variation

The third method is specifically developed to obtain variation in degrees. The actors are divided in four groups: one group with high indegrees and high outdegrees, one group with low indegrees and high outdegrees, one group with high indegrees and low outdegrees, and one group with low indegrees and low outdegrees. The procedure starts with selecting independently two integers X and Y between 1 and the network size n. Actors with an index lower than X obtain high outdegrees and actors with an index lower than Y obtain high indegrees. Again, actors with lower indices have higher outdegrees and indegrees in this way, but again this is not a problem.

More specifically, the procedure generates α_{ij} uniformly from $[\frac{2}{3}, 1]$ if $i < X$ and $j < Y$; α_{ij} is generated uniformly from $[0, \frac{1}{3}]$ if $i \geq X$ and $j \geq Y$; and α_{ij} is generated uniformly from $[\frac{1}{3}, \frac{2}{3}]$ otherwise. Besides variation in degrees, this method provides variation in density as well.

4. Structural Combinations

I use six given network structures for the fourth method. The matrices of these structures are in order of increasing density:

- the identity matrix, $\boldsymbol{I}$,
- a matrix with the first row of elements equal to 1 and the other off-diagonal elements equal to 0, $\begin{pmatrix} 1 & \mathbf{1}' \\ \mathbf{0} & \boldsymbol{I} \end{pmatrix}$,
- a matrix with the first column of elements equal to 1 and the other off-diagonal elements equal to 0, $\begin{pmatrix} 1 & \mathbf{0}' \\ \mathbf{1} & \boldsymbol{I} \end{pmatrix}$,
- a matrix with the elements of the first row and column equal to 1 and 0 elsewhere, $\begin{pmatrix} 1 & \mathbf{1}' \\ \mathbf{1} & \boldsymbol{I} \end{pmatrix}$,

- a matrix with the elements of the upper triangle including the diagonal equal to 1 and 0 elsewhere, $\begin{pmatrix} 1 & 1 & \cdots & 1 \\ 0 & \ddots & \ddots & \vdots \\ \vdots & \ddots & \ddots & 1 \\ 0 & \cdots & 0 & 1 \end{pmatrix}$, and
- the all-one matrix, $\boldsymbol{J} = \mathbf{1}\mathbf{1}'$.

Each of these six structures is selected independently for inclusion in the network with probability $\frac{1}{2}$, under the condition that at least one structure is selected. (By mistake, the identity matrix was included twice each with probability $\frac{1}{2}$ in my final program.) Next, the mean of the selected matrices is determined. Finally, a random component is added to every matrix element uniformly generated from $[-\frac{1}{4}, \frac{1}{4}]$, controlling that elements do not become larger than 1 or smaller than 0. By using a matrix that is a combination of standard structures, variation is obtained in the different network measures. The variation in density is obtained because the standard structures vary considerably in density. Variation in indegrees and outdegrees is obtained from the structures with one actor having a high indegree and/or outdegree. Finally, the triangular matrix induces more transitivity in the networks in which this structure is added.

Appendix C
Information on the MAT95 Questionnaire

This appendix contains concise translations of the questions from the survey on IT transactions. Translations of the original Dutch questions are given followed by the answer categories in parentheses. The questions are ordered as they were actually included in the questionnaire. Numbers of questions follow the codebook (Batenburg 1995/7a).

Computer Assisted Telephone Interview

Q220: Can you briefly describe the product? (After this description the product was categorized in *standard* (personal computers, standard software programs, etc.) or *complex* (mini computer, networks, main frames, tailor-made software, etc.) products).

Questionnaire

Section 1. The Product

Q1.2: Which of the following products/services were delivered at that time? (standard software, adjusted software, tailor-made software, sector-specific software, personal computers, workstation, network configuration, mini computer, mainframe, computer-controlled machines, side equipment, cabling, design, training, instruction, consultation, documentation, support).

Q1.4: How much was paid to the supplier, not including later supplements? (up to NLG 25,000, NLG 25,000–50,000, NLG 50,000–100,000, NLG 100,000–200,000, more than NLG 200,000).

Q1.6a: How important was this product for the automation of your firm? (unimportant, hardly important, moderately important, very important, of major importance).

Q1.6b: How important was this product for the profitability of your firm? (unimportant, hardly important, moderately important, very important, of major importance).

Q1.7: Was it easy or difficult for you and your employees to judge the quality of the product at the time of delivery? (very easy, easy, somewhat difficult, difficult, very difficult).

Q1.8: Compared to other firms in your sector, how much experience did your firm have with automation? (none, little, some, much, very much).

Q1.10: How important was it that the product delivery time was met? (unimportant, hardly important, moderately important, very important, of major importance).

Q1.12a: How important was the long-term suitability of this product? (unimportant, hardly important, moderately important, very important, of major importance).

Q1.12b: How important was long-term support by the supplier? (unimportant, hardly important, moderately important, very important, of major importance).

Q1.12c: How important was the long-term compatibility of this product with other hardware and software? (unimportant, hardly important, moderately important, very important, of major importance).

Q1.13a: What would have been the damage, in terms of money and time spent on purchasing a new product, if the product had failed to function and had had to be replaced? (very small, small, moderate, large, very large).

Q1.13b: What would have been the damage, in terms of money and time spent on training personnel, if the product had failed to function and had had to be replaced? (very small, small, moderate, large, very large).

Q1.13c: What would have been the damage, in terms of money and time spent on data entry, if the product had failed to function and had had to be replaced? (very small, small, moderate, large, very large).

Q1.13d: What would have been the damage, in terms of money and time wasted in idle production, if the product had failed to function and had had to be replaced? (very small, small, moderate, large, very large).

Q1.15: Did your firm have the possibility to make or adapt this product? (no, very difficult, difficult, easy, very easy).

SECTION 2. THE CHOICE OF PRODUCT AND SUPPLIER

Q2.8: Was it difficult for your firm to compare tenders? (very easy, easy, somewhat difficult, difficult, very difficult).

Q2.9: Was it difficult for your firm to compare the product with other products? (very easy, easy, somewhat difficult, difficult, very difficult).

Q2.10: Was it difficult for your firm to compare the price-quality relation of potential suppliers? (very easy, easy, somewhat difficult, difficult, very difficult).

SECTION 3. THE RELATION WITH THE SUPPLIER

Q3.2: How many employees were working at the supplier's firm at that time? (less than 5, 5–9, 10–19, 20–49, more than 50).

Q3.6: Has your firm had any kind of business relation with this supplier before the purchase of this product? (no, yes).

Q3.7: For how long has your firm done business with the supplier before the purchase of this product? (about ... years).

Q3.8: How frequently has your firm done business with the supplier before the purchase of this product? (once, occasionally, quite regular, regular, often).

Q3.9: How extensively has your firm done business with the supplier before the purchase of this product? (minimal, small, quite extensive, extensive, very extensive).

Q3.10: How satisfied was your firm with the business with the supplier before the purchase of this product? (very unsatisfied, unsatisfied, quite satisfied, satisfied, very satisfied).

Q3.13: To what extent did you expect that your firm would continue business with this supplier before the purchase of this product? (no business, incidental business of limited size, some business of limited size, regular and/or extensive business, very regular and/or very extensive business).

Q3.19: Please think about other firms that you know to be or think to be customers of the supplier at that time? How many of such firms do you know? (... other customers).

Q3.19ab–3.19db: Please, fill out in the following diagram the initials of at most four other customers of the supplier. If you know more than four other customers, select the four most important for the supplier.

Q3.19ac–3.19dc: For each of the (at most four) customers mentioned above, estimate the experience of this firm with respect to automation compared to the experience of your own firm at that time. (much smaller, smaller, similar, larger, much larger).

Q3.19ad–3.19dd: For each of the (at most four) customers mentioned above, estimate the importance of this firm for the supplier compared to the importance of your own firm for the supplier at that time. (much smaller, smaller, similar, larger, much larger).

Q3.19ae–3.19de: For each of the (at most four) customers mentioned above, how frequently did your firm have contacts with each of these firms at that time. (less than once a year, at least once a year, at least once in six months, at least once a month, at least once a week).

Q3.19bf–3.19dh: For each pair of the (at most four) customers mentioned above, estimate how frequently these two firms had contacts with each other at that time. (less than once a year, at least once a year, at least once in six months, at least once a month, at least once a week).

SECTION 4. THE CONTRACT

Q4.12: Was the main contract a more or less adapted version of a contract that your firm used before? (no, yes).

Q4.14b: For each of the following financial and legal clauses, can you indicate how they were arranged? (only verbally, in a written document, not at all arranged).

Issues (24): price determination, price level, price changes, payment terms, sanctions on late payment, delivery time, liability supplier, force majeure, warranties supplier, quality (norms), intellectual property, protection against privacy, restrictions on product use, non-disclosure, insurance supplier, duration service, reservation spare-parts, duration maintenance, updating, arbitration, calculation R&D costs, joint management during transaction, technical specifications, and termination.

Q4.20: Every firm has its standard procedures. Regarding the negotiations and agreements with this supplier concerning the product as a whole: To what extent could these be considered to be standard procedures? (hardly, to some extent, to a moderate extent, largely, completely).

Section 6. About Your Firm and Yourself

Q6.1a: How many full-time employees are working at your firm now? (number of full-time employees: ...).

Q6.1b: How many full-time employees were working at your firm at the time of the purchase of this product? (number of full-time employees: ...).

Q6.3ab: Does your firm have employees with expertise on automation? (no, yes).

Q6.3bb: Does your firm have an automation department? (no, yes).

Q6.3ac: Does your firm have employees with expertise on legal issues? (no, yes).

Q6.3bc: Does your firm have a legal department? (no, yes).

Appendix D
The Vignette Experiment

This appendix contains the text of the English and Dutch versions of the vignette experiment.[1] All the screens that were presented to the subjects are shown below. First, the subjects obtained a short bilingual introduction. After the choice for one language was made, all screens used the selected language. Subjects had the possibility for going back in the program by pressing "b" at every moment in the experiment. The answers were only stored at the end of the experiment, which implied that if subjects went back to a previous screen, they had to fill out the whole screen again. Because I did not want to encourage going back and forth too much during the experiment, the possibility for moving back did not appear at every screen.

Unfortunately, it is not possible to reproduce the colors used at the screen. The background color was always blue and the text was in white. For the lines that included an instruction to type a certain text or press a button, the background color was changed to red. The vignette at the right side of the screen had background color green in the Chicago experiments and dark grey in the Dutch experiments.

[1]The Pascal code of the program used in the experiment is available from the author.

The Bilingual Part

Screen 1:

> Typ het sessienummer dat u krijgt van de experimentleider en druk "Enter".
> Type the session number provided by the experiment leader followed by "Enter".
>
> Typ het computernummer dat u krijgt van de experimentleider en druk "Enter".
> Type the computer number provided by the experiment leader followed by "Enter".
>
> Uw casenummer is X.
> Your case number is X.
>
> Controleer a.u.b. het sessie- en computernummer.
> Please check the session and computer number.
>
> Druk hoofdletter "C" als het goed is, druk "b" om iets te verbeteren.
> Press capital "C" if everything is OK, press "b" to make any corrections.

Screen 2:

> HET KOPEN VAN EEN TWEEDEHANDS AUTO
>
> BUYING A USED CAR
>
> Druk "1" om te beginnen.
> Press "1" to start.

Screen 3:

> Wilt u verder gaan in het Nederlands, druk op "1".
> If you want to proceed in English, press "2".
>
> U kunt altijd een scherm terug door "b" te drukken.
> You can always return to the previous screen by pressing "b".

THE ENGLISH VERSION

Screen 4:

SCENARIO

Imagine the following situation:

- Congratulations, you just graduated from college. Your first job has provided you with a bonus.
- As a reward for completing your degree, you have decided to use the bonus to purchase a gift. You want something nice, but you want to spend your bonus wisely.
- You decide to buy a car, a used car because it is within your budget. You find a car you like although you have some concern. The garage selling the car is a local dealer called The Autoshop.
- The quality of the car is not guaranteed and you will not be able to have the car inspected before you buy it.
- You are nervous because you have seen a show on television documenting how dishonest garages sell used cars at inflated prices.

To continue, press "1".

Screen 5:

TASK

Now we will show you two situations, each describing a different situation for purchasing the car from The Autoshop. Imagine yourself in each of the situations and then decide which one of the two situations you would prefer. The scenario described above holds for all situations.

Once you have decided, we will ask you to indicate for the same pair of situations, how much you preferred the situation you chose to the one you did not choose.

All together, we will ask you to make these decisions in 10 pairs of situations.

To continue, press "1".
If you want to see the scenario again, press "b".

Screen 6, 8, 10, 12, 14, 16, 18, 20, 22, and 24:[2]

1	2
- You can buy a car for about $4000. - You bought a car from The Autoshop before and you were satisfied. - You do not expect to move out of town soon. - The Autoshop is a well-known garage and has many customers in your neighborhood. - You have friends who bought a car from The Autoshop before and they were satisfied. - The owner of the garage and you are members of the same football team.	- You can buy a car for about $4000. - You never bought a car from The Autoshop before. - You will move to the other side of the country in a few weeks. - The Autoshop is an unknown garage in your neighborhood. - As far as you know, none of your friends have bought a car from The Autoshop before. - You do not have a close social link with the owner of The Autoshop.

If you prefer situation 1, press "1".
If you prefer situation 2, press "2".

Screen 7, 9, 11, 13, 15, 17, 19, 21, 23, and 25 (X indicates the appropriate number, 1 or 2):

1	2
- You can buy a car for about $4000. - You bought a car from The Autoshop before and you were satisfied. - You do not expect to move out of town soon. - The Autoshop is a well-known garage and has many customers in your neighborhood. - You have friends who bought a car from The Autoshop before and they were satisfied. - The owner of the garage and you are members of the same football team.	- You can buy a car for about $4000. - You never bought a car from The Autoshop before. - You will move to the other side of the country in a few weeks. - The Autoshop is an unknown garage in your neighborhood. - As far as you know, none of your friends have bought a car from The Autoshop before. - You do not have a close social link with the owner of The Autoshop.

If your preference for situation X is far from clear, press "1".
If your preference for situation X is rather clear, press "2".
If your preference for situation X is clear, press "3".
If your preference for situation X is very clear, press "4".

[2] In this example, vignette 1 shows the formulations for a certain type of embeddedness that is present and vignette 2 for a type that is absent.

Screen 26:

To what degree do you agree with the following statements?

I buy in my neighborhood, because I know the people around.

When I buy a product, I am more concerned about the product's trademark than about the person who sells the product.

If I can, I prefer to purchase a good from a person I know rather than from a total stranger.

I prefer buying from a person my friends know over buying from a person my friends do not know.

I tell my friends if I bought a product and it does not meet the expectations the seller gave me.

do not agree at all, press "1".
do not agree, press "2".
neutral, press "3".
agree, press "4".
totally agree, press "5".

Screen 27:

The choices I had to make during the experiment are similar to decisions I have to make in real life.

I can judge the quality of a used car if I can take a close look at it.

I buy more often used products, such as a computer or audio system, with a quality that is difficult to judge.

People prefer to buy products from a person they know instead of buying from strangers.

If people buy a poor product, more than likely they are going to tell their friends about it.

do not agree at all, press "1".
do not agree, press "2".
neutral, press "3".
agree, press "4".
totally agree, press "5".

Screen 28:

Finally, some questions about yourself.

How old are you?

Type your age followed by "Enter".

Are you a woman or a man?

If you are a woman, press "1".
If you are a man, press "2".

What is your major? If you have a degree, indicate the area.
Type the name of the area followed by "Enter".

Area:

In which town or city do you live? How big is that town or city?

Type the name of the city followed by "Enter" and then the number of inhabitants followed by "Enter".

City:
Number of inhabitants:

THE DUTCH VERSION

Screen 4:

SCENARIO

Stelt u zich de volgende situatie voor:

- U bent net afgestudeerd. U heeft een aardige baan gevonden zodat u wat extra geld te besteden heeft.
- U heeft wat geld gespaard door te werken als studentassisent, waarvan u een deel wilt gebruiken als beloning voor het voltooien van de studie. Daarvoor wilt u uiteraard echt iets goeds kopen.
- U wilt graag een tweedehands auto kopen, maar de prijzen bij officiële dealers passen niet bij wat u wilt uitgeven voor een bepaalde auto. Uiteindelijk komt u bij garage The Autoshop toch iets van uw gading tegen, maar The Autoshop is niet aangesloten bij BOVAG of een ander garantiefonds.
- Er is onlangs nogal wat publiciteit geweest over twijfelachtige garages die tweedehands auto's verkopen waarbij er achteraf wat gebreken blijken te zijn en dan blijkt de garagehouder opeens niet thuis te geven.
- Zelf heeft u weinig mogelijkheden om de kwaliteit van de aangeboden auto van te voren in te schatten.

Om verder te gaan, druk "1".

Screen 5:

OPDRACHT

U krijgt steeds twee situaties voorgelegd, waarbij iedere situatie de koop van een tweedehands auto bij The Autoshop weergeeft. Probeert u zich in iedere situatie afzonderlijk in te leven en bepaalt u dan in welke van de twee situaties u het liefst de auto zou kopen. Het scenario dat we hierboven beschreven hebben, geldt voor alle situaties.

Daarna krijgt u bij hetzelfde paar situaties de vraag om aan te geven hoe sterk uw voorkeur voor deze situatie is boven de andere situatie.

In totaal zullen we u 10 paren van situaties voorleggen.

Om verder te gaan, druk "1".
Wilt u het scenario nog een keer zien, druk "b".

Screen 6, 8, 10, 12, 14, 16, 18, 20, 22, and 24:[3]

1	2
- U kunt een tweedehands auto kopen van ongeveer 8000 gulden. - U heeft al eens een auto gekocht bij The Autoshop die goed bevallen is. - U verwacht niet dat u op korte termijn zult verhuizen. - In de omgeving waar u vandaan komt, is The Autoshop een bekende garage met een groot klantenbestand. - U heeft een paar vrienden die bij The Autoshop een auto hebben gekocht en dat is goed bevallen. - De garagehouder en u zijn samen lid van hetzelfde voetbalteam.	- U kunt een tweedehands auto kopen van ongeveer 8000 gulden. - U heeft nog nooit een auto gekocht bij The Autoshop. - U verhuist binnenkort naar de andere kant van het land. - In de omgeving waar u vandaan komt, is The Autoshop een tamelijk onbekende garage. - U heeft geen vrienden waarvan u weet dat ze ooit bij The Autoshop een auto gekocht hebben. - U heeft geen sociale link met de eigenaar van The Autoshop.

Als u de voorkeur geeft aan situatie 1, druk "1".
Als u de voorkeur geeft aan situatie 2, druk "2".

Screen 7, 9, 11, 13, 15, 17, 19, 21, 23, and 25 (X indicates the appropriate number, 1 or 2):

1	2
- U kunt een tweedehands auto kopen van ongeveer 8000 gulden. - U heeft al eens een auto gekocht bij The Autoshop die goed bevallen is. - U verwacht niet dat u op korte termijn zult verhuizen. - In de omgeving waar u vandaan komt, is The Autoshop een bekende garage met een groot klantenbestand. - U heeft een paar vrienden die bij The Autoshop een auto hebben gekocht en dat is goed bevallen. - De garagehouder en u zijn samen lid van hetzelfde voetbalteam.	- U kunt een tweedehands auto kopen van ongeveer 8000 gulden. - U heeft nog nooit een auto gekocht bij The Autoshop. - U verhuist binnenkort naar de andere kant van het land. - In de omgeving waar u vandaan komt, is The Autoshop een tamelijk onbekende garage. - U heeft geen vrienden waarvan u weet dat ze ooit bij The Autoshop een auto gekocht hebben. - U heeft geen sociale link met de eigenaar van The Autoshop.

Als uw voorkeur voor situatie X nauwelijks duidelijk was, druk "1".
Als uw voorkeur voor situatie X enigszins duidelijk was, druk "2".
Als uw voorkeur voor situatie X duidelijk was, druk "3".
Als uw voorkeur voor situatie X zeer duidelijk was, druk "4".

[3]In this example, vignette 1 shows the formulations for a certain type of embeddedness that is present and vignette 2 for a type that is absent.

Screen 26:

In hoeverre bent u het met de volgende stellingen eens?

Ik koop de meeste dingen bij mij in de buurt omdat ik daar de mensen goed ken.

Ik ben niet zozeer geïnteresseerd in wie een bepaald product verkoopt, als het maar van een goed merk is.

Ik koop liever iets bij iemand die ik ken dan bij een totaal onbekend persoon.

Ik koop liever iets bij iemand die mijn vrienden kennen dan bij iemand die vrienden van mij niet kennen.

Als ik iets heb gekocht en het voldoet niet aan de verwachtingen zoals de verkoper mij die had voorgespiegeld, dan vertel ik dat aan mijn vrienden.

helemaal niet mee eens, druk "1".
niet mee eens, druk "2".
neutraal, druk "3".
mee eens, druk "4".
helemaal mee eens, druk "5".

Screen 27:

Tijdens het kiezen tussen de situaties heb ik een aantal keer serieus zaken tegen elkaar afgewogen, die ik herken uit overwegingen in het dagelijks leven.

Als ik een tweedehands auto goed kan bekijken, kan ik de waarde daarvan behoorlijk goed inschatten.

Ik koop vaker tweedehands spullen, b.v. een computer of geluids-installatie, waarvan de kwaliteit moeilijk is in te schatten.

Ik denk dat anderen liever iets kopen bij iemand die ze kennen dan bij een totaal onbekend persoon.

Ik denk dat anderen hun slechte ervaringen met verkopers van tweedehands producten aan hun vrienden vertellen.

helemaal niet mee eens, druk "1".
niet mee eens, druk "2".
neutraal, druk "3".
mee eens, druk "4".
helemaal mee eens, druk "5".

Screen 28:

Tenslotte nog enkele vragen over uzelf.

Hoe oud bent u?

Typ uw leeftijd gevolgd door "Enter".

Bent u een vrouw of man?

Als u een vrouw bent, druk "1".
Als u een man bent, druk "2".

Welke studie heeft u gedaan of volgt u momenteel?
Typ de naam van de studie gevolgd door "Enter".

Area:

In welke plaats woont u nu en hoeveel inwoners heeft deze plaats ongeveer?

Typ eerst de plaatsnaam gevolgd door "Enter" en daarna het aantal inwoners gevolgd door "Enter".

Plaats:
Aantal inwoners:

References

Abreu, D. (1988). On the theory of infinitely repeated games with discounting. *Econometrica*, 56:383–396.

Akerlof, G. A. (1970). The market for 'lemons': Quality uncertainty and the market mechanism. *Quarterly Journal of Economics*, 89:488–500.

Akkermans, S. T. M. and Van Lint, J. H. (1970). *Algebra en Analyse*. Wolters-Noordhoff, Groningen. (in Dutch).

Altmann, M. (1993). Reinterpreting network measures for models of disease transmission. *Social Networks*, 15:1–7.

Alves, W. M. and Rossi, P. H. (1978). Who should get what? Fairness judgments of the distribution of earnings. *American Journal of Sociology*, 84:541–564.

Amemiya, T. (1973). Regression analysis when the dependent variable is truncated normal. *Econometrica*, 41:997–1016.

Arrow, K. J. (1974). *The Limits of Organization*. W. W. Norton & Company, New York.

Axelrod, R. (1984). *The Evolution of Cooperation*. Basic Books, New York.

Axelrod, R. (1986). An evolutionary approach to norms. *American Political Science Review*, 80:1095–1111.

Bacharach, M. and Gambetta, D. (2001). Trust in signs. In Cook, K. S., editor, *Trust in Society*, pages 148–184. Russell Sage, New York.

Bailey, N. T. J. (1957). *The Mathematical Theory of Epidemics*. Charles Griffin, London.

Bailey, N. T. J. (1964). *The Elements of Stochastic Processes with Applications to the Natural Sciences*. Wiley, New York.

Bailey, N. T. J. (1975). *The Mathematical Theory of Infectious Diseases and Its Applications*. Charles Griffin, London, 2nd edition.

Baker, W. E., Faulkner, R. R., and Fisher, G. A. (1998). Hazards of the market: The continuity and dissolution of interorganizational market relationships. *American Sociological Review*, 63:147–177.

Bala, V. and Goyal, S. (2000). A noncooperative model of network formation. *Econometrica*, 68:1181–1229.

Barley, S. R., Freeman, J., and Hybels, R. C. (1992). Strategic alliances in commercial biotechnology. In Nohria, N. and Eccles, R. G., editors, *Networks and Organizations: Structure, Form, and Action*, pages 311–347. Harvard Business School Press, Boston.

Bartholomew, D. J. (1982). *Stochastic Models for Social Processes*. Wiley, New York, 3rd edition.

Batenburg, R. S. (1995/7a). The external management of automation 1995: Codebook of MAT95. ISCORE Paper 58, Utrecht University.

Batenburg, R. S. (1995/7b). The external management of automation 1995 (MAT95). fieldwork, response, and non-response. ISCORE Paper 59, Utrecht University.

Batenburg, R. S. and Raub, W. (1995). Het externe management van automatisering 1995. [data set] Utrecht, ISCORE.

Batenburg, R. S., Raub, W., and Snijders, C. (2002). Contacts and contracts: Temporal embeddedness and the contractual behavior of firms. *Research in the Sociology of Organization*, (forthcoming).

Bellman, R. E. (1957). *Dynamic Programming*. Princeton University Press, Princeton, NJ.

Berman, A. and Plemmons, R. J. (1979). *Nonnegative Matrices in the Mathematical Sciences*. Academic Press, New York.

Bernard, H. R., Killworth, P. D., Kronenfeld, D., and Sailer, L. (1985). On the validity of retrospective data: The problem of informant accuracy. *Annual Review of Anthropology*, 13:495–517.

Bernard, H. R., Killworth, P. D., and Sailer, L. (1981). A review of informant accuracy in social network data. In Hummell, H. J. and Sodeur, W., editors, *Modelle für Ausbreitungsprozesse in sozialen Strukturen*, pages 153–187. Sozialwissenschaftliche Kooperative, Duisburg.

Bienenstock, E. J. and Bonacich, P. (1997). Network exchange as a cooperative game. *Rationality and Society*, 9:37–65.

Binmore, K. (1994). *Game Theory and the Social Contract. Volume 1: Playing Fair*. MIT Press, Cambridge, MA.

Binmore, K. (1998). *Game Theory and the Social Contract. Volume 2: Just Playing*. MIT Press, Cambridge, MA.

Blau, P. M. ([1964] 1996). *Exchange and Power in Social Life*. Transaction Publishers, New Brunswick, NJ.

Blumberg, B. F. (1997). *Das Management von Technologiekooperationen: Partnersuche und Verhandlungen mit dem Partner aus empirisch-theoretischer Perspektive*. Thesis Publishers, Amsterdam. (in German).

Bollen, K. A. (1989). *Structural Equations with Latent Variables*. Wiley, New York.

Box, G. E. P. and Cox, D. R. (1964). An analysis of transformations. *Journal of the Royal Statistical Society, Series B*, 26:211–243.

Bradley, R. A. and Terry, M. E. (1952). The rank analysis of incomplete block designs: I. The method of paired comparison. *Biometrika*, 39:324–345.

Burt, R. S. (1992). *Structural Holes: The Social Structure of Competition*. Harvard University Press, Cambridge, MA.

Burt, R. S. (1993). The social structure of competition. In Swedberg, R., editor, *Explorations in Economic Sociology*, pages 56–103. Russell Sage, New York.

Burt, R. S. (2001). Bandwidth and echo: Trust, information, and gossip in social networks. In Rauch, J. E. and Casella, A., editors, *Networks and Markets*, pages 30–74. Russell Sage, New York.

Burt, R. S., Janotta, J. E., and Mahoney, J. T. (1998). Personality correlates of structural holes. *Social Networks*, 20:63–87.

Burt, R. S. and Knez, M. (1995a). Kinds of third-party effects on trust. *Rationality and Society*, 7:255–292.

Burt, R. S. and Knez, M. (1995b). Trust and third parties. Working paper, Graduate School of Business, University of Chicago.

Buskens, V. (1998). The social structure of trust. *Social Networks*, 20:265–289.

Buskens, V. (2000). Trust in triads: Effects of exit, control, and learning. *Games and Economic Behavior*, (forthcoming).

Buskens, V., Batenburg, R., and Weesie, J. (2002). Choosing the 'right' supplier: The importance of embeddedness for partner selection. *Research in the Sociology of Organization*, (forthcoming).

Buskens, V. and Raub, W. (2002). Embedded trust: Control and learning. *Advances in Group Processes*, (forthcoming).

Buskens, V., Raub, W., and Weesie, J. (2000). Networks and contracting in information technology transactions. In Raub, W. and Weesie, J., editors, *The Management of Durable Relations: Theoretical and Empirical Models for Organizations and Households*. Thela Thesis, Amsterdam.

Buskens, V. and Snijders, C. (1997). 'Individual heuristics and the dynamics of cooperation in large groups': Additional results using analytical methods. *Psychological Review*, 104:792–800.

Buskens, V. and Weesie, J. (2000a). Cooperation via networks. *Analyse und Kritik*, 22:44–74.

Buskens, V. and Weesie, J. (2000b). An experiment on the effects of embeddedness in trust situations: Buying a used car. *Rationality and Society*, 12:227–253.

Buskens, V. and Yamaguchi, K. (1999). A new model for information diffusion in heterogeneous social networks. In Sobel, M. E. and Becker, M. P., editors, *Sociological Methodology 1999*, pages 281–325. Blackwell, Oxford.

Camerer, C. (1995). Individual decision making. In Kagel, J. H. and Roth, A. E., editors, *Handbook of Experimental Economics*, pages 587–703. Princeton University Press, Princeton, NJ.

Camerer, C. and Weigelt, K. (1988). Experimental tests of a sequential equilibrium reputation model. *Econometrica*, 56:1–36.

Chiles, T. H. and McMackin, J. F. (1996). Integrating variable risk preferences, trust, and transaction cost economics. *Academy of Management Review*, 21:73–99.

Coleman, J. S. (1964). *Introduction to Mathematical Sociology*. The Free Press, London.

Coleman, J. S. (1972). Systems of social exchange. *Journal of Mathematical Sociology*, 2:145–163.

Coleman, J. S. (1973). *The Mathematics of Collective Action*. Academic Press, New York.

Coleman, J. S. (1990). *Foundations of Social Theory*. The Belknap Press of Harvard University Press, Cambridge, MA.

Colman, A. (1982). *Game Theory and Experimental Games: The Study of Strategic Interactions*. Pergamon Press, Oxford.

Cook, K. S. and Emerson, R. M. (1978). Power, equity, and commitment in exchange networks. *American Sociological Review*, 43:721–739.

Cripps, M. W. and Thomas, J. P. (1997). Reputation and perfection in repeated common interest games. *Games and Economic Behavior*, 18:141–158.

Dasgupta, P. (1988). Trust as a commodity. In Gambetta, D., editor, *Trust: Making and Breaking Cooperative Relations*, pages 49–72. Blackwell, Oxford.

David, H. A. (1963). *The Method of Paired Comparison*. Hafner Publishing Company, New York.

Dieudonné, J. A. (1960). *Foundation of Modern Analysis*. Academic Press, New York.

DiMaggio, P. and Louch, H. (1998). Socially embedded consumer transactions: For what kinds of purchases do people most often use networks? *American Sociological Review*, 63:619–637.

Ellickson, R. C. (1991). *Order Without Law: How Neighbors Settle Disputes*. Harvard University Press, Cambridge, MA.

Ensminger, J. (2001). Reputation, trust, and the principal agent problem. In Cook, K. S., editor, *Trust in Society*, pages 185–201. Russell Sage, New York.

Faia, M. A. (1980). The vagaries of vignette world: A comment on Alves and Rossi. *American Journal of Sociology*, 85:951–954.

Fechner, G. T. (1860). *Elemente der Psychophysik*. Breitkopf und Härtel, Leipzig. (in German).

Fedorov, V. V. (1972). *Theory of Optimal Experiments*. Academic Press, New York.

Feller, W. (1950). *An Introduction to Probability Theory*. Wiley, New York.

Flache, A. (1996). *The Double Edge of Networks: An Analysis of the Effect of Informal Networks on Cooperation in Social Dilemmas*. Thesis Publishers, Amsterdam.

Flache, A. and Macy, M. W. (1996). The weakness of strong ties: Collective action failure in highly cohesive groups. *Journal of Mathematical Sociology*, 21:3–28.

Flap, H. D. (1988). *Conflict, Loyalty, and Violence*. Peter Lang, Frankfurt am Main.

Flap, H. D. and De Graaf, N. D. (1986). Social capital and attained occupational status. *Netherlands' Journal of Sociology*, 22:145–161.

Frank, R. H., Gilovich, T., and Regan, D. T. (1993). Does studying economics inhibit cooperation? *Journal of Economic Perspectives*, 7:159–171.

Freeman, L. C. (1979). Centrality in social networks: Conceptual clarification. *Social Networks*, 1:215–239.

Freeman, L. C. (1992). Filling in the blanks: A theory of cognitive categories and the structure of social affiliation. *Social Psychology Quarterly*, 55:118–227.

Friedkin, N. E. (1991). Theoretical foundations for centrality measures. *American Journal of Sociology*, 96:1478–1504.

Friedman, D. and Hechter, M. (1988). The contribution of rational choice theory to macrosociological research. *Sociological Theory*, 6:201–218.

Friedman, J. W. (1971). A non-cooperative equilibrium for supergames. *Review of Economic Studies*, 38:1–12.

Friedman, J. W. (1986). *Game Theory with Applications to Economics*. Oxford University Press, New York.

Fudenberg, D. and Levine, D. K. (1998). *The Theory of Learning in Games*. MIT Press, Cambridge, MA.

Fudenberg, D. and Maskin, E. (1990). Evolution and cooperation in noisy repeated games. *American Economic Review*, 80:274–279.

Fudenberg, D. and Tirole, J. (1991). *Game Theory*. MIT Press, Cambridge, MA.

Gautschi, T. (2002). *Trust and Exchange*. Thela Thesis, Amsterdam.

Gellner, E. (1988). Trust, cohesion, and social order. In Gambetta, D., editor, *Trust: Making and Breaking Cooperative Relations*, pages 142–157. Blackwell, Oxford.

Gerlach, M. L. (1992). The Japanese corporate network: A blockmodel analysis. *Annual Review of Sociology*, 16:435–463.

Gibbons, R. (2001). Trust in social structures: Hobbes and Coase meet repeated games. In Cook, K. S., editor, *Trust in Society*, pages 332–353. Russell Sage, New York.

Gilles, R. P. (1990). *Core and Equilibria of Socially Structured Economies: The Modelling of Social Constraints in Economic Behavior*. Tilburg University, Tilburg.

Gilovich, T. (1987). Secondhand information and social judgement. *Journal of Experimental Social Psychology*, 23:59–74.

Goldberg, D. E. (1989). *Genetic Algorithms in Search, Optimization and Machine Learning*. Addison-Wesley, New York.

Gouldner, A. W. (1960). The norm of reciprocity: A preliminary statement. *American Sociological Review*, 25:161–178.

Granovetter, M. S. (1973). The strength of weak ties. *American Journal of Sociology*, 78:1360–1380.

Granovetter, M. S. (1979). The theory-gap in social network analysis. In Holland, P. W. and Leinhardt, S., editors, *Perspectives on Social Network Research*, pages 501–518. Academic Press, New York.

Granovetter, M. S. (1985). Economic action and social structure: The problem of embeddedness. *American Journal of Sociology*, 91:481–510.

Green, E. J. and Porter, R. H. (1984). Noncooperative collusion under imperfect price information. *Econometrica*, 52:87–100.

Greene, W. H. (1993). *Econometric Analysis*. Prentice-Hall, Englewood Cliffs, NJ, 2nd edition.

Greif, A. (1989). Reputation and coalitions in medieval trade: Evidence on the Maghribi traders. *Journal of Economic History*, 49:857–882.

Gulati, R. (1995a). Does familiarity breed trust? The implications of repeated ties for contractual choice in alliances. *Academy of Management Journal*, 38:85–112.

Gulati, R. (1995b). Social structure and alliance formation patterns: A longitudinal study. *Administrative Science Quarterly*, 40:619–652.

Gulati, R. and Gargiulo, M. (1999). Where do interorganizational networks come from? *American Journal of Sociology*, 104:1439–1493.

Harary, F., Norman, R. Z., and Cartwright, D. (1965). *Structural Models: An Introduction to the Theory of Directed Graphs*. Wiley, New York.

Harsanyi, J. C. (1967–68). Games with incomplete information played by 'Bayesian' players I–III. *Management Science*, 14:159–182, 320–334, 486–502.

Harsanyi, J. C. (1977). *Rational Behavior and Bargaining Equilibria in Games and Social Situations*. Cambridge University Press, Cambridge.

Harsanyi, J. C. (1995). A new theory of equilibrium selection for games with complete information. *Games and Economic Behavior*, 8:91–122.

Harsanyi, J. C. and Selten, R. (1988). *A General Theory of Equilibrium Selection in Games*. MIT Press, Cambridge, MA.

Hart, O. (1987). Incomplete contracts. In Eatwell, J., Milgate, M., and Newman, P., editors, *The New Palgrave: Allocation, Information and Markets*, pages 163–179. Macmillan, London.

Harvey, A. (1976). Estimating regression models with multiplicative heteroscedasticity. *Econometrica*, 44:461–465.

Hechter, M. and Kanazawa, S. (1997). Sociological rational choice theory. *Annual Review of Sociology*, 23:377–420.

Heckathorn, D. D. (1996). The dynamics and dilemmas of collective action. *American Sociological Review*, 61:250–277.

Hegselmann, R. (1996). Cellular automata in the social sciences: Perspectives, restrictions, and artefacts. In Hegselmann, R., Mueller, U., and Troitzsch, K. G., editors, *Modeling and Simulation in the Social Sciences from the Philosophy of Science Point of View*, pages 209–234. Kluwer Academic Publishers, Dordrecht.

Hermkens, P. L. J. (1983). *Oordelen over de Rechtvaardigheid van Inkomens*. Uitgeverij Kobra, Amsterdam. (in Dutch).

Hirschman, A. O. (1970). *Exit, Voice, and Loyalty: Responses to Decline in Firms, Organizations, and States*. Harvard University Press, Cambridge, MA.

Huber, P. J. (1967). The behavior of maximum likelihood estimates under nonstandard conditions. *Proceedings of the Fifth Berkeley Symposium on Mathematical Statistics and Probability*, 1:221–233.

Jasso, G. and Rossi, P. H. (1977). Distributive justice and earned income. *American Sociological Review*, 42:639–651.

Jones, C., Hesterly, W. S., and Borgatti, S. P. (1997). A general theory of network governance: Exchange conditions and social mechanisms. *Academy of Management Review*, 22:911–945.

Kelley, H. H. and Thibaut, J. W. (1978). *Interpersonal Relations: The Theory of Interdependence*. Wiley, New York.

Kemeny, J. G. and Snell, J. L. (1960). *Finite Markov Chains*. D. Van Nostrand, New York.

Klein, D. B. (1997a). *Reputation: Studies in the Voluntary Elicitation of Good Conduct*. University of Michigan Press, Ann Arbor, MI.

Klein, D. B. (1997b). Trust for hire: Voluntary remedies of quality and safety. In Klein, D. B., editor, *Reputation: Studies in the Voluntary Elicitation of Good Conduct*, pages 97–133. University of Michigan Press, Ann Arbor, MI.

Klein, D. B., editor (2000). *Assurance and Trust in a Great Society*. The Foundation for Economic Education, Irvington-on-Hudson, NY.

Kogut, B., Shan, W., and Walker, G. (1992). The make-or-cooperate decision in the context of an industry network. In Nohria, N. and Eccles, R. G., editors, *Networks and Organizations: Structure, Form, and Action*, pages 348–365. Harvard Business School Press, Boston.

Kollock, P. (1994). The emergence of exchange structures: An experimental study of uncertainty, commitment, and trust. *American Journal of Sociology*, 100:313–345.

Krackhardt, D. (1987). Cognitive social structures. *Social Networks*, 9:109–134.

Krackhardt, D. (1992). The strength of strong ties: The importance of *philos* in organizations. In Nohria, N. and Eccles, R. G., editors, *Networks and Organizations: Structure, Form, and Action*, pages 216–239. Harvard Business School Press, Boston.

Kramer, R. M. and Tyler, T. R., editors (1996). *Trust in Organizations: Frontiers of Theory and Research*. Sage, Thousand Oaks, CA.

Kreps, D. M. (1990a). Corporate culture and economic theory. In Alt, J. and Shepsle, K., editors, *Perspectives on Positive Political Economy*, pages 90–143. Cambridge University Press, Cambridge.

Kreps, D. M. (1990b). *A Course in Microeconomic Theory*. Harvester Wheatsheaf, New York.

Kreps, D. M., Milgrom, P., Roberts, J., and Wilson, R. (1982). Rational cooperation in the finitely repeated Prisoners' Dilemma. *Journal of Economic Theory*, 27:245–252.

Kumbasar, E., Romney, A. K., and Batchelder, W. H. (1994). Systematic biases in social perception. *American Journal of Sociology*, 100:477–505.

Lahno, B. (1995). Trust, reputation, and exit in exchange relationships. *Journal of Conflict Resolution*, 39:495–510.

Larson, A. (1992). Network dyads in entrepreneurial settings: A study of the governance of exchange relationships. *Administrative Science Quarterly*, 37:76–114.

Laumann, E. O. and Knoke, D. (1987). *The Organizational State: Social Choice in National Policy Domains*. The University of Wisconsin Press, Madison.

Lazega, E. and Van Duijn, M. (1997). Position in formal structure, personal characteristics, and choices of advisors in a law firm: A logistic regression model for dyadic network data. *Social Networks*, 19:375–397.

Leenders, R. T. A. J. (1995). *Structure and Influence: Statistical Models for the Dynamics of Actor Attributes, Network Structure and Their Interdependence*. Thesis Publishers, Amsterdam.

Levine, D. K. and Martinelli, C. (1998). Reputation with noisy precommitment. *Journal of Economic Theory*, 78:55–75.

Lieberson, S. (1985). *Making It Count: The Improvement of Social Research and Theory*. University of California Press, Berkeley, CA.

Lindenberg, S. M. (1992). The method of decreasing abstraction. In Coleman, J. S. and Fararo, T. J., editors, *Rational Choice Theory: Advocacy and Critique*, pages 3–20. Sage, London.

Lomborg, B. (1996). The evolution of social structure in the iterated Prisoner's Dilemma. *American Sociological Review*, 61:278–307.

Lorenz, E. H. (1988). Neither friends nor strangers: Informal networks of subcontracting in French industry. In Gambetta, D., editor, *Trust: Making and Breaking Cooperative Relations*, pages 94–107. Blackwell, Oxford.

Luce, R. D. and Raiffa, H. (1957). *Games and Decisions: Introduction and Critical Survey*. Wiley, New York.

Luhmann, N. (1988). Familiarity, confidence, trust: Problems and alternatives. In Gambetta, D., editor, *Trust: Making and Breaking Cooperative Relations*, pages 94–107. Blackwell, Oxford.

Lyons, B. R. (1994). Contracts and specific investments: An empirical test of transaction cost theory. *Journal of Economics and Management Strategy*, 3:257–278.

Macaulay, S. (1963). Non-contractual relations in business: A preliminary study. *American Sociological Review*, 28:55–67.

Macy, M. W. (1990). Learning theory and the logic of critical mass. *American Sociological Review*, 55:809–826.

Macy, M. W. (1993). Backward-looking social control. *American Sociological Review*, 58:819–836.

Macy, M. W. (1996). Natural selection and social learning in Prisoner's Dilemma: Co-adaptation with genetic algorithms and artificial neural networks. *Sociological Methods and Research*, 25:103–137.

Macy, M. W. and Skvoretz, J. (1998). The evolution of trust and cooperation between strangers: A computational model. *American Sociological Review*, 63:638–660.

Maddala, G. S. (1983). *Limited-Dependent and Qualitative Variables in Econometrics*. Cambridge University Press, Cambridge.

Mahajan, V. and Peterson, R. A. (1985). *Models for Innovation Diffusion*. Sage, Beverly Hills, CA.

Markovsky, B., Willer, D., and Patton, T. (1988). Power relations in exchange networks. *American Journal of Sociology*, 53:220–236.

McFadden, D. (1973). Conditional logit analysis of qualitative choice behavior. In Zarembka, P., editor, *Frontiers in Econometrics*, pages 105–142. Academic Press, New York.

Merry, S. E. (1984). Rethinking gossip and scandal. In Black, D., editor, *Towards a General Theory of Social Control, Vol. 1*, pages 271–302. Academic Press, New York.

Messick, D. D. and Liebrand, W. B. G. (1995). Individual heuristics and the dynamics of cooperation in large groups. *Psychological Review*, 102:131–145.

Milgrom, P., North, D. C., and Weingast, B. R. (1990). The role of institutions in the revival of trade: The law merchants. *Economics and Politics*, 2:1–23.

Milgrom, P. and Roberts, J. (1992). *Economics, Organization and Management*. Prentice-Hall, Englewood Cliffs, NJ.

Misztal, B. A. (1996). *Trust in Modern Societies*. Polity Press, Cambridge.

Mokken, R. J. (1970). *A Theory and Procedures of Scale Analysis: With Applications in Political Research*. Mouton, The Hague.

Molenaar, I. W. (1982). Mokken scaling revisited. *Kwantitatieve Methoden*, 3:145–164.

Morris, M. (1993). Epidemiology and social networks: Modeling structured diffusion. *Sociological Methods and Research*, 22:99–126.

Mosteller, F. (1951). Remarks on the method of paired comparison: I. The least squares solution assuming equal standard deviations and equal correlations. II. The effect of an aberrant standard deviation when equal standard deviations and equal correlations are assumed. III. A test of significance for paired comparison when equal standard deviations and equal correlations are assumed. *Psychometrika*, 16:3–9, 203–206, 207–218.

Nash, J. F. (1951). Non-cooperative games. *Annals of Mathematics*, 54:286–295.

Neral, J. and Ochs, J. (1992). The sequential equilibrium theory of reputation building: A further test. *Econometrica*, 60:1151–1169.

Nock, S. L. and Rossi, P. H. (1978). Ascription versus achievement in the attribution of family social status. *American Journal of Sociology*, 84:565–590.

Nock, S. L. and Rossi, P. H. (1979). Household types and social standing. *Social Forces*, 57:1325–1345.

Nohria, N. (1992). Information and search in the creation of new business ventures: The case of 128 venture group. In Nohria, N. and Eccles, R. G., editors, *Networks and Organizations: Structure, Form, and Action*, pages 240–261. Harvard Business School Press, Boston.

Nohria, N. and Eccles, R. G., editors (1992). *Networks and Organizations: Structure, Form, and Action*. Harvard Business School Press, Boston.

Norde, H., Potters, J., Reijnierse, H., and Vermeulen, D. (1996). Equilibrium selection and consistency. *Games and Economic Behavior*, 12:219–225.

Nowak, A., Szamrej, J., and Latané, B. (1990). From private to public opinion: A dynamic theory of social impact. *Psychological Review*, 97:362–376.

Nowak, M. and Sigmund, K. (1993). A strategy of Win-Stay, Loose-Shift that outperforms Tit-For-Tat in the Prisoner's Dilemma Game. *Nature*, 364:56–58.

Orbell, J., Dawes, R. M., and Schwartz-Shea, P. (1994). Trust, social categories, and individuals: The case of gender. *Motivation and Emotion*, 18:109–128.

Parry, J. (1967). *The Psychology of Human Communication*. University of London Press, London.

Parsons, T. (1937). *The Structure of Social Action*. McGraw-Hill, New York.

Piore, M. J. and Sabel, C. E. (1984). *The Second Industrial Divide: Possibility for Prosperity*. Basic Books, New York.

Porter, R. H. (1983). Optimal cartel trigger-price strategies. *Journal of Economic Theory*, 29:313–338.

Pukelsheim, F. (1993). *Optimal Design of Experiments*. Wiley, New York.

Rapoport, A. (1951). Nets with distance bias. *Bulletin of Mathematical Biophysics*, 13:85–91.

Rapoport, A. (1953a). Spread of information through a population with sociostructural bias: I. Assumption of transitivity. *Bulletin of Mathematical Biophysics*, 15:523–533.

Rapoport, A. (1953b). Spread of information through a population with sociostructural bias: II. Various models with partial transitivity. *Bulletin of Mathematical Biophysics*, 15:535–546.

Rapoport, A. (1957). Contribution to the theory of random and biased nets. *Bulletin of Mathematical Biophysics*, 19:257–277.

Rapoport, A. (1979). A probabilistic approach to networks. *Social Networks*, 2:1–18.

Rasmusen, E. (1994). *Games and Information: An Introduction to Game Theory*. Blackwell, Oxford, 2nd edition.

Raub, W. (1996). Effects of temporal embeddedness on ex ante planning under incomplete information. ISCORE Paper 87, Utrecht University.

Raub, W. (1997). *Samenwerking in Duurzame Relaties en Sociale Cohesie*. Thesis Publishers, Amsterdam. (in Dutch).

Raub, W. (1998). A simple contract game and some hypotheses on contractual behavior in interfirm relations. ISCORE Paper 119, Utrecht University.

Raub, W. and Keren, G. (1993). Hostages as a commitment device: A game-theoretic model and empirical test of some scenarios. *Journal of Economic Behavior and Organization*, 21:43–67.

Raub, W. and Weesie, J. (1990). Reputation and efficiency in social interactions: An example of network effects. *American Journal of Sociology*, 96:626–654.

Raub, W. and Weesie, J. (1993a). The management of matches: Decentralized mechanism for cooperative relations with applications to organizations and households (revised version). ISCORE Paper 1, Utrecht University.

Raub, W. and Weesie, J. (1993b). Symbiotic arrangements: A sociological perspective. *Journal of Institutional and Theoretical Economics*, 149:716–724.

Raub, W. and Weesie, J. (2000a). The management of matches: A research program on solidarity in durable social relations. *Netherlands' Journal of Social Sciences*, 36:71–88.

Raub, W. and Weesie, J. (2000b). Trust via hostages. *Analyse und Kritik*, 22:19–43.

Rogers, E. M. (1995). *Diffusion of Innovations*. The Free Press, New York, 4th edition.

Rogers, W. M. (1993). Regression standard errors in clustered samples. *Stata Technical Bulletin*, 13:19–23.

Rooks, G. (2002). *Contract en Conflict: Strategisch Management van Inkooptransaties*. Thela Thesis, Amsterdam. (in Dutch).

Rooks, G., Raub, W., Selten, R., and Tazelaar, F. (2000). Cooperation between buyer and supplier: Effects of social embeddedness on negotiation effort. *Acta Sociologica*, 43:123–137.

Rossi, P. H. (1979). Vignette analysis: Uncovering the normative structure of complexity. In Merton, R. K., Coleman, J. S., and Rossi, P. H., editors, *Qualitative and Quantitative Social Research: Papers in Honor of Paul F. Lazarsfeld*, pages 176–186. The Free Press, New York.

Rossi, P. H. and Nock, S. L., editors (1982). *Measuring Social Judgments: The Factorial Survey Approach*. Sage, Beverly Hills, CA.

Rossi, P. H., Sampson, W. A., Bose, C. E., Jasso, G., and Passel, J. (1974). Measuring household standing. *Social Science Research*, 3:169–190.

Roth, A. E. (1995). Introduction to experimental economics. In Kagel, J. H. and Roth, A. E., editors, *Handbook of Experimental Economics*, pages 3–109. Princeton University Press, Princeton, NJ.

Rubinstein, A. (1998). *Modeling Bounded Rationality*. MIT Press, Cambridge, MA.

Sahlins, M. (1972). *Stone Age Economics*. Aldine, Chicago.

Sampson, W. A. and Rossi, P. H. (1975). Race and family social standing. *American Sociological Review*, 40:201–214.

Samuelson, L. (1997). *Evolutionary Games and Equilibrium Selection*. MIT Press, Cambridge, MA.

Schüßler, R. A. (1989). Exit threats and cooperation under anonymity. *Journal of Conflict Resolution*, 33:728–749.

Schwartz, R. D. (1954). Social factors in the development of legal control: A case study of two Israeli settlements. *Yale Law Journal*, 63:471–491.

Scott, D. (1983). Trust differences between men and women in superior-subordinate relationships. *Groups and Organizations Studies*, 8:319–336.

Selten, R. (1965). Spieltheoretische Behandlung eines Oligopolmodells mit Nachfrageträgheit. *Zeitschrift für die gesamte Staatswissenschaft*, 121:301–324, 667–689. (in German).

Smelser, N. J. and Swedberg, R., editors (1994). *The Handbook of Economic Sociology*. Russell Sage, New York.

Snijders, C. (1996). *Trust and Commitments*. Thesis Publishers, Amsterdam.

Snijders, C. and Buskens, V. (2001). How to convince someone that you can be trusted? The role of 'hostages'. *Journal of Mathematical Sociology*, (forthcoming).

Snijders, C. and Keren, G. (2001). Do you trust? Whom do you trust? When do you trust? *Advances in Group Processes*, 18:129–160.

Snijders, T. A. B. (1981). The degree of variance: An index of graph heterogeneity. *Social Networks*, 3:163–174.

Snijders, T. A. B. (2001). The statistical evaluation of social network dynamics. In Sobel, M. E. and Becker, M. P., editors, *Sociological Methodology 2001*, pages 361–395. Blackwell, Oxford.

Spence, A. M. (1973). Job market signaling. *Quarterly Journal of Economics*, 87:355–374.

Stern, H. (1992). Are all linear paired comparison models empirically equivalent? *Mathematical Social Sciences*, 23:103–117.

Stinchcombe, A. L. (1990). *Information and Organizations*. University of California Press, Berkeley, CA.

Stokman, F. N. and Zeggelink, E. P. H. (1996). Is politics power or policy oriented? A comparative analysis of dynamic access models in policy networks. *Journal of Mathematical Sociology*, 21:77–111.

Swedberg, R., editor (1993). *Explorations in Economic Sociology*. Russell Sage, New York.

Taylor, M. (1987). *The Possibility of Cooperation*. Cambridge University Press (Revised edition of *Anarchy and Cooperation*, London: Wiley 1976), Cambridge.

Thurstone, L. L. (1927a). The method of paired comparison for social values. *Journal of Abnormal and Social Psychology*, 21:384–400.

Thurstone, L. L. (1927b). Psychophysical analysis. *American Journal of Psychology*, 38:368–389.

Tobin, J. (1958). Estimation of relationships for limited dependent variables. *Econometrica*, 26:24–36.

Uzzi, B. (1996). The sources and consequences of embeddedness for the economic performance of organizations: The network effect. *American Sociological Review*, 61:674–698.

Uzzi, B. (1997). Social structure and competition in interfirm networks: The paradox of embeddedness. *Administrative Science Quarterly*, 42:35–67.

Valente, T. W. (1995). *Network Models of the Diffusion of Innovations*. Hampton Press, Cresskill.

Van Berkum, E. E. (1985). *Optimal Paired Comparison Design for Factorial Experiments*. Centrum voor Wiskunde en Informatica, Amsterdam.

Van Damme, E. E. C. (1987). *Stability and Perfection of Nash Equilibria*. Springer-Verlag, Berlin.

Van den Brink, R. (1994). *Relational Power in Hierarchical Organizations*. Tilburg University, Tilburg.

Van der Bunt, G. G. (1997). The challenge of (longitudinal) inter-organizational social network research (in the Netherlands). *Bulletin de Methodologie Sociologique*, 56:50–70.

Vanberg, V. and Congleton, R. D. (1992). Rationality, morality, and exit. *American Political Science Review*, 86:418–431.

Voss, T. (1982). Rational actors and social institutions: The case of the organic emergence of norms. In Raub, W., editor, *Theoretical Models and Empirical Analyses: Contributions to the Explanation of Individual Actions and Collective Phenomena*, pages 101–128. Explanatory Sociology Publications, Utrecht.

Voss, T. (1985). *Rationale Akteure und soziale Institutionen*. Oldenbourg Verlag, München. (in German).

Wallis, W. A. and Friedman, M. (1942). The empirical derivation of indifference functions. In Lange, O., McIntyre, F., and Yntema, T. O., editors, *Studies in Mathematical Economics and Econometrics in Memory of Henry Schultz*, pages 267–300. University of Chicago Press, Chicago.

Wasserman, S. and Faust, K. (1994). *Social Network Analysis: Methods and Applications*. Cambridge University Press, Cambridge.

Weber, M. (1921). *Wirtschaft und Gesellschaft*. Mohr 1976, Tübingen, 5th edition. (in German).

Wechsberg, J. (1966). *The Merchant Bankers*. Bedminster Press, New York.

Weesie, J. (1988). *Mathematical Models for Competition, Cooperation, and Social Networks*. Utrecht University, Utrecht.

Weesie, J. (1994). Social orientations in symmetric 2 × 2 games. ISCORE Paper 17, Utrecht University.

Weesie, J. (1996). Disciplining via exit and voice. ISCORE Paper 88, Utrecht University.

Weesie, J., Buskens, V., and Raub, W. (1998). The management of trust relations via institutional and structural embeddedness. In Doreian, P. and Fararo, T., editors, *The Problem of Solidarity: Theories and Models*, pages 113–138. Gordon and Breach, Amsterdam.

Weesie, J. and Van Houwelingen, H. (1983). Gepcam user's manual: Generalized principal components analysis with missing values. Institute of Mathematical Statistics, Utrecht University.

Weibull, J. (1995). *Evolutionary Game Theory*. MIT Press, Cambridge, MA.

White, H. (1980). A heteroscedasticity-consistent covariance matrix estimator and a direct test for heteroscedasticity. *Econometrica*, 48:817–830.

Williamson, O. E. (1975). *Markets and Hierarchies: Analysis and Antitrust Implications*. The Free Press, New York.

Williamson, O. E. (1985). *The Economic Institutions of Capitalism*. The Free Press, New York.

Williamson, O. E. (1996). *The Mechanisms of Governance*. Oxford University Press, Oxford.

Wilson, R. (1985). Reputations in games and markets. In Roth, A. E., editor, *Reputations in Games and Markets*, pages 267–300. Cambridge University Press, Cambridge.

Wittek, R. (1999). *Interdependence and Informal Control in Organizations.* Thela Thesis, Amsterdam.

Wittek, R. (2001). Mimitec trust and intra-organizational network dynamics. *Journal of Mathematical Sociology*, 25:109–138.

Wu, J. and Axelrod, R. (1995). How to cope with noise in the iterated Prisoner's Dilemma. *Journal of Conflict Resolution*, 39:183–189.

Yamagishi, T. and Kakiuchi, R. (2000). It takes venturing into a tiger's cave to steal a baby tiger: Experiments in the development of trust relationships. In Raub, W. and Weesie, J., editors, *The Management of Durable Relations: Theoretical and Empirical Models for Organizations and Households*. Thela Thesis, Amsterdam.

Yamaguchi, K. (1994a). The flow of information through social networks: Diagonal-free measures of inefficiency and the structural determinants of inefficiency. *Social Networks*, 16:57–86.

Yamaguchi, K. (1994b). Some accelerated failure-time regression models derived from diffusion process models: An application to a network diffusion analysis. In Marsden, P. V., editor, *Sociological Methodology*, pages 267–300. Blackwell, Oxford.

Yamaguchi, K. (1996). Power in networks of substitutable and complementary exchange: A rational-choice model and an analysis of power centralization. *American Sociological Review*, 61:308–332.

Zeggelink, E. P. H., Hiramatsu, H., Stokman, F. N., Van Duijn, M., and Wasseur, F. (1998). Friendship formation over time among sociology students: A comparison between Japan and the Netherlands. Paper presented at Sunbelt XVIII and Fifth European International Social Networks Conference, Sitges, Spain, May 28–31.

Zeggelink, E. P. H., Stokman, F. N., and Van der Bunt, G. G. (1996). The emergence of groups in the evolution of friendship networks. *Journal of Mathematical Sociology*, 21:29–55.

About the Author

Vincent Buskens holds a degree in technical mathematics with a specialization in discrete mathematics, a degree in technology and development sciences, and a Ph.D. in sociology from the Interuniversity Center for Social Science Theory and Methodology (ICS). The research reported in this book is a result of his work at the ICS. Starting from July 2002, he is research fellow of the Royal Netherlands Academy of Arts and Sciences (KNAW) at the Department of Sociology / ICS at Utrecht University.

Author Index

Abreu, D., 47
Akerlof, G. A., 3
Akkermans, S. T. M., 217
Altmann, M., 95
Alves, W. M., 165
Amemiya, T., 78
Arrow, K. J., 5
Axelrod, R., 11–12, 21, 49, 206–207
Bacharach, M., 25
Bailey, N. T. J., 95
Baker, W. E., 12
Bala, V., 208
Barley, S. R., 21
Bartholomew, D. J., 95
Batchelder, W. H., 137
Batenburg, R. S., 13, 126, 130, 132, 139, 144, 147, 151, 196, 229
Bellman, R., 102, 213
Berman, A., 65
Bernard, H. R., 136–137, 209
Bienenstock, E. J., 207
Binmore, K., 125, 206
Blau, P. M., 11, 207
Blumberg, B. F., 12, 18, 57, 152, 188, 196, 200
Bollen, K. A., 154
Bonacich, P., 207
Borgatti, S. P., 21
Bose, C. E., 165
Box, G. E. P., 111
Bradley, I., 179
Burt, R. S., 11, 16, 21–22, 31, 37, 209
Camerer, C., 13–14, 51, 129, 165, 210
Cartwright, D., 32
Chiles, T. H., 24
Coleman, J. S., 1, 5–8, 11, 17, 22, 26, 86, 95, 189, 191, 205, 207
Colman, A., 13
Congleton, R. D., 18, 57
Cook, K. S., 207
Cox, D. R., 111
Cripps, M. W., 51
Dasgupta, P., 6, 51, 55
David, H. A., 171–173
Dawes, R. M., 177
De Graaf, N. D., 22
Dieudonné, J. A., 71
DiMaggio, P., 166, 170
Eccles, R. G., 21
Ellickson, R. C., 20
Emerson, R. M., 207
Ensminger, J., 20–21
Faia, M. A., 165
Faulkner, R. R., 12
Faust, K., 31–33, 63, 192
Fechner, G. T., 172
Fedorov, V. V., 173, 225
Feller, W., 225
Fisher, G. A., 12
Flache, A., 52, 206, 210
Flap, H. D., 22, 189
Frank, R. H., 177
Freeman, J., 21
Freeman, L. C., 34–35, 39, 104, 137
Friedkin, N. E., 95, 104
Friedman, D., 5
Friedman, J. W., 47–48, 62
Friedman, M., 165
Fudenberg, D., 42, 46–47, 49, 64, 205–207
Gambetta, D., 25
Gargiulo, M., 12
Gautschi, T., 14
Gellner, M. R., 20
Gerlach, M. L., 22
Gibbons, R., 46
Gilles, R. P., 207
Gilovich, T., 122, 177
Goldberg, D. E., 206
Gouldner, A. W., 11
Goyal, S., 208

Granovetter, M., 1, 10–11, 16, 31, 37, 40
Greene, W. H., 110
Green, E. J., 207
Greif, A., 25
Gulati, R., 12, 22, 157
Harary, F., 32, 106
Harsanyi, J., 42, 46, 50, 65, 205
Hart, O., 127
Harvey, A., 110
Hechter, M., 5
Heckathorn, D. D., 49
Hegselmann, R., 50
Hermkens, P. L. J., 165
Hesterly, W. S., 21
Hiramatsu, H., 209
Hirschman, A. O., 15
Huber, P. J., 77, 146
Hybels, R. C., 21
Jannotta, J. E., 31
Jasso, G., 165
Jones, C., 21
Kakiuchi, R., 13
Kanazawa, S., 5
Kelley, H. H., 6
Kemeny, J. G., 69, 100
Keren, G., 24, 177, 187
Killworth, P. D., 136–137
Klein, D. B., 25
Knez, M., 11, 16, 21, 209
Knoke, D., 94
Kogut, B., 21
Kollock, P., 14
Krackhardt, D., 138, 209
Kramer, R. M., 21
Kreps, D. M., 6, 11, 24–25, 47, 49–50, 55, 126, 193, 213
Kronenfeld, D., 136
Kumbasar, E., 137
Lahno, B., 18, 57
Larson, A., 12
Latané, B., 50
Laumann, E. O., 94
Lazega, E., 209
Leenders, R. Th. A. J., 209
Levine, D. K., 51, 205–206
Lieberson, S., 164
Liebrand, W. B. G., 50, 206
Lindenberg, S. M., 205
Lomborg, B., 49
Lorenz, E. H., 16, 18, 150, 200
Louch, H., 166, 170
Luce, R. D., 7
Luhmann, N., 5
Lyons, B. R, , 8, 12, 150
Macaulay, S., 8, 126–127
Macy, M. W., 52, 206
Maddala, G. S., 157
Mahajan, V., 95
Mahoney, J. T., 31
Markovsky, B., 207
Martinelli, C., 51
Maskin, R., 207
McFadden, D., 179
McMackin, J. F., 24
Merry, S. E., 25
Messick, D. M., 50, 206
Milgrom, P., 25, 49–50, 127
Misztal, B. A., 5
Mokken, R. J., 133
Molenaar, I. W., 133
Morris, M., 95
Mosteller, F., 179
Nash, J. F., 43
Neral, J., 13, 51
Nock, S. L., 165–166
Nohria, N., 21, 26, 139, 157
Norde, H., 46
Norman, R. Z., 32
North, D. C., 25
Nowak, A., 50
Nowak, M., 206
Ochs, J., 13, 51
Orbell, J., 177
Parry, J., 122
Parsons, T., 5
Passel, J., 165
Patton, T., 207
Peterson, R. A., 95
Piore, M. J., 26
Plemmons, R. J., 65
Porter, R. H., 207
Potters, J., 46
Pukelsheim, F., 173, 225
Raiffa, H., 7
Rapoport, A., 95
Rasmusen, E., 42–44, 46–47
Raub, W., 5, 10, 13, 24–26, 50, 55, 66, 69, 71, 86, 126, 129–130, 144, 151, 164, 193
Regan, D. T., 177
Reijnierse, H., 46
Roberts, J., 50, 127
Rogers, E. M., 36, 95
Rogers, W. M., 77, 110, 146, 180
Romney, A. K., 137
Rooks, G., 132, 164, 166, 170–171, 188, 196
Rossi, P. H., 165–166
Roth, A. E., 165
Rubinstein, A., 205
Russell, B., 71
Sabel, C. E., 26
Sahlins, M., 20
Sailer, L., 136–137
Sampson, W. A., 165
Samuelson, L., 205

Schwartz-Shea, P., 177
Schwartz, R. D., 25
Schüßler, R. A., 18, 57
Scott, D., 177
Selten, R. M. K. P., 164
Selten, R., 45–46, 65
Shan, W., 21
Sigmund, K., 206
Skvoretz, J., 206
Smelser, N. J., 21
Snell, J. L., 69, 100
Snijders, C., 6, 9–10, 13, 25, 66, 89, 129, 151, 177, 186–187, 206
Snijders, T. A. B., 38, 208
Spence, M. A., 25
Stern, H., 179
Stinchcombe, A. L., 24
Stokman, F. N., 208–209
Swedberg, R., 21
Szamrej, J., 50
Taylor, M., 11
Tazelaar, F., 164
Terry, M. E., 179
Thibaut, J. W., 6
Thomas, J. P., 51
Thurstone, L. L., 172, 179
Tirole, J., 42, 46–47, 49, 64
Tobin, J., 78
Tyler, T. R., 21
Uzzi, B., 12
Valente, T. W., 95
Van Berkum, E. E. M., 173
Van Damme, E. E. C., 46
Van den Brink, R., 207
Van der Bunt, G. G., 208–209
Van Duijn, M., 209
Van Houwelingen, H., 141
Van Lint, J. H., 217
Vanberg, V., 18, 57
Vermeulen, D., 46
Voss, T., 11
Walker, G., 21
Wallis, W. A., 165
Wasserman, S., 31–33, 63, 192
Wasseur, F., 209
Weber, M., 4, 20
Wechsberg, J., 3, 20, 125
Weesie, J., 5–6, 18, 25–26, 39, 50, 55, 57, 63, 66–67, 69–71, 86, 141, 193
Weibull, J., 205
Weigelt, K., 13–14, 51, 129, 210
Weingast, B. R., 25
White, H., 77
Willer, D., 207
Williamson, O. E., 6, 18, 23–24, 126, 128, 200
Wilson, R., 3, 50
Wittek, R., 209
Wu, J., 206–207
Yamagishi, T., 13
Yamaguchi, K., 39, 54, 61, 74, 91, 93–98, 104, 194, 199, 207
Zeggelink, E. P. H., 208–209

Topic Index

absorbing state, 100–102, 121–122
alliances, 12, 22
asset specificity, 23
backward-looking, 52
beliefs, 8, 10, 16–17, 21, 50, 217
blockmodel, 33, 35, 37, 63, 225
censoring, 78–79, 81, 84, 86
centrality, 34, 38, 95, 101
  betweenness, 104
  closeness, 104
  immediate effects, 104
  receiver, 101, 104–106, 109, 120–121
  transmitter, 101, 104–121
centralization, 38–40, 54, 71, 85, 87–88, 118–121, 191–192, 194–195, 203–204
chain length, 69–70
clustered observations, 74, 76–77, 81, 110, 146, 180, 184–185
coalitions, 25
cohesion, 20–21
commitments, 24
common knowledge, 43, 47, 54, 170, 208
complexity, 128–129, 131, 133, 139–140, 142–143, 145, 147–148, 153–155, 158, 164, 196, 201
components, 128–129, 132, 139–140, 142–143, 145, 147–148, 153, 158, 196
conditional cooperation, 11, 17, 47–48, 193
constituent game, 47, 55–57, 60, 62, 64, 73, 81, 89, 216
contract, 8, 12–13, 23–24, 126–127, 129, 132–134, 142, 147, 150, 154, 156–160, 167, 196, 202, 204, 210, 232
  (in)complete, 127, 160
control, 4–5, 10–14, 16–23, 25–29, 32, 41, 49, 51–53, 55, 57, 65, 69–70, 87, 94, 119–121, 135–136, 149–150, 155, 159–161, 163–164, 166, 169–170, 177, 181–183, 187–188, 192–193, 195–198, 201, 203–204, 207, 211
  institutionalized, 25
coordination, 127
correlation, 39, 70, 75–76, 78, 80–81, 83–84, 86, 91, 110, 116, 118, 120, 142, 152, 155–156, 202
  spatial, 77, 83
degree, 136, 143, 148–159, 161, 201–202
dense networks, 3–5, 16–17, 21–22, 53, 125, 160
density, 21, 26, 28, 34, 38–41, 54, 63, 67, 69, 72–90, 95, 105, 107–121, 136–138, 143–144, 148–149, 159, 161, 163–164, 167–171, 175, 181–182, 184–185, 188–189, 191–192, 194–198, 201, 203, 223, 225–228
dependence, 128–129, 139–145, 147–148, 151–153, 158, 196
diamond merchants, 3–4, 17, 20, 125
diffusion, 39, 70, 93, 95, 97
  information, 4, 10, 15–16, 28, 34, 36, 39, 41, 53, 57, 61, 93–97, 99, 102–104, 106, 110, 118–119, 122, 194–195, 199, 203
  innovation, 95
discount factor, 47, 49, 54, 60–61, 66–69, 76, 78–81, 89, 103
distrust, 16–17, 21
drop-out rate, 46, 49, 57, 59, 61, 67–68, 76, 78–81
efficiency, 22, 40, 56, 60, 64, 68, 70, 142
end node, 42, 45
endogeneity, 152, 154, 161, 164, 202
epidemics, 95
equilibrium path, 45, 48, 64
equilibrium selection, 44, 46, 65
equilibrium, 7, 44, 46–49, 51, 54–55, 63, 66
  Nash, 21, 43–45, 206
  subgame-perfect, 45–48, 56, 64–65, 67–68, 213–214, 217–220
exchange, 207
exit network, 16, 18, 23
exit, 15, 18, 57, 168
experiment, 9, 13–14, 202, 210
  abstract, 165

concrete, 165
vignette, 165
Folk theorem, 47, 64
formal arrangements, 4, 8, 12–13, 20, 23–24
bilateral, 24
forward-looking, 52
future, 4, 11, 13, 17, 49, 128, 135–136, 143–145, 148–151, 159, 164–165, 167–171, 175–176, 178, 181–185, 187–188, 192–193, 196, 198, 201–202
genetic algorithms, 206
geographical distance, 138, 143–145, 147–151, 196
governance, 12, 23–24, 173
heteroscedasticity, 110, 146
multiplicative, 86, 110, 146, 185
hierarchies, 24
hybrid forms, 24
implicit function, 71
incentive, 9–10, 14, 23, 55, 73, 76, 78–81, 87–89, 126, 128–129, 151, 192–193
long-term, 2, 11, 54
short-term, 2–3, 11, 49, 54
indegree quality, 36, 41, 75, 84–85, 117, 120–121
indegree variance, 34, 39, 41, 75, 84–85, 116–119
indegree, 34–36, 38–39, 41, 54, 74–75, 84–85, 88, 90, 106, 109–113, 116–118, 120, 136–137, 143–145, 148–149, 164, 167–169, 171, 175, 181–184, 188, 190–191, 195–198, 203, 226–228
informant accuracy, 135, 137, 208
information content, 17, 94, 120, 195, 199–200
information set, 43–44
information, 3, 28, 41, 44, 52, 94, 101, 120–121, 144, 149, 168–169, 188, 195, 197, 199, 211
(a)symmetric, 2, 44–45, 125, 166, 205
(im)perfect, 44–45, 205
(in)complete, 13, 44–45, 50–52, 54, 89–90, 129, 144, 159–160, 188–190, 197–201, 205, 210–211
third-party, 16, 177, 183, 188
interdependent relations, 1, 4
isolated encounters, 9–10, 46, 177
law merchants, 25
learning, 4–5, 10–14, 16–17, 21–22, 26, 28–30, 32, 49–52, 54, 70, 93–94, 120–121, 135–136, 147, 150, 159–161, 164, 166, 169–170, 181–183, 187–188, 192–193, 195–200, 203–205, 211
legal expertise, 142–143, 145, 147–148
linearization, 54, 71, 73, 194
local indegree density, 37–38, 41, 75–76, 84–85, 117–118
local outdegree density, 37, 41, 75–76, 84–86, 117–118
longitudinal data, 204, 209
markets, 24
Markov chain, 69, 97–100, 107, 121, 215
middlemen, 25
mimicry, 25
monitoring problems, 128–129, 140–143, 145, 147–149, 153, 159, 196
Nature, 42–45, 50–51, 55
network activities, 153
network embeddedness, 5, 10, 15–16, 21, 23, 26, 29, 69, 77, 87, 89, 132, 136, 147–148, 150–151, 154–155, 158, 161, 163, 170–171, 177, 181–183, 187–188, 191, 197–198, 200–202, 204, 211
network governance, 21
network parameters, 26–27, 31–32, 34, 41, 54, 61, 63, 71, 74–77, 80, 82–83, 85, 91, 94–96, 103–104, 109, 119–121, 136, 164, 167, 194–196, 204
global, 26, 28–29, 34, 41, 54, 75, 84–85, 87, 113, 117, 136, 164, 189, 192, 194, 198, 203, 208–209
individual, 27–29, 34, 37, 41, 54, 75, 84, 87, 113, 117, 136, 163–164, 189, 192, 194, 198, 203, 209
network size, 34, 41, 75, 78, 82, 84, 86, 107–109, 111–113, 115–117, 120
node, 32, 34–35
noise, 90, 122, 185, 200, 206
opportunism, 2–3, 16, 19, 23–25, 126–127, 129, 133
optimal punishment, 207
ostracism, 4, 18
outdegree quality, 36, 41, 75, 82, 84–85, 116–121
outdegree variance, 34, 39, 41, 75, 84–85, 116–119
outdegree, 34–35, 38–39, 41, 54, 67, 70–75, 78–90, 95, 106, 109–121, 136–137, 143–145, 148–149, 164–165, 167–171, 175, 178, 181–185, 187–188, 190–192, 194–198, 203, 223, 226–228
outdegree-indegree covariance, 34, 39–41, 75, 84–85, 105, 117–118
Pareto optimality, 46, 65, 67–68, 70, 217, 219
past, 3–4, 11–13, 15–16, 49, 134–135, 143–145, 147–151, 153, 159, 167–168, 171, 174–176, 181–184, 192, 197
payoff dominance, 46, 48, 65, 72
payoffs, 6, 9, 32, 42, 47, 49, 54, 60–61, 126–129, 196
principal agent theory, 126
principal components analysis, 139–141
Prisoner's Dilemma, 7, 11, 13, 21, 50, 206
probit model, 180–181, 184–185
public sources, 53, 95, 97, 122, 200
quality, 2–4, 14, 24, 125, 132, 166, 205
random utility model, 173, 179, 181, 184
recall, 58
imperfect, 58, 205
perfect, 58
reception rate, 34, 41, 96

reciprocity, 11
redundancy, 22, 37, 85, 90, 95, 199
relation-specific investments, 13, 18
repeated games, 14, 46, 49, 55
reputation, 3–4, 11, 13–14, 16, 20, 25, 50, 53, 144, 157, 159, 169, 187, 197–198
response rate, 131
risk, 1–3, 8, 191
monetary, 9
safeguards, 4, 6, 126–127, 129, 132–133, 135, 138, 142–152, 154, 156–160, 196, 201
sample stratification, 130–131, 138, 155
sanction costs, 54, 66–68, 73, 76, 78–81, 87–89, 129, 144, 152, 170, 193–194
sanction, 4, 10–11, 13, 15, 17–18, 20, 22, 24–25, 32, 47, 54, 65, 135, 137, 151, 155, 159, 163, 169, 183, 192–193, 197, 200, 203, 207
third-party, 4, 18–19, 94, 204
search, 13, 21, 23, 26, 153–154
extensive, 153–154
formal, 153–154
informal, 153
intensive, 153–155, 157
sector density, 138, 143–151, 155
selectivity, 156, 160, 202
self-selection, 164
shadow of the future, 12, 69
shadow of the past, 12
signaling, 25
simulation, 54, 61, 74, 90, 109, 194–195, 206
singleton, 43–44
size buyer, 142–143, 147–148, 153
size supplier, 142–143, 147–148, 153, 158
social capital, 22, 189
social context, 3–4, 10, 17
social dilemma, 7
social networks, 5, 10
definition, 33
directed, 32–33
discrete, 33–34
heterogeneous, 29, 33, 74, 77, 86
homogeneous, 33, 54, 67, 73, 77, 86, 107–109, 111, 121, 194–195
valued, 32–35, 38, 96, 192
solution, 42, 44, 55, 60, 65, 67, 89
standard errors, 76, 83, 180
Huber, 77, 79, 84, 113, 117, 146, 148, 153, 181, 184
robust, 77, 110, 184
standardization procedures, 142–143, 145, 147–148, 159
stock exchange, 4, 20
strategy, 42–43
trigger, 47–48, 50, 54, 62–68, 89, 193, 213–214, 216–218
structural holes, 22, 31, 37
subgame, 45, 64
temporal embeddedness, 4, 10, 12, 16–17, 23, 29, 32, 46, 66, 68, 132, 147–149, 154–155, 158–159, 163, 170–171, 181–183, 187, 191, 197–198, 200, 204
temptation, 9
third parties, 5, 10, 15–18, 23, 138, 160, 188, 197, 200
Tit-for-Tat, 11, 50, 206
tobit regression, 78
transaction characteristics, 6, 128, 132–133, 139, 143, 147, 149–151, 154–156, 158–159, 192, 194, 196, 202, 209
transaction cost theory, 6, 23–24, 126
transaction costs, 23
transaction management, 23–24, 126–127, 151, 184, 208
transactions
repeated, 3, 10, 24, 54, 166, 169
transient state, 100
transitivity, 34, 40–41, 75–76, 83–86, 90, 95, 105, 109, 116–118, 120–121, 199, 204
transmission rate, 34, 41, 93–94, 96
triad, 40, 76
Trust Game, 6–9, 13, 15, 18, 23, 31, 42–47, 50–51, 54–56, 126, 156, 165, 196
Heterogeneous, 55–56, 60, 64, 89, 127–128
Iterated Heterogeneous, 56, 60, 64–65, 71, 160, 213, 218
Iterated, 47, 49, 56, 60
one-shot, 42, 47, 89, 213
repeated, 11, 13–14, 29, 46, 51, 126, 190, 193, 210
trust, 4–5
definition, 6–8
example, 1–4, 62
functions, 5
hypothesis, 87–89, 119–121
relations, 1, 4–5
trustfulness, 8–9, 186
trustworthiness, 2, 8–9, 16, 21, 24, 128
uncertainty, 20, 24–25, 44, 160, 188, 197, 200, 207
utility, 6, 9, 32, 47, 167, 179, 181
vertical integration, 24
voice network, 16
voice, 15, 18
volume, 139, 143, 145, 147–148, 152–153, 167–168, 170–176, 180, 184–185, 189
financial, 128–129, 132, 139, 158, 164, 196
Wald test, 81, 180–181, 183, 185–186

THEORY AND DECISION LIBRARY

SERIES C: GAME THEORY, MATHEMATICAL PROGRAMMING AND OPERATIONS RESEARCH

Editor: H. Peters, *Maastricht University, The Netherlands*

1. B.R. Munier and M.F. Shakun (eds.): *Compromise, Negotiation and Group Decision.* 1988 ISBN 90-277-2625-6
2. R. Selten: *Models of Strategic Rationality.* 1988 ISBN 90-277-2663-9
3. T. Driessen: *Cooperative Games, Solutions and Applications.* 1988 ISBN 90-277-2729-5
4. P.P. Wakker: *Additive Representations of Preferences.* A New Foundation of Decision Analysis. 1989 ISBN 0-7923-0050-5
5. A. Rapoport: *Experimental Studies of Interactive Decisions.* 1990 ISBN 0-7923-0685-6
6. K.G. Ramamurthy: *Coherent Structures and Simple Games.* 1990 ISBN 0-7923-0869-7
7. T.E.S. Raghavan, T.S. Ferguson, T. Parthasarathy and O.J. Vrieze (eds.): *Stochastic Games and Related Topics.* In Honor of Professor L.S. Shapley. 1991 ISBN 0-7923-1016-0
8. J. Abdou and H. Keiding: *Effectivity Functions in Social Choice.* 1991 ISBN 0-7923-1147-7
9. H.J.M. Peters: *Axiomatic Bargaining Game Theory.* 1992 ISBN 0-7923-1873-0
10. D. Butnariu and E.P. Klement: *Triangular Norm-Based Measures and Games with Fuzzy Coalitions.* 1993 ISBN 0-7923-2369-6
11. R.P. Gilles and P.H.M. Ruys: *Imperfections and Behavior in Economic Organization.* 1994 ISBN 0-7923-9460-7
12. R.P. Gilles: *Economic Exchange and Social Organization.* The Edgeworthian Foundations of General Equilibrium Theory. 1996 ISBN 0-7923-4200-3
13. P.J.-J. Herings: *Static and Dynamic Aspects of General Disequilibrium Theory.* 1996 ISBN 0-7923-9813-0
14. F. van Dijk: *Social Ties and Economic Performance.* 1997 ISBN 0-7923-9836-X
15. W. Spanjers: *Hierarchically Structured Economies.* Models with Bilateral Exchange Institutions. 1997 ISBN 0-7923-4398-0
16. I. Curiel: *Cooperative Game Theory and Applications.* Cooperative Games Arising from Combinatorial Optimization Problems. 1997 ISBN 0-7923-4476-6
17. O.I. Larichev and H.M. Moshkovich: *Verbal Decision Analysis for Unstructured Problems.* 1997 ISBN 0-7923-4578-9
18. T. Parthasarathy, B. Dutta, J.A.M. Potters, T.E.S. Raghavan, D. Ray and A. Sen (eds.): *Game Theoretical Applications to Economics and Operations Research.* 1997 ISBN 0-7923-4712-9
19. A.M.A. Van Deemen: *Coalition Formation and Social Choice.* 1997 ISBN 0-7923-4750-1
20. M.O.L. Bacharach, L.-A. Gérard-Varet, P. Mongin and H.S. Shin (eds.): *Epistemic Logic and the Theory of Games and Decisions.* 1997 ISBN 0-7923-4804-4
21. Z. Yang (eds.): *Computing Equilibria and Fixed Points.* 1999 ISBN 0-7923-8395-8
22. G. Owen: *Discrete Mathematics and Game Theory.* 1999 ISBN 0-7923-8511-X
23. F. Patrone, I. Garcia-Jurado and S. Tijs (eds.): *Game Practice.* Contributions from Applied Game Theory. 1999 ISBN 0-7923-8661-2

THEORY AND DECISION LIBRARY: SERIES C

24. J. Suijs: *Cooperative Decision-Making under Risk.* 1999 ISBN 0-7923-8660-4
25. J. Rosenmüller: *Game Theory: Stochastics, Information, Strategies and Cooperation.* 2000 ISBN 0-7923-8673-6
26. J.M. Bilbao: *Cooperative Games on Combinatorial Structures.* 2000 ISBN 0-7923-7782-6
27. M. Slikker and A. van den Nouweland: *Social and Economic Networks in Cooperative Game Theory.* 2000 ISBN 0-7923-7226-3
28. K.J.M. Huisman: *Technology Investment: A Game Theoretic Real Options Approach.* 2001 ISBN 0-7923-7487-8
29. A. Perea: *Rationality in Extensive Form Games.* 2001 ISBN 0-7923-7540-8

KLUWER ACADEMIC PUBLISHERS – DORDRECHT / BOSTON / LONDON